ADAM, OR APE

ADAM, OR APE

A Sourcebook of Discoveries About Early Man

EDITED BY

L. S. B. LEAKEY

AND

JACK AND STEPHANIE PROST

WITH THE ASSISTANCE OF
RONALD GOODMAN

SCHENKMAN PUBLISHING COMPANY
Cambridge, Massachusetts, U.S.A.
and London, England

Library of Congress Catalog Card #67-29326
Copyright © 1971
Schenkman Publishing Company, Inc.
Cambridge, Massachusetts 02138

PRINTED IN THE UNITED STATES OF AMERICA

ISBN 0-87073-701-5; — 700-7

TABLE OF CONTENTS

Contents

Prologue

by
L. S. B. Leakey

"Mother, where did I come from?" This is a question that is asked by every intelligent child, sooner or later. Similarly, the intelligent man and woman today asks of the scientists, "Why am I different from the other mammals? How did I come to be what I am?" Although we are still a very long way from providing the final and complete answer to this question, we realize that once we accept the fact that we are the result of evolutionary processes like all other forms of life, it behooves us to find the means of unfolding this mystery and answering this puzzling question.

The sciences of anthropology and paleontology are essentially scientific detective work. They involve searching for, isolating, sorting, and studying a whole series of facts—the different parts, if you like, of a jigsaw puzzle—and then gradually and slowly interpreting those random facts correctly and setting them together as a picture. Unlike the modern jigsaw puzzle where we know we are starting with all the different parts and that we can get all of the pieces in the "correct" position, our puzzle is of such a nature that we shall never have all the pieces. Consequently, at each stage of our knowledge, we have to be content with the available facts and such parts of the puzzle as have been found.

Man has been trying to unravel his origins for a long time but during the last hundred years or so he has greatly intensified his search for clues. Today, we begin to see part of the picture clearly. Nevertheless, a very great deal more is still very hazy. As modern technological advances give us new ways to find clues, we are able to reconstruct those parts of the picture that were foggy and dim and with each year, the picture becomes clearer.

Exactly as in the case with crime detection, some of the facts were obvious at an early stage of our study, some were found with relative ease, while others required long and diligent search by specialists. It must be stressed that the better we are trained to observe and see the smallest clues, the better our chances of finding them. The more we use reason and patience and take into account the research work of sister sciences, the more successful we will be in searching for evidence of man's ancestry and the less time and money we will waste in our work. Above all, those who wish to carry out the work must be wholly and utterly dedicated. This is not the sort of task that can be taken up for a few years with quick success. It is a study that requires patience, perseverance, and a willingness to put up with very difficult and hard living conditions. Men who search for answers to our origins must accept the psychological fact that they will never have the complete answer, however many fossils they find. Just around the corner will be another piece of the puzzle and they will live in the knowledge that after their time much else will be found by their successors.

The gradual unfolding of the story, as we know it at the time of my writing this Prologue, has been long, slow, and arduous, and in this book we will show some of the steps that have brought us to the present state of our knowledge. Every day new things are being uncovered, new approaches to the problems are being developed, and those who read this book can be fully assured that if they wish to work ultimately in this exciting scientific detective field, there is a vast amount awaiting them.

When we search for an understanding of our origins, we are no longer content only with studying fossils and digging up the archeological remains of extinct animals, stone age cultures, or civilizations. We take the broader view today that there is much we can learn, to help us in our interpretation of man's past, by studying the behavior pattern of modern primates, both those relatively close to us like the great apes and those more distantly removed like the monkey. We are finding, too, that in the field of biochemistry, the study of blood groups and other aspects of our physiology can play an important part in throwing light on some problems of our evolution. Then again, in recent years our detective work has been very greatly aided by the development of new studies in the fields of physics and chemistry, such as the chemical constituents of fossil bone, studies of the argon gases in certain minerals for dating purposes, or the decay rate of carbon, for Carbon 14 dating. Modern advances in techniques of transportation and travel now greatly facilitate the search for sites of early man. The light airplane, the helicopter, and the four-wheel-drive motor vehicle, have all contributed greatly and made it possible for the archeologist today to reach places where he could never go before. New techniques, too, of preserving delicate fossils and even fragments of carbonized vegetable materials of the past have altered our whole idea of what can be retrieved from a site.

During the last few years the search for evidence of earliest man and of his stone age cultures, as well as the remains of man's prehuman ancestors has concentrated, greatly, on the continent of Africa, although work has continued in other continents. Why should Africa be attracting so much attention and why should it be yielding such a rich harvest of results? Charles Darwin, nearly 100 years ago, put forward the suggestion that the evidence would some day be found to show that it was in the African continent that man himself, his cousins the great apes, and his more remote cousins the tailed old world monkeys had all evolved. He did not make this prophesy as the result of idle guesswork, but through scientific detective thinking, because he came to realize that the living fauna of Africa included a wider spectrum of the genera and species of the primates than any other continent. It looked, therefore, as though Africa had been the center of dispersal of this group. Using his preliminary reasoning as a guide, others followed in his steps realizing that large parts of Europe and North America had been adversely affected by climatic changes, at least during the last chapters of the earth's history, at the time of true man's emergence from a mere animal. Africa, however, because of its geographical position astride the equator and because of its geological structures which have given it a range of altitudes—from high mountains covered with snow and glaciers through a series of magnificent plateaus ranging from 10,000 feet down to sea level—always had some area with an optimum climate, both for animals and for man who, in his early states, hunted them for food. Africa has great potential as a field in which to search for everything concerning man's ancestry because its rocks and waters have in the past often been rich in mineral content, and so can be expected to have preserved the bones of past generations of animals and man himself, rather than allowing them to decay and disappear. Africa too has been subjected, in recent geological history, to major earthquakes and upheavals of the earth's crust, resulting in the Great Rift Valley System and in wholly new river drainage patterns. These two factors have combined to expose great natural cuts through the more recent layers of the earth's crust, and thus facilitate the task of those searching for buried clues to man's ancestry.

The fact that so much attention has been concentrated on Africa in the recent search for clues of early man's ancestors (from the Oligocene deposits of the Faiyum, now being studied by E. L. Simons of the Peabody Museum, to the Miocene and Pleistocene deposits of East Africa, which have so long been studied by this writer and his colleagues, on to South Central Africa where men like Broom, Robinson, Dart, Tobias, and Singer have uncovered so much) should not imply that there is not also a wealth of evidence still undiscovered in Asia. We know, now, that the type of man represented by the

Java and Peking fossil skulls probably originated in Africa. Yet between Africa and the nearest site in the Far East with ancient men of this type, lie tens of thousands of miles, the rocks of which must contain remains of these men and their ancestors who gradually moved out of Africa to China and Java. There must be hundreds of sites and exciting discoveries to be made in Syria, Persia, Iraq, Afgan Turkistan, Afghanistan, Pakistan, and places further to the East. I say this because by the end of the Miocene period the protohuman stock which is represented in East Africa by the fossil *Kenyapithecus* had reached the Siwalik Hills of India. Somewhere between those two places there must be evidence of that migration. We know that in the same Siwalik deposits of India there are remains of the ancestoral orangutan, our living cousin, which is now found so much further to the east. We know that in China there lived a creature, known as *Cigantopithecus*, whose remains have now turned up in India. There must be a great deal that still remains buried in ancient deposits.

Just what is man? There was a time when our definition of man was: "Man begins at that state of primate evolution when the creatures begin to make tools to a set and regular pattern." That definition was rendered invalid a few years ago by the research of Jane van Lawick-Goodall, who found that chimpanzees living under natural wild conditions in Tanzania, habitually made and used simple tools of perishable material, for a variety of purposes.

For the time being we are inclined to define man as "the primate that makes cutting tools"; but I fear this definition is not necessarily a good one.

Whatever we may, or may not, say in an attempt to classify ourselves, one thing is certain, namely that man is full of curiosity about how he came to be what he is today—the dominant living creature of the whole world. Zoologically we quite definitely are mammals. We are born with a placenta, we suckle our young, and we have the same general structure of our skeleton and our soft parts as do other mammals. We are covered with hair rather than with feathers or scales, and we are warm-blooded.

Equally clearly, we stand much closer to the apes and to the monkeys than we do to cats, or dogs, or horses, or any of the other mammals that inhabit the world. It is only necessary to look at a picture of a newborn monkey, or to visit a zoo and watch some of the great apes, to realize how very much in their gestures and facial grimaces and the set of their eyes they resemble us. We are, in short, mammals and above all, we are members of the Order Primates, which includes the apes and monkeys. Yet we know very well that we differ from all the other mammals—differ, indeed from our closest cousins the gorillas and chimpanzees—by very many distinctive characteristics. We are capable of walking wholly upright on the soles of our feet with our bodies so balanced that our hands are completely free and are not needed for support when we move or when we stand. We have fingers and thumbs capable of a precision grip which we use in writing, in painting, in science, in music, and in all the other multitude of things that we do with our hands. This precision grip, moreover, is controlled by a brain that has become a marvelous natural computer—a brain that can plan and reason; a brain that can pick up lines of evidence and assess them and formulate a good answer to whatever problems are posed. Because of this combination of a brain with the power to reason and the development of a language which includes numerous words for abstract ideas, we have learned to think and to plan using abstract terms. Through this we have developed our ideas or religion, music, science, and literature. Because we possess these attributes we call ourselves, "psycho-social man" and believe that we have entered into a phase of evolution that goes far beyond the purely physical development of our forebears.

How did we come to be what we are today—psycho-social man? The search for evidence which will fill in the gaps of this part of the puzzle will concentrate on the time period closest to the present day, perhaps the last 150,000 to 50,000 years, after man became *Homo sapiens*. In this part of the study we know a great deal from the small, limited area of Eastern Central Europe. We know a little of the story for Africa, but for Asia we know almost nothing and the same is true for America.

For many years it has been wrongly believed that psycho-social man only came to the American continent between 10,000 and 20,000 years ago, but this is not the case. There is growing evidence that he must have migrated to the Americas between 60,000 and 100,000 years ago, and there is room for a vast army of trained scientific detectives to uncover the story of man in America.

Wherever one chooses to go, whatever part of the story one wishes to unfold, there is a vast and highly exciting field awaiting those who care to train themselves adequately and dedicate themselves wholly to this fascinating study. This book is a brief "retelling"—in the words of the men who did the work—of the search, discovery and reasoning which produced that much of the story of our origins as we know today.

SECTION I

EVOLUTIONARY THEORY:
CONCEPT AND CONTROVERSY

On the Tendency of Species to Form Varieties; and on the Perpetuation of Varieties and Species by Natural Means of Selection

by
Charles Darwin and Alfred Wallace

(Read 1 July 1858)

London, June 30th, 1858.

My Dear Sir,

The accompanying papers, which we have the honour of communicating to the Linnean Society, and which all relate to the same subject, viz. the Laws which affect the production of varieties, races, and species, contain the results of the investigations of two indefatigable naturalists, Mr Charles Darwin and Mr Alfred Wallace.

These gentlemen having, independently and unknown to one another, conceived the same very ingenious theory to account for the appearance and perpetuation of varieties and of specific forms on our planet, may both fairly claim the merit of being original thinkers in this important line of inquiry; but neither of them having published his views, though Mr Darwin has for many years past been repeatedly urged by us to do so, and both authors having now unreservedly placed their papers in our hands, we think it would best promote the interests of science that a selection from them should be laid before the Linnean Society.

Taken in the order of their dates, they consist of:

3

I. Extracts from a MS. work on species,[1] by Mr Darwin, which was sketched in 1839, and copied in 1844, when the copy was read by Dr Hooker, and its contents afterwards communicated to Sir Charles Lyell. The first part is devoted to 'The variation of organic beings under domestication and in their natural state'; and the second chapter of that part, from which we propose to read to the Society the extracts referred to, is headed, 'On the variation of organic beings in a state of nature; on the natural means of selection; on the comparison of domestic races and true species.'

II. An abstract of a private letter addressed to Professor Asa Gray, of Boston, U.S., in October 1857, by Mr Darwin, in which he repeats his views, and which shows that these remained unaltered from 1839 to 1857.

III. An Essay by Mr Wallace, entitled 'On the tendency of varieties to depart indefinitely from the original type'. This was written at Ternate in February 1858, for the perusal of his friend and correspondent Mr Darwin, and sent to him with the expressed wish that it should be forwarded to Sir Charles Lyell, if Mr Darwin thought it sufficiently novel and interesting. So highly did Mr Darwin appreciate the value of the views therein set forth, that he proposed, in a letter to Sir Charles Lyell, to obtain Mr Wallace's consent to allow the Essay to be published as soon as possible. Of this step we highly approved, provided Mr Darwin did not withhold from the public, as he was strongly inclined to do (in favour of Mr Wallace), the memoir which he had himself written on the same subject, and which, as before stated, one of us had perused in 1844, and the contents of which we had both of us been privy to for many years. On representing this to Mr Darwin, he gave us permission to make what use we thought proper of his memoirs, etc,; and in adopting our present course, of presenting it to the Linnean Society, we have explained to him that we are not solely considering the relative claims to priority of himself and his friend, but the interests of science generally; for we feel it to be desirable that views founded on a wide deduction from facts, and matured by years of reflection, should constitute at once a goal from which others may start, and that, while the scientific world is waiting for the appearance of Mr Darwin's complete work, some of the leading results of his labours, as well as those of his able correspondent, should together be laid before the public.

We have the honour to be yours very obediently,

Charles Lyell
Jos. D. Hooker

J. J. Bennett, Esq.
  Secretary of the Linnean Society

[1]This MS. work was never intended for publication, and therefore was not written with care. C. D. 1858.

I

On the Variation of Organic Beings in a
State of Nature
On the Natural Means of Selection; on the
Comparison of Domestic Races and
True Species

By Charles Darwin

De Candolle, in an eloquent passage, has declared that all nature is at war, one organism with another, or with external nature. Seeing the contented face of nature, this may at first well be doubted: but reflection will inevitably prove it to be true. The war, however, is not constant, but recurrent in a slight degree at short periods, and more severely at occasional more distant periods; and hence its effects are easily overlooked. It is the doctrine of Malthus applied in most cases with tenfold force. As in every climate there are seasons, for each of its inhabitants, of greater and less abundance, so all annually breed; and the moral restraint which in some small degree checks the increase of mankind is entirely lost. Even slow-breeding mankind has doubled in twenty-five years; and if he could increase his food with greater ease, he would double in less time. But for animals without artificial means, the amount of food for each species must, *on an average*, be constant, whereas the increase of all organisms tends to be geometrical, and in a vast majority of cases at an enormous ratio. Suppose in a certain spot there are eight pairs of birds, and that *only* four pairs of them annually (including double hatches) rear only four young, and that these go on rearing their young at the same rate, then at the end of seven years (a short life, excluding violent deaths, for any bird) there will be 2048 birds, instead of the original sixteen. As this increase is quite impossible, we must conclude either that birds do not rear nearly half their young, or that the average life of a bird is, from accident, not nearly seven years. Both checks probably concur. The same kind of calculation applied to all plants and animals affords results more or less striking, but in very few instances more striking than in man.

Many practical illustrations of this rapid tendency to increase are on record, among which, during peculiar seasons, are the extraordinary numbers of certain animals; for instance, during the years 1826 to 1828, in La Plata, when from drought some millions of cattle perished, the whole country actually *swarmed* with mice. Now I think it cannot be doubted that during the breeding season all the mice (with the exception of a few males or females in excess) ordinarily pair, and therefore that this astounding increase during three years must be attributed to a greater number than usual surviving the first year, and then breeding, and so on till the third year, when their numbers were brought down to their usual limits on the return of wet weather. Where man has introduced plants and animals into a new and favourable country, there are many accounts in how surprisingly few years the whole country has become stocked with them. This increase would necessarily stop as soon as the country was fully stocked; and yet we have every reason to believe, from what is known of wild animals, that *all* would pair in the spring. In the majority of cases it is most difficult to imagine where the check falls—though generally, no doubt, on the seeds, eggs, and young; but when we remember how impossible, even in mankind (so much better known than any other animal), it is to infer from repeated casual observations what the average duration of life is, or to discover the different percentage of deaths to births in different countries, we ought to feel no surprise at our being unable to discover where the check falls in any animal or plant. It should always be remembered, that in most cases the checks are recurrent yearly in a small, regular degree, and in an extreme degree during unusually cold, hot, dry, or wet years, according to the constitution of the being in question. Lighten any check in the least degree, and the geometrical powers of increase in every organism will almost instantly increase the average number of the favoured species. Nature may be compared to a surface on which rest ten thousand sharp wedges touching each other and driven inwards by incessant blows. Fully to realize these views, much reflection is requisite. Malthus on man should be studied; and all such cases as those of the mice in La Plata, of the cattle and horses when first turned out in South America, of the birds by our calculation, etc., should be well considered. Reflect on the enormous multiplying power *inherent and annually in action* in all animals; reflect on the countless seeds scattered by a hundred ingenious contrivances, year after year, over the whole face of the land; and yet we have every reason to suppose that the average percentage of each of the inhabitants of a country usually remains constant. Finally, let it be borne in mind that this average number of individuals (the external conditions remaining the same) in each country is kept up by recurrent struggles against other species or against external nature (as on the borders of the arctic regions, where the cold checks life), and that ordinarily each individual of every species holds its place, either by its own struggle and capacity of acquiring nourishment in some period of its life, from the egg upwards; or by the struggle of its parents (in short-lived organisms, when the main check occurs at longer intervals) with other individuals of the *same* or *different* species.

But let the external conditions of a country alter. If in a small degree, the relative proportions of the inhabitants will in most cases simply be slightly changed; but let the number of inhabitants be small, as on an island, and free access to it from other countries be circumscribed, and let the change of conditions continue progressing (forming new stations), in such a case the original inhabitants must cease to be as perfectly adapted to the changed conditions as they were originally. It has been shown in a former part of this work, that such changes of external conditions would, from their acting on the reproductive system, probably cause the organization of those beings which were most affected to become, as under domestication, plastic. Now, can it be doubted, from the struggle each individual has to obtain subsistence, that any minute variation in structure, habits, or instincts, adapting that individual better to the new conditions, would tell upon its vigour and health? In the struggle it would have a better *chance* of surviving; and those of its offspring which inherited the variation, be it ever so slight, would also have a better *chance*. Yearly more are bred than can survive; the smallest grain in the balance, in the long run, must tell on which death shall fall, and which shall survive. Let this work of selection on the one hand, and death on the other, go on for a thousand generations, who will pretend to affirm that it would produce no effect, when we remember what, in a few years, Bakewell effected in cattle, and Western in sheep, by this identical principle of selection?

To give an imaginary example from changes in progress on an island: let the organization of a canine animal which preyed chiefly on rabbits, but sometimes on hares, become slightly plastic; let these same changes cause the number of rabbits very slowly to decrease, and the number of hares to increase; the effect of this would be that the fox or dog would be driven to try to catch more hares: his organization, however, being slightly plastic, those individuals with the lightest forms, longest limbs, and best eyesight, let the difference be ever so small, would be slightly favoured, and would tend to live longer, and to survive during that time of the year when food was scarcest; they would also rear more young, which would tend to inherit these slight peculiarities. The less fleet ones would be rigidly destroyed. I can see no more reason to doubt that these causes in a thousand generations would produce a marked effect, and adapt the form of the fox or dog to the catching of hares instead of rabbits, than that greyhounds can be improved by selection and careful breeding. So would it be with plants under similar circumstances. If the number of individuals of a species with plumed seeds could be increased by greater powers of dissemination within its own area (that is, if the check to increase fell chiefly on the seeds), those seeds which were provided with ever so little more down, would in the long run be most disseminated; hence a greater number of seeds thus formed would germinate, and would tend to produce plants inheriting the slightly better-adapted down.[1]

Besides this natural means of selection, by which those individuals are preserved, whether in their egg, or larval, or mature state, which are best adapted to the place they fill in nature, there is a second agency at work in most unisexual animals, tending to produce the same effect, namely the struggle of the males for the females. These struggles are generally decided by the law of battle, but in the case of birds, apparently, by the charms of their song, by their beauty or their power of courtship, as in the dancing rock-thrush of Guiana. The most vigorous and healthy males, implying perfect adaptation, must generally gain the victory in their contests. This kind of selection, however, is less rigorous than the other; it does not require the death of the less successful, but gives to them fewer descendants. The struggle falls, moreover, at a time of year when food is generally abundant, and perhaps the effect chiefly produced would be the modification of the secondary sexual characters, which are not related to the power of obtaining food, or to defence from enemies, but to fighting with or rivalling other males. The result of this struggle amongst the males may be compared in some respects to that produced by those agriculturists, who pay less attention to the careful selection of all their young animals, and more to the occasional use of a choice male.

II

Abstract of a Letter from Charles
Darwin to Professor Asa Gray
of Boston, U.S.A., Dated Down,
5 September 1857

It is wonderful what the principle of selection by man, that is the picking out of individuals with any desired quality, and breeding from them, and again picking out, can do. Even breeders have been astounded at their own results. They can act on differences inappreciable to an uneducated eye. Selection has been *methodically* followed in *Europe* for only the last half century; but it was occasionally, and even in some degree methodically, followed in the most ancient times. There must have been also a kind of unconscious selection from a remote period, namely in the preservation of

[1] I can see no more difficulty in this, than in the planter improving his varieties of the cotton plant. C. D. 1858.

the individual animals (without any thought of their offspring) most useful to each race of man in his particular circumstances. The 'roguing', as nurserymen call the destroying of varieties which depart from their type, is a kind of selection. I am convinced that intentional and occasional selection has been the main agent in the production of our domestic races; but however this may be, its great power of modification has been indisputably shown in later times. Selection acts only by the accumulation of slight or greater variations, caused by external conditions, or by the mere fact that in generation the child is not absolutely similar to its parent. Man, by this power of accumulating variations, adapts living beings to his wants—may be said to make the wool of one sheep good for carpets, of another for cloth, etc.

Now suppose there were a being who did not judge by mere external appearances, but who could study the whole internal organization, who was never capricious, and should go on selecting for one object during millions of generations; who will say what he might not effect? In nature we have some *slight* variation occasionally in all parts; and I think it can be shown that changed conditions of existence is the main cause of the child not exactly resembling its parents; and in nature geology shows us what changes have taken place, and are taking place. We have almost unlimited time; no one but a practical geologist can fully appreciate this. Think of the Glacial period, during the whole of which the same species at least of shells have existed; there must have been during this period millions on millions of generations.

I think it can be shown that there is such an unerring power at work in *Natural Selection* (the title of my book), which selects exclusively for the good of each organic being. The elder de Candolle, W. Herbert, and Lyell have written excellently on the struggle for life; but even they have not written strongly enough. Reflect that every being (even the elephant) breeds at such a rate, that in a few years, or at most a few centuries, the surface of the earth would not hold the progeny of one pair. I have found it hard constantly to bear in mind that the increase of every single species is checked during some part of its life, or during some shortly recurrent generation. Only a few of those annually born can live to propagate their kind. What a trifling difference must often determine which shall survive, and which perish!

Now take the case of a country undergoing some change. This will tend to cause some of its inhabitants to vary slightly—not but that I believe most beings vary at all times enough for selection to act on them. Some of its inhabitants will be exterminated; and the remainder will be exposed to the mutual action of a different set of inhabitants, which I believe to be far more important to the life of each being than mere climate. Considering the infinitely various methods which living beings follow to obtain food by struggling with other organisms, to escape danger at various times of life, to have their eggs or seeds disseminated, etc., I cannot doubt that during millions of generations individuals of a species will be occasionally born with some slight variation, profitable to some part of their economy. Such individuals will have a better chance of surviving, and of propagating their new and slightly different structure; and the modification may be slowly increased by the accumulative action of natural selection to any profitable extent. The variety thus formed will either coexist with, or, more commonly, will exterminate its parent form. An organic being like the woodpecker or mistletoe may thus come to be adapted to a score of contingencies—natural selection accumulating those slight variations in all parts of its structure, which are in any way useful to it during any part of its life.

Multiform difficulties will occur to every one, with respect to this theory. Many can, I think, be satisfactorily answered. *Natura non facit saltum* answers some of the most obvious. The slowness of the change, and only a very few individuals undergoing change at any one time, answers others. The extreme imperfection of our geological records answers still others.

Another principle, which may be called the principle of divergence, plays, I believe, an important part in the origin of species. The same spot will support more life if occupied by very diverse forms. We see this in the many generic forms in a square yard of turf, and in the plants or insects on any little uniform islet, belonging almost invariably to as many genera and families as species. We can understand the meaning of this fact amongst the higher animals, whose habits we understand. We know that it has been experimentally shown that a plot of land will yield a greater weight if sown with several species and genera of grasses, than if sown with only two or three species. Now, every organic being, by propagating so rapidly, may be said to be striving its utmost to increase in numbers. So it will be with the offspring of any species after it has become diversified into varieties, or subspecies, or true species. And it follows, I think, from the foregoing facts, that the varying offspring of each species will try (only few will succeed) to seize on as many and as diverse places in the economy of nature as possible. Each new variety or species, when formed, will generally take the place of, and thus exterminate its less well-fitted parent. This I believe to be the origin of the classification and affinities of organic beings at all times; for organic beings always *seem* to branch and sub-branch like the limbs of a tree from a common trunk, the flourishing and diverging twigs destroying the less vigorous—the dead and lost branches rudely representing extinct genera and families.

This sketch is *most* imperfect; but in so short a space I cannot make it better. Your imagination must fill up very wide blanks.

III

On the Tendency of Varieties to
Depart Indefinitely from the
Original Type

By Alfred Russell Wallace

One of the strongest arguments which have been adduced to prove the original and permanent distinctness of species is, that *varieties* produced in a state of domesticity are more or less unstable, and often have a tendency, if left to themselves, to return to the normal form of the parent species; and this instability is considered to be a distinctive peculiarity of all varieties, even of those occurring among wild animals in a state of nature, and to constitute a provision for preserving unchanged the originally created distinct species.

In the absence or scarcity of facts and observations as to *varieties* occurring among wild animals, this argument has had great weight with naturalists, and has led to a very general and somewhat prejudiced belief in the stability of species. Equally general, however, is the belief in what are called 'permanent or true varieties',—races of animals which continually propagate their like, but which differ so slightly (although constantly) from some other race, that the one is considered to be a *variety* of the other. Which is the *variety* and which the original *species*, there is generally no means of determining, except in those rare cases in which the one race has been known to produce an offspring unlike itself and resembling the other. This, however, would seem quite incompatible with the 'permanent invariability of species', but the difficulty is overcome by assuming that such varieties have strict limits, and can never again vary further from the original type, although they may return to it, which, from the analogy of the domesticated animals, is considered to be highly probable, if not certainly proved.

It will be observed that this argument rests entirely on the assumption, that *varieties* occurring in a state of nature are in all respects analogous to or even identical with those of domestic animals, and are governed by the same laws as regards their permanence or further variation. But it is the object of the present paper to show that this assumption is altogether false, that there is a general principle in nature which will cause many *varieties* to survive the parent species, and to give rise to successive variations departing further and further from the original type, and which also produces, in domesticated animals, the tendency of varieties to return to the parent form.

The life of wild animals is a struggle for existence. The full exertion of all their faculties and all their energies is required to preserve their own existence and provide for that of their infant offspring. The possibility of procuring food during the least favourable seasons, and of escaping the attacks of their most dangerous enemies, are the primary conditions which determine the existence both of individuals and of entire species. These conditions will also determine the population of a species; and by a careful consideration of all the circumstances we may be enabled to comprehend, and in some degree explain, what at first sight appears so inexplicable—the excessive abundance of some species, while others closely allied to them are very rare.

The general proportion that must obtain between certain groups of animals is readily seen. Large animals cannot be so abundant as small ones; the Carnivora must be less numerous than the Herbivora; eagles and lions can never be so plentiful as pigeons and antelopes; the wild asses of the Tartarian deserts cannot equal in numbers the horses of the more luxuriant prairies and pampas of America. The greater or less fecundity of an animal is often considered to be one of the chief causes of its abundance or scarcity; but a consideration of the facts will show us that it really has little or nothing to do with the matter. Even the least prolific of animals would increase rapidly if unchecked, whereas it is evident that the animal population of the globe must be stationary, or perhaps, through the influence of man, decreasing. Fluctuations there may be; but permanent increase, except in restricted localities, is almost impossible. For example, our own observation must convince us that birds do not go on increasing every year in a geometrical ratio, as they would do, were there not some powerful check to their natural increase. Very few birds produce less than two young ones each year, while many have six, eight or ten; four will certainly be below the average; and if we suppose that each pair produce young only four times in their life, that will also be below the average, supposing them not to die either by violence or want of food. Yet at this rate how tremendous would be the increase in a few years from a single pair! A simple calculation will show that in fifteen years each pair of birds would have increased to nearly ten millions! whereas we have no reason to believe that the number of the birds of any country increases at all in fifteen or in one hundred and fifty years. With such powers of increase the population must have reached its limits, and have become stationary, in a very few years after the origin of each species. It is evident, therefore, that each year an immense number of birds must perish—as many in fact as are born; and as on the lowest calculation the progeny are each year twice as numerous as their parents, it follows that, whatever be the average number of individuals existing in any given country, *twice that number must perish annually*—a striking result, but one which seems at least highly probable, and is perhaps under rather than over the truth. It would therefore appear that, as far as the continuance of the species and the keeping up the average number of individuals are concerned, large broods are superfluous. On the average all above *one* become food for hawks and kites, wild cats and weasels, or perish of cold and hunger as winter comes on. This is strikingly proved by the case of particular species; for we find that their abundance in individuals bears no relation whatever to their fertility in producing offspring. Perhaps the most remarkable instance of an immense bird population is that of the passenger pigeon of the United States, which lays only one, or at most two eggs, and is said to rear generally but one young one. Why is this bird so extraordinarily abundant, while others producing two or three times as many young are much less plentiful? The explanation is not difficult. The food most congenial to this species, and on which it thrives best, is abundantly distributed over a very extensive region, offering such differences of soil and climate, that in one part or another of the area the supply never fails. The bird is capable of a very rapid and long-continued flight, so that it can pass without fatigue over the whole of the district it inhabits, and as soon as the supply of food begins to fail in one place is able to discover a fresh feeding-ground. This example strikingly shows that procuring a constant supply of wholesome food is almost the sole condition requisite for ensuring the rapid increase of a given species, since neither the limited fecundity, nor the unrestrained attacks of birds of prey and of man are here sufficient to check it. In no other birds are these peculiar circumstances so strikingly combined. Either their food is more liable to failure, or they have not sufficient power of wing to search for it over an extensive area, or during some season of the year it becomes very scarce, and less wholesome substitutes have to be found; and thus, though more fertile in offspring, they can never increase beyond the supply of food in the least favourable seasons. Many birds can only exist by migrating, when their food becomes scarce, to regions possessing a milder, or at least a different climate, though, as these migrating birds are seldom excessively abundant, it is evident that the countries they visit are still deficient in a constant and abundant supply of wholesome food. Those whose organization does not permit them to migrate when their food becomes periodically scarce, can never attain a large population. This is probably the reason why woodpeckers are scarce with us, while in the tropics they are among the most abundant of solitary birds. Thus the house sparrow is more abundant than the redbreast, because its food is more constant and plentiful—seeds of grasses being preserved during the winter, and our farmyards and stubble-fields furnishing an almost inexhaustible supply. Why, as a general rule, are aquatic, and especially sea birds, very numerous in individuals? Not because they are more prolific than others, generally the contrary; but because their food never fails, the sea-shores and river-banks daily swarming with a fresh supply of small

Mollusca and Crustacea. Exactly the same laws will apply to mammals. Wild cats are prolific and have few enemies; why then are they never as abundant as rabbits? The only intelligible answer is, that their supply of food is more precarious. It appears evident, therefore, that so long as a country remains physically unchanged, the numbers of its animal population cannot materially increase. If one species does so, some others requiring the same kind of food must diminish in proportion. The numbers that die annually must be immense; and as the individual existence of each animal depends upon itself, those that die must be the weakest—the very young, the aged, and the diseased—while those that prolong their existence can only be the most perfect in health and vigour—those who are best able to obtain food regularly, and avoid their numerous enemies. It is, as we commenced by remarking, 'a struggle for existence', in which the weakest and least perfectly organized must always succumb.

Now it is clear that what takes place among the individuals of a species must also occur among the several allied species of a group—viz. that those which are best adapted to obtain a regular supply of food, and to defend themselves against the attacks of their enemies and the vicissitudes of the seasons, must necessarily obtain and preserve a superiority in population; while those species which from some defect of power or organization are the least capable of counteracting the vicissitudes of food supply, etc., must diminish in numbers, and, in extreme cases, become altogether extinct. Between these extremes the species will present various degrees of capacity for ensuring the means of preserving life; and it is thus we account for the abundance or rarity of species. Our ignorance will generally prevent us from accurately tracing the effects to their causes; but could we become perfectly acquainted with the organization and habits of the various species of animals, and could we measure the capacity of each for performing the different acts necessary to its safety and existence under all the varying circumstances by which it is surrounded, we might be able even to calculate the proportionate abundance of individuals which is the necessary result.

If now we have succeeded in establishing these two points; first, *that the animal population of a country is generally stationary, being kept down by a periodical deficiency of food, and other checks*; and, secondly, *that the comparative abundance or scarcity of the individuals of the several species is entirely due to their organization and resulting habits, which, rendering it more difficult to procure a regular supply of food and to provide for their personal safety in some cases than in others, can only be balanced by a difference in the population which has to exist in a given area*—we shall be in a condition to proceed to the consideration of *varieties*, to which the preceding remarks have a direct and very important application.

Most or perhaps all the variations from the typical form of a species must have some definite effect, however slight, on the habits or capacities of the individuals. Even a change of colour might, by rendering them more or less distinguishable, affect their safety; a greater or less development of hair might modify their habits. More important changes, such as an increase in the power or dimensions of the limbs or any of the external organs, would more or less affect their mode of procuring food or the range.of country which they inhabit. It is also evident that most changes would affect, either favourably or adversely, the powers of prolonging existence. An antelope with shorter or weaker legs must necessarily suffer more from the attacks of the feline carnivora; the passenger pigeon with less powerful wings would sooner or later be affected in its powers of procuring a regular supply of food; and in both cases the result must necessarily be a diminution of the population of the modified species. If, on the other hand, any species should produce a variety having slightly increased powers of preserving existence, that variety must inevitably in time acquire a superiority in numbers. These results must follow as surely as old age, intemperance, or scarcity of food produce an increased mortality. In both cases there may be many individual exceptions; but on the average the rule will invariably be found to hold good. All varieties will therefore fall into two classes—those which under the same conditions would never reach the population of the parent species, and those which would in time obtain and keep a numerical superiority. Now, let some alteration of physical conditions occur in the district—a long period of drought, a destruction of vegatation by locusts, the irruption of some new carnivorous animal seeking 'pastures new'—any change in fact tending to render existence more difficult to the species in question, and tasking its utmost powers to avoid complete extermination; it is evident that, of all the individuals composing the species, those forming the least numerous and most feebly organized variety would suffer first, and, were the pressure severe, must soon become extinct. The same causes continuing in action, the parent species would next suffer, would gradually diminish in numbers, and with a recurrence of similar unfavourable conditions might also become extinct. The superior variety would then alone remain, and on a return to favourable circumstances would rapidly increase in numbers and occupy the place of the extinct species and variety.

The *variety* would now have replaced the *species*, of which it would be a more perfectly developed and more highly organized form. It would be in all respects better adapted to secure its safety, and to prolong its individual existence and that of the race. Such a variety *could not* return to the original form; for that form is an inferior one, and could never compete with it for existence. Granted, therefore, a 'tendency' to reproduce the original type of the species, still the variety must ever remain preponderant in numbers, and under adverse physical conditions *again alone survive*. But this new, improved, and populous race might itself, in course of time, give rise to new varieties, exhibiting several diverging modifications of form, any of which, tending to increase the facilities for preserving existence, must, by the same general law, in their turn become predominant. Here, then, we have *progression and continued divergence* deduced from the general laws which regulate the existence of animals in a state of nature, and from the undisputed fact that varieties do frequently occur. It is not, however, contended that this result would be invariable; a change of physical conditions in the district might at times materially modify it, rendering the race which had been the most capable of supporting existence under the former conditions now the least so, and even causing the extinction of the newer and, for a time, superior race, while the old or parent species and its first inferior varieties continued to flourish. Variations in unimportant parts might also occur, having no perceptible effect on the life-preserving powers; and the varieties so furnished might run a course parallel with the parent species, either giving rise to further variations or returning to the former type. All we argue for is, that certain varieties have a tendency to maintain their existence longer than the original species, and this tendency must make itself felt; for though the doctrine of chances or averages can never be trusted to on a limited scale, yet, if applied to high numbers, the results come nearer to what theory demands, and, as we approach to an infinity of examples, become strictly accurate. Now the scale on which nature works is so vast—the numbers of individuals and periods of time with which she deals approach so near to infinity, that any cause however slight, and however liable to be veiled and counteracted by accidental circumstances, must in the end produce its full legitimate results.

Let us now turn to domesticated animals, and inquire how varieties produced among them are affected by the principles here enunciated. The essential difference in the condition of wild and domestic animals is this, that among the former, their well-being and very existence depend upon the full exercise and healthy condition of all their senses and physical powers, whereas, among the latter, these are only partially exercised, and in some cases are absolutely unused. A wild animal has to search, and often to labour, for every mouthful of food—to exercise sight, hearing, and smell in seeking it, and in avoiding dangers, in procuring shelter from the inclemency of the seasons, and in providing for the subsistence and safety of its offspring. There is no muscle of its body that is not called into daily and hourly activity; there is no sense or faculty that is not strengthened by continual exercise. The domestic animal, on the other hand, has food provided for it, is sheltered, and often confined, to guard it against the vicissitudes of the seasons, is carefully secured from the attacks of its natural enemies, and seldom even rears its young without human assistance. Half of its senses and faculties are quite useless; and the other half are but occasionally called into feeble exercise, while even its muscular system is only irregularly called into action.

Now when a variety of such an animal occurs, having increased power or capacity in any organ or sense, such increase is totally useless, is never called into action, and may even exist without the animal ever becoming aware of it. In the wild animal, on the contrary, all its faculties and powers being brought into full action for the necessities of existence, any increase becomes immediately available, is strengthened by exercise, and must even slightly modify the food, the habits, and the whole economy of the race. It creates as it were a new animal, one of superior powers, and which will necessarily increase in numbers and outlive those inferior to it.

Again, in the domesticated animal all variations have an equal chance of continuance; and those which would decidedly render a wild animal unable to compete with its fellows and continue its existence are no disadvantage whatever in a state of domesticity. Our quickly fattening pigs, short-legged sheep, pouter pigeons, and poodle dogs could never have come into existence in a state of nature, because the very first step towards such inferior forms would have led to the rapid extinction of the race; still less could they now exist in competition with their wild allies. The great speed but slight endurance of the race horse, the unwieldy strength of the ploughman's team, would both be useless in a state of nature. If turned wild on the pampas, such animals would probably soon become extinct, or under favourable circumstances might each lose those extreme qualities which would never be called into action, and in a few generations would revert to a common type, which must be that in which the various powers and faculties are so proportioned to each other as to be best adapted to procure food and secure safety—that in which by the full exercise of every part of his organization the animal can alone continue to live. Domestic varieties, when turned wild, *must* return to something near the type of the original wild stock, *or become altogether extinct.*

We see, then, that no inferences as to varieties in a state of nature can be deduced from the observation of those occurring among domestic animals. The two are so much opposed to each other in every circumstance of their existence, that what applies to the one is almost sure not to apply to the other. Domestic animals are abnormal, irregular, artificial; they are subject to varieties which never occur and never can occur in a state of nature: their very existence depends altogether on human care, so far are many of them removed from that just proportion of faculties, that true balance of organization, by means of which alone an animal left to its own resources can preserve its existence and continue its race.

The hypothesis of Lamarck—that progressive changes in species have been produced by the attempts of animals to increase the development of their own organs, and thus modify their structure and habits—has been repeatedly and easily refuted by all writers on the subject of varieties and species, and it seems to have been considered that when this was done the whole question has been finally settled; but the view here developed renders such an hypothesis quite unnecessary, by showing that similar results must be produced by the action of principles constantly at work in nature. The powerful retractile talons of the falcon and the cat tribes have not been produced or increased by the volition of those animals; but among the different varieties which occurred in the earlier and less highly organized forms of these groups, *those always survived longest which had the greatest facilities for seizing their prey*. Neither did the giraffe acquire its long neck by desiring to reach the foliage of the more lofty shrubs, and constantly stretching its neck for the purpose, but because any varieties which occurred among its antetypes with a longer neck than usual *at once secured a fresh range of pasture over the same ground as their shorter-necked companions, and on the first scarcity of food were thereby enabled to outlive them*. Even the peculiar colours of many animals, especially insects, so closely resembling the soil or the leaves or the trunks on which they habitually reside, are explained on the same principle; for though in the course of ages varieties of many tints may have occurred, *yet those races having colours best adapted to concealment from their enemies would inevitably survive the longest*. We have also here an acting cause to account for that balance so often observed in nature—deficiency in one set of organs always compensated by an increased development of some others—powerful wings accompanying weak feet, or great velocity making up for the absence of defensive weapons; for it has been shown that all varieties in which an unbalanced deficiency occurred could not long continue their existence. The action of this principle is exactly like that of the centrifugal governor of the steam engine, which checks and corrects any irregularities almost before they become evident; and in like manner no unbalanced deficiency in the animal kingdom can ever reach any conspicuous magnitude, because it would make itself felt at the very first step, by rendering existence difficult and extinction almost sure soon to follow. An origin such as is here advocated will also agree with the peculiar character of the modifications of form and structure which obtain in organized beings—the many lines of divergence from a central type, the increasing efficiency and power of a particular organ through a succession of allied species, and the remarkable persistence of unimportant parts such as colour, texture of plumage and hair, form of horns or crests, through a series of species differing considerably in more essential characters. It also furnishes us with a reason for that 'more specialized structure' which Professor Owen states to be a characteristic of recent compared with extinct forms, and which would evidently be the result of the progressive modification of any organ applied to a special purpose in the animal economy.

We believe we have now shown that there is a tendency in nature to the continued progression of certain classes of *varieties* further and further from the original type—a progression to which there appears no reason to assign any definite limits—and that the same principle which produces this result in a state of nature will also explain why domestic varieties have a tendency to revert to the original type. This progression, by minute steps, in various directions, but always checked and balanced by the necessary conditions, subject to which alone existence can be preserved, may, it is believed, be followed out so as to agree with all the phenomena presented by organized beings, their extinction and succession in past ages, and all the extraordinary modifications of form, instinct, and habits which they exhibit.

Review of Charles Darwin's
"On the Origin of Species"

by
Bishop Samuel Wilberforce

Art. VII.—On the Origin of Species, by means of Natural Selection; or the Preservation of Favoured Races in the Struggle for Life. By Charles Darwin, M.A., F.R.S. London, 1860.

Any contribution to our Natural History literature from the pen of Mr. C. Darwin is certain to command attention. His scientific attainments, his insight and carefulness as an observer, blended with no scanty measure of imaginative sagacity, and his clear and lively style, make all his writings unusually attractive. His present volume on the 'Origin of Species' is the result of many years of observation, thought, and speculation; and is manifestly regarded by him as the 'opus' upon which his future fame is to rest. It is true that he announces it modestly enough as the mere precursor of a mightier volume. But that volume is only intended to supply the facts which are to support the completed argument of the present essay. In this we have a specimen-collection of the vast accumulation; and, working from these as the high analytical mathematician may work from the admitted results of his conic sections, he proceeds to deduce all the conclusions to which he wishes to conduct his readers.

Now, the main propositions by which Mr. Darwin's conclusion is attained are these:—

1. That observed and admitted variations spring up in the course of descents from a common progenitor.

2. That many of these variations tend to an improvement upon the parent stock.

21

3. That, by a continued selection of these improved specimens as the progenitors of future stock, its powers may be unlimitedly increased.

4. And, lastly, that there is in nature a power continually and universally working out this selection, and so fixing and augmenting these improvements.

Mr. Darwin's whole theory rests upon the truth of these propositions, and crumbles utterly away if only one of them fail him. These therefore we must closely scrutinise. We will begin with the last in our series, both because we think it the newest and the most ingenious part of Mr. Darwin's whole argument, and also because, whilst we absolutely deny the mode in which he seeks to apply the existence of the power to help him in his argument, yet we think that he throws great and very interesting light upon the fact that such a self-acting power does actively and continuously work in all creation around us.

Mr. Darwin finds then the disseminating and improving power, which he needs to account for the development of new forms in nature, in the principle of 'Natural Selection,' which is evolved in the strife for room to live and flourish which is evermore maintained between themselves by all living things. One of the most interesting parts of Mr. Darwin's volume is that in which he establishes this law of natural selection; we say establishes, because—repeating that we differ from him totally in the limits which he would assign to its action—we have no doubt of the existence or of the importance of the law itself.

That such a struggle for life then actually exists, and that it tends continually to lead the strong to exterminate the weak, we readily admit; and in this law we see a merciful provision against the deterioration, in a world apt to deteriorate, of the works of the Creator's hands. Thus it is that the bloody strifes of the males of all wild animals tend to maintain the vigour and full development of their race; because, through this machinery of appetite and passion, the most vigorous individuals become the progenitors of the next generation of the tribe. And this law, which thus maintains through the struggle of individuals the high type of the family, tends continually, through a similar struggle of species, to lead the stronger species to supplant the weaker.

This indeed is no new observation: Lucretius knew and eloquently expatiated on its truth:—

'Multaque tum interiisse animantum secla necesse est,
Nec potuisse propagando procudere prolem.
Nam, quaecumque vides vesci vitalibus auris
Aut dolus, aut virtus, aut denique mobilitas, est,
Ex ineunte aevo, genus id tutata reservant.'*

*Lucret., 'De Rer. Nat.,' lib. v.

And this, which is true in animal, is no less true in vegetable life. Hardier or more prolific plants, or plants better suited to the soil or conditions of climate, continually tend to supplant others less hardy, less prolific, or less suited to the conditions of vegetable life in those special districts. Thus far, then, the action of such a law as this is clear and indisputable.

But before we can go a step further, and argue from its operation in favour of a perpetual improvement in natural types, we must be shown first that this law of competition has in nature to deal with such favourable variations in the individuals of any species, as truly to exalt those individuals above the highest type of perfection to which their least imperfect predecessors attained—above, that is to say, the normal level of the species;—that such individual improvement is, in truth, a rising above the highest level of any former tide, and not merely the return in its appointed season of the feebler neap to the fuller spring-tide;—and then, next, we must be shown that there is actively at work in nature, co-ordinate with the law of competition and with the existence of such favourable variations, a power of accumulating such favourable variation through successive descents. Failing the establishment of either of these last two propositions, Mr. Darwin's whole theory falls to pieces. He has accordingly laboured with all his strength to establish these, and into that attempt we must now follow him.

Mr. Darwin begins by endeavouring to prove that such variations are produced under the selecting power of man amongst domestic animals. Now here we demur *in limine*. Mr. Darwin himself allows that there is a plastic habit amongst domesticated animals which is not found amongst them when in a state of nature. 'Under domestication, it may be truly said that the whole organization becomes in some degree plastic.'—(p. 80.) If so, it is not fair to argue, from the variations of the plastic nature, as to what he himself admits is the far more rigid nature of the undomesticated animal. But we are ready to give Mr. Darwin this point, and to join issue with him on the variations which he is able to adduce, as having been produced under circumstances the most favourable to change. He takes for this purpose the domestic pigeon, the most favourable specimen no doubt, for many reasons, which he could select, as being a race eminently subject to variation, the variations of which have been most carefully observed by breeders, and which, having been for some 4000 years domesticated, affords the longest possible period for the accumulation of variations. But with all this in his favour, what is he able to show? He writes a delightful chapter upon pigeons. Runts and fantails, short-faced tumblers and long-faced tumblers, long-beaked carriers and pouters, black barbs, jacobins, and turgits, coo and tumble, inflate their oesophagi, and pout and spread out their tails before us. We learn that 'pigeons have been watched and tended with the utmost care, and loved by many people.' They have been domesticated for thousands of years in several quarters of the world. The earliest known record of pigeons is in the fifth Egyptian dynasty, about 3000 B.C., though 'pigeons are given in a bill of fare' (what an autograph would be that of the chef-de-cuisine of the day!) 'in the previous dynasty' (pp. 27, 28): and so we follow pigeons on down to the days of 'that most skilful breeder Sir John Sebright,' who 'used to say, with respect to pigeons, that "he would produce any given feather in three years, but it would take him six years to produce beak and head." '–(p. 31.)

Now all this is very pleasant writing, especially for pigeon-fanciers; but what step do we really gain in it at all towards establishing the alleged fact that variations are but species in the act of formation, or in establishing Mr. Darwin's position that a well-marked variety may be called an incipient species? We affirm positively that no single *fact* tending even in that direction is brought forward. On the contrary, every one points distinctly towards the opposite conclusion; for with all the change wrought in appearance, with all the apparent variation in manners, there is not the faintest beginning of any such change in what that great comparative anatomist, Professor Owen, calls 'the characteristics of the skeleton or other parts of the frame upon which specific differences are founded.'* There is no tendency to that great law of sterility which, in spite of Mr. Darwin, we affirm ever to mark the hybrid; for every variety of pigeon, and the descendants of every such mixture, breed as freely, and with as great fertility, as the original pair; nor is there the very first appearance of that power of accumulating variations until they grow into specific differences, which is essential to the argument for the transmutation of species; for, as Mr. Darwin allows, sudden returns in colour, and other most altered appearances, to the parent stock continually attest the tendency of variations not to become fixed, but to vanish, and manifest the perpetual presence of a principle which leads not to the accumulation of minute variations into well-marked species, but to a return from the abnormal to the original type. So clear is this, that it is well known that any relaxation in the breeder's care effaces all the established points of difference, and the fancy-pigeon reverts again to the character of its simplest ancestor.

Nor let our readers forget over how large a lapse of time our opportunities of observation extend. From the early Egyptian habit of embalming, we know that for 4000 years at least the species of our own domestic animals, the cat, the dog, and others, has remained absolutely unaltered.

Yet it is in the face of such facts as these that Mr. Darwin ventures, first, to declare that 'new races of animals and plants are produced under domestication by man's methodical and unconscious power of selection, for

*'On the Classification of Mammalia,' p. 98.

his own use and pleasure,' and then to draw from the changes introduced amongst domesticated animals this caution for naturalists: 'May they not learn a lesson of caution when they deride the idea of species in a state of nature being lineal descendants of other species?' (p. 29.)

Nor must we pass over unnoticed the transference of the argument from the domesticated to the untamed animals. Assuming that man as the selector can do much in a limited time, Mr. Darwin argues that Nature, a more powerful, a more continuous power, working over vastly extended ranges of time, can do more. Buy why should Nature, so uniform and persistent in all her operations, tend in this instance to change? why should she become a selector of varieties? Because, most ingeniously argues Mr. Darwin, in the struggle for life, *if* any variety favourable to the individual were developed, that individual would have a better chance in the battle of life, would assert more proudly his own place, and, handing on his peculiarity to his descendants, would become the progenitor of an improved race; and so a variety would have grown into a species.

We think it difficult to find a theory fuller of assumptions; and of assumptions not grounded upon alleged facts in nature, but which are absolutely opposed to all the facts we have been able to observe.

1. We have already shown that the variations of which we have proof under domestication have never, under the longest and most continued system of selections we have known, laid the firm foundation of a specific difference, but have always tended to relapse, and not to accumulated and fixed persistence.

But, 2ndly, all these variations have the essential characteristics of *monstrosity* about them; and *not one* of them has the character which Mr. Darwin repeatedly reminds us is the *only one* which nature can select, viz. of being an advantage to the selected individual in the battle of life, *i.e.* an improvement upon the normal type by raising some individual of the species not to the highest possible excellence within the species, but to some excellence above it. So far from this, every variation introduced by man is for man's advantage, not for the advantage of the animal. Correlation is so certainly the law of all animal existence that man can only develop one part by the sacrifice of another. The bull-dog gains in strength and loses in swiftness; the grayhound gains in swiftness but loses in strength. Even the English race-horse loses much which would enable it in the battle of life to compete with its rougher ancestor. So too with our prize-cattle. Their greater tendency to an earlier accumulation of meat and fat is counterbalanced, as is well known, by loss of robust health, fertility, and of power of yielding milk, in proportion to their special development in the direction which man's use of them as food requires. There is not a shadow of ground for saying that man's variations ever improve the typical character of the animal as an animal; they do but by some monstrous development make it more useful to himself; and hence it is that Nature, according to her universal law with monstrosities, is ever tending to obliterate the deviation and to return to the type.

The applied argument then, from variation under domestication, fails utterly. But further, what does observation say as to the occurrence of a single instance of such favourable variation? Men have now for thousands of years been conversant as hunters and other rough naturalists with animals of every class. Has any one such instance ever been discovered? We fearlessly assert not one. Variations have been found: rodents whose teeth have grown abnormally; animals of various classes of which the eyes, from the absence of light in their dwellings, have been obscured and obliterated; but *not one* which has tended to raise the individual in the struggle of life above the typical conditions of its own species. Mr. Darwin himself allows that he finds none; and accounts for their absence in existing fauna only by the suggestion, that, in the competition between the less improved parent-form and the improved successor, the parent will have yielded in the strife in order to make room for the successor; and so 'both the parent and all the transitional varieties will generally have been exterminated by the very process of formation and perfection of the new form' (p. 172),–a most unsatisfactory answer as it seems to us; for why–since if this is Nature's law these innumerable changes must be daily occurring–should there never be any one produceable proof of their existence?

Here then again, when subjected to the stern Baconian law of the observation of facts, the theory breaks down utterly; for no natural variations from the specific type favourable to the individual from which nature is to select can anywhere be found.

But once more. If these transmutations were actually occurring, must there not, in some part of the great economy of nature round us, be somewhere at least some instance to be quoted of the accomplishment of the change? With many of the lower forms of animals, life is so short and generations so rapid in their succession that it would be all but impossible, if such changes were happening, that there should be no proof of their occurrence; yet never have the longing observations of Mr. Darwin and the transmutationists found one such instance to establish their theory, and this although the shades between one class and another are often most lightly marked. For there are creatures which occupy a doubtful post between the animal and the vegetable kingdoms–half-notes in the great scale of nature's harmony. Is it credible that all favourable varieties of turnips are tending to become men, and yet that the closest microscopic observation has never detected the faintest tendency in the highest of the Algae to improve into the very lowest Zoophyte?

Again, we have not only the existing tribes of animals out of which to cull, if it were possible, the instances which the transmutationists require to make their theory defensible consistently with the simplest laws of inductive science, but we have in the earth beneath us a vast museum of the forms which have preceded us. Over so vast a period of time does Mr. Darwin extend this collection that he finds reasons for believing that 'it is not improbable that a longer period than 300,000,000 years has elapsed since the latter part of the secondary (geological) period' alone. (p. 287.) Here then surely at last we must find the missing links of that vast chain of innumerable and separately imperceptible variations, which has convinced the inquirer into Nature's undoubted facts of the truth of the transmutation theory. But no such thing. The links are wholly wanting, and the multiplicity of these facts and their absolute rebellion against Mr. Darwin's theory is perhaps his chief difficulty. Here is his own statement of it, and his mode of meeting it:—

> 'Why then is not every geological formation and every stratum full of such intermediate links? Geology assuredly does not reveal any such finely graduated organic chain; and this, perhaps, is the most obvious and gravest objection which can be urged against my theory. The explanation lies, as I believe, in the extreme imperfection of the geological record.'—p. 280.

This 'Imperfection of the Geological Record,' and the 'Geological Succession,' are the subjects of two laboured and ingenious chapters, in which he tries, as we think utterly in vain, to break down the unanswerable refutation which is given to his theory by the testimony of the rocks. He treats the subject thus:—1. He affirms that only a small portion of the globe has been explored with care. 2. He extends at will to new and hitherto unsuggested myriads of years the times which have elapsed between successive formations in order to account for the utter absence of everything like a succession of ascertainable variations in the successive inhabitants of the earth.

Mr. Darwin then argues (pp. 285, 286) that 'faults' proclaim the vastness of these durations. To establish this, he supposes that the result of a great fracture was the severing of strata once continuous, so as to throw them relatively a thousand feet apart from their original position, and thus form a cliff which stood up vertically on one side of that dislocation; and so he imagines that countless ages must have elapsed, *according to the present waste of land*, to account for the wearing down of these outlines, so as to have left (as is often the case) no trace of the great dislocation upon the present surface of the land. But, with hardly an exception, every sound geologist would repudiate as a 'petitio principii' this whole method of reasoning; for though a few geologists would explain these great dislocations on the hypothesis of intermittent successive movements severally of small amount, yet in the judgment of far the larger number, and the more judicious of those who have made geology their study, they were undoubtedly the result of sudden movements, produced by internal efforts of central heat and gas to escape, and were infinitely more intense and spasmodic (catastrophic if you will) than any of those similar causes which, in a minor way, now produce our earthquakes and oscillations of the surface to the extent of a few feet only. Hence these great breaks and fractures were of such a nature as to render it impossible that any cliff should, at the period of their formation, have stood up on one side of the fracture. The very violence of the movement, accompanied as it must have been by the translation of vast masses of water sweeping away the rubbish, may, on the instant, have almost entirely smoothed down the ruptured fragments; the more so, as most of these great dislocations are believed to have taken place *under the sea*. The flattening down of all superficial appearances was therefore most probably the direct result of the catastrophe, and the countless ages of Darwin were, in all probability, at the longest, nothing more than a few months or years of our time.

Now it is proved to demonstration by Sir Roderick Murchison, and admitted by all geologists, that we possess these earlier formations, stretching over vast extents, perfectly unaltered, and exhibiting no signs of life. Here we have, as nearly as it is possible in the nature of things to have, the absolute proof of a negative. If these forms of life had existed they must have been found. Even Mr. Darwin shrinks from the deadly gripe of this argument. 'The case,' he says (p. 308) 'at present must remain inexplicable, and may be truly urged as a valid argument against the views here entertained.' More than once indeed does he make this admission. One passage we have quoted already from p. 280 of his work. With equal candour he says further on:—

> 'I do not pretend that I should ever have suspected how poor a record of the mutations of life the best preserved geological section presented, had not the difficulty of our not discovering innumerable transitional links between the species which appeared at the commencement and close of each formation pressed so hardly on my theory.'—p. 302.

And, once more—

> 'Why does not every collection of fossil remains afford plain evidence of the gradation and mutation of the forms of life? We

meet with no such evidence, and this is the most obvious and
forcible of the many objections which may be urged against my
theory.'—p. 463.

But though this objection is that which is rated highest by himself, there is
another which appears to us in some respects stronger still, and to which we
deem Mr. Darwin's answers equally insufficient,—we mean the law of sterility
affixed to hybridism. If it were possible to proclaim more distinctly by one
provision than another that the difference between various species was a law
of creation, and not, as the transmutationists maintain, an ever-varying
accident, it would surely be by the interposing such a bar to change as that
which now exists in the universal fruitlessness which is the result of all known
mixtures of animals specifically distinct. Mr. Darwin labours hard here, but
his utmost success is to reveal a very few instances from the vegetable world,
with its shadowy image of the procreative animal system, as exceptions to the
universal rule. As to animals, he is compelled by the plainness of the
testimony against him to admit that he 'doubts whether any case of a
perfectly fertile hybrid animal can be considered as thoroughly well
authenticated' (p. 252); and his best attempts to get rid of this evidence are
such suggestions as that 'the common and the true ring-necked pheasant
intercross' (p. 253), though every breeder of game could tell him that, so far
from there being the slightest ground for considering these as distinct species,
all experience shows that the ring-necked almost uniformly appears where the
common pheasant's eggs are hatched under the domestic hen. How then does
Mr. Darwin dispose of this apparently impassable barrier of nature against the
transmutation-theory? He urges that it depends not upon any great law of
life, but mainly, first, on the early death of the embryo, or, secondly, upon
'the common imperfection of the reproductive system' in the male offspring.
How he considers this to be any answer to the difficulty it is beyond our
power to conceive. We can hardly imagine any clearer way of stating the
mode in which an universal law, if it existed, must act, than that in which he
describes it, to disprove its existence.

We come then to these conclusions. All the facts presented to us in the
natural world tend to show that none of the variations produced in the fixed
forms of animal life, when seen in its most plastic condition under
domestication, give any promise of a true transmutation of species; first, from
the difficulty of accumulating and fixing variations within the same species;
secondly, from the fact that these variations, though most serviceable for
man, have no tendency to improve the individual beyond the standard of his
own specific type, and so to afford matter, even if they were infinitely
produced, for the supposed power of natural selection on which to work;
whilst all variations from the mixture of species are barred by the inexorable

law of hybrid sterility. Further, the embalmed records of 3000 years show that there has been no beginning of transmutation in the species of our most familiar domesticated animals; and beyond this, that in the countless tribes of animal life around us, down to its lowest and most variable species, no one has ever discovered a single instance of such transmutation being now in prospect; no new organ has ever been known to be developed—no new natural instinct to be formed—whilst, finally, in the vast museum of departed animal life which the strata of the earth imbed for our examination, whilst they contain far too complete a representation of the past to be set aside as a mere imperfect record, yet afford no one instance of any such change as having ever been in progress, to give us anywhere the missing links of the assumed chain, or the remains which would enable now existing variations, by gradual approximations, to shade off into unity.

In the name of all true philosophy we protest equally against such a mode of dealing with nature, as utterly dishonourable to all natural science, as reducing it from its present lofty level as one of the noblest trainers of man's intellect and instructors of his mind, to being a mere idle play of the fancy, without the basis of fact or the discipline of observation. In the 'Arabian Nights' we are not offended as at an impossibility when Amina sprinkles her husband with water and transforms him into a dog, but we cannot open the august doors of the venerable temple of scientific truth to the genii and magicians of romance. We plead guilty to Mr. Darwin's imputation that

> 'the chief cause of our natural unwillingness to admit that one species has given birth to other and distinct species is that we are always slow in admitting any great change of which we do not see the intermediate steps.'—p. 481.

In this tardiness to admit great changes suggested by the imagination, but the steps of which we cannot see, is the true spirit of philosophy.

> 'Analysis,' says Professor Sedgwick, 'consists in making experiments and observations, and in drawing general conclusions from them by induction, and admitting of no objections against the conclusions but such as are taken from experiments or other certain truths; for hypotheses are not to be regarded in experimental philosophy.'*

The other solvent which Mr. Darwin most freely and, we think, unphilosophically employs to get rid of difficulties, is his use of time. This he shortens or prolongs at will by the mere wave of his magician's rod. Thus the duration of whole epochs, during which certain forms of animal life prevail, is gathered up into a point, whilst an unlimited expanse of years, impressing his

*'A Discourse on the Studies of the University,' by A. Sedgwick, p. 102.

mind with a sense of eternity, is suddenly interposed between that and the next series, though geology proclaims the transition to have been one of gentle and, it may be, swift accomplishment. All this too is made the more startling because it is used to meet the objections drawn from facts. 'We see none of your works,' says the observer of nature; 'we see no beginnings of the portentous change; we see plainly beings of another order in creation, but we find amongst them no tendencies to these altered organisms.' 'True,' says the great magician, with a calmness no difficulty derived from the obstinacy of facts can disturb; 'true, but remember the effect of time. Throw in a few hundreds of millions of years more or less, and why should not all these changes be possible, and, if possible, why may I not assume them to be real?'

Mr. Darwin writes as a Christian, and we doubt not that he is one. We do not for a moment believe him to be one of those who retain in some corner of their hearts a secret unbelief which they dare not vent; and we therefore pray him to consider well the grounds on which we brand his speculations with the charge of such a tendency. First, then, he not obscurely declares that he applies his scheme of the action of the principle of natural selection to Man himself, as well as to the animals around him. Now, we must say at once, and openly, that such a notion is absolutely incompatible not only with single expressions in the word of God on that subject of natural science with which it is not immediately concerned, but, which in our judgment is of far more importance, with the whole representation of that moral and spiritual condition of man which is its proper subject-matter. Man's derived supremacy over the earth; man's power of articulate speech; man's gift of reason; man's free-will and responsibility; man's fall and man's redemption; the incarnation of the Eternal Son; the indwelling of the Eternal Spirit,—all are equally and utterly irreconcilable with the degrading notion of the brute origin of him who was created in the image of God, and redeemed by the Eternal Son assuming to himself his nature. Equally inconsistent, too, not with any passing expressions, but with the whole scheme of God's dealings with man as recorded in His word, is Mr. Darwin's daring notion of man's further development into some unknown extent of powers, and shape, and size, through natural selection acting through that long vista of ages which he casts mistily over the earth upon the most favoured individuals of his species. We care not in these pages to push the argument further. We have done enough for our purpose in thus succinctly intimating its course. If any of our readers doubt what must be the result of such speculations carried to their logical and legitimate conclusion, let them turn to the pages of Oken, and see for themselves the end of that path the opening of which is decked out in these pages with the bright hues and seemingly innocent deductions of the transmutation-theory.

Nor can we doubt, secondly, that this view, which thus contradicts the revealed relation of creation to its Creator, is equally inconsistent with the fulness of His glory. It is, in truth, an ingenious theory for diffusing throughout creation the working and so the personality of the Creator. And thus, however unconsciously to him who holds them, such views really tend inevitably to banish from the mind most of the peculiar attributes of the Almighty.

Equally startling is the contrast between the flighty anticipations of the future in which Mr. Darwin indulges, and the sober philosophy with which Owen restrains the flight of his own more soaring imagination:—

> 'In the distant future I see,' says Darwin, 'open fields for far more important researches. Psychology will be based on a new foundation—that of the necessary acquirement of each mental power and capacity by gradation. Light will be thrown on the origin of man and his history.'—pp. 488-9.

> 'Judging from the past, we may safely infer that not one living species will transmit its unaltered likeness to a distant futurity, and of the species now living very few will transmit progeny to a far-distant futurity.... We may look with some confidence to a secure future of equally inappreciable length. And as natural selection works solely by and for the good of each being, all corporeal and mental endowments will tend to progress towards perfection.'—p. 489.

> 'There is grandeur in this view of life, with its several powers, and having been originally breathed by the Creator into a few forms or into one; and that, whilst this planet has gone cycling on according to the fixed law of gravity, from so simple a beginning endless forms most beautiful and most wonderful have been and are being evolved!'—p. 490.

Surely there is a far grander tone of vaticination about these words of caution from a far greater philosopher:—

> 'As to the successions or coming in of new species, one might speculate on the gradual modifiability of the individual; on the tendency of certain varieties to survive local changes, and thus progressively diverge from an older type; on the production and fertility of monstrous offspring; on the possibility, *e.g.* of a variety of auk being occasionally hatched with a somewhat longer winglet and a dwarfed stature; on the probability of such a variety better adapting itself to the changing climate or other conditions than the old type; of such an origin of *Alca torda, e.g.*;—but to what purpose? Past experience of the chance-aims of human fancy, unchecked and unguided by observed facts, shows how widely they have ever glanced away from the gold centre of truth.'—*Owen on the Classification of Mammalia*, p. 58.

'Turning from a retrospect into past time for the prospect of time to come . . . . . . I may crave indulgence for a few words. . . . . . . There seems to have been a time when life was not; there may, therefore, be a period when it will cease to be . . . . The end of the world has been presented to man's mind under divers aspects:—as a general conflagration; as the same, preceded by a millennial exaltation of the world to a paradisiacal state, the abode of a higher and blessed state of intelligences. If the guide-post of palaeontology may seem to point to a course ascending to the condition of the latter speculation, it points but a very short way, and on leaving it we find ourselves in a wilderness of conjecture, where to try to advance is to find ourselves "in wandering mazes lost." '—p. 61.

It is by putting such a restraint upon fancy that science is made the true trainer of our intellect:—

'A study of the Newtonian philosophy,' says Sedgwick, 'as affecting our moral powers and capacities, does not terminate in mere negations. It teaches us to see the finger of God in all things animate and inanimate, and gives us an exalted conception of His attributes, placing before us the clearest proof of their reality; and so prepares, or ought to prepare, the mind for the reception of that higher illumination which brings the rebellious faculties into obedience to the Divine will.'—*Studies of the University*, p. 14.

It is by our deep conviction of the truth and importance of this view for the scientific mind of England that we have been led to treat at so much length Mr. Darwin's speculation. The contrast between the sober, patient, philosophical courage of our home philosophy, and the writings of Lamarck and his followers and predecessors, of MM. Demailet, Bory de Saint Vincent, Virey, and Oken,* is indeed most wonderful; and it is greatly owing to the noble tone which has been given by those great men whose words we have quoted to the school of British science. That Mr. Darwin should have wandered from this broad highway of nature's works into the jungle of fanciful assumption is no small evil. We trust that he is mistaken in believing

---

*It may be worth while to exhibit to our readers a few of Dr. Oken's postulates or arguments as specimens of his views:—

'I wrote the first edition of 1810 in a kind of inspiration.

'4. Spirit is the motion of mathematical ideas.

'10. Physio-philosophy has to . . . . portray the first period of the world's development from nothing; how the elements and heavenly bodies originated; in what method by self-evolution into higher and manifold forms they separated into minerals, became finally organic, and in man attained self-consciousness.

'42. The mathematical monad is eternal.

'43. The eternal is one and the same with the zero of mathematics.'

that he may count Sir C. Lyell as one of his converts. We know indeed the strength of the temptations which he can bring to bear upon his geological brother. The Lyellian hypothesis, itself not free from some of Mr. Darwin's faults, stands eminently in need for its own support of some such new scheme of physical life as that propounded here. Yet no man has been more distinct and more logical in the denial of the transmutation of species than Sir C. Lyell, and that not in the infancy of his scientific life, but in its full vigour and maturity.

Sir C. Lyell devotes the 33rd to the 36th chapter of his 'Principles of Geology' to an examination of this question. He gives a clear account of the mode in which Lamarck supported his belief of the transmutation of species; he 'interrupts the author's argument to observe that no positive fact is cited to exemplify the substitution of some *entirely new* sense, faculty, or organ—because no examples were to be found; and remarks that when Lamarck talks' of 'the effects of internal sentiment,' &c., as causes whereby animals and plants may acquire *new organs*, he substitutes names for things, and with a disregard to the strict rules of induction resorts to fictions.

He shows the fallacy of Lamarck's reasoning, and by anticipation confutes the whole theory of Mr. Darwin, when gathering clearly up into a few heads the recapitulation of the whole argument in favour of the reality of species in nature. He urges:—

1. That there is a capacity in all species to accommodate themselves to a certain extent to a change of external circumstances.

4. The entire variation from the original type . . . may usually be effected in a brief period of time, after which no further deviation can be obtained.

5. The intermixing distinct species is guarded against by the sterility of the mule offspring.

6. It appears that species have a real existence in nature, and that each was endowed at the time of its creation with the attributes and organization by which it is now distinguished.*

We trust that Sir C. Lyell abides still by these truly philosophical principles; and that with his help and with that of his brethren this flimsy speculation may be as completely put down as was what in spite of all denials we must venture to call its twin though less-instructed brother, the 'Vestiges of Creation.' In so doing they will assuredly provide for the strength and continually growing progress of British science.

Indeed, not only do all laws for the study of nature vanish when the great principle of order pervading and regulating all her processes is given up, but all that imparts the deepest interest in the investigation of her wonders will

*'Principles of Geology,' edit. 1853.

have departed too. Under such influences man soon goes back to the marvelling stare of childhood at the centaurs and hippogriffs of fancy, or if he is of a philosophic turn, he comes like Oken to write a scheme of creation under 'a sort of inspiration;' but it is the frenzied inspiration of the inhaler of mephitic gas. The whole world of nature is laid for such a man under a fantastic law of glamour, and he becomes capable of believing anything: to him it is just as probable that Dr. Livingstone will find the next tribe of negroes with their heads growing under their arms as fixed on the summit of the cervical vertebrae; and he is able, with a continually growing neglect of all the facts around him, with equal confidence and equal delusion, to look back to any past and to look on to any future.

On the Relations of
Man to the Lower Animals

by
Thomas H. Huxley

"Man's Place in Nature"
January, 1863,

On all sides I shall hear the cry—"We are men and women, not a mere better sort of apes, a little longer in the leg, more compact in the foot, and bigger in brain than your brutal Chimpanzees and Gorillas. The power of knowledge—the conscience of good and evil—the pitiful tenderness of human affections, raise us out of all real fellowship with the brutes, however closely they may seem to approximate us."

To this I can only reply that the exclamation would be most just and would have my own entire sympathy, if it were only relevant. But, it is not I who seek to base Man's dignity upon his great toe, or insinuate that we are lost if an Ape has a hippocampus minor. On the contrary, I have done my best to sweep away this vanity. I have endeavoured to show that no absolute structural line of demarcation, wider than that between the animals which immediately succeed us in the scale, can be drawn between the animal world and ourselves; and I may add the expression of my belief that the attempt to draw a psychical distinction is equally futile, and that even the highest faculties of feeling and of intellect begin to germinate in lower forms of life. At the same time, no one is more strongly convinced than I am of the vastness of the gulf between civilised man and the brutes; or is more certain that whether *from* them or not, he is assuredly not *of* them. No one is less disposed to think lightly of the present dignity, or despairingly of the future hopes, of the only consciously intelligent denizen of this world.

We are indeed told by those who assume authority in these matters, that the two sets of opinions are incompatible, and that the belief in the unity of origin of man and brutes involves the brutalization and degradation of the former. But is this really so? Could not a sensible child confute by obvious arguments, the shallow rhetoricians who would force this conclusion upon us? Is it, indeed, true, that the Poet, or the Philosopher, or the Artist whose genius is the glory of his age, is degraded from his high estate by the undoubted historical probability, not to say certainty, that he is the direct descendant of some naked and bestial savage, whose intelligence was just sufficient to make him a little more cunning than the Fox, and by so much more dangerous than the Tiger? Or is he bound to howl and grovel on all fours because of the wholly unquestionable fact, that he was once an egg, which no ordinary power of discrimination could distinguish from that of a Dog? Or is the philanthropist, or the saint, to give up his endeavours to lead a noble life, because the simplest study of man's nature reveals, at its foundations, all the selfish passions, and fierce appetites of the merest quadruped? Is mother-love vile because a hen shows it, or fidelity base because dogs possess it?

The common sense of the mass of mankind will answer these questions without a moment's hesitation. Healthy humanity, finding itself hard pressed to escape from real sin and degradation, will leave the brooding over speculative pollution to the cynics and the "righteous overmuch" who, disagreeing in everything else, unite in blind insensibility to the nobleness of the visible world, and in inability to appreciate the grandeur of the place Man occupies therein.

Nay more, thoughtful men, once escaped from the blinding influences of traditional prejudice, will find in the lowly stock whence Man has sprung, the best evidence of the splendour of his capacities; and will discern in his long progress through the Past, a reasonable ground of faith in his attainment of a nobler Future.

They will remember that in comparing civilised man with the animal world, one is as the Alpine traveller, who sees the mountains soaring into the sky and can hardly discern where the deep shadowed crags and roseate peaks end, and where the clouds of heaven begin. Surely the awe-struck voyager may be excused if, at first, he refuses to believe the geologist, who tells him that these glorious masses are, after all, the hardened mud of primeval seas, or the cooled slag of subterranean furnaces—of one substance with the dullest clay, but raised by inward forces to that place of proud and seemingly inaccessible glory.

But the geologist is right; and due reflection on his teachings, instead of diminishing our reverence and our wonder, adds all the force of intellectual sublimity to the mere aesthetic intuition of the uninstructed beholder.

And after passion and prejudice have died away, the same result will attend the teachings of the naturalist respecting that great Alps and Andes of the living world—Man. Our reverence for the nobility of manhood will not be lessened by the knowledge that Man is, in substance and in structure, one with the brutes; for, he alone possesses the marvellous endowment of intelligible and rational speech, whereby, in the secular period of his existence, he has slowly accumulated and organised the experience which is almost wholly lost with the cessation of every individual life in other animals; so that, now, he stands raised upon it as on a mountain top, far above the level of his humble fellows, and transfigured from his grosser nature by reflecting, here and there, a ray from the infinite source of truth.

Summation for the State
from the Scopes Trial

by
William Jennings Bryan

"Christianity welcomes truth from whatever source it comes and is not afraid that any real truth from any source can interfere with the divine truth that comes by inspiration from God Himself. It is not scientific truth to which Christians object, for true science is classified knowledge and nothing therefore can be scientific unless it is true.

"Evolution is not truth, it is merely an hypothesis—it is millions of guesses strung together. It had not been proved in the days of Darwin; he expressed astonishment that with two or three million species it had been impossible to trace any species to any other species. It had not been proved in the days of Huxley, and it has not been proved up to today.

"It is less than four years ago that Professor Bateson came all the way from London to Canada to tell the American scientists that every effort to trace one species to another had failed—every one. He said he still had faith in evolution, but had doubts about the origin of species.

"But of what value is evolution if it cannot explain the origin of species? While many scientists accept evolution as if it were a fact, they all admit when questioned that no explanation has been found of how one species developed into another.

"Darwin suggested two laws, sexual selection and natural selection. Sexual selection has been laughed out of the class room, and natural selection is being abandoned, and no new explanation is satisfactory even to scientists. Some of the more rash advocates of evolution are wont to say that evolution is as firmly established as the law of gravitation or the Copernician theory.

"The absurdity of such a claim is apparent when we remember that any one can prove the law of gravitation by throwing a weight into the air and

41

that any one can prove the roundness of the earth by going around it, while no one can prove evolution to be true in any way whatever.

"Chemistry is an insurmountable obstacle in the path of evolution. It is one of the greatest of the sciences; it separates the atoms—isolates them and walks about them, so to speak. If there were in nature a progressive force, an eternal urge, chemistry would find it. But it is not there.

"All of the ninety-two original elements are separate and distinct; they combine in fixed and permanent proportions. Water is H_2O, as it has been from the beginning. It was here before life appeared and has never changed; neither can it be shown that anything else has materially changed.

"There is no more reason to believe that man descended from some inferior animal than there is to believe that a stately mansion has descended from a small cottage. Resemblances are not proof—they simply put us on inquiry. As one fact, such as the absence of the accused from the scene of the murder, outweighs all the resemblances that a thousand witnesses could swear to, so the inability of science to trace any one of the millions of species to another species outweighs all the resemblances upon which evolutionists rely to establish man's blood relationship with the brutes.

"But while the wisest scientists cannot prove a pushing power, such as evolution is supposed to be, there is a lifting power that any child can understand. The plant lifts the mineral up into a higher world, and the animal lifts the plant up into a world still higher. So, it has been reasoned by analogy, man rises, not by a power within him, but only when drawn upward by a higher power. There is a spiritual gravitation that draws all souls toward heaven, just as surely as there is a physical force that draws all matter on the surface of the earth toward the earth's center.

"Christ is our drawing power; He said, 'I, if I be lifted up from the earth, will draw all men unto me,'[1] and His promise is being fulfilled daily all over the world.

"It must be remembered that the law under consideration in this case does not prohibit the teaching of evolution up to the line that separates man from the lower form of animal life. The law might well have gone further than it does and prohibit the teaching of evolution in lower forms of life; the law is a very conservative statement of the people's opposition to an anti-Biblical hypothesis. . . .

"Most of the people who believe in evolution do not know what evolution means. One of the science books taught in the Dayton High School has a chapter on 'The Evolution of Machinery.' This is a very common misuse of the term. People speak of the evolution of the telephone, the automobile, and

[1] John 12:32.

the musical instrument. But these are merely illustrations of man's power to deal intelligently with inanimate matter; there is no growth from within in the development of machinery.

"Equally improper is the use of the word 'evolution' to describe the growth of a plant from a seed, the growth of a chicken from an egg, or the development of any form of animal life from a single cell. All these give us a circle, not a change from one species to another.

"Evolution—the evolution involved in this case, and the only evolution that is a matter of controversy anywhere—is the evolution taught by defendant, set forth in the books now prohibited by the State law, and illustrated in the diagram printed on page 194 of Hunter's 'Civic Biology.'

"The author estimates the number of species in the animal kingdom at 518,900. These are divided into eighteen classes, and each class is indicated on the diagram by a circle. It begins with protozoa and ends with the mammals.

"No circle is reserved for man alone. He is, according to the diagram, shut up in the little circle entitled 'mammals,' with 3,499 other species of mammals. Does it not seem a little unfair not to distinguish between man and lower forms of life?

"What shall we say of the intelligence, not to say religion, of those who are so particular to distinguish between fishes and reptiles and birds, but put a man with an immortal soul in the same circle with the wolf, the hyena, and the skunk? What must be the impression made upon children by such a degradation of man?

"In the preface of this book the author explains that it is for children, and adds that 'the boy or girl of average ability upon admission to the secondary school is not a thinking individual.'

"Whatever may be said in favor of teaching evolution to adults, it surely is not proper to teach it to children who are not yet able to think.

"The evolutionist does not undertake to tell us how protozoa, moved by interior and resident forces, sent life up through all the various species, and cannot prove that there was actually any such compelling power at all. And yet, the school children are asked to accept guesses and build a philosophy of life upon them.

"If it were not so serious a matter, one might be tempted to speculate upon the various degrees of relationship that, according to evolutionists, exist between man and other forms of life. It might require some very nice calculation to determine at what degree of relationship the killing of a relative ceases to be murder and the eating of one's kin ceases to be cannibalism.

"But it is not a laughing matter when one considers that evolution not only offers no suggestions regarding a Creator, but tends to put the creative act so far away to cast doubt upon creation itself. And, while it is shaking faith in God as a beginning, it is also creating doubt regarding a heaven at the end of life.

"Evolutionists do not feel that it is incumbent upon them to show how life began or at what point in their long drawn out scheme of changing species man became endowed with hope and promise of immortal life. God may be a matter of indifference to the evolutionists, and a life beyond may have no charm for them, but the mass of mankind will continue to worship their Creator and continue to find comfort in the promise of their Saviour that He has gone to prepare a place for them.

"Christ has made of death a narrow, star-lit strip between the companionship of yesterday and the reunion of tomorrow; evolution strikes out the stars and deepens the gloom that enshrouds the tomb.

"If the results of evolution were unimportant, one might require less proof in support of the hypothesis, but before accepting a new philosophy of life, built upon a materialistic foundation, we have reason to demand something more than guesses; 'We may well suppose' is not a sufficient substitute for 'Thus saith the Lord.'

"If you, your Honor, and you, gentlemen of the jury, would have an understanding of the sentiment that lies back of the statute against the teaching of evolution, please consider the facts that I shall now present to you. First, regarding the animals to which evolutionists would have us trace our ancestry. The following is Darwin's family tree, as you will find it set forth on pages 180-181 of his 'Descent of Man':

" 'The most ancient progenitors in the kingdom of vertebrata, at which we are able to obtain an obscure glance, apparently consisted of a group of marine animals resembling the larvae of existing ascidians. These animals probably gave rise to a group of fishes, as lowly organized as the lancelot; and from these the ganoids, and other fishes like the Lepidosiren, must have been duplicated.

" 'From such fish a very small advance would carry us on to the amphibians. We have seen that birds and reptiles were once intimately called together, and the Monotremata now connect mammals with reptiles in a slight degree.

" 'But no one can at present say by what line of descent the three higher and related classes, namely mammals, birds, and reptiles, were derived from the two lower vertebrate classes, namely amphibians and fishes. In the class of mammals the steps are not difficult to conceive which led from the ancient Monotremata to the ancient Marsupials and from these to the early progenitors of the placental mammals. We may thus ascend to the Lemuridae; and the interval is not very wide from these to the Simiadae.

" 'The Simiadae then branched off into two great stems, the New World and Old World monkeys; and from the latter, at a remote period, man, the wonder and glory of the universe, proceeded. Thus we have given to a man a pedigree of prodigious length, but not, it may be said, of noble quality.'

"Note the words implying uncertainty: 'obscure glance,' 'apparently,' 'resembling,' 'must have been,' 'slight degree,' and·'conceive.'

"Darwin, on page 171 of the same book, tries to locate his first man—that is, the first man to come down out of the trees—in Africa. After leaving man in company with gorillas and chimpanzees, he says: 'But it is useless to speculate on this subject.' If he had only thought of this earlier the world might have been spared much of the speculation that his brute hypothesis has excited.

"On page 79, Darwin gives some fanciful reasons for believing that man is more likely to have descended from the chimpanzee than from the gorilla. His speculations are an excellent illustration of the effect that the evolutionary hypothesis has in cultivating the imagination. Professor J. Arthur Thomson says that the 'idea of evolution is the most potent thought-economizing formula the world has yet known.' It is more than that; it dispenses with thinking entirely and relies on the imagination.

"On page 141, Darwin attempts to trace the mind of man back to the mind of lower animals. On pages 113 and 114, he endeavors to trace man's moral nature back to the animals. It is all animal, animal, animal, with never a thought of God or of religion.

"Our first indictment against evolution is that it disputes the truth of the Bible account of man's creation and shakes faith in the Bible as the work of God. This indictment we prove by comparing the processes described as evolutionary with the text of Genesis. It not only contradicts the Mosaic record on the beginning of human life, but it disputes the Bible doctrine of reproduction according to kind—the greatest scientific principle known.

"Our second indictment is that the evolutionary hypothesis carried to its logical conclusion disputes every vital truth of the Bible. Its tendency, natural if not inevitable, is to lead those who really accept it, first to agnosticism and then to atheism. Evolutionists attack the truth of the Bible, not openly at first, but by using weasel words like 'poetical,' 'symbolical,' and 'allegorical' to suck the meaning out of the inspired record of man's creation.

"We call as our first witness Charles Darwin. He began life a Christian. On page 39, Volume I, of the 'Life and Letters of Charles Darwin,' by his son, Francis Darwin, he says, speaking of the period from 1828 to 1831, 'I did not then in the least doubt the strict and literal truth of every word in the Bible.'

"On page 412 of Volume II of the same publication, he says, 'When I was collecting facts for the "Origin," my belief in what is called a personal God was as firm as that of Dr. Pusey himself.' It may be a surprise to your Honor and to you, gentlemen of the jury, as it was to me, to learn that Darwin spent three years at Cambridge studying for the ministry.

"This was Darwin as a young man, before he came under the influence of doctrine that man came from a lower order of animals. The change wrought in his religious views will be found in a letter written to a German youth in 1879, and printed on page 277 of Volume I of the 'Life and Letters' above referred to. The letter begins: 'I am much engaged, an old man, and out of health, and I cannot spare time to answer your questions fully—nor indeed can they be answered. Science has nothing to do with Christ, except in so far as the habit of scientific research makes a man cautious in admitting evidence. For myself, I do not believe that there ever has been any revelation. As for a future life, every man must judge for himself between conflicting vague probabilities.'

"Note that 'science has nothing to do with Christ, except in so far as the habit of scientific research makes a man cautious in admitting evidence.' Stated plainly, that simply means that 'the habit of scientific research' makes one cautious in accepting the only evidence that we have of Christ's existence, mission, teachings, crucifixion, and resurrection, namely the evidence found in the Bible.

"To make this interpretation of his words, the only possible one, he adds: 'For myself, I do not believe that there ever has been any revelation.'

"In rejecting the Bible as a revelation from God, he rejects the Bible's conception of God, and he rejects also the supernatural Christ, of whom the Bible, and the Bible alone, tells. And, it will be observed, he refuses to express any opinion on a future life.

"Now let us follow with his son's exposition of his father's views as they are given in extracts from a biography written in 1876. Here is Darwin's language as quoted by his son:

" 'During these two years—October, 1838, to January, 1839—I was led to think much about religion. Whilst on board the *Beagle* I was quite orthodox and I remember being heartily laughed at by several of the officers—who thought themselves orthodox—for quoting the Bible as an unanswerable authority on some point of morality. When thus reflecting I felt compelled to look for a First Cause, having an intelligent mind in some degree analogous to man, and I deserved to be called an atheist.

" 'This conclusion was strong in my mind about the time, as far as I can remember, when I wrote the "Origin of Species"; it is since that time that it has very gradually, with many fluctuations, become weaker. But then arises the doubt, can the mind of man, which has, as I fully believe, been developed from a mind as low as that possessed by the lowest animals, be trusted when it draws such grand conclusions?

" 'I cannot pretend to throw the least light on such abstruse problems. The mystery of the beginning of all things is insoluble by us; and I for one must be content to remain an agnostic.'

"When Darwin entered upon his scientific career he was 'quite orthodox and quoted the Bible as an unanswerable authority on some point of morality.' Even when he wrote 'The Origin of Species' the thought of 'a First Cause, having an intelligent mind in some degree analogous to man' was strong in his mind. It was after that time that 'very gradually, with many fluctuations,' his belief in God became weaker.

"He traces this decline for us and concludes by telling us that he cannot pretend to throw the least light on such abstruse problems—the religious problems above referred to. Then comes the flat statement that he 'must be content to remain an agnostic'; and to make clear what he means by the word 'agnostic,' he says that 'the mystery of the beginning of all things is insoluble by us'—not by him alone, but by everybody. Here we have the effect of evolution upon its most distinguished exponent; it led him from an orthodox Christian, believing every word of the Bible and in a personal God, down and down and down to helpless and hopeless agnosticism.

"But there is one sentence upon which I reserved comment—it throws light upon his downward pathway. 'Then arises the doubt, can the mind of man which has, as I fully believe, been developed from a mind as low as that possessed by the lowest animals, be trusted when it draws such grand conclusions?'

"Here is the explanation; he drags man down to the brute level, and then, judging man by brute standards, he questions whether man's mind can be trusted to deal with 'God and immortality.'

"Our third indictment against evolution is that it diverts attention from pressing problems of great importance to trifling speculations. While one evolutionist is trying to imagine what happened in the dim past, another is trying to pry open the door of the distant future.

"One recently grew eloquent over ancient worms, and another predicted that 75,000 years hence every one will be bald and toothless. Both those who endeavor to clothe our remote ancestors with hair and those who endeavor to remove the hair from the heads of our remote descendants ignore the present with its imperative demands. The science of 'how to live' is the most important of all the sciences, but it is necessary to know how to live.

"Christians desire that their children shall be taught all the sciences, but they do not want them to lose sight of the Rock of Ages while they study the age of rocks; neither do they desire them to become so absorbed in measuring the distance between the stars that they will forget Him who holds the stars in His hand.

"While not more than two per cent of our population are college graduates, these, because of enlarged powers, need a 'heavenly vision' even more than those less learned, both for their own restraint and to assure society that their enlarged powers will be used for the benefit of society and not against the public welfare.

"The cry in the business world, in the industrial world, in the professional world, in the political world—even in the religious world—is for consecrated talents—for ability plus a passion for service.

"Our fourth indictment against the evolutionary hypothesis is that, by paralyzing the hope of reform, it discourages those who labor for the improvement of man's condition. Every upward-looking man or woman seeks to lift the level upon which mankind stands, and they trust that they will see beneficent changes during the brief span of their own lives.

"Evolution chills their enthusiasm by substituting eons for years. It obscures all beginnings in the mists of endless ages. It is represented as a cold and heartless process, beginning with time and ending in eternity, and acting so slowly that even the rocks cannot preserve a record of the imaginary changes through which it is credited with having carried an original germ of life that appeared some time from somewhere.

"Its only program for man is scientific breeding, a system under which a few supposedly superior intellects, self-appointed, would direct the mating and the movements of the mass of mankind—an impossible system. Evolution, disputing the miracle, and ignoring the spiritual in life, has no place for the regeneration of the individual. It recognizes no cry of repentance and scoffs at the doctrine that one can be born again.

"It is thus the intolerant and unrelenting enemy of the only process that can redeem society through the redemption of the individual. An evolutionist would never write such a story as 'The Prodigal Son'; it contradicts the whole theory of evolution. The two sons inherited from the same parents and, through their parents, from the same ancestors, proximate and remote.

"And these sons were reared at the same fireside and were surrounded by the same environment during all the days of their youth; and yet they were different. If Mr. Darrow is correct in the theory applied to Loeb, namely, that his crime was due either to inheritance or to environment, how will he explain the difference between the elder brother and the wayward son?

"The evolutionist may understand from observation, if not by experience, even though he cannot explain, why one of these boys was guilty of every immorality, squandered the money the father had laboriously earned and brought disgrace upon the family name; but his theory does not explain why a wicked young man underwent a change of heart, confessed his sin, and begged for forgiveness.

"And because the evolutionists cannot understand this fact, one of the most important in the human life, he cannot understand the infinite love of the Heavenly Father who stands ready to welcome home any repentant sinner, no matter how far he has wandered, how often he has fallen, or how deep he has sunk in sin.

"Your Honor has quoted from a wonderful poem written by a great Tennessee poet, Walter Malone. I venture to quote another stanza which puts into exquisite language the new opportunity which a merciful God gives to every one who will turn from sin to righteousness:

> *Though deep in mire, wring not your hands and weep;*
> *I lend my arm to all who say 'I can.'*
> *No shame-faced outcast ever sank so deep*
> *But he might rise and be again a man.*

"There are no lines like these in all that evolutionists have ever written. Darwin says that science has nothing to do with the Christ who taught the spirit embodied in the words of Walter Malone, and yet this spirit is the only hope of human progress. A heart can be changed in the twinkling of an eye and a change in the life follows a change in the heart.

"It is because Christians believe in individual regeneration and in the regeneration of society through the regeneration of individuals that they pray, 'Thy kingdom come, Thy will be done on earth as it is in Heaven.' Evolution makes a mockery of the Lord's Prayer.

"Our fifth indictment of the evolutionary hypothesis is that if taken seriously and made the basis of a philosophy of life, it would eliminate love and carry man back to a struggle of tooth and claw.

"The Christians who have allowed themselves to be deceived into believing that evolution is a beneficent, or even a rational, process have been associating with those who either do not understand its implications or dare not avow their knowledge of these implications. Let us give you some authority on this subject. I will begin with Darwin, the high priest of evolution, to whom all evolutionists bow.

"On pages 149 and 150, in 'The Descent of Man,' already referred to, he says:

" 'With savages the weak in body or mind are soon eliminated, and those that survive commonly exhibit a vigorous state of health. We civilized men, on the other hand, do our utmost to check the process of elimination; we build asylums for the imbecile, the maimed, and the sick; we institute poor laws; and our medical men exert their utmost skill to save the life of every one to the last moment. There is reason to believe that vaccination has preserved thousands who from a weak constitution would formerly have succumbed to smallpox. Thus the weak members of civilized society propagate their kind.

" 'The aid which we feel impelled to give to the helpless is mainly an incidental result of the instinct of sympathy, which was originally acquired as part of the social instincts, but subsequently rendered, in the manner previously indicated, more tender and more widely diffused. Nor could we check our sympathy, even at the urging of hard reason, without deterioration in the noblest part of our nature. We must therefore bear the undoubtedly bad effects of the weak serving and propagating their kind.'

"Let us analyze the quotation just given. Darwin speaks with approval of the savage custom of eliminating the weak, so that only the strong will survive, and complains that 'we civilized men do our utmost to check the process of elimination.' How inhuman such a doctrine as this!

"He thinks it injurious to 'build asylums for the imbecile, the maimed and the sick, or to care for the poor.' All of the sympathetic activities of civilized society are condemned because they enable 'the weak members to propagate their kind.'

"Then he drags mankind down to the level of the brute and compares the freedom given to man unfavorably with the restraint that we put on barnyard beasts.

"Let no one think that this acceptance of barbarism as the basic principle of evolution died with Darwin. Within three years a book has appeared whose author is even more frankly brutal than Darwin. The book is entitled 'The New Decalogue of Science' and has attracted wide attention. One of our most reputable magazines has recently printed an article by him defining the religion of a scientist.

"In his preface he acknowledges indebtedness to twenty-one prominent scientists and educators, nearly all of them 'doctors' and 'professors.' One of them, who has recently been elevated to the head of a great state university, read the manuscript over twice 'and made many invaluable suggestions.'

"The author describes Nietzsche, who, according to Mr. Darwin, made a murderer out of 'Babe' Leopold, as 'the bravest soul since Jesus.'

"He admits that Nietzsche was 'gloriously wrong,' not certainly, but 'perhaps,' 'in many details of technical knowledge,' but he affirms that 'Nietzsche was gloriously right in his fearless questioning of the universe and of his own soul.'

"In another place the author says 'most of our morals today are jungle products,' and then he affirms that 'it would be safer, biologically, if they were more so now.' After these two samples of his views you will not be surprised when I read you the following (see page 34):

" 'Evolution is a bloody business, but civilization tries to make it a pink tea. Barbarism is the only process by which man has ever organically progressed, and civilization is the only process by which he has ever organically declined. Civilization is the most dangerous enterprise upon which man ever set out. For when you take man out of the bloody, brutal but beneficent hand of natural selection you place him at once in the soft, perfumed, daintily gloved, but far more dangerous hand of artificial selection. And unless you call science to your aid and make this artificial selection as efficient as the rude methods of nature you bungle the whole task.'

"This aspect of evolution may amaze some of the ministers who have not been admitted to the inner circle of the iconoclasts whose theories menace all the ideals of civilized society. Do these ministers know that 'evolution is a bloody business'? Do they know that 'civilization is the only process by which man has ever organically declined?' Do they know that 'the bloody, brutal hand of natural selection' is 'beneficent' and that 'the artificial selection' found in civilization is 'dangerous'? What shall we think of the distinguished educators and scientists who read the manuscript before publication and did not protest against this pagan doctrine?

"To show that this is a world-wide matter, I now quote from a book issued from the press in 1918, seven years ago. The title of the book is 'The Science of Power,' and its author, Benjamin Kidd, being an Englishman, could not have any national prejudice against Darwin. On pages 46 and 47 we find Kidd's interpretation of evolution:

" 'Darwin's presentation of the evolution of the world as the product of natural selection in never-ceasing war—as a product, that is to say, of a struggle in which the individual efficient in the fight for his own interests was always the winning type—touched the profoundest depths of the psychology of the West. The idea seemed to present the whole order of progress in the world as the result of a purely mechanical and materialistic process resting on force. In so doing it was a conception which reached the springs of that heredity born of the unmeasured ages of conquest out of which the Western mind has come.' Within half a century the 'Origin of Species' had become the Bible of the doctrine of the omnipotence of force.

"Kidd goes so far as to charge that 'Nietzsche's teaching represented the interpretation of the popular Darwinism delivered with the fury and intensity of genius.' And Nietzsche, be it remembered, denounced Christianity as the 'doctrine of the degenerate,' and democracy as 'the refuge of weaklings.'

"Kidd says that Nietzsche gave Germany the doctrine of Darwin's efficient animal in the voice of his superman, and that Bernhardi and the military textbooks in due time gave Germany the doctrine of the superman translated into the national policy of the superstate aiming at world power. (Page 67.)

"And what else but the spirit of evolution can account for the popularity of the selfish doctrine, 'each one for himself, and the devil take the hindmost,' that threatens the very existence of the doctrine of brotherhood.

"In 1900—twenty-five years ago—while an international peace congress was in session in Paris, the following editorial appeared in *L 'Universe*:

" 'The spirit of peace has fled the earth because evolution has taken possession of it. The plea for peace in past years has been inspired by faith in the divine nature and the divine origin of man; men were then looked upon as children of apes. What matters it whether they are slaughtered or not?'

"When there is poison in the blood, no one knows on what part of the body it will break out, but we can be sure that it will continue to break out until the blood is purified. One of the leading universities of the South (I love the state too well to mention its name) published a monthly magazine entitled 'Journal of Social Forces.' In the January issue of this year, a contributor has a lengthy article on 'Sociology and Ethics,' in the course of which he says:

" 'No attempt will be made to take up the matter of the good or evil of sexual intercourse among humans aside from the matter of conscious procreation, but as an historian it might be worth while to ask the exponents of the impurity complex to explain the fact that, without exception, the great periods of cultural efflorescence have been those characterized by a large amount of freedom in sex relations, and that those of the greatest cultural degradation and decline have been accomplished with greater sex repression and purity.'

"No one charges or suspects that all or any large percentage of the advocates of evolution sympathize with this loathsome application of evolution to social life, but it is worth while to inquire why those in charge of a great institution of learning allow such filth to be poured out for the stirring of the passions of its students.

"Let us, then, hear the conclusion of the whole matter. Science is a magnificent material force, but it is not a teacher of morals. It can perfect machinery, but it adds no moral restraints to protect society from the misuse of the machine. It can also build gigantic intellectual ships, but it constructs no moral rudders for the control of storm-tossed human vessels. It not only fails to supply the spiritual element needed, but some of its unproven hypotheses rob the ship of its compass and thus endanger its cargo.

"In war, science has proven itself an evil genius; it has made war more terrible than it ever was before. Man used to be content to slaughter his fellowmen on a single plane—the earth's surface. Science has taught him to go down into the water and shoot up from below, and to go up into the clouds and shoot down from above, thus making the battlefield three times as bloody as it was before; but science does not teach brotherly love.

"Science has made war so hellish that civilization was about to commit suicide; and now we are told that newly discovered instruments of destruction will make the cruelties of the late war seem trivial in comparison with the cruelties of wars that may come in the future.

"If civilization is to be saved from the wreckage threatened by intelligence not consecrated by love, it must be saved by the moral code of the meek and lowly Nazarene. His teachings, and His teachings alone can solve the problems that vex the heart and perplex the world.

"The world needs a saviour more than it ever did before, and there is only one name under heaven given among men whereby we must be saved. It is this name that evolution degrades, for, carried to its logical conclusion, it robs Christ of the glory of a Virgin birth, of the majesty of His deity and mission, and of the triumph of His resurrection. It also disputes the doctrine of the atonement.

"This case is no longer local; the defendant ceases to play an important part. The case has assumed the proportions of a battle royal between unbelief that attempts to speak through so-called science and the defenders of the Christian faith, speaking through the legislators of Tennessee.

"It is again a choice between God and Baal; it is also a renewal of the issue in Pilate's court.

"In that historic trial—the greatest in history—force, impersonated by Pilate, occupied the throne. Behind it was the Roman Government, mistress of the world, and behind the Roman Government were the legions of Rome. Before Pilate stood Christ, the Apostle of love. Force triumphed; they nailed him to the tree and those who stood around mocked and jeered and said, 'He is dead.' But from that day the power of Caesar waned and the power of Christ increased. In a few centuries the Roman Government was gone and its legions forgotten; while the crucified and risen Lord has become the greatest fact in history and the growing figure of all time.

"Again force and love meet face to face, and the question, 'What shall I do with Jesus?' must be answered. A bloody, brutal doctrine—evolution—demands, as the rabble did 1900 years ago, that He be crucified. That cannot be the answer of this jury, representing a Christian State and sworn to uphold the laws of Tennessee.

"Your answer will be heard throughout the world; it is eagerly awaited by a praying multitude. If the law is nullified, there will be rejoicing wherever God is repudiated, the Saviour scoffed at, and the Bible ridiculed. Every unbeliever of every kind and degree will be happy.

"If, on the other hand, the law is upheld and the religion of the school children protected, millions of Christians will call you blessed and, with hearts full of gratitude to God, will sing again that grand old song of triumph:

Faith of our Fathers, living still,
    In spite of dungeon, fire and sword;
O, how our hearts beat high with joy,
    Whene'er we hear that glorious word!
Faith of our fathers—holy faith;
    We will be true to thee till death!

Statement for the Defense
from the Scopes Trial

by
Clarence Darrow

"I am going to begin with some of the simpler reasons why it is absolutely absurd to think that this statute, indictment, or any part of the proceedings in this case are legal; and I think the sooner we get rid of it in Tennessee the better for the people of Tennessee, and the better for the pursuit of knowledge in the world.

"This legislation–this legislation and all similar legislation that human ingenuity and malice can concoct–is void because it violates Section 13, Section 12, and Section 3 [of the Tennessee Constitution].

"I want to call attention to that, your Honor. Section 12 is the section providing that the State should cherish science, literature, and learning. Now, your Honor, I make it a rule to try and not argue anything that I do not believe in, unless I am caught in a pretty close corner, and I want to say that the construction the Attorney General has given to that, I think, is correct.

"It shows the policy of the State. It shows what the State is committed to. I don't believe that a statute could be set aside as unconstitutional simply because the Legislature did not see fit to pass proper acts to enlighten and educate the yeomen of Tennessee.

"The State by Constitution is committed to the doctrine of education, committed to schools. It is committed to teaching, and I assume when it is committed to teaching it is committed to teaching the truth–ought to be anyhow–plenty of people to do the other.

"It is committed to teaching literature and science. My friend has suggested that literature and science might conflict. I cannot quite see how, but that is another question; but that indicates the policy of the State of Tennessee, and whenever it is used in construing the constitutionality of this act, it can only

55

be used as an indication of what the State meant, and you could not pronounce a statute void on it; but we insist that this statute is absolutely void because it contravenes Section 3, which is headed 'The Right of Free Worship.'

"It is impossible, if you leave freedom in the world, to mold the opinions of one man upon the opinions of another—only tyranny can do it—and your constitutional provision providing freedom of religion was to meet that emergency.

"I will go further. There is nothing else since man—I don't know whether I dare say evolved; still, this isn't a school—since man was created out of the dust of the earth—out of hand—there is nothing else, your Honor, that has caused the difference of opinion, the bitterness, hatred, war, and cruelty, that religion has caused. With that, of course, it has given consolation to millions, but only if these particular things that should be are left solely between the individual and his Maker, or his God, or whatever takes His place with him, and it is no one else's concern.

"How many creeds and cults are there in this whole world over? No man could enumerate them. At least, as I have said, five hundred different Christian creeds,—all made up of differences, your Honor, every one of them, and these subdivided into small differences, until they reach that number in every congregation. Because to think is to differ. And then there are any number of creeds older, and any number of creeds younger, than the Christian creed, any number of them; the world has had them forever. They have come, and they have gone. They have abided their time and have passed away. Some of them are here still, some may be here forever; but there has been a multitude, due to the multitude and manifold differences in human beings, and it was meant by the Constitutional Convention of Tennessee to leave these questions of religion between man and whatever he worshiped,—to leave him free.

"Has the Mohammedan any right to stay here and cherish his creed? Has the Buddhist a right to live here and cherish his creed? Can the Chinaman who comes here to wash our clothes, can he bring his joss and worship it? Is there any man that holds a religious creed, no matter where he came from, or how old it is, or how false it is,—is there any man that can be prohibited by any act of the Legislature of Tennessee? Impossible!

"The Constitution of Tennessee, as I understand it, was copied from the one that Jefferson wrote—so clear, simple, direct—to encourage the freedom of religious opinion. It said in substance that no act shall ever be passed to interfere with complete religious liberty.

"Now, wait—is this it or not? What do you say? What does it do?

"We will say I am a scientist. No, I will take that back—I am a pseudo-scientist, because I believe in evolution,—pseudo-scientist, named by somebody, who neither knows or cares what science is, except to grab it by the throat and throttle it to death. I am a pseudo-scientist, and I believe in evolution. Can a legislative body say, 'You cannot read a book or take a lesson, or make a talk on science until you first find out whether you are saying anything against Genesis'? Can it? It can, unless that constitutional provision protects me.

"Can it say to the astronomer, 'You cannot turn your telescope upon the infinite planets and suns and stars that fill space unless you find that the earth is not the center of the universe and there is not any firmament between us and the Heaven'? Can it? It could, except for the work of Thomas Jefferson which has been woven into every state constitution of the Union, and has stayed there like the flaming sword to protect the rights of man against ignorance and bigotry. And when it is permitted to overwhelm them, then we are taken in a sea of blood and ruin that compared with it all the miseries and tortures and wars of the Middle Ages would be as nothing.

"They would need to call back these men once more. But are the provisions of the constitutions that they left, are they enough to protect you and me, and everyone else in a land which we thought was free?

"Now, let us see what it says: 'All men have a natural and indefeasible right to worship Almighty God according to the dictates of their own conscience.'

"That takes care even of the despised Modernist, who dares to be intelligent.

" 'That no man can of right be compelled to attend, erect, or support any place of worship, or to maintain any minister against his consent; that no human authority can in any case whatever control or interfere with the rights of conscience in any case whatever.'

"Let us see. Here is the State of Tennessee, living peacefully, surrounded by its beautiful mountains, each one of which contains evidence that the earth is millions of years old. Here is a state going along in its own business, teaching evolution for years: state boards handing out books on evolution, professors in colleges, teachers in schools, lawyers at the bar, physicians, ministers,—a great percentage of the intelligent citizens of the State of Tennessee, evolutionists, have not even thought it was necessary to leave their Church.

"They believed that they could appreciate and understand and make their own simple and human doctrine of the Nazarene, to love their neighbors, be kindly with them, not to place a fine on and not to try to send to jail some man who did not believe as they believed. And they got along all right with it, too, until something happened.

"They have not thought it necessary to give up their Church because they believed that all that was here was not made on the first six days of creation, or that it had come by a slow process of developments extending over the ages, or that one thing grew out of another.

"They are people who believed that organic life and the plants and the animals and man, and the mind of man, and the religion of man are the subjects of evolution, and they have not got through, and that the God in which they believed did not finish creation on the first day, but that he is still working to make something better and higher still out of human beings, who are next to God, and that evolution has been working forever and will work forever—they believe it.

"And along comes somebody who says we have got 'to believe it as I believe it; it is a crime to know more than I know.' And they publish a law to inhibit learning. Now what is in the way of it?

"First, what does the law say? This law says that it shall be a criminal offense to teach in the public schools any account of the origin of man that is in conflict with the divine account in the Bible. It makes the Bible the yardstick to measure every man's intellect, to measure every man's intelligence, and to measure every man's learning.

"Are your mathematics good? Turn to Elijah i, 2. Is your philosophy good? See Samuel ii, 3. Is your astronomy good? See Genesis, chapter ii, verse 7. Is your chemistry good? See—well, chemistry, see Deuteronomy 6, or anything that tells about brimstone. Every bit of knowledge that the mind has must be submitted to a religious test.

"Now, let us see. It is a travesty upon language, it is a travesty upon justice, it is a travesty upon the Constitution, to say that any citizen of Tennessee can be deprived of his rights by a legislative body in the face of the Constitution.

"Your life and my life and the life of every American citizen depends after all upon the tolerance and forebearance of his fellow men. If men are not tolerant, if men cannot respect each other's opinions, if men cannot live and let live, then no man's life is safe.

"Here is a country made up of Englishmen, Irishmen, Scotch, Germans, Europeans, Asiatics, Africans,—men of every sort and men of every creed and men of every scientific belief. Who is going to begin this sorting out and say: 'I shall measure you. I know you are a fool or worse. I know, and I have read a creed telling what I know, and I will make people go to Heaven even if they don't want to go with me. I will make them do it.' Where is the man that is wise enough to do it?

"This statute is passed under the police power of this State. Is there any kind of question about that? Counsel have argued that the Legislature has the right to say what shall be taught in the public school. Yes, within limits, they have. We do not doubt it, but they probably cannot say writing and arithmetic could not be taught, and certainly they cannot say nothing can be taught unless it is first ascertained that it agrees with the Scriptures. Certainly, they cannot say that.

"But this is passed under the police power. Let me call your Honor's attention to this,—this is a criminal statute, nothing else. It is not any amendment to the school law of the State. It makes it a crime in the caption to teach evolution and in the body of the act to teach something else.

"Any law passed under the police power must be uniform in its application—must be uniform. What do you mean by a police law? Well, your Honor, that calls up visions of policemen and penitentiaries and electro-cutionary establishments, and all that, and wickedness of heart.

"I do not imagine evolution hurts the health of anyone, probably not the morals, excepting as all enlightenment may, and the ignorant think of course that it does. But it is not passed for them, your Honor. Oh, no; it is not passed because it is best for the public morals that they shall not know anything about evolution, but because it is contrary to the divine account contained in Genesis. That is all—that is the basis of it.

"Here is a law which makes it a crime to teach evolution in the caption. I don't know whether we have discussed that or not, but it makes it a crime in the body of the act to teach any theory of the origin of man excepting that contained in the divine account, which we find in the Bible. All right. Now that applies to what? Teachers in the public schools.

"Now, I have seen somewhere a statement of Mr. Bryan's that the fellow that made the pay check had a right to regulate the teachers. All right. Let us see. I do not question the right of the Legislature to fix the courses of study, but the State of Tennessee has no right under the police power of the State to carve out a law which applies to school teachers, a law which is a criminal statute and nothing else; which makes no effort to prescribe the school law or course of study. It says that John Smith, who teaches evolution, is a criminal if he teaches it in the public schools.

"There is no question about this act; there is no question where it belongs; there is no question of its origin. Nobody would claim for a minute that the act could be passed excepting that teaching evolution was in the nature of a criminal act; and that therefore the State should forbid it.

"Now, if this is the subject of a criminal act, then it cannot make a criminal out of a teacher in the public schools and [at the same time] leave a man free to teach it in a private school.

"It cannot make it criminal for this teacher to teach evolution and permit books upon evolution to be sold in every store in the State of Tennessee, and to permit the newspapers from foreign cities to bring into your peaceful community the horrible utterances of evolution. Oh, no, nothing like that.

"Now, your Honor, there is an old saying that nits are made of lice. I don't know whether you know what it makes possible down here in Tennessee. I know; I was raised in Ohio. It is a good idea to clear the nits—safer and easier.

"To strangle puppies is good, when they grow up into mad dogs, maybe. I will tell you what is going to happen, and I do not pretend to be a prophet, but I do not need to be a prophet to know.

"Your Honor knows that fires have been lighted in America to kindle religious bigotry and hate. You can take judicial notice of them, if you cannot of anything else.

"If today you can take a thing like evolution and make it a crime to teach it in the public schools, tomorrow you can make it a crime to teach it in the private schools, and next year you can make it a crime to teach it to the hustings or in the church. At the next session you may ban books and the newspapers. Soon you may set Catholic against Protestant, and Protestant against Protestant, and try to foist your own religion upon the minds of men.

"If you can do one, you can do the other. Ignorance and fanaticism are ever busy and need feeding. Always they are feeding and gloating for more. Today it is the public school teachers, tomorrow the private, the next day the preachers and the lecturers, the magazines, the books, the newspapers.

"After a while, your Honor, it is the setting of man against man and creed against creed, until with flying banners and beating drums we are marching backward to the glorious ages of the sixteenth century when bigots lighted fagots to burn the men who dared to bring any intelligence and enlightenment and culture to the human mind."

The Concept of Natural Selection:
A Centennial View

by
I. Michael Lerner
Professor of Genetics, University of California, Berkeley

Commemoration of the Centennial of the Publication of
The Origin of Species *by Charles Darwin, Annual Meeting
of the American Philosophical Society, April, 1959.*

Several years ago, Sir Isaiah Berlin in writing an essay on Tolstoy's philosophy of history took his text from a fragment of the Greek poet Archilochus, which said: "The fox knows many things, but the hedgehog knows one big thing." Berlin's imaginative interpretation of this line was that writers, thinkers, or perhaps, all of humanity, can be divided into the two classes of foxes and hedgehogs. The ideas of the foxes are centrifugal, diffuse; they range over a variety of levels not integrated by a single theme; they lack a unifying focal point. In the realm of thought and creation the foxes follow many ends which may be unrelated and which do not form a cohesive system. The hedgehogs, on the other hand, are characterized by centripetal thinking directed towards a unitary inner vision. They are single-minded in their intellectual pursuits and, no matter how versatile they may be in their endeavors, the hedgehogs point to and are guided by the one big thing. Aristotle, Shakespeare, Balzac were foxes. Plato, Dante, Dostoyevsky were hedgehogs. Had Berlin considered biologists, he might well have placed Pasteur among the foxes. Darwin would most certainly have stood supreme as a hedgehog.

The one big thing towards which Darwin's thoughts and writings were directed was, perhaps, not so much Evolution as the principle of Natural Selection. This was the concept that allowed the formulation of an acceptable theory of secular change in organic nature. Evolution had been discussed for more than two millennia before Darwin and Wallace. The idea, however, lacked conviction because, in the face of so much evidence for it, no generally comprehensible way in which evolution could have occurred was apparent to its proponents. Even the notion of natural selection was not exactly brand new in 1858. As an explanation of the presence of adaptations within species it had been considered by one or another natural philosopher from classical antiquity onwards. But as a mechanism for the origin of species, natural selection was apparently advanced only in the nineteenth century. The South Carolina-born Dr. Wells mentioned it as if he took it for granted in "An account of a white female, part of whose skin resembles that of a Negro" some forty years before Darwin and Wallace. Patrick Matthew apparently alluded even more casually to natural selection a few years later in an appendix to a volume on *Naval Timber and Arboriculture*. Yet the revelation that a single principle can embrace the evolutionary changes in all systematic categories, that the same basic process is operative at all levels of life wherever self-replicating units exist, came from Darwin and Wallace.

Their one big thing, natural selection, set at rest the doctrine of special creation. In combination with our knowledge of Mendelian inheritance acquired since Darwin's day, it rendered obsolete such alternative theories of evolution as were based on extra-mechanical agencies, or on direct adaptation of organisms to their immediate environment (that is, on inheritance of acquired characters), and exposed them as sins against Occam's razor. Natural selection furnished the binding principle for a general or unified theory of historical change in the living world. It made evolution not only understandable and acceptable but, beyond that, caused it to become of commanding significance in man's thinking about himself.

Objections to Natural Selection

This is not to say that the doctrine of natural selection was generally accorded, immediately upon its appearance, the status of dogma. In fact, over the last hundred years the thesis of natural selection has been doubted, questioned, derided, ridiculed, and on several occasions buried with considerable pride, pomp, and circumstance. Nevertheless, over the passage of years the concept has weathered its criticisms and survived its funerals, gathering strength after each successive interment. No serious student of biology today questions the actuality of organic evolution. Neither is there any disagreement as to the reality of natural selection, although its importance relative to other phenomena responsible for descent with modification may be in dispute. Even those considered to be militant foes of the view that natural selection is of primary significance in all phases of the evolutionary process, acknowledge, as for example did the late Richard Goldschmidt, that "every biologist agrees that selection and isolation are the basic working methods of evolution." The objection that Goldschmidt took towards what he used to call hyper-selectionists was not addressed to their belief in selection but rather to their ideas as to what was being selected. Thus arguments may still flourish as to whether selection operates with respect to minor or major mutational steps, how exclusive an agent it is under one or another circumstance, in what particular way it interacts with other processes in determining a given evolutionary change, whether it has been completely suspended in man under the recent developments in combatting sterility, disease, and old age, and with respect to many other issues. But there is no longer any doubt that natural selection is more than a theoretical possibility—it is unquestionably a logically imperative necessity in any accounting for evolution.

Generally speaking, there have been six kinds of criticisms raised against natural selection. The gravamen of the first kind was against evolution itself rather than natural selection as such. This issue is of no significance today. Secondly, teleologically minded biologists objected to the apparent purposelessness of natural selection. Condemnation on these grounds has little validity in the climate of present-day science, though I shall have occasion to return to this point in another connection. Thirdly, Darwin's own hypothesis regarding the basis of hereditary transmission created difficulties for the concept of natural selection. They were, however, dispelled when Mendelism entered the scene. Fourthly, Mendelian inheritance itself was misguidedly used to buttress the opposition to natural selection. Population geneticists have effectively demolished criticisms of this type; moveover they have demonstrated how particulate inheritance following Mendelian principles greatly augments the probable role of natural selection in evolution. Fifthly, objections have been raised, undoubtedly justifiably, against the intemperate support of natural selection by its earlier proponents, who attributed to the process consequences which we now know are ascribable to mating system, isolation, chance, and interactions of these factors with each other and with selection. And lastly, the most common and continually recurring opposition to natural selection is based on a misunderstanding of what is meant by the term. In spite of the fact that in recent years Fisher, Wright, Haldane, Muller, Dobzhansky, Ford, Simpson, Mayr, Stebbins, and countless others have repeatedly expounded the concept of natural selection, it still seems to remain an uncrossable *pons asinorum* for many refractory naturalists. It is difficult to know what, if anything more, should be done about this class of objections.

None of these categories of dissent from the idea of natural selection is a matter of serious concern at the present. Proof of the participation of natural selection in some situations is, of course, not tantamount to proof of its sufficiency to account for all evolutionary change. But no serious student of the subject insists on this extreme view. It is enough to say that the notion of natural selection as a major component of the evolutionary process has not only been theoretically established and empirically observed in the wild and in the laboratory, but it no longer falls entirely within the qualitative realm of science: natural selection can now be quantitatively treated and in many instances has been actually measured.

Thanks to post-Mendelian studies on the bases of hereditary transmission, and particularly to the developments in both theoretical and experimental population genetics in the last thirty years, our understanding of the operation of selection in nature has been vastly increased. Because of that, a prodigious embarrassment of riches on which to base a general discussion faces any reviewer of the subject. I shall therefore confine myself to a few aspects of the issue at large, trusting that other contributions to this program will cover at least some of the territory I neglect. In particular, I propose to pass over the speciation or splitting level of evolution, since it involves interaction with isolation, which is to be considered here by others infinitely more versed than I in this question. I should also note that, in considering post-Darwinian advances in the field of natural selection, I prefer omitting all mention of individual contributions to the risk of finding myself sire to an invidious, or even a merely provocative, list of names.

The Definition of Natural Selection

It may be appropriate at this point to define natural selection. Darwin himself did so in a number of ways. Thus (quoting from the sixth edition of *The Origin of Species*), he says:

> As many more individuals of each species are born than can possibly survive; and as, consequently, there is a frequently recurring struggle for existence, it follows that any being, if it vary however slightly in any manner profitable to itself, under the complex and sometimes varying conditions of life, will have a better chance of surviving, and thus be *naturally selected*. From the strong principle of inheritance, any selected variety will tend to propagate its new and modified form.

Elsewhere we read:

> This preservation of favourable individual differences and variations, and the destruction of those which are injurious, I have called Natural Selection, or the Survival of the Fittest.

Some exegesis of the operative words in these passages is called for. In particular, three questions may be asked. Is Darwin's term *selection* synonymous with *choice*? Is *survival* to be taken in the precise meaning of the word or is it used figuratively, including the ability to reproduce? What does the term *fittest* which Darwin adopted from Herbert Spencer, signify in the context of the rest of the definition?

Regarding the first question, Darwin says:

> In the literal sense of the word, no doubt, natural selection is a false term, but who ever objected to chemists speaking of the elective affinities of the various elements?—and yet acid cannot strictly be said to elect the base with which it in preference combines. It has been said that I speak of natural selection as an active power of Deity; but who objects to an author speaking of the attraction of gravity as ruling the movements of the planets? Everyone knows what is meant and is implied by such metaphorical expressions; and they are almost necessary for brevity. So again it is difficult to avoid personifying the word Nature; but I mean by Nature, only the aggregate action and product of many natural laws, and by laws the sequence of events as ascertained by us.

It seems clear that, despite the fact that Darwin in his argument leaned very heavily on analogies between the results of purposeful and directed artificial selection of plants and animals by man with what is observed in the wild, he did not see in selection a process in which deliberative judgment or choice on the part of any agency plays a part.

With respect to the second question, the meaning of survival, the vast majority of writers on evolution take Darwin's usage of this word literally. They assume that Darwin meant that discrimination between what he considered the fit and the unfit was entirely by death and did not involve the broader and more relevant differences in ability to produce living offspring. Darwin, however, was not as naive as he is often represented. In discussing struggle for existence, he says: "I should premise that I use this term in a large and metaphorical sense including dependence of one being on another, and including (which is more important) not only the life of the individual, but success in leaving progeny." Thus, although Darwin may have erroneously accepted the view that survival is necessarily the major component of natural selection, he understood that the crux of the selection process lies not merely in the ability of an individual to survive longer than others, but in its greater capacity for production of living offspring; that is to say, not only in survival of individuals within a generation, but of groups over a period of generations.

This fact enables us to answer the third question, that regarding the interpretation which must be given the word *fittest*, or rather, the term *fitness*. The expressiveness of Spencer's superlative seduced Darwin into accepting "survival of the fittest" as being equivalent to "natural selection." As a result, many early evolutionists and a fair proportion of those naturalists of today whom the literature of population genetics has bypassed attached anthropomorphic value judgments to selection. Yet neither strength of character nor moral goodness, neither extreme size nor high intelligence, nor even long life *per se* causes an individual to produce more offspring, that is to say, make it fit in Darwin's sense. Indeed, often organisms which are totally undistinguished by any physical standards, organisms exhibiting average dimensions for various properties, in fine, individuals which are mediocre for any traits obvious to the human eye, are the ones that are most successful in propagating themselves. They are therefore the *fittest*. If there is one thing upon which the most factious partisans of various currents of evolutionary thought agree, it is that fitness of an individual, in the context of the natural selection principle, can mean only the extent to which the organism is represented by descendants in succeeding generations. Fitness can be discussed in absolute terms or expressed relatively to the average of a group. Immediate or more remote generations of descent may be chosen as a point of reference. Enumeration of offspring or some other way of assessing the "amount" of progeny left may be resorted to. But in all instances, fitness must refer to the ability of an organism to leave surviving offspring.

A habitual fallacy, shared by both the opponents and the supporters of evolution by natural selection, is the idea that any part of evolution may be explained by saying that the fittest individuals have the most offspring. When fitness is considered with reference to evolutionary phenomena, such statement is logically circular and begs the question. If capacity of reproduction is the criterion of fitness, the only connecting proposition between reproduction and fitness which avoids tautology is that individuals having most offspring are the fittest ones. This is neither an assumption, nor a hypothesis to be proven, but merely a definition.

Darwin's description of natural selection can now be paraphrased to say (1) that in nature individuals differ among themselves, (2) that their differences are in part determined by heredity, and (3) that, therefore, whenever these differences are correlated with fitness, that is, success in leaving offspring, the properties of the more fit individuals will be represented in succeeding generations to an increasing extent. Thus, changes in the make-up of successive generations are determined in a measure by the inequalities between the reproductive rates of individuals differing in hereditary endowment, that is to say, by different *genotypes*. More concisely, natural selection then is the *differential reproduction of genotypes*. The carriers of various genetic constitutions have *phenotypes* (to wit, somatic properties whether or not they happen to be apparent to the human observer) which differ in their capacity to produce surviving progeny in their particular environment. The genotypic composition of the next generation is then modified, and changes in phenotypes are produced to the degree to which phenotypes are genetically determined.

Advances Since Darwin

Darwin and Wallace arrived at their conclusions about the role of natural selection in evolution by deduction. Assuming the validity of their basic premises, natural selection can be inferred as a consequence independently of actual experience. *The Origin of Species* was essentially an attempt at *a posteriori* justification of Darwin's thesis based on the mustering of a great volume of descriptive evidence in its support. Since 1859 the premises underlying Darwin's chain of reasoning have been subjected to test many times. Thus, differential reproduction of individuals could often be ascertained by counting and statistical analysis of only a moderate degree of sophistication. Similarly, the dependence of such differential reproduction at least in part on hereditary differences was demonstrated both by verifiable inference from observation in nature and by laboratory experiment. But our achievements since Darwin are not limited merely to a further accumulation of examples (including those in ultramicroscopic organisms not even dreamt of in Darwin's philosophy) or to the development of less equivocal proofs of evolution that Darwin had at his disposal. Much more can be said about post-Darwinian advances in the study of natural selection. A sampling of illustrations chosen from different areas of evolutionary knowledge charted in recent decades bespeaks this fact.

The first of these may be provided by the insight that has been acquired into the basis of hereditary transmission. It is this knowledge that furnished the necessary link between selection and evolution. Darwin made somewhat vague references in *The Origin of Species* to the operation of the "strong principle of inheritance." He was fully aware of the deficiencies in his knowledge of the mechanism of heredity. They led him to formulate a speculative and somewhat improbable, even in the light of a century ago, hypothesis of blending inheritance. This principle in turn forced Darwin to espouse the postulate that acquired characters were transmissable, because otherwise continued variability in natural populations could not be accounted for. It was not until Mendelian theory was developed that such pathetically artless conjectures as, for instance, the direct hereditary effects of use and disuse of organs and parts of the body, become superfluous. Three aspects of Mendelism were especially important in this connection: (1) the particulate basis of the units of inheritance to which we may refer as *genes*. (2) the distinction between phenotype and genotype, and (3) the statistical nature of the phenomena of heredity. It was also in large part Mendelian inheritance that resolved the problem of persistent variation and, more generally, led to the possibility of quantifying evolutionary processes.

Symbolic representation of evolution, taking into account all but unique events, has now been arrived at. It is based on the description of the evolutionary process in terms of changes in the frequencies of alternative genes (or chromosomes) in a population. Indeed, the expression "survival of the fittest" can be applied with much more justice to the behavior of genes over many generations than to that of individual organisms within one. From the quantitative approach an understanding of the components of selection-induced alterations in fitness (those due not only to changes in gene frequencies, but also to modifications of the environment and of the mating system, as well as to gene interaction) has been gained. Methods for estimating the extent to which a population can be transformed by selection have been devised. Quantitative bases for systems of correlated response (i.e., effects on traits which themselves are not being subjected to selection pressure) characterizing changes under selection have been established. The utility of these developments for breeding practice is obvious. But equally important are the possibilities they have opened for a quantitative approach to selection in terms of observations of living beings in nature or of the paleontological record.

Another sphere of study which has contributed to an increased comprehension of a natural selection is that dealing with the materials on which selection operates. The notion that individuals differ in hereditary endowment presupposes that a mechanism by which such differences can arise exists. Selection experiments, followed by the discovery of artificial means of producing mutations in the hereditary material, and the many elaborate investigations on the nature of mutational changes and effects, made it clear that hereditary variants on the gene level do not arise as a consequence of selection. Variability for selection to act upon must therefore be supplied by mutation (or subsequent to mutation, by hybridization). It is not entirely correct to say, as has often been done, that the mutation process is a completely haphazard one. The structures that mutated genes can assume are not random. For instance, not all possible combinations of the elements of which genes are made possess the power of self-duplication, without which genes would not exist. But the non-randomness of mutations does not mean that selection determines the direction of phenotypic effect which gene mutations have.

More recent studies, including those on the physical chemistry of hereditary material, may be expected to clarify eventually many related points which are still obscure. For example, the question of how random the genes subjected to selection are with respect to their spatial relations within organized units of higher order, such as chromosomes, needs additional elucidation which breeding experiments with any of the higher organisms are incapable of supplying efficiently. Similarly, the relation between the amount of actual structural change involved in a gene mutation and the degree of phenotypic effect the change may lead to in the developing or adult organism still remains to be explored. The relative importance in different circumstances of the hierarchy of selection materials—genes, chromosomes, genomes, total genotypes, populations—is another aspect of evolution on which more light may be expected to be forthcoming.

On another level, the relationships between natural selection and adaptation has been illuminated by the semantic analysis of the term fitness. The early evolutionists chose their examples of adaptive traits, presumed to have originated by selection, on the basis of entirely anthropomorphic interpretations as to what constitutes an advantage to a plant or animal. We now know that adaptive traits are those contributing to increased fitness in any way whatever, rather than only those with spectacular manifestations on the ingenuous level of Kipling's *Just So Stories*. The important effects of natural selection are more subtle than the provision of tigers with stripes or leopards with spots for alleged purposes of camouflage. Physiological and biochemical properties very often are more likely to be of significance in determining an individual's fitness than are conspicuous morphological differences which sometimes may be by-products rather than criteria of selection. Moreover, fitness is determined by a combination of a great many somatic features, or rather by the phenotype as a whole. It follows from this: (1) that the selective value of any one character may vary, depending on the particular totality of traits in which it is found, (2) that the selection pressure applied to any single trait (which, of course, is an abstraction by an investigator from the total phenotype) is bound to be very small, and (3) that, considered with respect to single genes, the process of natural selection is usually very slow. These deductions accord well with the evidence on the rate and complexity of evolutionary change in nature which tended to puzzle the early Darwinians.

They also lead to the idea that the most adapted kind of individual is not one conforming to some phenotypic norm, but rather one whose development and reproductive life history is adjustable to varying environmental conditions in such a manner as to preserve high fitness. The most successful population is similarly one that can meet the challenge of environmental changes between generations. In other words, homeostatic devices stabilizing the individual's own reproductive performance have a high selective value, while a heterogeneous genetic make-up, even behind a uniform phenotypic facade within a single generation, may be an advantage to a population. These considerations, backed by ever-accumulating experimental and descriptive evidence, suggest the importance in evolutionary thought of such concepts as buffered and balanced genotypes, integrated gene pools, and coadaptation, which no doubt will be discussed on this occasion by others.

I would, nevertheless, like to call attention to these general ideas, without entering into the exposition of their full meaning, in alluding to some other aspects of natural selection. For one thing, they are of significance in the process in which natural selection, by utilizing interactions between components of genotypes, endows whole populations with properties transcending those attributable to their individual members. For another, these concepts are relevant to the currently controversial issue regarding the autonomy of single genes in the selection process.

Reducing the argument to its simplest terms, there is, on the one hand, the belief that the selective values of genes are reasonably independent of the genotypic combinations in which they occur. That is to say, genes which are found to be highly deleterious to fitness when forming part of one genotype are, in this view, considered extremely unlikely to be advantageous in another genotype. Ranged on the opposing side is the opinion that, since selection is primarily concerned with genotypes, the effects of individual genes in a given genetic context are not necessarily predictable from their behavior in another genetic background, be it only different with respect to a single member of a gene pair. Needless to say, the proponents of neither view claim that their interpretation entirely excludes the contrary one. Rather, the argument relates to the comparative importance of the two kinds of genes (those with predictable and those with unpredictable behavior) in evolution and in breeding practice. The same question can also be raised, with some poignancy, with reference to the human species, since, for example, estimates of the extent of genetic damage produced by ionizing radiation differ on the alternative hypotheses of gene action.

These broad issues also bear upon the relative importance of the different types of selection which we have learned to distinguish since Darwin's day. Thus *directional* selection produces transformation of a population along the time axis, while *disruptive* selection may result in the splitting of a group into subgroups. These two kinds of selection are progressive, in the limited sense of leading to new forms of life. *Stabilizing* selection is conservative. It operates by rejection of variants and maintains the population at an equilibrium. Of the several forms of pressure antagonistic to the preservation of fitness which selection must counterbalance, those of mutation and segregation are of greatest import. Elimination of deleterious mutants by selection is a process that has been long recognized. The significance of selection against non-optimal genotypes which arise in every generation as a result of segregation of chromosomes in the process of germ-cell formation, however, has been appreciated only recently. Studies from many fields, for example, those on wild and cage populations of *Drosophila*, on artificial irradiation, on the use of hybrid vigor in breeding economic plants and animals, on cytogenetics of grasshoppers, on aberrant forms appearing under intense inbreeding, and many others, argue for at least as great an evolutionary importance of selection against segregation as of that against mutation. Mutations are needed to provide a basis for further evolution. But the ones not useful at any given time in the phylogeny of a population are eliminated or kept from increasing in frequency by selection. Without selection against segregation genetic variability already present could be lost. William Blake's affirmation that "to be an error and to be cast out is a part of God's design" seems to be an apt description of selection against both mutation and segregation, though invoking Blake in this connection leaves me open to the charge of citing the Scriptures to my own purpose.

Another evolutionary precept which has been recognized since Darwin (in fact, in contradiction to Darwin) is that selection, far from being blind, operating entirely by chance, and begetting successful kinds of organisms only as a result of improbable accidents, may be correctly described as a *creative* process. This term can, of course, be used in a variety of senses. In reference to natural selection its meaning is well illustrated by quoting what Michelangelo conceived the process of creation to be. The opening lines of one of his best known sonnets says in a somewhat free translation:

> The best of artists has that thought alone
> Which is contained within the marble shell;
> The sculptor's hand can only break the spell
> To free the figures slumbering in the stone.

In the same way, natural selection does not originate its own building blocks in the form of mutations of genes. But from them it does create complexes; it solves in a diversity of ways the great variety of problems that successful individuals and populations face; it builds step by step, even if by trial and error, entities of infinite complexity, ingenuity, and be one inclined to say so, beauty. Granted that it needs appropriate raw materials, that it may not necessarily be able to make a silk purse out of a sow's ear; yet, interacting with other evolutionary mechanisms, it has created the human species out of stuff which in its primordial stage may have looked no more promising.

Miscellaneous Implications

The epithet creative is often interpreted to mean *effectively* causing, in the Aristotelean sense. Indeed, taking mutant genes and higher order components of genotypes as the *material* cause of evolutionary change, application of the adjective creative to natural selection is undoubtedly sanctioned by our present knowledge of the process. Nonetheless, the term raises some fundamental questions regarding causalities in evolution and may even provoke charges of teleology, long a dirty word in science. I do not mean, of course, that any mystical doctrines of ends involving inner perfecting principles or entelechy can be imputed to modern evolutionists. Neither design by supernatural agencies, nor an *elan vital*, from a comprehensive laboratory analysis of which we are supposedly forever barred, nor yet any guiding plan or morphological and physiological perfection, needs detain us in this discussion. Indeed, Bergson and other militant teleologists of yesteryear would find little comfort in the distinct possibility that, if there is an Aristotelean final cause of evolution which directed all preceding events in the animate world, it may turn out to be the Gotterdammerung initiated by man's mastery of subatomic forces. Be that as it may, there is no necessity to assume that increased adaptation of organisms under natural selection represents the purposive end of the evolutionary process. Adaptation and adaptability simply provide means toward increased fitness; they should be viewed not as causes but as consequences of natural selection.

At the same time it must be realized that natural selection depends, in addition to variation (production of materials for selection to work on) and heredity (perpetuation of successful variants), on still a third factor, namely, the *potentiality* to produce young in excess of parental numbers. Only in the presence of this factor can inequalities of rate of reproduction between individuals exist in a group not heading for extinction. When the inequalities systematically relate to genotypic differences between individuals, natural selection is said to take place. In other words, while capacity for propagation beyond that needed to maintain constant population size does not ensure that natural selection will occur, it is a necessary condition for natural selection in any group which is to survive.

Darwin, who was, of course, mechanistically minded, spoke somewhat obscurely of the laws of Growth and Reproduction underlying selection. Samuel Butler came out directly with the vitalistic tenet that there exists a "universal innate desire on the part of every organism to live beyond its income." We may instead talk of an empirically discovered biological analogy to the first law of motion, namely that living matter if left alone will tend to increase itself indefinitely. Whatever the formulation, natural selection must always operate to maintain or to increase the frequency of genotypes which have the highest relative fitness. This process as a rule cannot lead to a decrease in absolute fitness except under special circumstances involving changes in the direction of selection or in mating system. The exceptions do not invalidate the proposition that natural selection *defined* as inequality of reproductive ability, that is to say, of fitness, also *causes* fitness to increase. Thus we are either attributing immanency to natural selection, or at the least, after having eliminated one tautology by our definition of fitness, we have come upon another. Logical dilemmas of this sort are, of course, not unique to the issues involved in natural selection or, indeed, to biology in general. I am sure that any competent philosopher could easily solve seeming paradoxes of this kind. The difficulty is that no two schools of philosophy seem to agree on the correct solution. It was for good reason that Bertrand Russell once said that causality is one of the two great scandals (induction being the other) in the philosophy of science. I have mentioned the problem here merely to indicate that, with all of the knowledge now acquired on the process of selection in nature, its logical status in evolution is still uncertain and undoubtedly controversial.

It was very likely misplaced confidence in their comprehension of natural selection or, perhaps, confusion between evolution as a law and natural selection as its instrumentality, that has led numerous social scientists and political philosophers of various hues and persuasions to project the notion of natural selection from biological to cultural systems. Such terms as progressive adaptation, struggle for existence, survival of the fittest, proved to be equally irresistible to materialists and idealists, to mechanists and teleologists, to prophets of *laissez faire* capitalism and to heralds of the proletarian revolution. Yet, as has already been noted, the only value connotation that natural selection in its proper interpretation has refers to reproductive ability. Furthermore, it operates in a self-perpetuating system of particulate units, the relative proportions of which in a population change as a consequence of selection. Is there really an exact or even a moderate analogy of this principle in social evolution?

If so, it does not seem to have been established by any of the varieties of self-styled social Darwinists, especially when social institutions are dealt with. It is, indeed, possible that intergroup selection occurs between religious or cultural segments of the human species whenever they differ in birth rates. But the often-asserted inevitability of communist domination of the world, for example, is not rooted in unequal reproductive rates. Again, ethically dubious business practices allegedly sanctioned by the purported natural law of dog-eat-dog, seem remote from the biological phenomenon from which they are supposed to derive support. Perhaps, the source of confusion does lie in the value constructs of "steady advance," "struggle for survival" and so forth, which have become attached to natural selection by its early enthusiasts. Darwin himself, taking the cue from Wallace, Galton, and Spencer, has unfortunately contributed to these mists of error, especially in *The Descent of Man*, though even in that book he confined himself, broadly speaking, to biological and not to social aspects of "natural selection as affecting civilized nations."

That organic evolution is based on natural selection can be considered to be demonstrated. Whether cultural evolution, in which generations communicate with each other by means different from information coded within replicates of the units of hereditary transmission, also is, remains to be seen. Needless to say, Mendelism is not a prerequisite to natural selection. Cytoplasmic transmission of particles, whatever its role in evolution is, can, no doubt, be shown to be subject to the same process. But self-propagation is essential to natural selection, whereas systematic historical changes in the extra-biological aspects of the world surrounding us could have happened without natural selection in the biological sense of the term.

A possible exception to this dictum may be found in the events leading to the origin of life. If autocatalytic processes of reproduction can be said to have occurred before protoplasm made its appearance on earth, chemical evolution culminating in living matter could have depended, as has been suggested by some, on natural selection. On the other hand, if the view is taken that self-reproduction is the exclusive property of living matter, natural selection cannot have antedated life.

One more point with reference to common misinterpretations of the basis of natural selection may be considered. It has often been said that the development of modern medicine and other technological advances combined with certain humanitarian and religious notions has led to the suspension of natural selection in man. As evidence, exercise of therapeutic measures against various congenital diseases is cited and examples are given from an increasing list of defects which used to be, but no longer are, disabling. It is assumed that carriers of genotypes predisposing to such conditions were in the past at a selective disadvantage, while currently their reproductive ability is not under any handicap. Hence, it is argued, natural selection is being interfered with by euthenic measures. More often than not, a dire warning that the human race is thereby slowly committing suicide is added.

It is entirely true that many genotypes which rendered their possessors unfit in earlier days do so no more. Natural selection now, therefore, is not based on the same components of fitness or results in the same directional changes as before. But this is by no means the same thing as saying that natural selection is not operative. What has happened is that the environment, the adjudicator of which genotypes are fit, has been altered. The therapy that has become available is a feature of the new environment. The determinants of fitness may have become changed, but inequalities in reproduction were not thereby eliminated. An analogy is provided by one of the classical cases of empirically observed natural selection in a lower form of life.

In certain species of moths dark and light colored forms occur. The dark kind is generally hardier and hence would have been expected to be more fit. However, its melanic pigmentation makes it more conspicuous to predators. Therefore, in early observations at certain localities the light forms were generally found to be more numerous than the dark ones. Since the Industrial Revolution, however, increasing amounts of soot and similar waste products began to spread around the countryside. This provided increased protection to the melanic forms in manufacturing districts. As a result, their higher reproductive capacity now gave them an advantage over the light forms so that in many industrial areas the latter now approach extinction. Natural selection here has reversed its direction. A gene that was deleterious in its net effects in the earlier environment has now become advantageous. The basis of fitness has been changed, but natural selection still went on. This kind of change has undoubtedly occurred many times in the past history of man, for instance, when fire-making tools were invented, thereby affording protection to some genotypes which were formerly disadvantageous.

Susceptibility to many diseases may then not contribute any more to differences in fitness of man. It is not impossible that resistance became in some instances an encumbrance. More likely, however, major importance in determining fitness was assumed by genes in control of other phenotypic traits. For instance, the genetically determined aspects of the ability to provide young with food obtained by strength may have now lost their positive selective value. On the other hand, genes for philoprogenitiveness in a world in which conception is under man's volitional control may have become of correspondingly greater import in the selective process.

Exactly how disgenic in terms of human values today's natural selection may be is difficult to tell. Selection which might have the most serious potential consequences to mankind could be that operating through the medium of differential reproductive rates of groups with differing intelligence. However, there are reasons to believe that this process may be of the stabilizing kind, maintaining constant genotypic frequencies rather than shifting them in a direction commonly agreed to be an undesirable one.

Generally speaking, selection in man is probably not as stringent as it was in the past, though this is by no means certain. The immense increase in the average number of surviving offspring which occurred in the last century does not of itself constitute conclusive evidence for lowered selection intensity. In any case, the actual reproductive rate in man is, of course, still greatly below its biological maximum, which means that there is still considerable opportunity for selection to occur. Evidence that inequalities in fitness currently observable are independent of genotypic constitutions would doubtlessly be difficult to obtain. Even so, it would seem that only when man has achieved such complete mastery over his environment that all possible human genotypes will be equally likely to produce the average number of surviving progeny, can we be sure that natural selection has ceased in our species.

In Conclusion

I have ranged somewhat widely, even if not deeply, over the subject assigned to me. Before closing I would like to make it clear that population genetics, the discipline which has contributed most to our present understanding of natural selection, is only entering the stage of adolescence. Its attainment of maturity depends on a synthesis with its sibling doctrines of physiological, biochemical, and other branches of genetics, which should bring into fuller clarity our picture of evolution, and should fill the numerous gaps in our knowledge of the organic world. Evolution is the most fundamental biological law yet discovered. Natural selection is the basic mechanism implementing it. The principle of descent with modification, creatively, albeit opportunistically, husbanded by natural selection, is as firmly established as any concept in biology. But what we have learned so far about natural selection is obviously only the beginning. What remains to be learned is immeasurably more. Truth, said Bacon, is the daughter of Time, and one hundred years is not a long period in the history of mankind. Furthermore, giant-slayers abound in the scientific woods through which we have to travel to our goal of understanding ourselves and the living universe. It is then not inconceivable that the role now assigned to natural selection some day may have to be re-evaluated. However, if more adequate explanations are found for the phenomena in the animate world which we currently view as being consequent to natural selection, the ensuing revolution in our thought will have to be as great as that produced by Darwin and Wallace a century ago.

The Nature of the Fossil Record

by
Norman D. Newell
Curator of Historical Geology and Fossil Invertebrates,
American Museum of Natural History;
Professor of Geology, Columbia University

Commemoration of the Centennial of the Publication of
The Origin of Species *by Charles Darwin, Annual Meeting*
of the American Philosophical Society, April, 1959.

Introduction

The past two decades have witnessed a remarkable revival of interest in organic evolution and the emergence of a broad new discipline, the study of evolution, which integrates and synthesizes evidence derived from systematic biology, genetics, and paleontology. In the resulting rapid growth of knowledge of evolution, paleontology has played a leading role far beyond that envisioned by Darwin of supplying proofs that evolution has, indeed, occurred. Broadly defined, paleontology is the *geological history of life*, and as such it is vast in scope, and diffuse. In spite of the fact that the number of dedicated investigators in this field has always been small, progress has been phenomenal in the century since publication of *The Origin of Species*, not only in continued discoveries of new fossils from a seemingly inexhaustible supply but also in their scientific interpretations as once-living organisms.

When Charles Darwin turned to the geological implications of his theory of evolution, his first major concern was to learn the nature of the fossil record. It is a measure of his genius that two geological chapters, ten and eleven, in *The Origin of Species* demonstrate a profound grasp of the subject far beyond that of any paleontologist of his time. It is the purpose of the present discussion to undertake briefly an evaluation of the fossil record in the light of a century of discovery since publication of *The Origin of Species*.

Darwin argued that the fossils known to science in his day represented a very small part of the potentially available record. He also understood that all of the fossils that ever existed must constitute only a very incomplete and fragmentary record of past life. These conclusions we still endorse, even though we now know immeasurably more about fossils than did Darwin. We cannot learn everything about past life from fossils, but we have learned much and the potentially knowable record is still far greater than the known record for most fossil groups. Paleontological exploration of the past is a sampling procedure in which provisional estimates of the whole are made from small, frequently biased, samples. Knowledge is cumulative and sampling errors are gradually corrected as the process is repeated over and over again by independent workers.

Darwin's Geological Background

It is perhaps often overlooked that during his youth Darwin was by interest and training as much geologist as biologist, and it must be granted that his conclusions about organic evolution would have been significantly different had he not learned to view organisms against the historical background provided by geology. At Cambridge University he had studied under Adam Sedgwick, who, with Murchison, was shortly to work out the British early Paleozoic sequence of rocks and fossils; but his greatest inspiration in geology undoubtedly came from Charles Lyell whose ideas were sweeping across Europe in the 1830's and bringing about a revolution in geology that had been quietly started half a century before by James Hutton.

Lyell's Contribution

When, in 1831, Darwin was ready to embark on the voyage of the *Beagle*, his friend, Cambridge botany professor and amateur geologist, John Henslow, gave him the first volume of Lyell's *Principles of Geology*, and the second volume, containing Lyell's views on evolution and the fossil record, was sent to him in Montevideo a year later. Henslow's gift was not only a great boon to Darwin who had not yet read Lyell's book, but it was of inestimable benefit to future science. Lyell's book freed Darwin of many of the crippling prejudices held by a majority of contemporary geologists. Lyell extended the age of the earth by millions of years and gave the rudiments of a scientific history of the earth at a time when scholars were still following Archbishop Ussher's pronouncement that the earth was created in 4004 B.C. It was Lyell who disseminated and popularized Hutton's Uniformitarian views about the adequacy of known natural laws to explain the geologic past in contra-distinction to the prevailing belief, usually attributed inaccurately to Cuvier, that earth history had been characterized by successive episodes of creation and catastrophic destruction. While Lyell was not an evolutionist, his reasoned arguments against organic evolution doubtless stimulated young Darwin to consider both sides of the question and perhaps to draw parallels between Lyell's record of orderly changes in the planet and the evolutionary changes in organisms described by Lamarck.

Darwin, the Fossil Collector

It is important that Darwin thought as a geologist. His enthusiasm for the science of the earth is revealed in a letter from South America to his sisters, written in the idiom of the country gentleman (he was one of the elite and had made the Grand Tour):

> I wish any of you could enter into my feelings of excessive pleasure which Geology gives me as soon as one partly understands the nature of a country. . . . There is nothing like Geology. The pleasure of the first day's hunting cannot be compared to finding a fine group of fossil bones which tell their story of former times with almost a living tongue.

On an Argentine pampa he collected remains of extinct mammals of gigantic size and he pondered deeply on the fact that, although they clearly belonged to extinct forms, they were constructed on the same basic plan as the small living sloths and armadillos of the region. This experience started him thinking about the fossil sequence of faunas and floras, the causes of extinction, and the origin of new forms that have replaced successively old ones in the fossil record.

Darwin and the Missing Links

In 1859 the fossil record still was poorly sampled and practically all paleontologic studies had been concerned with the description and stratigraphic documentation of fossil assemblages. Nevertheless, many important generalizations could be made. Although it often is denied, the known record gave strong support to Darwin and he made full use of available knowledge of fossils. The evidence that he gleaned from the fossil record showed that the prevalent theory of multiple special creations and catastrophic extinctions could not possibly explain the fossil record as a whole.

The Stratigraphic Succession

Late in the eighteenth century Cuvier, Alexandre Brogniart, William Smith, and many others had shown the value of fossils as indicators of stratigraphic

position and geologic age. Out of their observations there quickly developed
the conception of a geological time scale, and the stage was set for the
organization of a scientific history of the earth. In the first two decades of
the nineteenth century, paleontologists were recognizing a sequence of three
great time-stratigraphic units, Primary, Secondary, and Tertiary, based mainly
on their fossils; and by the time Darwin returned to England from his voyage,
the broad outlines of the time-stratigraphic system now in general use had
been worked out in Great Britain and on the Continent (fig. 1).

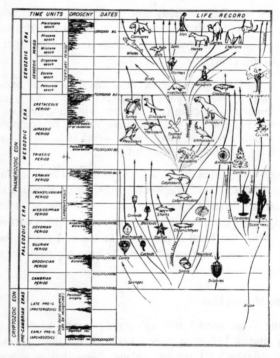

Fig. 1. The sequence of fossil floras and faunas provides the basis for a
geologic time scale and worldwide correlations of events in geologic history
(Dunbar, *Historical Geology*, John Wiley and Sons, 1949).

The Succession Is Gradational

Lyell had shown that the recent biota had not appeared abruptly in its
entirety, as required by special creation, but gradually, a few species at a time
in the Tertiary rocks, replacing one after another species that are now extinct;
and these new species and their near relatives were commonly widely

distributed, making their appearance in different regions at nearly the same stratigraphic position. Darwin was deeply impressed by this and by the discoveries of de Verneuil, d'Archiac, Barrande, Adolph Brogniart, and others. They showed that there is a characteristic succession of fossil forms through time in all studied rock sequences in various parts of the world. Darwin wrote:

> Scarcely any paleontological discovery is more striking than the fact that the forms of life change almost simultaneously throughout the world. . . . Thus, as it seems to me, the parallel, and, taken in a large sense, simultaneous, succession of the same forms of life throughout the world, accords well with the principle of new species having been formed by dominant species spreading widely and varying. . . . As new and improved groups spread throughout the world, old groups disappear from the world; and the succession of forms everywhere tends to correspond both in their first appearance and final disappearance.

Connecting Forms

Fossils structurally intermediate between distantly related living animals were known in Darwin's day and they, of course, influenced the strictly morphological taxonomy of the time. Many paleontologists had noted that fossil forms in some cases join together living families and even orders. For example, the fossil *Zeuglodon* was regarded as intermediate between whales and aquatic carnivores, and, after its discovery in 1861, *Archaeopteryx* was properly placed in a position intermediate between reptiles and birds, but before Darwin there was little reason to consider the phylogenetic implications of these discoveries.

Casual Gaps in the Record

Two kinds of interruptions in the fossil record attracted Darwin's attention and the attention of every paleontologist since. One of these is a local, or casual, deficiency which results from insufficient collecting, migrations of original organisms, unfavorable biotic environment, nondeposition, nonpreservation after burial, or destruction by erosion. With continued and geographically extended search aided by improved techniques of collecting and preparing fossils, these gaps in the record gradually are filled in as "missing links" are discovered.

Within ten years of the publication of *The Origin of Species*, Waagen had published evidence in support of an ammonite phylogeny and five years thereafter Kowalevsky had worked out a graded sequence of fossil horses in Europe. The record of horse evolution was quickly improved and amplified by Marsh's discoveries in America (fig. 2). Thus, Darwin lived to see the support from paleontology that he had confidently expected. There are now innumerable illustrations of graded temporal series of fossils from both animal and plant kingdoms, and there are few paleontologists in the world today who doubt that the fossil record gives convincing support to Darwin's thesis that species gradually become modified with time.

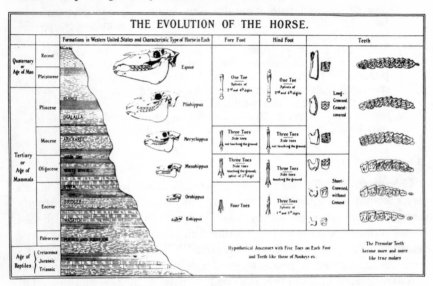

Fig. 2. The fossil record of the horse family illustrates gradual but comparatively rapid morphological change during some 60 million years (Matthew and Chubb, *Guide Leaflet Ser.* 36, Amer. Mus. Nat. Hist., 1921).

Systematic Gaps in the Record

The second kind of paleontological break is systematic. This is, it reflects a genuine deficiency of the record not dependent on insufficient collecting or chance factors of sedimentation. The earliest members of higher categories, phyla, classes, orders, and superfamilies generally have all of the basic characteristics of those categories rather than dominantly ancestral characters. Thus, the higher categories tend to be separated sharply from other related groups with little or no tendency for intergradation. The meaning of this morphological isolation of higher categories has troubled students of the fossil record and was explained by pre-Darwinian paleontologists as indicative of special creation. It is true that a few stratigraphic levels are characterized by the "simultaneous" appearance of several higher categories, for example, at the base of the Triassic system; but for the most part the first appearances are scattered through the stratigraphic record. The idea of piecemeal special creations was not what most of the early paleontologists had in mind. A very few modern students have attributed these sudden appearances of group characteristics as evidence of large gene mutations, macroevolution, but there are alternatives that are considered more acceptable to the majority of modern evolutionists. This is the problem of the origin of higher categories.

From time to time discoveries are made of connecting links that provide clues to the relationships, as between fishes and amphibians, amphibians and reptiles, and reptiles and mammals. These isolated discoveries, of course, stimulate hope that more complete records will be found and other gaps closed. These finds are, however, rare; and experience shows that the gaps which separate the highest categories may never be bridged in the fossil record. Many of the discontinuities tend to be more and more emphasized with increased collecting.

The early history of the flowering plants, the angiosperms, is a case in point. Their rich fossil record begins with great abruptness in the lower Cretaceous rocks (fig. 3). The first angiosperm flora of some sixteen families appears almost simultaneously in such remote places as Transcaucasia, Portugal, England, Maryland, Texas, and New Zealand; and before the close of the Cretaceous period the flowering plants had become the dominant land vegetation probably occupying most of the present niches. In spite of their initial diversity, a long and determined search for Jurassic ancestors of the

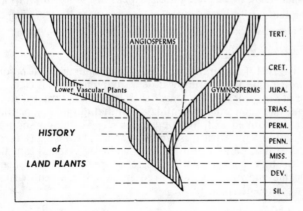

Fig. 3. The flowering plants, or angiosperms, of uncertain ancestry, appear abruptly in the fossil record and almost immediately become the dominant flora (Dorf, 1955).

angiosperms has produced only a few doubtfully related forms. We can conclude only that the character of terrestrial vegetation throughout the world underwent a radical change within a period of time that was quite brief geologically but sufficient for differentiation and worldwide spread of the angiosperms, or that a long antecedent history of these plants took place in upland habitats that have not been preserved (Axelrod, 1952).

The trilobites of Paleozoic seas also illustrate very well the phenomenon of the systematic discontinuity. Judging from their fossils, the trilobites may well have been the most highly organized, abundant, and diverse animals during the first 100 million years of their existence. Several superfamilies comprising many families appear abruptly near the base of the lower Cambrian; others are introduced somewhat higher in the lower Cambrian. Of the ten superfamilies of lower Cambrian trilobites, not a single ancestor is known. Several of these major groups drop out at the top of the Cambrian without known descendants. Among the post-Cambrian forms ten of the superfamilies have long and well-documented records in the later Paleozoic. But of these, seven cannot be related confidently to any of the known Cambrian groups by means of intermediate fossils. Continued collecting has only emphasized the separation of these groups in the known record.

The abrupt appearance of the trilobites near the base of the Paleozoic rocks is part of a larger problem of the origin of the Cambrian fauna. A majority of the major invertebrate phyla comprising some five hundred known species, many of which belonged to highly organized animals, are known in this fauna.

On the other hand, most pre-Cambrian rocks are unfossiliferous and very few pre-Cambrian fossils are on record. Many of these have been discredited either as inorganic in origin or younger than pre-Cambrian in age. Darwin addressed himself to this problem as follows:

> If the theory [of evolution] be true, it is indisputable that before the lowest Cambrian stratum was deposited long periods elapsed, as long as, or probably far longer than, the whole interval from the Cambrian age to the present day; and that during vast periods the world swarmed with living creatures. . . . To the question of why we do not find rich fossiliferous deposits belonging to these assumed earliest periods prior to the Cambrian system, I can give no satisfactory answer. . . . The case at present must remain inexplicable and may be truly urged as a valid argument against the views here entertained.

A century of intensive search for fossils in the pre-Cambrian rocks has thrown very little light on this problem. Early theories that those rocks were dominantly nonmarine or that once-contained fossils have been destroyed by heat and pressure have been abandoned because the pre-Cambrian rocks of many districts physically are very similar to younger rocks in all respects except that they rarely contain any records whatsoever of past life.

In Finland and the United States rare pre-Cambrian coal-like deposits have been found that may have been formed from the lowest forms of plants (Barghoorn, 1957). More convincing fossil evidence that simple plants existed nearly two billion years ago has been secured recently in Ontairo by Tyler and Barghoorn (1954). Unequivocal evidence of early animal life seems to be limited to trails and burrows of soft-bodied wormlike creatures (Schindewolf, 1956). These sparse records tell us nothing about the origin of life or the course of evolution during the first three-fourths of the time that life is known to have existed on earth.

Students of trilobites, impressed by the advanced state of evolution of the earliest trilobites of the lower Cambrian, believe with Darwin that they must have had a long antecedent history in the pre-Cambrian when their skeletons may have contained little or no calcium carbonate (Whittington, 1954). It is a well-known fact that the chitinous exoskeletons of *Limulus* and other arthropods are destroyed quickly by certain bacteria and only those groups that have heavily calcified skeletons are common fossils even in Tertiary and Quaternary rocks. This explanation, however, does not take into account the fact that unequivocal fossils of soft-bodied invertebrates, although by no means common, are known in many places and should have turned up in pre-Cambrian rocks by now. The mid-Cambrian Burgess shale of British Columbia has yielded thousands of specimens of upward of 130 species of soft-bodied animals, most of which are unknown elsewhere. They are preserved with minute details as tissue-thin films of carbon imprinted on bedding planes. Many of these fossils (trilobitomorphs) are similar to trilobites but they did not possess calcareous skeletons.

A clue to the meaning of some of the systematic deficiencies of the fossil record is provided by the recent discovery of living coelacanth fishes and monoplacophoran molluscs long known from the fossil record and supposed to be extinct since the Cretaceous and Devonian periods, respectively. There are many such illustrations in the fossil record of stragglers from once widespread and abundant groups that have become greatly restricted geographically, living on in some isolated area for millions of years after their disappearance in other areas. For example, blastoids died out in early Pennsylvanian times over most of the world, but they survived well into the Permian period in Indonesia, a time span of forty or fifty million years. These facts simply mean that probabilities of discovery of a fossil record or a living population are poor in those groups that are not abundant and widely distributed.

Darwin noted that our fossil record is pretty much limited to sedimentary basins. That is, low swampy areas, deltas, lakes, the sea. Organisms of upland areas and other ecological zones characterized by erosion, such as the seashore, are rarely represented in the fossil record. It has often been suggested that the angiosperms may have diverged from the gymnosperms in upland areas subject to persistent denudation. Axelrod (1958) has suggested that the late pre-Cambrian fauna may have evolved in the littoral zone of the sea, a habitat rich in ecological niches, but one which rarely is preserved in the stratigraphic record.

Simpson (1953a) has shown that the systematic discontinuities in the fossil record are most satisfactorily explained as an effect of sampling error in small, isolated populations. Many of these populations were in rapid transition, undergoing "quantum evolution" between adaptive zones. Sampling is less reliable for very rapidly evolving than for slowly evolving groups. Thus, while a few connecting links are discovered between higher categories, these are relatively rare and many systematic gaps tend to persist in spite of continued collecting.

In contrast to the many fossil groups that display innumerable gaps in the record, there are a few in which the known record is relatively complete and inferred phylogenies are secure, e.g., the ammonites.

Abundance of Fossils

One of the earliest discoveries about the paleontologic record is that fossils actually are more abundant in fossil-bearing rocks than might be assumed from cursory inspection. In many cases it may be suspected that even those forms represented in collections by a few specimens, or only one, are numerous or abundant within the rocks.

Now, the problem of locating fossils is enormously complicated by the fact that fossiliferous strata are partly or wholly concealed in most areas by a cover of superficial rubble, soil, and vegetation. Consequently, our ideas about the abundance of fossils usually are colored by the character and extent of suitable rock exposures.

Strata considered to be only sparsely fossiliferous as judged from superficial inspection actually may be abundantly so. The degree to which this is true is clearly shown by methods of mass collecting fossils, wherein a volume of fossiliferous clay or marl is dug by hand shovel, or power machinery, washed with water, and sieved for fossils. This method has long been used widely for microscopic fossils such as spores and Foraminifera, but it also is coming into use for larger invertebrates and bones and teeth of small vertebrates. The number of fossils thus obtained is usually greater per unit volume of rock than per unit surface and fossils collected in matrix have an advantage that they are damaged less frequently by weathering than those found at the surface.

Small fossils are incredibly numerous in certain strata, where they may be a major component of the rocks. Leidy once estimated a quarter of a million Foraminifera in an ounce of marine sediment. A cubic inch of diatomaceous earth contains as high as fifteen million diatoms per cubic inch and there are many cubic miles of pure diatomite in the Tertiary rocks of California alone. Robert Broom, the distinguished South African paleontologist estimated that there are about eight hundred billion skeletons of vertebrate animals in the Karroo formation. While such estimates are not really meaningful in themselves, they stress the vast difference between the paleontological sample and the astronomic numbers of fossils remaining in the rocks. The abundance of individual fossils is, of course, not directly related to their diversity. Teichert (1956) has undertaken an interesting estimate of the total number of fossil species of animals and plants. He has taken as a premise that those organisms with skeletal parts make up most of the fossil record and he omits consideration of soft-bodied organisms or insects as quantitatively unimportant. In this he errs on the side of conservatism because very many of these are known fossils. Among living organisms the numbers of species most susceptible to preservation as fossils are:

Invertebrates	170,000
Vertebrates	49,000
Vascular plants	350,000
"Preservable species"	569,000

Taking twelve million years as the average longevity of a species, he concludes that the number of species of animals and plants preserved in the rocks may reach a total of ten million. According to an estimate made by Muller and Campbell (1954), about ninety-two thousand fossil species of animals are now described (fig. 4), and I think that the plants would bring the total to around one hundred thousand or only one per cent of Teichert's estimate of the ultimate richness of the fossil record. These speculations are useful in stressing the fact that the fossil record still is poorly known, and they indicate something of the magnitude of the opportunities and the task ahead.

Publication rates provide a rough measure of the rates of discovery of new categories of fossils. A long sustained or increasing rate of publication of new genera, for example, is strong circumstantial evidence that there has not been a decline in the rate of new discoveries. Minor fluctuations in publication

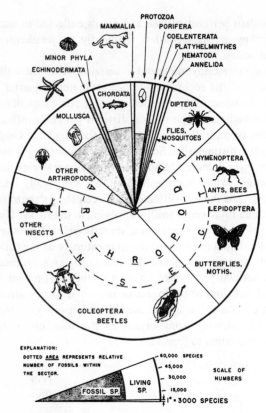

Fig. 4. Relative numbers of known species of animals (Muller and Campbell, *Systematic Zool.*, 1954).

rates are produced by the sporadic appearance of monographs, by differences in initiative and taxonomic philosophy among authors; and larger fluctuations are caused by war, depression, and other vicissitudes of life. Long term trends may be significant in terms of the development of knowledge about fossil groups. Discovery rates in Foraminifera and fossil mammals seem to be expanding; there is no indication but that most of the distinctive kinds of fossils have been discovered. On the other hand, discovery of new living mammals has about ceased, and there is a suggestion that the rate of discovery of new ammonoids is declining. This may indicate that most of the basically different kinds of ammonoids have been found, but it is too early to be sure of this.

Bias in the Fossil Record

It is an exciting experience, charged with emotion, to sit in a canoe quietly drifting down a stream surrounded by a tropical forest teeming with life or to submerge oneself along a coral reef and to inspect closely this biota. To the paleontologist these are momentary situations in a changing scene—single frames in the motion picture of earth history. How much is likely to be preserved in the fossil record? I have examined the alluvial deposits of the tropical river bank for recently deposited organic remains and I have studied broken fragments of living coral reefs piled above sea level by great storm waves. In both cases, the contrast between the living and the dead is very great. Practically all of the organic substances readily decomposable by aerobic bacteria and fungi disappear within days or weeks. In the river alluvium there are remains of perhaps ten or fifteen species of the total of ten thousand. In the reef limestone fifty to seventy-five species of the living three thousand are recognizable after depredations of bacteria and scavengers. But note this: even though the living communities are not preservable in the aggregate, the few preserved species, studied in context with the sediments, tell eloquently of a specific habitat.

Darwin showed clearly that the fossil record probably is never a random sample of life of the past. This idea extends back to Cuvier and beyond.

A Record of Skeletons

Aside from extremely rare examples of preservation of animal tissues in comparatively young rocks and small arthropods and spores in fossil amber, nearly all fossil remains consist of comparatively resistant hard parts. Complete skeletons with all of the parts in position of articulation are on the whole exceptional or even unknown for many groups of plants and animals, so that paleontological studies usually are based on scattered and fragmentary parts of skeletons. Although there are exceptions, the organs and other tissues, details of form, coloration, behavior, and many other characteristics of living organisms commonly are not preserved. The great hosts of soft-bodied plants and animals that make up a large part of any biota likewise rarely are preserved so that their very existence in the past must be inferred by analogy with communities of organisms of the present.

Unequal Preservation of Habitats

There are puzzling systematic deficiencies in the records of many groups of organisms with skeletal parts well adapted for fossilization. The incomplete-ness of the record in many cases probably originates in low population density, location of habitat far from sites of deposition of sediments, and in the habits of organisms. For example, as already noted, the fossil record throughout the world is very poor in remains of upland animals and plants. Probabilities of quick and permanent burial of these forms are slight because they live at a distance from the low places where sediments finally come to rest in depositional basins. Likewise, arboreal mammals and birds tend to be consumed by scavengers before burial and they are poorly represented as fossils. There is scarcely any record of desert plants. Desert deposits are deficient in fossils of all kinds because of a characteristic sparseness of desert life, and oxidizing conditions and leaching reach far below the surface. Organic remains are destroyed here about as fast as they are buried; desert deposits tend to be coarse-grained. The sediment fragments grind up organic remains as they are transported in violent floods that characterize stream deposition in the desert.

Without going into all the various factors operative in these systematic deficiencies in the fossil record, it seems safe to conclude that very many organisms did not frequent sites of persistent and quiet accumulation of sediments. For one reason or another they did not occur in abundance in places where they might be buried quickly. The extreme rareness of fossil remains of early man is a case in point. Man and many other mammals make use of their intelligence in escaping flood waters and in avoiding quicksands and bogs.

On the other hand, aquatic organisms and those that live near water are in close association with the deposition of sediments and are favorably situated for quick burial before they are consumed. Consequently, the greatest part of the fossil record consists of the skeletal remains and traces of organisms that lived in water, especially in the sea, or near the margins of streams, lakes, or swamps. Thus, in a very real sense, most of the fossil record is the record of lowland or marine basins of aqueous sedimentation. Even under the most favorable conditions, however, quick burial and preservation of organic remains must be a rare event as compared with the total number of organisms that live at one time.

Biological Factors

Population density and distribution must also be an important factor affecting the frequency with which organisms have been preserved. It seems certain that preservation of organisms in the fossil record is such a very rare event that thousands or millions of individuals are destroyed for each one that is incorporated in the record. Thus, organisms that are abundantly represented in an environment favorable for quick burial have a better chance of preservation than those that are not so abundant. In general, small organisms reproduce more rapidly and produce larger populations than do large organisms. It is perhaps partly because of this that fossil Foraminifera are more abundant in the rocks than, say, mammals. Probably the relative sparseness of larger fossils as compared with microscopic forms is a reflection of differences in relative abundance.

The structure of the plant body is not well adapted to preservation as a single unit and the most common plant fossils are detached spores, pollen leaves, stems, or fragments of wood. Well-preserved seeds, fruits, and particularly flowers are rare. There also is occasionally a close resemblance of form among the leaves of different families and orders. These difficulties are overcome by careful consideration of all the fine details of shape, texture, character of margin, and apex of leaves, character of primary and secondary venation, and particularly by the microscopic structure of the cuticle of leaves and reproductive organs. Epidermal characters are often well preserved and directly comparable to those of living plants. Thus, conclusions are not based solely on a few leaves but on a whole complex of characters and on the plant associations which, although incomplete, are nevertheless composed of dominant members of harmonious communities and therefore indicative of specific habitats.

Physical Factors

Fossils may be destroyed quickly by weathering or gradually by changes that take place after burial. These changes are more rapid in certain kinds of skeletons than in others so that there is selective preservation of some fossil groups over others.

The processes of sedimentation in many cases complicate interpretation of the associations of fossils, particularly the small forms that are easily moved by wind or water. The dead remains of various forms may be transported from diverse habitats and deposited together in associations that do not reflect any single life environment. Under these conditions there is much winnowing and sorting of organic remains by size, shape, and effective specific gravity. The remains of young and small organisms thus may be separated from those of older and larger forms. Less commonly, the fossils of an older rock formation are weathered free of rock matrix and become incorporated in a younger formation in association with fossil forms that lived much later and under quite different conditions.

These are all complicating factors that try to the utmost the skill and patience of the paleontologist. Nevertheless, they do not provide insurmountable obstacles to correct interpretations of the record. As in all scientific research, paleontological interpretations may be from time to time independently tested by additional work and new discoveries.

In spite of the shortcomings of the fossil record, many extinct animal and plant groups favored by the factors of preservation are becoming quite well known. The record provides documents of organic evolution and still incomplete but very meaningful histories of many important groups of organisms through hundreds of millions of years. It serves as the basis for a scale of geologic time that has been adopted generally and found accurate in broad outline throughout the world. The sequence of fossil faunas and floras enables the paleontologist to date rock formations in terms of this standard geologic scale and thus to correlate contemporaneous strata and geological events in widely separated regions.

Reliability of the Record

I have discussed at some length the shortcomings of the fossil record as a representative sample of past life. Darwin understood very well most of the cited limitations. He was optimistic about the future of paleontology, and the remarkable advances in the past century of discovery and collecting surely have far exceeded his expectations. But how can we evaluate our knowledge of the record? What are the confidence limits of our present inferences? How much will we have to modify our conclusions as more information is gathered? These questions cannot be answered readily, but past experience may help us in formulating tentative judgments.

The Test of Adequacy

Experience from past discoveries shows that our ideas still are changing rapidly in some areas of knowledge as new evidence accumulates. In other areas, there has been little or no fundamental change in broad perspective for several decades in spite of continuous study. For example, the early nineteenth century paleontologists knew that the trilobites were quite varied and complex at their first appearance in the lower Cambrian, that they soon deployed greatly in the higher Cambrian and Ordovician rocks, and that they then gradually diminished in variety until their disappearance from the record near the top of the Paleozoic.

Even if the known range of the trilobites is extended through future discoveries of pre-Cambrian or Triassic trilobites, it would be unreasonable in the present advanced state of knowledge to consider seriously the possibility that the new finds would reveal widespread and diverse faunas at the new limits of range that had been completely overlooked previously. Such new discoveries are not likely to affect greatly our present conclusions about the presently known record.

Studies of fossils over the past century have confirmed many generalizations held in Darwin's day, and, in retrospect, we can recognize steady confirmations as well as refutations of general conclusions. We still believe that the dinosaurs, marine reptiles, and the ammonites dropped out in the late Cretaceous. Gymnosperms are still considered dominant in Jurassic and Triassic rocks; angiosperms and mammals are dominant in Tertiary rocks. Of course, revolutionary discoveries occur from time to time, but usually they result in modification and adjustment of details, not in wholesale abandonment of broad generalizations arrived at empirically after much sampling. The known record is spotty indeed, but it is very good for the more abundant and well-preserved groups of fossils. When fossils are rare or poorly preserved, conclusions are more tentative and they vary greatly in order of probability.

Evolutionary Patterns

The great times of expansion and recession of the better-known major groups have been known for a long time and the general outlines of knowledge here are not likely to undergo major revision. Some major groups display what appears to have been a sort of ecological incompatibility, successively and gradually replacing one another in time as more successful groups wrested one niche after another from competing inferior groups. Darwin anticipated this phenomenon and suggested how competition could lead to the extinction of all of the less well-adapted organisms without concurrent changes in the inorganic factors of the environment. Illustrations of replacement in competing groups are the trilobites, shelled cephalopods, and bony fishes; the creodonts and fissipeds; and the perissodactyls and ruminant artiodactyls (fig. 5). Among plants, the expansion of the angiosperms was accompanied by restriction and elimination of many groups of gymnosperms and lower land plants (fig. 3).

Rates of Evolution

Studies by G. G. Simpson and others have shown that the known fossil record now is sufficient for accurate measurement of rates of evolution, a subject of great importance in connection with understanding evolutionary mechanisms and also of interest from the standpoint of geological chronology (Simpson, 1953a). It now is well established that rates of evolution vary greatly within and between related groups. Furthermore, there is no simple correlation between reproduction rate and evolutionary rate. Certain groups of small Foraminifera, with reproductive rates thousands of the times those

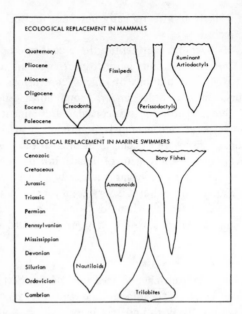

Fig. 5. Replacement among competing major groups of animals. The patterns of increasing and decreasing diversity suggest progressive ecological displacement of less successful by more successful groups. (Data on mammals after Simpson, 1953, Columbia Univ. Press.)

of mammals, have evolved very much more slowly than the latter, but other Foraminifera have evolved as fast as any group of mammals. High, intermediate, and low rates are recognized and these are dependent on the Darwinian factors of variability and selection pressure (fig.2).

Phylogeny

Phylogenies in paleontology are inferred from morphological series distributed chronologically through the stratigraphic succession. Innumerable examples have been worked out for Foraminifera, corals, molluscs, echinoderms, arthropods, hemichordates, vertebrates, and vascular plants. The evidence in many fossil groups is so well documented and voluminous that few neontologists would think of ignoring paleontologic data in making phylogenetic interpretations. For example, Florin (1944) has shown that the mutual relationships among modern conifers can be understood only by taking into account the many extinct Permian forms which had fructifications unlike those of any living forms. It has been shown many times that modern animals and plants are the ends of evolutionary lines which usually are more specialized in at least a few characters than the most closely related ancestral forms in the fossil record. Thus, hypothetical phylogenies based solely on living genera and species cannot express the true relationships. In order to understand the ancestry of, and connections between, living genera and families, it is necessary to know the fossil record. Conversely, the evidence from fossils is incomplete without reference to distributions, ecology, anatomy, and adaptions of living forms.

Paleontologists have pioneered studies of growth and morphogenesis and they have provided many illustrations from the fossil record of correlated growth (allometric) gradients in both ontogeny and phylogeny.

One outstanding contribution of paleontology that would otherwise be completely unknown is the repeated demonstration of long evolutionary trends in which two or more separate but related lineages pass independently through the same sequence of morphological changes, either simultaneously or at different times. Many illustrations are known among both animals and plants. For example, there was a persistent tendency for many lines of primitive graptolites to change direction of colony growth from downward to horizontal to vertical. This trend extended through several families and it frequently enables the stratigrapher to determine the general geological age of a graptolite assemblage from evolutionary stage without identification of the particular genera at hand (Bulman, 1955). Likewise, many families of the great groups of corals have evolved along a characteristic sequence from solitary or dendritic forms to tightly packed colonies with prismatic individuals (Wells, 1956). The independent development of saber-toothed "tigers" and carnivores in placental and marsupial mammals, the closely parallel changes in horse and horselike litopterns, the common trends for increased body size and brain size in mammals are other examples of parallel evolution recognizable as such only in the fossil record (Colbert, 1955).

Stebbins notes that "the great majority of evolutionary trends toward increased specialization in vascular plants can be explained as a result of three types of morphological trends, acting either separately or in conjunction with each other. These are reduction, fusion, and change in symmetry. The most widespread of these trends has been reduction" (Stebbins, 1950).

These parallel trends no longer have orthogenetic or vitalistic implications to the majority of paleontologists who now recognize the probability that these patterns are an adaptive expression of similar genetic organization in closely related lineages.

Fossil Populations

The fossil record supplies a wealth of data on changes in time and space in both populations and entire biotas during long spans of time. Thus, paleontology contributes evidence bearing on many principles of evolution and gives the paleontologist an advantage of an abundance of time that is denied the student of living organisms.

Many fossil samples are adequate for quantitative studies of various kinds. For example, Kurten (1953), Deevey (1955), and others have shown that relatively undisturbed fossil assemblages may be used effectively in studies of population dynamics. Samples suitable for the studies of population variability are quite easily obtained for some groups, especially microfossils; and statistical methods are used increasingly to refine discrimination and to establish the limits of fossil subspecies and species (Imbrie, 1957).

Paleoecology

Much attention has been given in recent years to ecological interpretations of fossil assemblages in order to learn about the mutual relationships between past organisms and their environments. This requires a disciplined synthesis of paleontology, stratigraphy, petrology, geochemistry, and sedimentation for the most complete utilization of all available evidence from fossils, rocks, and stratigraphy. By attacking paleoecological problems along all available lines of evidence, surprisingly detailed interpretations of past environments are possible and the fossils themselves acquire much added significance whenever they are studied in the full context of their geologic setting (e.g., Imbrie, 1955; Newell *et al.*, 1953; Bradley, 1931).

Fossils have provided most of the evidence for a quite detailed history of changes in distributions of land and sea, and many generalized paleogeographic maps have been published showing the location of major seaways and lands for the successive epochs of time (Dunbar, 1949). These maps are helpful in summarizing knowledge of the distributions of marine and nonmarine deposits and in working out hypothetical times and routes of migrations of organisms (Simpson, 1953*b*).

The evidence from fossil plants is in some respects less complete than that available from fossil animals, but plants tell us much more than animals do about past climates and there is an excellent record of the succession and migration of floras during geologic history.

The oldest known fossils are the remains of filamentous algae and fungi, but the record of past floras is quite poor before the upper Silurian by which time the continents of the world had become clothed with a diverse vegetation of vascular plants (fig. 3). Cosmopolitan floras of extraordinarily wide distribution of the middle Paleozoic are thought to indicate much milder world climates than at present with remarkably little zonation. The late Paleozoic and Triassic floras increasingly marked zonation roughly parallel with the present equator. This is succeeded in Jurassic and Cretaceous rocks by comparatively uniform floras throughtout the world. Evidence of latitudinal floral zones is again apparent throughout the Tertiary period which was a time of gradual cooling from generally subtropical conditions at intermediate lattitudes to the present conditions (fig. 6). The zonal distribution from fossil floras argues for stability of the poles and continents throughout the latter part of earth history (Chaney, 1940; Edwards, 1955), as opposed to extensive polar migrations or continental sliding as suggested by studies of paleomagnetism. The record of fossil invertebrates has been used in arguments for (Ma, 1957) and against (Stehli, 1957) migration of poles or continents. All paleontologists are agreed that the record indicates mild and surprisingly uniform climatic conditions throughout much of geologic time in contrast to the sharply zoned climate conditions of the past million years.

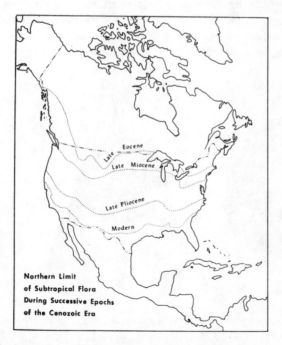

Fig. 6.   Evidence from fossil plants of progressive cooling of climate since the Cretaceous period. The glacial climates of the Pleistocene are not represented (Dorf, 1957).

Fossil spores long have been known in coal beds (fig. 7A), and in the past few decades plant micropaleontology, or palynology, as it is now termed, has produced a vast literature of thousands of papers on fossil spores and pollen, bearing particularly on stratigraphic zonation and correlation in coal basins and Quaternary nonmarine deposits. These fossils have assumed a significance for correlating and dating continental deposits comparable to that of the Foraminifera of marine rocks. The tiny plant fossils are chemically resistant and may be extracted successfully from rocks by chemical means. In 1900 the Swedish botanist Logerheim showed that the stratigraphic succession of spores and pollen in Quaternary deposits provided a detailed record of floral migrations under the influence of strong climatic changes. With the aid of these tiny plant remains, the complex climatic fluctuations of the Quaternary glacial and interglacial stages have been worked out in great detail.

Shortly after World War II, H. C. Urey showed that the ratio of the isotopes of oxygen O^{18}/O^{16} contained in unmodified calcium carbonate skeletons of aquatic organisms is a delicate indication of the temperature of the water in which the skeletons were secreted. Paleotemperatures of ancient marine molluscs as old as Cretaceous thus have been measured, but the greatest application of this chemical method has been to work out the detailed stratigraphy and temperature zonation of the Globigerina ooze that

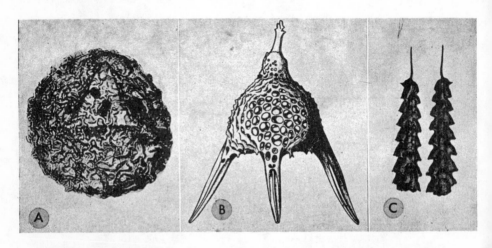

Fig. 7. Microscopic fossils. A, a plant spore, × 250, of Mississippian age, Nova Scotia (Hacquebard, 1957, *Micropaleontology*); B, a silica radiolarian, × 250, late Tertiary, Rotti (Riedel, *Jour. Paleont.*, 1953); C, an uncrushed graptolite colony of original chitinoid material, × 8, Ordovician of Oland (Bulman, *Archiv for Zoologi.*, 1936).

blankets much of the floor of the north Atlantic (Emiliani, 1958a). The records of climatic fluctuations over the north Atlantic basin throughout the glacial and interglacial stages of the past 300,000 years have been worked out in detail and correlated with climatic cycles in Europe and America determined by means of pollen analyses (Emiliani, 1958b).

Quality of Fossils

Much has been written and said about the imperfections of fossils which, for the most part, consist of incomplete, weathered, or fragmentary skeletons, or their impressions in matrix from which the skeletal remains have been dissolved by ground water. Fortunately, we do not have to depend solely on fossils of inferior quality for our information about past life. Steady improvement in techniques of collecting and of extracting fossils from rock matrix has effected a minor revolution in paleontology and has shown that there is a bountiful supply of well-preserved material available for study provided that it can be suitably prepared for study. The great impediment to progress in paleontology is not the imperfections of the fossil record, but rather the difficulties involved in freeing fossils from matrix or otherwise preparing them for study. A large part of the energies and time of paleontologists is spent in freeing fossils from matrix in the laboratory.

Animal skeletons and shells originally composed of phosphate or carbonate of lime, or of silica, and leaves, spores and the woody parts of plants form the bulk of the fossil record and these may be well preserved (fig. 7), but there are also examples of preservation of chitinous skeletons and soft tissues which provide valuable information not available in the more common fossils.

Preservation of Soft Parts of Organisms

For example, frozen mammoths with parts of the flesh and skin preserved have been reported from more than fifty localities in northern Siberia, and thousands of ivory tusks have been obtained from this source and marketed for the manufacture of art objects in China. In this case, continuous refrigeration since death has prevented bacterial decay. Fossils preserved in this way are limited to quite young fossils of the far north. A much more important mode of preservation is the embalming action of stagnant, oxygen-deficient waters of certain swamps, lakes, and marine basins. Anaerobic conditions prevail where products of decaying organic matter become so concentrated that they suppress the activities of decay bacteria.

Animal tissues decompose very slowly in the bottom sediments of stagnant waters. For example, a large number of human cadavers more than two thousand years old have been found within peat deposits of Denmark and Holland. Many of these are remarkable for the excellent preservation of tissues and organs which have suffered hardly any shrinkage or deformation. Experimental work by Franz Hecht indicates in a general way how animal tissues may be preserved for a long time after burial. The observations were made at the Senckenberg-am-Meer Institute near Wilhelmshaven (Hecht, 1933). Fish carcasses were buried in the fine-grained sediments of tidal flats or in aquaria and studied at intervals. The body of a shark, naturally stranded on tidal flats in 1924, was buried beneath three feet of sediment. It was unearthed in 1926 and again in 1931, and studied. Surprisingly, it had changed very little in form. From his studies Hecht concluded that the albuminous substances decomposed rapidly (presumably liberating ammonia in the process), but the fatty substances decomposed very slowly and gradually passed into the enclosing sediment sealing the organic mass concretion-like from ground waters and oxygen. Under certain conditions the environment was acid and the skeletons of associated clam shells were dissolved. Extreme anaerobic conditions prevailed when sulfate-reducing bacteria were active. In this case the interstitial water became alkaline because of replacement of the strongly acid sulfate radicle by sulfide, and calcareous skeletons were perfectly preserved. Hecht's work is so suggestive that further experiments along these lines should be undertaken.

Incompletely decayed plant remains accumulate in bogs as peat, and if the peat becomes buried by sediments, it may eventually form coal through a succession of chemical changes. Remains of bottom animals are not abundant in these deposits because bog waters are usually anaerobic and even toxic, but occasional insects and land animals find their way into bog deposits where, free from the depredations of scavengers, they may become preserved as fossils.

One of the most remarkable examples of preservation of organic tissues in antiseptic swamp waters is a "fossil graveyard" in Eocene lignite deposits of the Geisel Valley in central Germany. This was systematically studied by Johannes Weigelt of Halle University and his associates (Weigelt, 1935). Many animals, including groups rarely found as fossils, lower primates, snakes, and birds were trapped in several small, scattered bogs where they accumulated and were preserved from bacterial attack in stagnant oxygen-poor waters. More than six thousand remains of vertebrate animals and great numbers of insects, molluscs, and plants were found over a period of several years as the lignite was being mined.

The fossils that had been collected when Weigelt made his report in 1935 included more than fifteen hundred fish of many kinds, twenty frogs, a salamander, fifty-two crocodiles, two hundred tortoises, several snakes, and tree lizards, twenty different kinds of birds, seventeen species of lemuroids, five rodents, six archiac carnivores, three early horses, a bat, and many primitive herbivores.

The flattened and dessicated remains of soft tissues of these animals in many cases showed details of cellular structure. Some of the specimens had undergone little chemical modification, but among the frogs there are specimens in which the bones were leached away while the brain and spinal cord were preserved as *adipocere*, a calcium compound of fatty acids. This is a very unusual case of preservation of soft anatomical structures after destruction of the hard skeleton. Epithelial cells showing the nuclei were preserved in the skin of frog specimens. Small details of fly larvae and beetles, including the chitinous exoskeleton, muscular tissue, and tracheae were preserved. Muscular tissue, connective tissue showing microscopic details, and cartilage were found in fishes, frogs, salamanders, lizards, and mammals.

Several fossils contained remains of fat cells and pigment cells (chromatophores) with animal pigment. Well-preserved bits of hair, feathers, and scales probably are among the oldest known examples of essentially unmodified preservation of these structures. Stomach contents of beetles, amphibia, fishes, birds, and mammals provided direct evidence about eating habits. Bacteria of two kinds were found in the excrement of crocodiles and another on the trachea of a beetle. Fungi were identified on leaves, and the original plant pigments, chlorophyll and coproporphyrin, were found preserved in some of the leaves. From such ample fossil evidence it is possible to reconstruct the Eocene life of the Geisel Valley in considerable detail.

Fossil wood buried under the anaerobic conditions of stagnant swamps has in some cases endured with only little decay for amazingly long periods of time. For example, logs found in the Eocene lignites of Germany and in early Cretaceous clays of New Jersey are composed of unaltered wood and show perfectly preserved microscopic cellular structure of the original trees. They resemble ordinary wood and do not exhibit significant mineralization in spite of the fact that they are approximately fifty million years old in the first case, and one hundred million years old in the second.

The fossil amber deposits of the Baltic region are famous for the well-preserved insects and spiders found in the amber. These were trapped in tree gum long ago, in the Oligocene epoch, and have been protected from decomposition by the moisture-proof and air-proof cover.

Destruction of organic remains is retarded in impervious rocks which not only exclude oxygen but also prevent the circulation of ground water. Molluscs of Cretaceous age are abundant in the Coon Creek Clay of Tennessee. The mother-of-pearl shells and even chitinoid ligaments of clam shells are extraordinarily well preserved for faunas this old. Caster and

Waering (1951) discovered many remarkable skeletons of eurypterid *Megalograptus* in a clay deposit of Ordovician age. The original chitin is but little altered in these fossils and still retains a scorpionid color pattern, and many of the skeletons are articulated. Since chitin usually is quickly destroyed by bacterial decomposition, the preservation of these eurypterids illustrates the influence of the type of matrix on preservation of fossils. The horny substance of graptolites still is preserved in calcareous rocks of fine grain (fig. 7C).

Fossils Impregnated with Silica

The most effective preservative of fossils is fine-grained silica which may hermetically seal and protect organic remains from bacteria and ground water solutions for hundreds of millions of years. The most remarkable examples of this are filaments and spores of low algae and fungi found in the chert of the mid-Huronian Gunflint formation of Ontario. The oldest known fossils, they preserve traces of amino acids after 1,700 million years.

Until recently, the oldest known land flora was a lower Devonian peat bog, heavily impregnated with silica, found near Rhynie in the Scottish county of Aberdeen. Many species of beautifully preserved primitive vascular plants have been described from this locality together with the remains of many spiders, a mite, and a primitive wingless insect. Early Paleozoic protozoans (Chitinozoa) and graptolites are common in chert nodules. A great advance was made when Kozlowski discovered that many of these microscopic fossils are not appreciably altered from the original chitinoid condition and that they can be extracted from the hard matrix by means of hydrofluoric acid, which dissolves the silica but does not affect the fossils. Soft-bodied microscopic organisms, including the flagella of one-celled euglenoid forms, have been described in Cretaceous chert in several well-documented reports by Wetzel (1933).

Chemical Preparation of Fossils

Long ago, in the latter part of the nineteenth century, it was known that certain fossils may be extracted without damage from hard rock matrix by means of acids which either dissolve the matrix without harm to the fossils, or dissolve the fossils without affecting the matrix. In the latter case, the resulting cavity could be used as a mold to restore perfectly the external form of the organism or skeleton (fig. 8). Perhaps because of the relatively high cost of commercial acids in those days, this method of preparing fossils was never thoroughly explored until the past three decades. G. Arthur Cooper of the U.S. National Museum, more than any other, is responsible for an important revolution in paleontology through the development of "chemical" methods of preparation of fossils. In certain rock formations many of the calcareous fossils have been selectively replaced by silica. This was owing, presumably, to the catalytic effect of contained organic substances on silica-bearing solutions. The matrix commonly was not affected by the replacement. Consequently, the more soluble rock matrix may be carefully dissolved away from the fossils with hydrochloric or acetic acid. Cooper has combined the advantages of mass collecting with chemical preparation. From 30 tons of Permian limestone collected in the Glass Mountains of Texas, he has extracted three million individual invertebrate fossils, almost all of which are exquisitely preserved with many delicate structures intact. The morphology of a large proportion of these fossils now can be worked out for the first time. A single control block of limestone weighing one hundred and eighty-six pounds yielded ten thousand excellent specimens of invertebrates, including Foraminifera, brachiopods, bryozoans, gastropods, and pelecypods. Only a very few of these fossils were exposed on the surface of the rock and none could have been completely cleaned of matrix by mechanical means. A whole new fauna of mid-Ordovician trilobites preserved in this way has been worked out by H. B. Whittington and others.

Fig. 8. A nearly perfect restoration of a fossil amphibian prepared by dissolving the bones with acid from relatively insoluble rock matrix. The resulting natural molds of the individual bones were then used to cast replicas. The skeleton is about 5 feet long. A, original in matrix; B, reconstructed cast, Permian, New South Wales (Swinton, Brit. Mus. Nat. Hist.).

Extraordinarily well-preserved, uncrushed insects and other small arthropods with the body hairs and appendages clearly visible and some of the internal organs preserved were discovered by Bassett in calcareous nodules of Miocene age in the Calico Mountains, California. Palmer (1957) discovered that many of the insects have been impregnated, or coated, with silica so that they can be extracted in all exquisite detail from the matrix by means of acetic or formic acid. This discovery points the way to systematic examination and chemical preparation of calcareous nodules from other formations and areas. Bradley (1946) discovered well-preserved micro-organisms of several kinds in fossil coprolites of Eocene age in Wyoming. The fossil faeces belonging to reptiles and mammals contained a profusion of intestinal saprophytes closely similar to those of living forms. In addition, one of the mammalian coprolites contained large numbers of fresh-water algae. The bacteria and algae are preserved in silica and show fine structures in detail.

Fig. 9. Fossil skull of mammal-like reptile freed from rock matrix by softening and dissolving away the rock with acid. Triassic, South Africa. The skull is about 3½ inches long. A, nearly perfect jaw; B, original fossil before preparation; C, cleaned skull (Swinton, Brit. Mus. Nat. Hist.).

Calcium phosphate, the principal substance of vertebrate bones, conodonts, and certain brachiopods is nearly insoluble in acetic and formic acids which can, therefore, be used to dissolve calcareous matrix from these fossils. Many delicate and complex structures have been perfectly cleaned of hard matrix by this means (fig. 8). Usually the matrix contains much insoluble material so that chemical preparation must be supplemented with manual cleaning under a microscope.

Summary

The known fossil record is characterized by systematic deficiencies as pointed out long ago by Charles Darwin; but as a record of preservable lowland and aquatic organisms, it is rich beyond the most optimistic predictions of nineteenth-century paleontologists. As collecting continues, it is becoming evident that the unsampled record in the rocks far exceeds the known record. Well-preserved fossils of some groups are abundant, and it may be confidently asserted that new discoveries made possible by new techniques of collecting and preparing fossils will necessitate revision of many present concepts about past life; but most of the revision will pertain to details of phylogeny and the accommodation of new categories not yet discovered. Many early generalizations about the record, the broad outlines of the history of many of the major groups, have been independently tested and confirmed many times. These generalizations will not be so much affected by future discoveries.

The Study of Evolution:
Methods and Present Status of Theory

by
George Gaylord Simpson

From Behavior and Evolution, *1958, edited by Anne Roe and George Gaylord Simpson; reprinted by permission of the author and of the Yale University Press. The book is the publication of a conference held April 30–May 5, 1956, at Princeton. This chapter is a brief and simple review of certain main points of the modern synthetic theory of evolution, written by one of its principal architects. Dr. Simpson is Alexander Agassiz Professor of Vertebrate Paleontology at Harvard University.*

Samuel Butler said that a hen is an egg's way of producing another egg. Thus in the Darwinian epoch he foreshadowed a reorientation of evolutionary studies that did later occur. Without expressing it in that way, the evolutionary scientists of Butler's and earlier times held the commonsense view that an egg is a hen's way of producing another hen. They were trying to explain the evolution of the hen, not of the egg. It was the geneticists, after 1900, who came around to Butler's view that the essence of the matter is in the egg, not in the hen.[1]

Those contrasting points of view reflect different ideas as to the involvement of behavior in evolution. The 19th-century evolutionary theories of the naturalists were largely, if not primarily, behavioral. The behavioral

[1] Without, indeed, any real debt to Butler. That an egg somehow "knows" how to produce a hen and thus produces another egg that "knows" just a little more seems brilliantly apt in retrospect. But, like other flashes of Butler's peculiar genius, this bit of insight was so embedded in nonsense that it was not really helpful at the time and had no useful outcome.

element tended at first to be minimized in the 20th-century evolutionary theories of the geneticists, who might in some cases be accused of leaving the hen out of the picture altogether except as a means of learning what the egg "knows."

The first great issue in naturalistic evolutionary theory was between the neo-Lamarckians and the Darwinians. (There were and are nonnaturalistic alternative schools, such as those of vitalism or of finalism, but their metaphysics can legitimately be omitted from this brief account.) Lamarck, himself, stressed behavior almost to the point of considering it the sole effective cause of evolution. It is, he taught, the habitual actions of organisms—in other words, their behavior—that modify their morphology, and these modifications accumulated through the generations *are* evolution. It is true that Lamarck also believed in a perfecting principle that somehow has driven organisms up the *scala naturae*, but the neo-Lamarckians discarded that essentially nonnaturalistic element in his theory. The neo-Lamarckians also incorporated into their views the accumulation of direct results of the action of the environment on organisms, a hypothesis that is non-Lamarckian and nonbehavioral.

Darwin's theory of evolution was hardly less behavioral than Lamarck's. Darwin saw no reason to question the Lamarckian belief in the direct influence of behavior on evolution, through the induction of heritable modifications. Darwin's own main contribution, the theory of natural selection, also involved essential relationships between behavior and evolution. He saw and illustrated with many examples that the behavior of animals is often determined and always circumscribed by their heredity, although he knew even less than we do about the mechanisms involved. The behavior of animals is also obviously and crucially involved in their survival and success in reproduction. Thus natural selection provides another way, less direct but truer than the supposed Lamarckian way, in which behavior is bound in with the changes in heredity that constitute evolution.

Few now doubt that the Lamarckian and neo-Lamarckian views are essentially false, and we need pay no further attention to them here. The point is that Lamarck, Darwin, and their many colleagues and followers were all primarily interested in the behaving animal, the hen, rather than in the egg, which has no behavior in usual senses of the word, and that one of the things they sought and stressed was a relationship between behavior and evolution. It is a pity, in a way, that we cannot accept a direct and simple relationship, but Darwin pointed out a relationship that is surely present, in some degree, and that is all the more effective for being indirect and subtle.

Then came the shift of emphasis to the egg by the geneticists from about 1900 onward. In extreme form, their views practically eliminated behavior as an essential element in evolution. What a hen is and does depends on the egg, that is, on the mechanism of heredity complete within the fertilized egg. Evolutionary changes in the hen, so some of the early geneticists submitted and a dwindling few still hold, arise without any prior relationship to the hen and its behavior. Evolution is reduced to processes in the precursor cells of the gametes and in the confluence of gametes in the fertilized egg (zygote). The hen (the man, the tree) is largely irrelevant except, as Butler said, as a device for producing another egg.

The most widely held modern theory of evolution may be presented as a reconciliation between the naturalists' hen-evolution and the geneticists' egg-evolution. It reinstates behavior not merely as something to which evolution has happened but as something that is itself one of the essential determinants of evolution. Accepting the geneticists' knowledge of egg-processes, it shows that these are not autonomous but are strongly influenced by hen-processes. The means of that influence is, as Darwin thought, natural selection. In the course of this theoretical synthesis natural selection has turned out to be something broader than and in some respects different from Darwin's concept.[2]

Methods of Evolutionary Study

The topic assigned for this chapter requires some notice of methods before proceeding to summarize the present status of evolutionary theory. Methods are, indeed, so numerous and diverse that a catalogue of them would be redundant to those who are using them, confusing to those who are not, and of little interest or usefulness in either case. It will be best to avoid detail and to present only a few broad considerations as to aims, the ways of achieving them, and implications or criteria involved in those ways.

In the first place, most of the aims of evolutionary study involve either events or processes. The study of events is historical; it seeks to reconstruct the whole history of organisms on this planet. That (unattainable) goal is of course approached by accumulation of restricted studies of the histories of particular groups of organisms, of particular anatomical or physiological features, and the like. The procedure is by levels: comparative descriptive studies, then inferential placing of the unit of description in phylogenetic sequences, and finally, generalizations as to the kinds of sequences that have most frequently occurred and the conditions that accompany and therefore may determine a particular kind of sequence.

[2] In justice, however, it should be emphasized that practically nothing that Darwin wrote about natural selection is invalidated by the modern concept. Darwinian selection still stands, but its complexities and bearings are better understood and it becomes part of a more inclusive principle.

The objective data for historical study, the things described at the first level of research, are characteristics of (1) organisms or parts thereof, (2) their activities, (3) the conditions surrounding and influencing them, and (4) the temporal sequence of the items observed.[3] It is especially pertinent to the subject of this book that all four kinds of data are only very exceptionally available in any one study. There are in this respect two quite different cases, each with its distinct methodological problems. A temporal sequence long enough to involve marked evolutionary change usually extends into geological time, and the organisms involved are, or include, fossils. Then the documents are directly historical in nature, but their data are primarily of classes (1), mainly morphological, and (4), sequential. Observations of class (3), environmental, are limited and more often involve inferences than direct observation. Direct observations of class (2), including behavior, are almost entirely lacking.[4] Morphological evolution of, for instance, a bone in the lower jaw of a group of reptiles can sometimes be observed without the slightest ambiguity in a directly historical record. Behavioral evolution cannot be so observed. Inferences as to behavior can be based on the morphology of fossils and analogy with living animals. That can, for instance, usually be done for food habits and locomotion, but such possible inferences include little beyond what might be called elemental or first-order behavior. For example, practically all of the habitual or possible movements of a bird may be inferred from its fossilized skeleton, and those movements are the elements from which the bird's total behavior was necessarily compounded. But it would be impossible to infer just what series of movements occurred in courtship, an example of compound or second-order behavior. The evolution of first-order behavior is important and interesting, and we have some good examples documented by the fossil record, such as the evolution of locomotion in the horse family. Nevertheless, the evolution of second-order behavior is even more important and more interesting, and this is quite properly the principal preoccupation of the evolutionary psychologist. In that field the fossil record is of almost no direct (although it is of some indirect) help.

In the second main sort of historical study the documents are essentially contemporaneous. If the organisms under study are dead (fossils; the usual taxonomic collections of recent organisms; specimens for postmortem dissection) the limitations are even greater than for fossil sequences, and data

[3]The temporal order of a really long sequence is rarely directly observed but it is commonly on so factual a basis that it may be considered an objective datum.

[4]There are, to be sure, surprisingly numerous examples of what may be called "fossilized behavior"; tracks, burrows, wounds, and tooth marks, even animals fossilized in the act of parturition or copulation. Nevertheless I know of only one or two rather unimportant examples in which change, actual evolution, of behavior can be observed in such materials.

for the study of behavioral evolution are few, indeed. If, however, the subjects of study are living, data of classes (1), (2), and (3) are freely available. This is the source of practically all of our observational information on behavior. That is almost too obvious to require statement, but the point to be emphasized is that *such information is in itself completely nonhistorical*; it includes no data of class (4). Almost all students agree with that statement when it is made, but many of them do not really keep it in mind in their own work. In comparative anatomy some such sequence as dogfish-frog-cat-man is still frequently taught as "evolutionary," i.e., historical. In fact the anatomical differences among those organisms are in large part ecologically and behaviorally determined, are divergent and not sequential, and do not in any useful sense form a historical series. The same objection applies with perhaps even greater force to studies of behavior which state or assume an evolutionary (historical) sequence in, for instance, comparison of an insect[5] ("invertebrate level"), a rat[5] ("primitive mammalian level"), and a man.

The three main bases for inference from contemporaneous data to historical sequence are well known. (1) Related lineages often evolve more or less in parallel but some faster than others; at any one time, then, the contemporaneous representatives of the various lineages may form a series that approximates the historical sequence leading to the more advanced members of the group. (2) Certain historical trends (e.g., from smaller to larger size, from simpler to more complex behavior) are so frequent or logical that they may be assumed to have occurred in a given case. (3) Characteristics shared by contemporaneous organisms are likely to have been present in their common ancestry. There is no reason to doubt that methods based on these principles, long used in comparative anatomy, are equally pertinent for the historical study of behavior. There are, however, many pitfalls in these methods, and these are probably (at least in the present state of the subject) even more serious for behavioral studies than they have proved to be for morphological studies. Problems and precautions cannot be further discussed here than to indicate the general nature of a few of the more serious in each category. (1) Divergence is more common than parallelism, and a contemporaneous series may not at all resemble an ancestral sequence, different characteristics commonly evolve at different rates so that the animal most primitive in one respect may be most advanced in another; truly ancestral

[5] Apart from the point that there are hundreds of thousands of different kinds of insects, with almost incredibly diverse behavior patterns, and hundreds of kinds of rats, with much less but still important behavioral differences. In the conferences on which this symposium is based, the naturalists present repeatedly had occasion to call attention to the absurdity of speaking of "the insect," "the rat," or "the monkey" in studies of behavior, as if there were only one insect, rat, or monkey, or as if all insects, rats, or monkeys behaved alike.

stages are liable to complete replacement and are frequently totally unrepresented at the present time. (2) No trends have been universal and comparatively few are established as usual; trends may go in either direction, or both ways from the middle, and data without an objective time factor provide no directional signpost, any array of data can be arranged in a logical sequence, but if the data are contemporaneous the logical sequence may have no relationship to a true historical sequence. (3) Parallelism and convergence in evolution have been extremely common and they produce resemblances not present in a common ancestor; homoplasy is, therefore, widespread and is difficult to distinguish from homology, especially when, as in most studies of behavior, direct historical evidence is lacking.

The second main class of evolutionary studies involves processes rather than (historical) events. Study of a process necessarily includes study of the mechanism that performs it; joint study of genetic mechanisms and processes is an example more or less familiar to everyone with any interest in biology or evolution. The methods are for the most part experimental, and it is really not necessary to discuss them here; they are most familiar to the students least familiar with the matter of the present chapter, and they are richly exemplified in other chapters of this book. It is perhaps well just to point out that there is no natural, deep cleavage between the study of events and that of processes, or between the observational methods characteristic of the former and the experimental methods usual in the latter. Both sorts of methods are used to some extent in both fields, and the two can sometimes hardly be distinguished. Processes can to some extent be inferred from the historical record, and prior events lie implicitly behind existing processes. The importance and long-range effects of processes established by experimentation are best judged in the light of the historical record. Alternative possible interpretations of historical sequences must be judged by compatibility with known processes.

Elements of the Synthetic Theory of Evolution

Among students of evolution the world around there are still neo-Lamarckians, old-line Darwinians, vitalists, finalists, orthogeneticists, hologeneticists, mutationists, even spiritualists, not to mention theories so particular to certain individuals that they hardly fall into an -ism. All those now heterodox views are interesting, and many of them have points of emphasis, at least, that still should be kept in mind. Nevertheless, in a brief review of the present status of evolutionary theory it is now possible and proper to concentrate on a single school of theory. No one would maintain either that this theory is complete or that it is correct in all details. An overwhelming majority of students really familiar with the evidence do maintain that the theory has a sound basis and is proving most fertile in increasing understanding of the tremendously intricate course and process of evolution. This strong consensus, if not near unanimity, is a comparatively recent development. The name here preferred is the *synthetic theory*,[6] so-called because it is a new synthesis from all fields of biology and not the offspring exclusively of any one of the numerous preceding theories.

Genetic Mechanisms

The medium of evolution, the thing in which the processes of evolution occur and hence the thing that is actually evolving, is a population. A population, in this sense, is a group of organisms, similar among themselves and dissimilar from other organisms with which they live, descended from a not remote common ancestry, living in the same general region and environment, and with a continuity of many generations through time. The inclusiveness of the term is vague and necessarily variable. At its least inclusive it is synonymous with the deme or local population of the biogeographers and systematists or (in a biparental population) the so-called Mendelian population of the geneticists. At its most inclusive it is practically synonymous with the species of most modern students. In the usual case of biparental organisms, the population is also characterized and unified by interbreeding among its actively sexual members. In the less common case of uniparental (asexual, apomictic, etc.) organisms, the unity of the population is still real but is looser and the evolutionary mechanisms are simpler but less flexible and potent.

The characteristics of any individual organism within a population are determined by interaction of its heredity with its environment, in the broadest sense, as the organism develops and, to less extent, thereafter as long as it lives. Heredity may be determined in part by the nature and organization of directly inherited cytoplasm (in metazoans mostly or entirely maternal, in the egg) and sometimes by extranuclear bodies (plastids in plants, etc.), but to far greater degree it is determined by the chromosomes in the nucleus. Chromosomes are differentiated longitudinally, and the irreducible (or at least experimentally unreduced) units of that differentiation are called genes. Different genes have different effects (necessarily, in practice, because the

---

[6]Numerous other tags have been applied, especially "neo-Darwinian," because of the large role assigned to natural selection in the theory. But "neo-Darwinian" in this application is misleading on two important counts. First, natural selection (itself no longer purely Darwinian) is here synthesized with equally important factors unknown to Darwin and even in strong contradictions with his views, especially on heredity. Second, the label "neo-Darwinian" historically belongs to a school that was literally neo-Darwinian, quite distinct from the present synthetic theory and only one of the several forerunners incorporated in the synthesis.

genes are disinguishable or recognizable in no other way), but the whole
chromosomal complement acts and interacts, and it is that complement as a
complex unit that is the main determinant of heredity. It may be considered
as setting a reaction range, sometimes rigidly narrow and sometimes very
broad, within which the characteristics of the developing organism must lie.
The characteristics actually arising at one point or another of the reaction
range, for instance the exact size of an organism when the range permits
much variation in size, depend for the most part on environmental influences
during development.

The population as a whole has characteristics likewise determined by the
interaction of the genetic mechanism and of the environment. Its total
genetic structure at any one time usually depends almost entirely on the
kinds and combinations of chromosomes and genes present and their relative
frequencies. Continuity of the population depends on the processes of
reproduction in which sets of chromosomes are passed on from parent to
offspring. In asexual reproduction the parental set (generally double) is
simply passed on, usually unchanged. In sexual, biparental reproduction two
homologous sets (each usually single) are received, one from each parent.
Then there is reduction of a parental double set to a single set in the gamete,
and this involves the mechansim of meiosis, with two concomitants of special
importance for evolution: (1) the single chromosome set of the gamete is a
random assortment from each of the two sets of the parent, and (2)
occasional crossing over from one homologous parental chromosome to the
other produces different combinations of genes in the chromosomes received
by the offspring. Fusion of gametes into a zygote brings together sets of
homologous chromosomes from different sources. That factor means that the
combinations actually realized will be influenced by breeding structure and
habits in the population. The extent to which breeding is random or
promiscuous, monogamous, polygamous, etc., becomes important, and above
all any influence which makes individuals with certain genetic characteristics
more likely than others to have offspring. Also important is the likelihood of
hybridization between different populations or, much less commonly,
different species.

Changes in characteristics induced by changing environmental influences
on identical genetic reaction ranges are not heritable. Such changes may
affect evolution quite indirectly, but they cannot in themselves constitute
secular evolutionary change. True evolutionary change involves changes in the
genetics of the population, which are almost always changes in the relative
frequencies of the various kinds of genes and of chromosomes and of their
combinations. In sexual, biparental populations constant changes in individual combinations are guaranteed by the mechanisms already mentioned:

random assortment of chromosomes and crossing over in meiosis, and biparental origin of chromosomes. These may, but as will be seen, usually do not in themselves bring about changes in relative frequencies in the population as a whole.

The mechanisms hitherto mentioned make for constant and radical individual rearrangements of genetic factors already present in any biparental population. The appearance of new factors in both biparental and uniparental populations is due to mutations which, broadly speaking, include changes in the number of chromosomes, in the internal structure of chromosomes (other than by simple crossing over), and in genes. It is the past occurrence of mutations that guarantees that homologous chromosomes rarely have exactly the same forms (alleles) of homologous genes and often are structurally different (have, for instance, the genes arranged in different sequence). Occurrence of new mutations, unless counteracted in various ways, further tends slowly but steadily to change the genetics of a population.

Random Processes and Evolution

It is an extraordinary fact that most of the processes inherent in the genetic mechanisms of evolution occur at random. It must be understood that the word "random" in this connection (and, indeed, etymologically) does *not* mean that all of a number of possible outcomes are equally probable. It means that the results of the processes are not oriented toward some end external to the processes themselves. In evolution the relevant end is the adaptedness of the population as a whole, its capacity to continue through future generations within an available environment. The random genetic processes are those that are not inherently adaptive for the population. Assortment of chromosomes in meiosis does seem normally to be random not only in this sense but also in the fullest possible sense that all combinations are about equally probable. Crossing over, as it affects association of any two genes, has probabilities almost directly proportional to the distance (along the chromosome) between the genes, but still is random as regards adaptation. For reasons yet unknown, different genes mutate at quite different rates and mutations of a given gene to (or from) different alleles also have decidedly different rates, so that possible gene mutation—and the same is true also of chromosome mutations—have very diverse probabilities, but these processes are still random by the pertinent definition of that word. Mating or more broadly reproduction is usually not entirely random, a fact to be stressed in the next section, but it may be at least approximately so. Here randomness involves likelihood that parents of given genetic types occurring with given frequencies in the population tend to produce offspring in about the same frequencies, or, what comes to the same thing, that relatively higher production of offspring is not significantly correlated with genetic factors in the parents.[7]

If reproduction is random, in combination with the inherently random processes in meiosis, there is no statistical tendency for change in frequencies of genetic factors within a population; in other words there is no tendency for directional evolutionary change to occur. That is the so-called Hardy-Weinberg law, the mathematical expression and derivation of which are given in most textbooks of genetics. Even if mutation is taken into account, there is a point of equilibrium where a given mutation is balanced by back-mutation and random loss (see below), and there is no (or no further) tendency toward evolutionary change in the population. Thus the random genetic processes, all together, do *not* tend statistically to produce evolution. That statement applies equally to sexual populations with mutation, meiosis, and fertilization and to asexual populations with mutation and mitosis, only.

Although the random processes noted do not tend systematically to change the mean frequencies of genetic factors in a population, those frequencies through the generations do tend to fluctuate around the mean. Populations of organisms are of course always finite, and each generation is in effect a sample drawn from the long-range total population of all generations or from the purely theoretical infinite population of statistical estimation. The genetical constitution of each generation is thus subject to statistical sampling error, which is its departure from the mean of the long-range or infinite population. Such departures or statistical sampling errors also occur, and may be quite radical, when a new area is populated by a few individuals spreading from a larger population elsewhere, or when for any reason a segment of a large population becomes reproductively isolated from the rest of that population. Sampling errors are larger the smaller the population. In very large populations they are so small as to be negligible, at least in comparison with effects of selection (below), but they are never reduced to zero in populations of finite size.

Under the influence of random sampling error, commonly called "genetic drift" in this connection, the frequency of a given chromosome number or arrangement or of a given gene allele may increase, even to 100 per cent, or decrease, even to zero. Evolution has then obviously occurred, and as far as now known this is the *only* process by which random (unoriented with respect to adaptation) evolution can occur. That it does occur, for instance in the colonization of an oceanic island from a mainland, is beyond any

[7] Because of doubts or equivocation as to the precise meanings of "random" in application to these various processes, they are sometimes called "stochastic." Appropriate definition may, nevertheless, be as readily made for "random" as for "stochastic."

question. How commonly it occurs and how important it is in the over-all picture of evolution are still strongly disputed questions. The present consensus seems to be that it is rather common but that its importance in long evolutionary sequences or radical evolutionary transformations is largely, or almost completely, overshadowed by the nonrandom effects of selection. One special case of completely demonstrated reality has evidently played an important role in the diversification of plants, at least, on lower taxonomic levels. Polyploid mutants or hybrids, with increased (usually doubled) numbers of chromosomes, may be unable to breed back with a parental stock. If they do survive and increase to become populations, they are thus genetically distinct samples isolated forthwith from their ancestral populations.[8]

Oriented Processes and Adaptation

Thus the usual random processes of the genetic mechanism tend to produce either no evolutionary changes at all or changes that are sampling errors and that are nonadaptive or, so to speak, only accidentally adaptive. Yet it is perfectly clear that evolution does occur and that it is, to say the least, often adaptive and not entirely random. It was often urged against Darwin and, with more basis, against De Vries and other early geneticists who assigned too exclusive a role to mutation that evolution cannot have occurred "by accident." The fairly obvious answer, which was in fact already emphasized and soundly established by Darwin, is that the adaptive orientation of evolution must involve the one genetic process that is not necessarily or, as a matter of conclusive observation, usually random: reproduction. If reproduction is differential, if there is a correlation between distinctive genetic factors in the parents and their relatively greater success in reproduction, then there will be an increase in the frequencies of those genetic factors (and combinations of them) within the population from one generation to another. Evolution will occur, and it will be oriented, not random. That, in brief and shorn of numerous complications, is the modern concept of natural selection. Natural selection, as defined, is known really to exist and to be effective, both by observation in nature and by experimentation. No other nonrandom genetic factor has been objectively demonstrated, even though several have been postulated (e.g., Lamarckian influence of use or disuse, nonrandom mutation, inherent tendency—whatever that may mean—to progress toward a goal). Most students now believe that this only demonstrably real nonrandom process is also sufficient to account for all the

---

[8] It is not usual to consider the origin of a polyploid species as an example of sampling error, but it does seem logically to fall into that category as an example of random evolutionary change.

observed nonrandom events in the course of evolution. *Proving* sufficiency amounts to proving a negative, which is generally deemed impossible; but sufficiency is the stand of the synthetic theory, and the burden of proof would seem to lie with its (now few) opponents.

Reproductive success may be comparatively simple in asexual organisms. It often amounts only to this: a genetic difference arises by mutation, there is direct competition between mutant and nonmutant forms, members of one group or the other survive more often to reproduce, and the less successful group eventually disappears. Even there complications are ignored, and in biparental populations the matter becomes highly intricate. (1) Male and female must occur in proximity or must find each other. (2) In many, especially the more complex, animals they must be sexually acceptable to each other and must mate. (3) Fertilization must occur. (4) The gametes must be genetically compatible. (5) Normal embryological development must occur. (6) Offspring must survive to breeding age and become successful reproducers in their turn. Relatively greater or less success may occur at any one of these stages, and at substages within them, and selection depends on the total outcome.

Darwin was aware of the selective possibilities of all the listed stages, but he stressed (6) above all others, and some of his followers did so almost to the exclusion of any others. Thus Darwinian natural selection was based mainly on differential mortality, and the Darwinians and neo-Darwinians hardly grasped the whole process as one of differential reproduction. Darwin also devoted much attention to stage (2) as involving sexual selection, which he distinguished from natural selection.

Until quite recently it was generally implied or assumed that selection always favors individual survival or, more in the spirit of the modern theory, individual success in reproduction. Now it is evident that selection favors successful reproduction of the population and not necessarily of any or of all particular individuals within it. A striking, although rather exceptional, example of that fact is provided by the social insects, among which only a very small fraction actually reproduce although their success in reproduction is completely dependent on the nonreproducing individuals. Of more general import is the recently accumulating evidence that the most successful populations usually have considerable genetic heterogeneity and much heterozygosity in individuals. But that favored characteristic of a population can be maintained only at the expense of constantly producing a certain proportion of definitely inferior, less heterozygous individuals.

A central problem of evolutionary theory has always been the explanation of adaptation, and the synthetic theory maintains (as did Darwin, but with a different understanding of the mechanism) that adaptation is a result of natural selection. But it also demonstrates that natural selection always favors reproductive success of a population, and nothing else. It might be suitable to redefine adaptation as such reproductive success, but some confusion might arise from the fact that most of the characteristics generally considered adaptive seem to be so in the old Darwinian sense of promoting survival of the individual and seem to have little or nothing to do with population reproduction *per se*. The anomaly is only apparent, however, for clearly reproductive success of the population involves all phases of individual life cycles and will incomparably more often than not be favored by individual adaptation to the environment. Such adaptation will therefore almost always be favored by natural selection. Nevertheless the possibility remains that selection, as here defined, could favor population reproduction at the expense of individual adaptation. We have already noted that it does so, indeed, in the cases of homozygous individuals in heterotic populations. It has also been variously claimed that a species may become so specialized for reproductive ends, for example in development of sexual weapons and competition, as to put the whole population at a disadvantage in competition with other species. The reality or importance of such possible phenomena are not, however, clearly established.

An aspect of the synthetic theory especially pertinent here is that it again brings in behavior as a central element. It not only points the way to evolutionary, historical explanations of existing behavior patterns but also involves behavior as one of the factors that produce or guide evolution. Some phases of selection, as in zygote and embryo, are not directly behavioral, but aspects of breeding, care of young, and subsequent survival are pre-eminently so and are obviously crucial elements in selection.

Some Historical Generalizations and Principles

Those, in brief, are the most essential features of the mechanisms and processes now believed to underlie the phenomena of evolution. An understanding of comparative behavior, or other biological aspects of our comtemporary world, further involves consideration of what those phenomena have, in fact, been, of how the processes have worked out in the prodigious history of life. A review of the vast body of information and theory on this subject is of course beyond the present scope. There are, however, certain generalizations and principles that stand out from that record and that can be particularly useful in any reconstruction of behavioral (or other) evolution. Just a few of the most important of these will be mentioned.

Irrevocability, Opportunism, and Transformation

From a certain point of view all study and knowledge of nature can be divided into processes, immanent and changeless characteristics of the universe, and configurations that result from those processes, transient and historically cumulative states of the universe. The difference is that between gravity, a timeless structural feature of our world, and a falling stone, acted on by gravity but determined as to time, place, and condition by the whole previous history of the matter in the stone. The configuration of the living, as of any other, world depends from instant to instant on its last previous configuration and on how the immanent processes, the "laws" of nature, tend to act on any given configuration. Involved is historical causation, which includes everything that has ever happened and which is thus an inherently nonrepeatable accumulation.

In application to evolution, those rather abstract considerations mean that the actual course of evolution is determined not only by its processes but also by the cumulative total of *all* previous events. It follows that evolution is irrevocable. That law (it seems to be about as near to a true law as anything in the realm of biology) has two major corollaries. One is the famous doctrine of the irreversibility of evolution. No organism, no population, no community returns precisely to any antecedent structure or state. A gross but impressive example: whales are descended from fishes; they have returned to the water and resumed the ecological status of fishes; but they have not again become fishes, and every system, organ, tissue, or cell of a whale is radically distinct from that of any fish that is or ever was. The other corollary of irrevocability is that the effects of previous conditions are never wholly lost. A whale, again, carries not only in general but also in detail down to the last cell unmistakable effects of its ancestors' sojourn on the land.[9]

As each configuration is derived from the last, and from all previous ones, each can only be a modification of or an addition to what was already there. This gives evolution an opportunistic aspect. Changes take place on the basis of the previous condition and not as a wholly new construction most efficiently adapted to new conditions. Early fishes had lungs. In many later fishes the pre-existing lungs evolved into hydrostatic organs, which, in spite of their radically different function, did not arise *de novo*. In land animals the

---

[9]Exceptions to both aspects of irrevocability are conceivable, but none are known or likely. The genetic processes of evolution are all reversible, but that all should reverse to just the same extent in conjunction and within an intricate and changing environmental framework is so improbable that it is not likely to have happened in only a few billion years. An event such as a mutation may seem to be quite canceled out if the mutant allele is subsequently eliminated from the population, but again the probability that even the transient presence of the allele left no effects at all is infinitesimal.

lungs retained and considerably perfected their respiratory structure and function. Land snails, requiring an organ for the same function, had no lungs in their ancestry and did not evolve lungs, but a structure that was pre-existent, the mantle cavity, could and did evolve to serve that function.

When a way of life is changing in the course of evolution it is evidently simpler, that is, it is genetically more likely, to remodel the existing than to introduce something completely new. That is the principle of transformation. The evolution of lung to swim bladder, already mentioned, is an example. Another striking and widely familiar example is the incorporation of the bones hinging skull and jaw in early reptiles (quadrate and articular) into the middle ear of mammals (where they are renamed incus and malleus).

The principles of irrevocability, opportunism, and transformation are based mainly on anatomical and physiological data, but in the nature of things they must also apply, *mutatis mutandis*, to the evolution of behavior.

Trends and Orthogenesis

It is a common observation, backed by hundreds of concrete examples in the fossil record, that evolutionary change in a given direction once started may tend to continue for a long time. In terms of years, as nearly as highly inaccurate approximations permit conclusion, it is the rule for trending changes to continue for more than 10^6 years and common for them to last on the order of 10^7 years. Much longer trends, however, as of the order of 10^8 years without stop or pronounced change of direction, have apparently not been substantiated. For instance the recorded history of the horse family shows several well-marked trends, as has become common knowledge, but it is less widely known by nonspecialists that no single recognized trend in that family was continuous throughout the 6×10^7 years of its history. The longest of the known trends did not continue with even approximate constancy for more than about 2×10^7 years. Some trends reached an inherent limit, for instance the premolars (all but the first) once fully molarized could not become more so. Other trends stopped without having reached such an apparent limit; for instance increase in size stopped far short of any mechanical limit.

Similar trends often appear simultaneously or successively in multiple related lines, such as a tendency for the shells to become coiled in relatives of the oyster. Others may appear over and over again in widely diverse groups, for example increase in individual size. Yet there has been no universal trend, no trend that did not stop or change before about 10^8 years and usually much less, and even no trend that was not on occasion reversed.[10] The trend

[10]There has been some confusion on the subject of trends and the irreversibility of evolution, with the argument that either trends do not become reversed or else evolution

toward larger size noted above for some of the horses and here in a more general sense is probably the most widespread to be detected among animals. It has occurred repeatedly in groups as diverse as protozoans and primates. Yet it has obviously been neither universal nor, in any one group, constant. If it had been, all animals would by now be elephantine or cetacean in bulk. The opposite trend, toward smaller size, has evidently been less frequent but has certainly occurred many times, and absence of trend, maintenance of about the same size, has probably been the rule.

The foregoing and many other facts about trends lead to the essential conclusion that there is no mysterious, inherent tendency for evolution to proceed indefinitely in straight lines. It accords with everything really known about trends, to the limited extent that they do characterize evolution, to conclude that they occur only when and only as long as they are adaptive. This pre-eminently oriented feature of evolutionary history is adequately explained by the known orienting (nonrandom or antichance) process of evolution: natural selection. The opposite view, that trends may or do occur without relationship to natural selection generally is labeled as "orthogenesis," and there has been widespread belief that the fossil record supports or even proves the postulate of orthogenesis. That idea has always been most widespread among those least familiar with the fossil record. Most paleontologists have long since rejected it.

The facts that trends are adaptive, begin and end at fairly definite times, and rarely persist long, geologically speaking, have another bearing, harking back to methods of inference mentioned early in this chapter. In the absence of really historical documents, it is generally impossible to extrapolate far and accurately from brief sequences or by postulating a previous trend on the basis of comparative data on living animals. It is, for instance, unjustified to conclude that a behavioral sequence from simple to complex among recent primates can be correctly superimposed as a continuing historical trend from Paleocene prosimian to Recent man.

Patterns of Evolution

The fabric of evolution is phylogeny, and above the level of interbreeding and hybridization it has only two elements: splitting and succession. The basic process of evolutionary splitting is speciation, the rise of two or more species from a single species. Isolation of a segment of the population is accompanied or followed by genetic divergence, with more or less divergence

is reversible. The difficulty is semantic, only. A lineage that becomes smaller and to that degree more like an ancestral stage has not except in this one artificially segregated characteristic returned to the ancestral condition.

also in morphology, physiology, and behavior. In uniparental populations no genetic nexus unites the individuals and speciation is a comparatively simple result of mutation and selection. In biparental populations the crucial feature is the breaking of the nexus of interbreeding. Usually (some would say "always") an initial requirement is some degree of geographic separation. Isolating mechanisms that then reduce and finally stop interbreeding, even if the incipient species do come into contact, are almost innumerable. Many of them are behavioral, for instance in decreasing willingness to mate or success in mating. The eventual and complete barrier, which always does arise finally if the now separate species survive but which may be long delayed, is genetic divergence that makes the gametes so incompatible that hybrid zygotes cannot develop.

The significance of phylogenetic splitting in over-all evolutionary history is increase in diversity, with the occupation of new regions and environments and, within each area of occupation, a parceling out into increasingly numerous and narrow ecological niches, each occupied by a distinctive species. If we had no fossil record, it would be irresistible to visualize a single, broadly adapted, primordial marine species the descendants of which expanded to occupy all the waters and lands and specialized for close fit in each available niche. Expansion and diversification complete, evolution would end. Expansion and diversification are, of course, the main motifs in the rich fabric of life's history, but the whole pattern is astonishingly more complex. Most species, even though already well fitted into a niche or adaptive zone, continue to change. The overwhelming majority finally become extinct without issue and are replaced by other, perhaps quite different organisms.

A few organisms have reached a sort of evolutionary stasis, adequate adaptation to a sufficiently constant environment, and have continued without marked change thereafter to become "living fossils": the horseshoe crab, the opossum, and others. Most environments change enough so that the organisms in them must do so, too. The mere fact that some one species in a community changes, for any reason, means that the environment of all the others is different to some degree. The environmental change requiring adaptive adjustment for a species may even reside within the species, itself—that is probably true of many of the trends toward larger size, the smaller animals of a population always being at a slight competitive disadvantage compared with the larger. Such usually slow shifts of environment and adaptation are nearly, but not quite, universal and they account for the commonest trends in evolution.

Rarer but more striking events result from not merely maintaining adaptation in a changing world but also changing or improving the quality of adaptation. Then there is likely to occur on a smaller or larger scale what has been aptly called a break-through. Increased competitive efficiency may permit expansion into already occupied adaptive zones, with extinction for their former occupants, as among the fishes the teleosts have ousted all but a tithe of their ancient competitors. Or new ways of life may be achieved, as the reptiles spread over the lands then effectively empty of competitors. In such episodes more or less radical changes in structure, physiology, and behavior are involved. Selection is then particularly intense, and change is correspondingly rapid. The changes do usually take an appreciable time, apparently as a rule on the order of 10^6 years and upward, but the effect in the over-all picture is steplike, not a trend but a steep transition from one level to another. The behavioral change when man became adept with tools—supposing, as one must, that this was accompanied by a biological and not entirely a cultural evolutionary advance—was such an event, probably one of exceptional rapidity and certainly one of exceptional portent.

SECTION II

THE FOSSIL RECORD:

DISCOVERERS AND THEIR DISCOVERIES

An Historical Overview

by
J. H. Prost*

The papers which were read by Darwin and Wallace in 1858 expounded for the first time a clear and positive statement of evolutionary theory and its mechanism Natural Selection. They were followed in 1859 by Darwin's book *The Origin of Species*. In it Darwin presented a compilation of evidence on the process of Natural Selection and thus provided the scientific community with an evolutionary "force" which made the theory comprehensible. He was careful in his text to avoid any direct use of evolutionary thinking to explain the origins of man. He said "light would be thrown on the origin of man and his history" but went no further. Perhaps this was strategy on his part, an effort to keep debate about his theory free of that human prejudice which comes when men assess their own nature and destiny. Perhaps Darwin did not believe the fossil evidence gave him a secure base from which to speculate on the story of man's prehuman ancestors.

Darwin's close friend Thomas Huxley had no such qualms. In 1863 he published his book *Man's Place in Nature*, in which he placed "man" squarely in the midst of "nature," and speculated on the course of human evolution. Huxley compared man with the largest of the great apes, the Gorilla, and identified three of the significant anatomical complexes which must have changed through evolutionary time in order for the human species to have arisen from a more or less ape-like prehuman ancestor. He demonstrated that the skeleton and muscles of man's lower limbs were different from those of his primate collaterals and rightly attributed these differences to man's assumption of upright posture and locomotion. His second major complex involved the dentition, or teeth. Today we tend to think of the teeth and face as an integrated unit; the jaws and muscles of mastication being interrelated

*1968

127

with the teeth. Even the muscles of the neck can be viewed in terms of their actions in consonance with chewing, tearing and stripping food-stuffs. Man's small canines, small incisors, small jaws, small muscles of mastication and small posterior neck muscles all demonstrate a de-emphasis on forceful and habitual use of the teeth. In part, man's use of tools, and the cooking of his food, has produced this selective de-emphasis. Huxley's last major category was the brain. Man's large brain, with its concomitant sophisticated functions, is certainly his most distinctive and significant possession. Thus, Huxley identified three complexes which were the exclusive possession of man and which must have changed through time to bring an ape-like creature to the human condition. What Huxley was unable to fathom from the evidence he had at his disposal was how fast and how early these changes had occurred. Did man become a biped before his brain increased in size, or afterwards? Would the first signs of the earliest premen be signaled by changes in the teeth and face or in the hip bones and feet? The only way to answer these questions was to have evidence from the fossil record and Huxley had only two fossil men with which to reason his answers.

In 1863, at the time Huxley wrote his popular and controversial book, the profession had available only two really ancient fossil human remains. In 1848 a skull was discovered in a quarry in the face of the Rock of Gibraltar. The skull was sent to England and passed from museum to museum. Its true significance was not understood for almost 50 years. A second discovery, made a few years later, had a different history. It was the human skeleton found in a limestone cave in the Neander valley. The discovery was first brought to public attention by Hermann Schaaffhausen, a Professor of Anatomy at the University of Bonn. George Busk translated Schaaffhausen's report and Thomas Huxley gave it prominence by including the translation in his book. Neither Schaaffhausen nor Huxley could find in the anatomy of the Neanderthal skeleton dramatic differences from modern man. The few differences which they did find might have suggested to them the existence, 40,000 to 70,000 years ago, of a population just on the brink of evolving the anatomy and physiology characteristic of present *Homo sapiens*. Huxley and Schaaffhausen did not draw this conclusion because the Neanderthal skeleton was a single specimen and they could not accept it as documentation of the range of characters present in the entire ancient population. Further discoveries, such as those from Spy in Belgium, 1886, and Le Moustier and La Chapelle-aux-Saints in France, 1908, proved that the Neanderthal remains were not unique and that these ancient peoples were, in fact, different from modern *Homo sapiens*.

Eugene Dubois was a Dutch physician who had travelled to Sumatra and Java just before the turn of the century. Dubois was convinced he could find the fossil intermediate between apes and man, a "missing link," so called, in the islands just off the mainland of Asia. From 1890 to 1895 he worked deposits in Java and returned to Europe with the remains of a creature he called *Pithecanthropus erectus*, "erect ape-man." The creature had lived perhaps 400,000 to 500,000 years ago and was at least ten times as ancient as the remains from the Neander valley. The anatomy of its skull cap was far different from that of modern men and Dubois built these differences into his argument that indeed *Pithecanthropus* was the "missing link."

Up to 1910, the discoveries of fossil men seemed to be falling into a general pattern. The limb bones were always like those of modern men but the teeth and jaws, and, particularly, the brain varied from the modern conditon. Between the years of 1911 and 1915 discoveries in a gravel pit in Sussex, England, confounded this scheme, producing a mystery all of its own. The brain case showed that the brain had already reached the human size while the jaws, teeth, and perhaps the face had remained almost in an ape-like condition. The solution of the Piltdown mystery took more than thirty years for its solution. The full story of Piltdown will be left to its discoverers and to the scientific detectives who in the late 1940's solved its mystery.

While the Piltdown enigma was exercising human paleontologists, the march of fossil discoveries continued. In 1924 at Taungs in South Africa, the skull of an adolescent ape-like creature was brought to Raymond A. Dart, Professor of Anatomy at the University of Witwatersrand, Johannesburg. Dart published on the skull in 1925. He called the creature *Australopithecus africanus*, "southern ape from Africa." In retrospect, the *Australopithecus* find, or Taungs baby as it was colloquially called, was far more significant than Piltdown. Few workers suspected this in 1925.

Another discovery from Africa, around the same time, was Rhodesian man; a large, massive skull and some limb bones found at Broken Hill, Northern Rhodesia, in 1921. The circumstances of the discovery were clouded and an American Physical Anthropologist, Ales Hrdlicka, in 1925, went to Rhodesia to reconstruct the circumstances of the discovery. Rhodesian man was another isolated fossil, very much like Dart's Taungs baby and its status and interpretation had to await further evidence, which came in 1953 with the discovery of the Saldanha skull.

In Asia, 1926, fossils were found near Peking, in a site close to the town of Choukoutien. Davidson Black from the Department of Anatomy at the Peking Union Medical College, on the basis of a single tooth from the Choukoutien site, predicted that the site would yield a new type of fossil man. He called his predicted fossil man *Sinanthropus pekinensis*, "China man from Peking." We now know, from a larger collection of material, that Peking man was a later representative of the same stock as Dubois's Java man. The two are usually lumped together under the binomial terms *Homo erectus*.

Fragments of jaws and teeth from North India were discovered and described by G. E. Lewis, in 1934. The significance of Lewis's *Ramapithecus* and *Bramapithecus*, as he named them, was only vaguely known to Lewis at the time that he wrote. Further material and careful comparisons by E. L. Simons thirty years later brought the true relevance of *Ramapithecus* before the anthropological public.

The growth of evidence of the South African Australopithecines began in 1936. R. Broom, from the Transvaal Museum, Pretoria, South Africa, kept careful watch on several sites in the hope of finding adult specimens of creatures like Dart's Taungs baby. He announced his successes in 1936 and 1938. He had discovered adults of the *Australopithecus* form and specimens which were very much like *Australopithecus*, but not identical, which he called *Paranthropus*. Today we group these two similar forms together under the term "Australopithecines." Broom's discoveries began an epoch of almost thirty years during which immense numbers of Australopithecine remains have been found throughout Africa and the Near East. Further work by Dart and Broom and their colleagues Phillip Tobias and John Robinson in South Africa and L. S. B. Leakey at his site, Olduvai Gorge, in Tanzania has burgeoned the Australopithecine material until it has become the best documented group of fossils known today. The truly ancient age of these fossils and the wide distribution of the group was not fully appreciated until the discoveries by Leakey in the 1960s.

Just before World War II, under the direction of D. A. E. Garrod, an expedition excavated two ancient caves in Palestine (Israel) which yielded a wealth of fossil material. The work of this joint expedition was a classic example of careful and accurate field work. One of the caves contained a number of skeletons representing an almost modern form. The other cave contained remains which resembled the Neanderthal group, which by then had been well documented from European sites. This evidence from the Mount Carmel caves brought speculations about the coexistence of modern and Neanderthal populations living side by side, 35,000 to 70,000 years ago. Later discoveries, such as those at Shanidar, in Iraq, tended to corroborate these speculations.

Following World War II, with the resumption of excavations and world travel, fossil remains and sites which had been neglected throughout the War began to be reworked. The first group to draw concerted attention was the Australopithecines. W. E. Le Gros Clark, a British Anatomist of international reputation, re-examined the Australopithecine material and his analyses brought this long misunderstood group into proper focus.

Shortly thereafter, Saldanha man was added to the fossil catalogue, complementing Rhodesian man, which it resembled.

And finally, the Piltdown mystery was solved and forty years of needless debate came to an end.

Before the din of the Piltdown controversy had quieted, L. S. B. Leakey, after more than 20 years of searching at Olduvai Gorge, announced discoveries which brought attention to East Africa. Leakey not only added further material to the Australopithecine group, he also initiated a chain of radioactive dating tests which revised the time scale with which fossil man had been interpreted.

At about the same time E. L. Simons reassessed the *Ramapithecus* and *Bramapithecus* jaw fragments and demonstrated that they probably came from a Pliocene hominid form, the first acceptable evidence of premen from the Pliocene period. Soon after Simons' publication L. S. B. Leakey, at Fort Ternan in East Africa, discovered evidence of a creature much like *Ramapithecus*. This corroborated Simons' interpretation and proved that premen were certainly living during the Pliocene, and perhaps beyond.

Within the last few years, work at Olduvai Gorge has produced forms which resemble the Peking and Java men, called by Leakey "Chellean man," and a contemporary of *Zinjanthropus* whose morphology appears to be even closer to that of *Homo sapiens* than is that of the Australopithecines. Leakey called this latter creature *Homo habilis*. Lastly, and most recently, Leakey has announced presumptive evidence of tool-using in undoubted Miocene deposits. This combined with the fact that *Kenyapithecus* is dated to the Miocene opens the door to exciting speculations.

The papers in this book have been placed in juxtaposition to give the reader familiarity with the original reports of the investigators who discovered the more important specimens of fossil man. This selection also illustrates the processual nature of the science of human paleontology. It has passed from discovery to interpretation to further work and new discoveries, in an ongoing and unending sequence. Early workers, who believed in the concept of the "missing link," had hoped that the discovery of a "half man-half ape" would finalize forever the story of man's ancient history. In this belief they were simply wrong. Neither evolutionary theory nor the nature of science itself should have led them to this conclusion. The human species evolved by gradual change over an extensive period of time. At no instant was there a single "missing link." We can know the story of this historical continuum only when we have a continuous population series of fossils connecting an undoubted ape precursor to our immediate ancestors. No one can speculate on how long it would take to search for, discover and assess such a wealth of material. In the discipline of human paleontology, as well as elsewhere in the sciences, the processes of discovery and re-evaluation are unending. Absolute Truth is a chimera which the sciences chase but shall never cage.

On the Relations of Man to the
Lower Animals

T. H. Huxley*

The question of questions for mankind—the problem which underlies all others, and is more deeply interesting than any other—is the ascertainment of the place which Man occupies in nature and of his relations to the universe of things. Whence our race has come; what are the limits of our power over nature, and of nature's power over us; to what goal we are tending; are the problems which present themselves anew and with undiminished interest to every man born into the world. Most of us, shrinking from the difficulties and dangers which beset the seeker after original answers to these riddles, are contented to ignore them altogether, or to smother the investigating spirit under the feather-bed of respected and respectable tradition. But, in every age, one or two restless spirits, blessed with that constructive genius, which can only build on a secure foundation, or cursed with the spirit of mere scepticism, are unable to follow in the well-worn and comfortable track of their forefathers and contemporaries, and unmindful of thorns and stumbling-blocks, strike out into paths of their own. The sceptics end in the infidelity which asserts the problem to be insoluble, or in the atheism which denies the existence of any orderly progress and governance of things: the men of genius propound solutions which grow into systems of Theology or of Philosophy, or veiled in musical language which suggests more than it asserts, take the shape of the Poetry of an epoch.

Each such answer to the great question, invariably asserted by the followers of its propounder, if not by himself, to be complete and final, remains in high authority and esteem, it may be for one century, or it may be for twenty: but, as invariably, Time proves each reply to have been a mere approximation to the truth—tolerable chiefly on account of the ignorance of

*1863 (from his book *Man's Place in Nature*)

133

those by whom it was accepted, and wholly intolerable when tested by the larger knowledge of their successors.

In a well-worn metaphor, a parallel is drawn between the life of man and the metamorphosis of the caterpillar into the butterfly; but the comparison may be more just as well as more novel, if for its former term we take the mental progress of the race. History shows that the human mind, fed by constant accessions of knowledge, periodically grows too large for its theoretical coverings, and bursts them asunder to appear in new habiliments, as the feeding and growing grub, at intervals, casts its too narrow skin and assumes another, itself but temporary. Truly the imago state of Man seems to be terribly distant, but every moult is a step gained, and of such there have been many.

Since the revival of learning, whereby the Western races of Europe were enabled to enter upon that progress towards true knowledge, which was commenced by the philosophers of Greece, but was almost arrested in subsequent long ages of intellectual stagnation, or, at most, gyration, the human larva has been feeding vigorously, and moulting in proportion. A skin of some dimension was cast in the 16th century, and another towards the end of the 18th, while, within the last fifty years, the extraordinary growth of every department of physical science has spread among us mental food of so nutritious and stimulating a character that a new ecdysis seems imminent. But this is a process not unusually accompanied by many throes and some sickness and debility, or, it may be, by graver disturbances; so that every good citizen must feel bound to facilitate the process, and even if he have nothing but a scalpel to work withal, to ease the cracking integument to the best of his ability.

In this duty lies my excuse for the publication of these essays. For it will be admitted that some knowledge of man's position in the animate world is an indispensable preliminary to the proper understanding of his relations to the universe; and this again resolves itself, in the long run, into an inquiry into the nature and the closeness of the ties which connect him with those singular creatures whose history* has been sketched in the preceding pages.

The importance of such an inquiry is indeed intuitively manifest. Brought face to face with these blurred copies of himself, the least thoughtful of men is conscious of a certain shock, due perhaps, not so much to disgust at the aspect of what looks like an insulting caricature, as to the awakening of a sudden and profound mistrust of time-honoured theories and strongly-rooted prejudices regarding his own position in nature, and his relations to the

---

*It will be understood that, in the preceding Essay, I have selected for notice from the vast mass of papers which have been written upon the man-like Apes, only those which seem to me to be of special moment.

under-world of life; while that which remains a dim suspicion for the unthinking, becomes a vast argument fraught with the deepest consequences, for all who are acquainted with the recent progress of the anatomical and physiological sciences.

I now propose briefly to unfold that argument, and to set forth, in a form intelligible to those who possess no special acquaintance with anatomical science, the chief facts upon which all conclusions respecting the nature and the extent of the bonds which connect man with the brute world must be based: I shall then indicate the one immediate conclusion which, in my judgment, is justified by those facts, and I shall finally discuss the bearing of that conclusion upon the hypotheses which have been entertained respecting the Origin of Man.

A careful study of the resemblances and differences presented by animals has, in fact, led naturalists to arrange them into groups, or assemblages, all the members of each group presenting a certain amount of definable resemblance, and the number of points of similarity being smaller as the group is larger and *vice versa*. Thus, all creatures which agree only in presenting the few distinctive marks of animality form the *Kingdom Animalia*. The numerous animals which agree only in possessing the special characters of Vertebrates form one *Sub-kingdom* of this Kingdom. Then the Sub-kingdom *Vertebrata* is subdivided into the five *Classes*, Fishes, Amphibians, Reptiles, Birds, and Mammals, and these into smaller groups called *Orders*; these into *Families* and *Genera*; while the last are finally broken up into the smallest assemblages, which are distinguished by the possession of constant, not-sexual, characters. These ultimate groups are Species.

Every year tends to bring about a greater uniformity of opinion throughout the zoological world as to the limits and characters of these groups, great and small. At present, for example, no one has the least doubt regarding the characters of the classes Mammalia, Aves, or Reptilia; nor does the question arise whether any thoroughly well-known animal should be placed in one class or the other. Again, there is a very general agreement respecting the characters and limits of the orders of Mammals, and as to the animals which are structurally necessitated to take a place in one or another order.

Bearing this obvious course of zoological reasoning in mind, let us endeavour for a moment to disconnect our thinking selves from the mask of humanity; let us imagine ourselves scientific Saturnians, if you will, fairly acquainted with such animals as now inhabit the Earth, and employed in discussing the relations they bear to a new and singular "erect and featherless biped," which some enterprising traveller, overcoming the difficulties of space and gravitation, has brought from that distant planet for our inspection, well preserved, maybe, in a cask of rum. We should all, at once, agree upon placing him among the mammalian vertebrates; and his lower jaw, his molars, and his brain, would leave no room for doubting the systematic position of the new genus among those mammals, whose young are nourished during gestation by means of a placenta, or what are called the "placental mammals."

Further, the most superficial study would at once convince us that, among the orders of placental mammals, neither the Whales, nor the hoofed creatures, nor the Sloths and Ant-eaters, nor the carnivorous Cats, Dogs, and Bears, still less the Rodent Rats and Rabbits, or the Insectivorous Moles and Hedgehogs, or the Bats, could claim our *Homo*, as one of themselves.

There would remain then but one order for comparison, that of the Apes (using the word in its broadest sense), and the question for discussion would narrow itself to this—is Man so different from any of these Apes that he must form an order by himself? Or does he differ less from them than they differ from one another, and hence must take his place in the same order with them?

Being happily free from all real, or imaginary, personal interest in the result of the inquiry thus set afoot, we should proceed to weigh the arguments on one side and on the other, with as much judicial calmness as if the question related to a new Opossum. We should endeavour to ascertain, without seeking either to magnify or diminish them, all the characters by which our new Mammal differed from the Apes; and if we found that these were of less structural value than those which distinguish certain members of the Ape order from others universally admitted to be of the same order, we should undoubtedly place the newly discovered tellurian genus with them.

I now proceed to detail the facts which seem to me to leave us no choice but to adopt the last-mentioned course.

It is quite certain that the Ape which most nearly approaches man, in the totality of its organisation, is either the Chimpanzee or the Gorilla; and as it makes no practical difference, for the purposes of my present argument, which is selected for comparison, on the one hand, with Man, and on the other hand, with the rest of the Primates,* I shall select the latter (so far as its organisation is known)—as a brute now so celebrated in prose and verse, that all must have heard of him, and have formed some conception of his appearance. I shall take up as many of the most important points of difference between man and this remarkable creature, as the space at my disposal will allow me to discuss, and the necessities of the argument demand;

*We are not at present thoroughly acquainted with the brain of the Gorilla, and therefore, in discussing cerebral characters, I shall take that of the Chimpanzee as my highest term among the Apes.

and I shall inquire into the value and magnitude of these differences, when placed side by side with those which separate the Gorilla from other animals of the same order.

In the general proportions of the body and limbs there is a remarkable difference between the Gorilla and Man, which at once strikes the eye. The Gorilla's brain-case is smaller, its trunk larger, its lower limbs shorter, its upper limbs longer in proportion than those of Man.

We may next consider the differences presented by the trunk, consisting of the vertebral column, or backbone, and the ribs and pelvis, or bony hipbasin, which are connected with it, in Man and in the Gorilla respectively.

In Man, in consequence partly of the disposition of the articular surfaces of the vertebrae, and largely of the elastic tension of some of the fibrous bands, or ligaments, the spinal column, as a whole, has an elegant S-like curvature, being convex forwards in the neck, concave in the back, convex in the loins, or lumbar region, and concave again in the sacral region; an arrangement which gives much elasticity to the whole backbone, and diminishes the jar communicated to the spine, and through it to the head, by locomotion in the erect position.

Furthermore, under ordinary circumstances, Man has seven vertebrae in his neck, which are called *cervical*; twelve succeed these, bearing ribs and forming the upper part of the back, whence they are termed *dorsal*; five lie in the loins, bearing no distinct, or free, ribs, and are called *lumbar*; five, united together into a great bone, excavated in front, solidly wedged in between the hip bones, to form the back of the pelvis, and known by the name of the *sacrum*, succeed these; and finally, three or four little more or less movable bones, so small as to be insignificant, constitute the *coccyx* or rudimentary tail.

In the Gorilla, the vertebral column is similarly divided into cervical, dorsal, lumbar, sacral, and coccygeal vertebrae, and the total number of cervical and dorsal vertebrae, taken together, is the same as in Man; but the development of a pair of ribs to the first lumbar vertebra, which is an exceptional occurrence in Man, is the rule in the Gorilla; and hence, as lumbar are distinguished from dorsal vertebrae only by the presence or absence of free ribs, the seventeen "dorso-lumbar" vertebrae of the Gorilla are divided into thirteen dorsal and four lumbar, while in Man they are twelve dorsal and five lumbar.

The vertebral column of the Gorilla, as a whole, differs from that of Man in the less marked character of its curves, especially in the slighter convexity of the lumbar region. Nevertheless, the curves are present, and are quite obvious in young skeletons of the Gorilla and Chimpanzee which have been prepared without removal of the ligaments. In young Orangs similarly preserved on the other hand, the spinal column is either straight, or even concave forwards, throughout the lumbar region.

Whether we take these characters then, or such minor ones as those which are derivable from the proportional length of the spines of the cervical vertebrae, and the like, there is no doubt whatsoever as to the marked difference between Man and the Gorilla; but there is as little, that equally marked differences, of the very same order, obtain between the Gorilla and the lower Apes.

The Pelvis, or bony girdle of the hips, of Man is a strikingly human part of his organisation; the expanded haunch bones affording support for his viscera during his habitually erect posture, and giving space for the attachment of the great muscles which enable him to assume and to preserve that attitude. In these respects the pelvis of the Gorilla differs very considerably from his (Fig. 1). But go no lower than the Gibbon, and see how vastly more he differs from the Gorilla than the latter does from Man, even in this structure. Look at the flat, narrow haunch bones—the long and narrow passage—the coarse, outwardly curved, ischiatic prominences on which the Gibbon habitually rests, and which are coated by the so-called "callosities," dense patches of

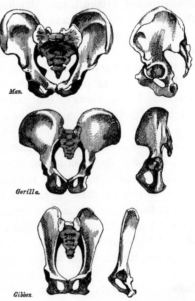

Fig. 1. Front and side views of the bony pelvis of Man, the Gorilla and Gibbon: reduced from drawings made from nature, of the same absolute length, By Mr. Waterhouse Hawkins.

skin, wholly absent in the Gorilla, in the Chimpanzee, and in the Orang, as in Man!

In the lower Monkeys and in the Lemurs the difference becomes more striking still, the pelvis acquiring an altogether quadrupedal character.

But now let us turn to a nobler and more characteristic organ—that by which the human frame seems to be, and indeed is, so strongly distinguished from all others,—I mean the skull. The differences between a Gorilla's skull and a Man's are truly immense (Fig. 2). In the former, the face, formed largely by the massive jawbones, predominates over the brain-case, or cranium proper: in the latter, the proportions of the two are reversed. In the Man, the occipital foramen, through which passes the great nervous cord connecting the brain with the nerves of the body, is placed just behind the centre of the base of the skull, which thus becomes evenly balanced in the erect posture; in the Gorilla, it lies in the posterior third of that base. In the Man, the surface of the skull is comparatively smooth, and the supraciliary ridges or brow prominences usually project but little—while, in the Gorilla, vast crests are developed upon the skull, and the brow ridges overhang the cavernous orbits, like great penthouses.

Sections of the skulls, however, show that some of the apparent defects of the Gorilla's cranium arise, in fact, not so much from deficiency of braincase as from excessive development of the parts of the face. The cranial cavity is not ill-shaped, and the forehead is not truly flattened or very retreating, its really well-formed curve being simply disguised by the mass of bone which is built up against it (Fig. 2).

But the roofs of the orbits rise more obliquely into the cranial cavity, thus diminishing the space for the lower part of the anterior lobes of the brain, and the absolute capacity of the cranium is far less than that of Man. So far as I am aware, no human cranium belonging to an adult man has yet been observed with a less cubical capacity than 62 cubic inches, the smallest cranium observed in any race of men by Morton, measuring 63 cubic inches; while, on the other hand, the most capacious Gorilla skull yet measured has a content of not more than 34½ cubic inches. Let us assume, for simplicity's sake, that the lowest Man's skull has twice the capacity of that of the highest Gorilla.

No doubt, this is a very striking difference, but it loses much of its apparent systematic value, when viewed by the light of certain other equally indubitable facts respecting cranial capacities.

The first of these is, that the difference in the volume of the cranial cavity of different races of mankind is far greater, absolutely, than that between the lowest Man and the highest Ape, while, relatively, it is about the same. For the largest human skull measured by Morton contained 114 cubic inches, that

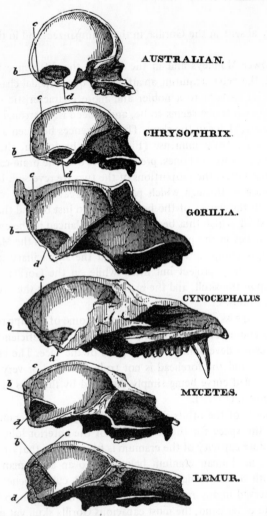

Fig. 2. Sections of the skulls of Man and various Apes, drawn so as to give the cerebral cavity the same length in each case, thereby displaying the varying proportions of the facial bones. The line *b* indicates the plane of the tentorium, which separates the cerebrum from the cerebellum; *d*, the axis of the occipital outlet of the skull. The extent of cerebral cavity behind *c*, which is a perpendicular erected on *b* at the point where the tentorium is attached posteriorly, indicates the degree to which the cerebrum overlaps the cerebellum—the space occupied by which is roughly indicated by the dark shading. In comparing these diagrams, it must be recollected, that figures on so small a scale as these simply exemplify the statements in the text, the proof of which is to be found in the objects themselves.

is to say, had very nearly double the capacity of the smallest; while its absolute perponderance, of 52 cubic inches—is far greater than that by which the lowest adult male human cranium surpasses the largest of the Gorillas (62–34½–27½). Secondly, the adult crania of Gorillas which have as yet been measured differ among themselves by nearly one-third, the maximum capacity being 34.5 cubic inches, the minimum 24 cubic inches; and, thirdly, after making all due allowance for difference of size, the cranial capacities of some of the lower Apes fall nearly as much, relatively, below those of the higher Apes as the latter fall below Man.

Thus, even in the important matter of cranial capacity, Men differ more widely from one another than they do from the Apes; while the lowest Apes differ as much in proportion, from the highest, as the latter does from Man. The last proposition is still better illustrated by the study of the modifications which other parts of the cranium undergo in the Simian series.

It is the large proportional size of the facial bones and the great projection of the jaws which confer upon the Gorilla's skull its small facial angle and brutal character.

But if we consider the proportional size of the facial bones to the skull proper only, the little *Chrysothrix* (Fig. 2) differs very widely from the Gorilla, and, in the same way, as Man does; while the Baboons (*Cynocephalus*, Fig. 2) exaggerate the gross proportions of the muzzle of the great Anthropoid, so that its visage looks mild and human by comparison with theirs. The difference between the Gorilla and the Baboon is even greater than it appears at first sight; for the great facial mass of the former is largely due to a downward development of the jaws; an essentially human character, superadded upon that almost purely forward, essentially brutal, development of the same parts which characterises the Baboon, and yet more remarkably distinguishes the Lemur.

Similarly, the occipital foramen of *Mycetes* (Fig. 2), and still more of the Lemurs, is situated completely in the posterior face of the skull, or as much further back than that of the Gorilla, as that of the Gorilla is further back than that of Man; while, as if to render patent the futility of the attempt to base any broad classificatory distinction on such a character, the same group of Platyrhine, or American monkeys, to which the *Mycetes* belongs, contains the *Chrysothrix*, whose occipital foramen is situated far more forward than in any other ape, and nearly approaches the position it holds in man.

Again, the Orang's skull is as devoid of excessively developed supraciliary prominences as a Man's, though some varieties exhibit great crests elsewhere; and in some of the Cebine apes and in the *Chrysothrix*, the cranium is as smooth and rounded as that of Man himself.

What is true of these leading characteristics of the skull, holds good, as may be imagined, of all minor features; so that for every constant difference between the Gorilla's skull and the Man's a similar constant difference of the same order (that is to say, consisting in excess or defect of the same quality) may be found between the Gorilla's skull and that of some other ape. So that, for the skull, no less than for the skeleton in general, the proposition holds good, that the differences between Man and the Gorilla are of smaller value than those between the Gorilla and some other Apes.

In connection with the skull, I may speak of the teeth—organs which have a peculiar classificatory value, and whose resemblances and differences of number, form, and succession, taken as a whole, are usually regarded as more trustworthy indicators of affinity than any others.

Man is provided with two sets of teeth—milk teeth and permanent teeth. The former consist of four incisors, or cutting teeth; two canines, or eye-teeth; and four molars or grinders, in each jaw, making twenty in all. The latter (Fig. 3) comprise four incisors, two canines, four small grinders, called premolars or false molars, and six large grinders, or true molars in each jaw—making thirty-two in all. The internal incisors are larger than the external pair, in the upper jaw, smaller than the external pair in the lower jaw. The crowns of the upper molars exhibit four cusps, or blunt-pointed elevations, and a ridge crosses the crown obliquely, from the inner, anterior cusp to the outer, posterior cusp (Fig. 3 m^2). The anterior lower molars have five cusps, three external and two internal. The premolars have two cusps, one internal and one external, of which the outer is higher.

In all these respects the dentition of the Gorilla may be described in the same terms as that of Man; but in other matters it exhibits many and important differences (Fig. 3).

Thus the teeth of man constitute a regular and even series—without any break and without any marked projection of one tooth above the level of the rest; a peculiarity which, as Cuvier long ago showed, is shared by no other mammal save one—as different a creature from man as can well be imagined—namely, the long extinct *Anoplotherium*. The teeth of the Gorilla, on the contrary, exhibit a break, or interval, termed the *diastema*, in both jaws: in front of the eyetooth, or between it and the outer incisor, in the upper jaw; behind the eye-tooth, or between it and the front false molar, in the lower jaw. Into this break in the series, in each jaw, fits the canine of the opposite jaw; the size of the eyetooth in the Gorilla being so great that it projects, like a tusk, far beyond the general level of the other teeth. The roots of the false molar teeth in the Gorilla, again, are more complex than in Man, and the proportional size of the molars is different. The Gorilla has the crown of the hindmost grinder of the lower jaw more complex, and the order of eruption of the permanent teeth is different; the permanent canines making their appearance before the second and third molars in Man, and after them in the Gorilla.

Thus, while the teeth of the Gorilla closely resemble those of Man in number, kind, and in the general pattern of their crowns, they exhibit marked differences from those of Man in secondary respects, such as relative size, number of fangs, and order of appearance.

But, if the teeth of the Gorilla be compared with those of an Ape, no further removed from it than a *Cynocephalus*, or Baboon, it will be found that differences and resemblances of the same order are easily observable; but

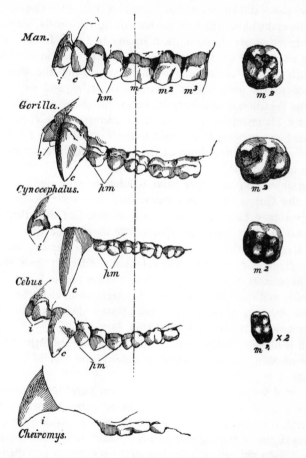

Fig. 3. Lateral views, of the same length, of the upper jaws of various Primates. *i*, incisors; *c*, canines; *pm*, premolars; *m*, molars. A line is drawn through the first molar of Man, *Gorilla, Cynocephalus,* and *Cebus,* and the grinding surface of the second molar is shown in each, its anterior and internal angle being just above the *m* of m^2

that many of the points in which the Gorilla resembles Man as those in which it differs from the Baboon; while various respects in which it differs from Man are exaggerated in the *Cynocephalus*. The number and the nature of the teeth remain the same in the Baboon as in the Gorilla and in Man. But the pattern of the Baboon's upper molars is quite different from that described above (Fig. 3), the canines are proportionally longer and more knife-like; the anterior premolar in the lower jaw is specially modified; the posterior molar of the lower jaw is still larger and more complex than in the Gorilla.

Passing from the old-world Apes to those of the new world, we meet with a change of much greater importance than any of these. In such a genus as *Cebus*, for example (Fig. 3), it will be found that while in some secondary points, such as the projection of the canines and the diastema, the resemblance to the great ape is preserved; in other and most important respects, the dentition is extremely different. Instead of 20 teeth in the milk set, there are 24: instead of 32 teeth in the permanent set, there are 36, the false molars being increased from eight to twelve. And in form, the crowns of the molars are very unlike those of the Gorilla, and differ far more widely from the human pattern.

The Marmosets, on the other hand, exhibit the same number of teeth as Man and the Gorilla; but, notwithstanding this, their dentition is very different, for they have four more false molars, like the other American monkeys—but as they have four fewer true molars, the total remains the same. And passing from the American apes to the Lemurs, the dentition becomes still more completely and essentially different from that of the Gorilla. The incisors begin to vary both in number and in form. The molars acquire, more and more, a many-pointed, insectivorous character, and in one Genus, the Aye-Aye (*Cheiromys*), the canines disappear, and the teeth completely simulate those of a Rodent (Fig. 3).

Hence it is obvious that, greatly as the dentition of the highest Ape differs from that of Man, it differs far more widely from that of the lower and lowest Apes.

The external form of the human hand is familiar enough to every one. It consists of a stout wrist followed by a broad palm, formed of flesh, and tendons, and skin, binding together four bones, and dividing into four long and flexible digits, or fingers, each of which bears on the back of its last joint a broad and flattened nail. The longest cleft between any two digits is rather less than half as long as the hand. From the outer side of the base of the palm a stout digit goes off, having only two joints instead of three; so short, that it only reaches to a little beyond the middle of the first joint of the finger next it; and further remarkable by its great mobility, in consequence of which it can be directed outwards, almost at a right angle to the rest. This digit is called the *"pollex,"* or thumb; and, like the others, it bears a flat nail upon the back of its terminal joint. In consequence of the proportions and mobility of the thumb, it is what is termed "Opposable"; in other words, its extremity can, with greatest ease, be brought into contact with the extremities of any of the fingers; a property upon which the possibility of our carrying into effect the conceptions of the mind so largely depends.

The external form of the foot differs widely from that of the hand; and yet, when closely compared, the two present some singular resemblances. Thus the ankle corresponds in a manner with the wrist; the sole with the palm; the toes with the fingers; the great toe with the thumb. But the toes, or digits of the foot, are far shorter in proportion than the digits of the hand, and are less moveable, the want of mobility being most striking in the great toe—which, again, is very much larger in proportion to the other toe than the thumb to the fingers. In considering this point, however, it must not be forgotten that the civilized great toe, confined and cramped from childhood upwards, is seen to a great disadvantage, and that in uncivilized and barefooted people it retains a great amount of mobility, and even some sort of opposability. The Chinese boatmen are said to be able to pull an oar; the artisans of Bengal to weave, and the Carajas to steal fishhooks by its help; though, after all, it must be recollected that the structure of its joints and the arrangement of its bones, necessarily render its prehensile action far less perfect than that of the thumb.

But to gain a precise conception of the resemblances and differences of the hand and foot, and of the distinctive characters of each, we must look below the skin, and compare the bony framework and its motor apparatus in each (Fig. 4).

The skeleton of the hand exhibits, in the region which we term the wrist, and which is technically called the *carpus*—two rows of closely fitted polygonal bones, four in each row, which are tolerably equal in size. The bones of the first row with the bones of the forearm form the wrist joint, and are arranged side by side, no one greatly exceeding or overlapping the rest.

Three of the bones of the second row of the carpus bear the four long bones which support the palm of the hand. The fifth bone of the same character is articulated in a much more free and moveable manner than the others, with its carpal bone, and forms the base of the thumb. These are called *metacarpal* bones, and they carry the *phalanges* or bones of the digits, of which there are two in the thumb, and three in each of the fingers.

The skeleton of the foot is very like that of the hand in some respects. Thus there are three phalanges in each of the lesser toes, and only two in the great toe, which answers to the thumb. There is a long bone, termed *metatarsal*, answering to the metacarpal, for each digit; and the *tarsus* which

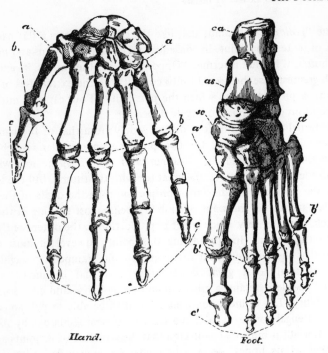

Hand.   *Foot.*

Fig. 4.   The skeleton of the Hand and Foot of Man reduced from Dr. Carter's drawings in Gray's *Anatomy*. The hand is drawn to a larger scale than the foot. The line *a a* in the hand indicates the boundary between the carpus and the metacarpus; *b b* that between the latter and the proximal phalanges; *c c* marks the ends of the distal phalanges. The line *a′ a′* in the foot indicates the boundary between the tarsus and metatarsus; *b′ b′* marks that between the metatarsus and the proximal phalanges; and *c′ c′* bounds the ends of the distal phalanges; *ca*, the calcaneum; *as*, the astragalus; *sc*, the scaphoid bone in the tarsus.

corresponds with the carpus, presents four short polygonal bones in a row, which correspond very closely with the four carpal bones of the second row of the hand. In other respects the foot differs very widely from the hand. Thus the great toe is the longest digit but one; and its metatarsal is far less moveably articulated with the tarsus than the metacarpal of the thumb with the carpus. But a far more important distinction lies in the fact that, instead of four more tarsal bones there are only three; and, that these three are not arranged side by side, or in a row. One of them, the *os calcis* or heel bone (*ca*), lies externally, and sends back the large projecting heel; another, the *astragalus* (*as*), rests on this by one face, and by another forms, with the bones of the leg, the ankle joint; while a third face, directed forwards, is separated from the three inner tarsal bones of the row next the metatarsus by a bone called the *scaphoid* (*sc*).

Thus there is a fundamental difference in the structure of the foot and the hand, observable when the carpus and the tarsus are contrasted: and there are differences of degree noticeable when the proportions and the mobility of the metacarpals and metatarsals, with their respective digits, are compared together.

The same two classes of differences become obvious when the muscles of the hand are compared with those of the foot.

Three principal sets of muscles, called "flexors," bend the fingers and thumb, as in clenching the fist, and three sets,—the extensors—extend them, as in straightening the fingers. These muscles are all "long muscles" that is to say, the fleshy part of each, lying in and being fixed to the bones of the arm, is at the other end, continued into tendons, or rounded cords, which pass into the hand, and are ultimately fixed to the bones which are to be moved. Thus, when the fingers are bent, the fleshy parts of the flexors of the fingers, placed in the arm, contract, in virtue of their peculiar endowment as muscles; and pulling the tendinous cords, connecting with their ends, cause them to pull down the bones of the fingers towards the palm.

Not only are the principal flexors of the fingers and of the thumb long muscles, but they remain quite distinct from one another throughout their whole length.

In the foot, there are also three principal flexor muscles of the digits or toes, and three principal extensors; but one extensor and one flexor are short muscles; that is to say, their fleshy parts are not situated in the leg (which corresponds with the arm), but in the back and in the sole of the foot—regions which correspond with the back and the palm of the hand.

Again, the tendons of the long flexor of the toes, and of the long flexor of the great toe, when they reach the sole of the foot, do not remain distinct from one another, as the flexors in the palm of the hand do, but they become united and commingled in a very curious manner—while their united tendons receive an accessory muscle connected with the heel-bone.

But perhaps the most absolutely distinctive character about the muscles of the foot is the existence of what is termed the *peronaeus longus*, a long muscle fixed to the outer bone of the leg, and sending its tendon to the outer ankle, behind and below which it passes, and then crosses the foot obliquely to be attached to the base of the great toe. No muscle in the hand exactly corresponds with this, which is eminently a foot muscle.

To resume—the foot of man is distinguished from his hand by the following absolute anatomical differences:—

1. By the arrangement of the tarsal bones.
2. By having a short flexor and a short extensor muscle of the digits.
3. By possessing the muscle termed *peronaeus longus*.

And if we desire to ascertain whether the terminal division of a limb, in other Primates, is to be called a foot or a hand, it is by the presence or absence of these characters that we must be guided, and not by the mere proportions and greater or lesser mobility of the great toe, which may vary indefinitely without any fundamental alteration in the structure of the foot.

Keeping these considerations in mind, let us now turn to the limbs of the Gorilla. The terminal division of the fore limb presents no difficulty—bone for bone and muscle for muscle, are found to be arranged essentially as in man, or with such minor differences as are found as varieties in man. The Gorilla's hand is clumsier, heavier, and has a thumb somewhat shorter in proportion than that of man; but no one has ever doubted it being a true hand.

At first sight, the termination of the hind limb of the Gorilla looks very hand-like, and as it is still more so in many of the lower apes, it is not wonderful that the appellation "Quadrumana," or four-handed creatures, adopted from the older anatomists by Blumenbach, and unfortunately rendered current by Cuvier, should have gained such wide acceptance as a name for the Simian group. But the most cursory anatomical investigation at once proves that the resemblance of the so-called "hind hand" to a true hand, is only skin deep, and that, in all essential respects, the hind limb of the Gorilla is as truly terminated by a foot as that of man. The tarsal bones, in all important circumstances of number, disposition, and form, resemble those of man (Fig. 5). The metatarsals and digits, on the other hand, are proportionally longer and more slender, while the great toe is not only proportionally shorter and weaker, but its metatarsal bone is united by a more moveable joint with the tarsus. At the same time, the foot is set more obliquely upon the leg than in man.

As to the muscles, there is a short flexor, a short extensor, and a *peronaeus longus*, while the tendons of the long flexors of the great toe and of the other toes are united together and with an accessory fleshy bundle.

The hind limb of the Gorilla, therefore, ends in a ture foot, with a very moveable great toe. It is a prehensile foot, indeed, but is in no sense a hand; it is a foot which differs from that of man not in any fundamental character, but in mere proportions, in the degree of mobility, and in the secondary arrangement of its parts.

It must not be supposed, however, because I speak of these differences as not fundamental, that I wish to underrate their value. They are important enough in their way, the structure of the foot being in strict correlation with that of the rest of the organism in each case. Nor can it be doubted that the greater division of physiological labour in Man, so that the function of support is thrown wholly on the leg and foot, is an advance in organization of very great moment to him; but, after all, regarded anatomically, the resemblances between the foot of Man and the foot of the Gorilla are far more striking and important than the differences.

I have dwelt upon this point at length, because it is one regarding which much delusion prevails; but I might have passed it over without detriment to my argument, which only requires me to show that, be the differences between the hand and foot of Man and those of the Gorilla what they may—the differences between those of the Gorilla, and those of the lower Apes are much greater.

It is not necessary to descend lower in the scale than the Orang for conclusive evidence on this head.

The thumb of the Orang differs more from that of the Gorilla than the thumb of the Gorilla differs from that of Man, not only by its shortness, but by the absence of any special long flexor muscle. The carpus of the Orang, like that of most lower apes, contains nine bones, while in the Gorilla, as in Man and the Chimpanzee, there are only eight.

The Orang's foot (Fig. 5) is still more aberrant; its very long toes and short tarsus, short great toe, short and raised heel, great obliquity of articulation

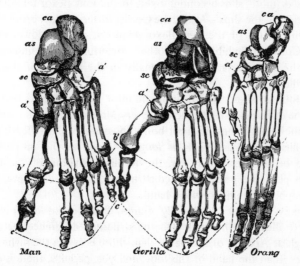

Fig. 5. Foot of Man, Gorilla, and Orang-Utan of the same absolute length, to show the differences in proportion of each. Letters as in Fig. 4. Reduced from original drawings by Mr. Waterhouse Hawkins.

with the leg, and absence of a long flexor tendon to the great toe, separating it far more widely from the foot of the Gorilla than the latter is separated from that of Man.

But, in some of the lower apes, the hand and foot diverge still more from those of the Gorilla, than they do in the Orang. The thumb ceases to be opposable in the American monkeys; is reduced to a mere rudiment covered by the skin in the Spider Monkey; and is directed forwards and armed with a curved claw like the other digits, in the Marmosets—so that, in all these cases, there can be no doubt but that the hand is more different from that of the Gorilla than the Gorilla's hand is from Man's.

And as to the foot, the great toe of the Marmoset is still more insignificant in proportion than that of the Orang—while in the Lemurs it is very large, and as completely thumb-like and opposable as in the Gorilla—but in these animals the second toe is often irregularly modified, and in some species the two principal bones of the tarsus, the *astragalus* and the *os calcis*, are so immensely elongated as to render the foot, so far, totally unlike that of any other mammal.

So with regard to the muscles. The short flexor of the toes of the Gorilla differ from that of Man by the circumstance that one slip of the muscle is attached, not to the heel bone, but to the tendons of the long flexors. The lower Apes depart from the Gorilla by an exaggeration of the same character, two, three, or more, slips becoming fixed to the long flexor tendons—or by a multiplication of the slips.—Again, the Gorilla differs slightly from Man in the mode of interlacing of the long flexor tendons: and the lower apes differ from the Gorilla in exhibiting yet other, sometimes very complex, arrangements of the same parts, and occasionally in the absence of the accessory fleshy bundle.

Throughout all these modifications it must be recollected that the foot loses no one of its essential characters. Every Monkey and Lemur exhibits the characteristic arrangement of tarsal bones, possesses a short flexor and short extensor muscle, and a *peronaeus longus*. Varied as the proportions and appearance of the organ may be, the terminal division of the hind limb remains, in plan and principle of construction, a foot, and never, in those respects, can be confounded with a hand.

Hardly any part of the bodily frame, then, could be found better calculated to illustrate the truth that the structural differences between Man and the highest Ape are of less value than those between the highest and the lowest Apes, than the hand or the foot; and yet, perhaps, there is one organ the study of which enforces the same conclusion in a still more striking manner—and that is the Brain.

But before entering upon the precise question of the amount of difference between the Ape's brain and that of Man, it is necessary that we should clearly understand what constitutes a great, and what a small difference in cerebral structure; and we shall be best enabled to do this by a brief study of the chief modifications which the brain exhibits in the series of vertebrate animals.

The brain of a fish is very small, compared with the spinal cord into which it is continued, and with the nerves which come off from it: of the segments of which it is composed—the olfactory lobes, the cerebral hemispheres, and the succeeding divisions—no one predominates so much over the rest as to obscure or cover them; and the so-called optic lobes are, frequently, the largest masses of all. In Reptiles, the mass of the brain, relatively to the spinal cord, increases and the cerebral hemispheres begin to predominate over the other parts; while in Birds this predominance is still more marked. The brain of the lowest Mammals, such as the duck-billed Platypus and the Opossums and Kangaroos, exhibits a still more definite advance in the same direction. The cerebral hemispheres have now so much increased in size as, more or less, to hide the representatives of the optic lobes, which remain comparatively small, so that the brain of a Marsupial is extremely different from that of a Bird, Reptile, or Fish. A step higher in the scale, among the placental Mammals, the structure of the brain acquires a vast modification—not that it appears much altered externally, in a Rat or in a Rabbit, from what it is in a Marsupial—nor that the proportions of its parts are much changed, but an apparently new structure is found between the cerebral hemispheres, connecting them together, at what is called the "great commissure" "corpus callosum." The subject requires careful reinvestigation, but if the currently received statements are correct, the appearance of the "corpus callosum" in the placental mammals is the greatest and most sudden modification exhibited by the brain in the whole series of vertebrated animals—it is the greatest leap anywhere made by Nature in her brain work. For the two halves of the brain being once thus knit together, the progress of cerebral complexity is traceable through a complete series of steps from the lowest Rodent, or Insectivore, to Man; and that complexity consists, chiefly, in the disproportionate development of the cerebral hemispheres and of the cerebellum, but especially of the former, in respect to the other parts of the brain.

In the lower placental mammals, the cerebral hemispheres leave the proper upper and posterior face of the cerebellum completely visible, when the brain is viewed from above; but, in the higher forms, the hinder part of each hemisphere, separated only by the tentorium from the anterior face of the cerebellum, inclines backwards and downwards, and grows out, as the so-called "posterior lobe," so as at length to overlap and hide the cerebellum. In all Mammals, each cerebral hemisphere contains a cavity which is termed the "ventricle"; and as this ventricle is prolonged, on the one hand, forwards, and on the other downwards, into the substance of the hemisphere, it is said to have two horns or "cornua," an "anterior cornu," and a "descending cornu." When the posterior lobe is well developed, a third prolongation of the ventricular cavity extends into it, and is called the "posterior cornu."

In the lower and smaller forms of placental Mammals the surface of the cerebral hemispheres is either smooth or evenly rounded, or exhibits a very few grooves, which are technically termed "sulci," separating ridges or "convolutions" of the substance of the brain; and the smaller species of all orders tend to a similar smoothness of brain. But, in the higher orders, and especially the larger members of these orders, the grooves, or sulci, become extremely numerous, and the intermediate convolutions proportionately more complicated in their meanderings, until, in the Elephant, the Porpoise, the higher Apes, and Man, the cerebral surface appears a perfect labyrinth of tortuous foldings.

Where a posterior lobe exists and presents its customary cavity—the posterior cornu—it commonly happens that a particular sulcus appears upon the inner and under surface of the lobe, parallel with and beneath the floor of the cornu—which is, as it were, arched over the roof of the sulcus. It is as if the groove had been formed by indenting the floor of the posterior horn from without with a blunt instrument, so that the floor should rise as a convex eminence. Now this eminence is what has been termed the "Hippocampus minor;" the "Hippocampus major" being a larger eminence in the floor of the descending cornu. What may be the functional importance of either of these structures we know not.

As if to demonstrate, by a striking example, the impossibility of erecting any cerebral barrier between man and the apes, Nature has provided us, in the latter animals, with an almost complete series of graduations from brains little higher than that of a Rodent, to brains little lower than that of Man. And it is a remarkable circumstance, that though so far as our present knowledge extends, there *is* one true structural break in the series of forms of Simian brains, this hiatus does not lie between Man and the man-like apes, but between the lower and the lowest Simians; or, in other words, between the old and new world apes and monkeys, and the Lemurs. Every Lemur which has yet been examined, in fact, has its cerebellum partially visible from above, and its posterior lobe, with the contained posterior cornu and hippocampus minor, more or less rudimentary. Every Marmoset, American monkey, old world monkey, Baboon, or Man-like ape, on the contrary, has its cerebellum entirely hidden, posteriorly, by the cerebral lobes, and possesses a large posterior cornu, with a well-developed hippocampus minor.

In many of these creatures, such as the Saimiri (*Chrysothrix*), the cerebral lobes overlap and extend much further behind the cerebellum, in proportion, than they do in man (Fig. 2)–and it is quite certain that, in all, the cerebellum is completely covered behind, by well developed posterior lobes. The fact can be verified by every one who possesses the skull of any old or new world monkey. For, inasmuch as the brain in all mammals completely fills the cranial cavity, it is obvious that a cast of the interior of the skull will reproduce the general form of the brain, at any rate with such minute and, for the present purpose, utterly unimportant differences as may result from the absence of the enveloping membranes of the brain in the dry skull. But if such a cast be made in plaster, and compared with a similar cast of the interior of a human skull, it will be obvious that the cast of the cerebral chamber, representing the cerebrum of the ape, as completely covers over and overlaps the cast of the cerebellar chamber, representing the cerebellum, as it does in the man (Fig. 6). A careless observer, forgetting that a soft structure like the brain loses its proper shape the moment it is taken out of the skull, may indeed mistake the uncovered condition of the cerebellum of an extracted and distorted brain for the natural relations of the parts; but his error must become patent even to himself if he try to replace the brain within the cranial chamber. To suppose that the cerebellum of an ape is naturally uncovered behind is a miscomprehension comparable only to that of one who should imagine that a man's lungs always occupy but a small portion of the thoracic cavity, because they do so when the chest is opened, and their elasticity is no longer neutralized by the pressure of the air.

And the error is the less excusable, as it must become apparent to every one who examines a section of the skull of any ape above a Lemur, without taking the trouble to make a cast of it. For there is a very marked groove in every such skull, as in the human skull–which indicates the line of attachment of what is termed the *tentorium*–a sort of parchment-like shelf, or partition, which, in the recent state, is interposed between the cerebrum and cerebellum, and prevents the former from pressing upon the latter. (See Fig. 2).

This groove, therefore, indicates the line of separation between that part of the cranial cavity which contains the cerebrum, and that which contains the cerebellum; and as the brain exactly fills the cavity of the skull, it is obvious that the relations of these two parts of the cranial cavity at once informs us of the relations of their contents. Now in man, in all the old world, and in all the new world Simiae, with one exception, when the face is directed forwards, this line of attachment of the tentorium, or impression for the lateral sinus, as it is technically called, is nearly horizontal, and the cerebral chamber invariably overlaps or projects behind the cerebellar chamber. In the Howler Monkey or *Mycetes* (see Fig. 2), the line passes obliquely upwards and backwards, and the cerebral overlap is almost nil; while in the Lemurs, as

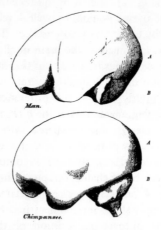

Fig. 6.   Drawings of the internal casts of a Man's and of a Chimpanzee's skull, of the same absolute length, and placed in corresponding positions, A. Cerebrum; B. Cerebellum. The former drawing is taken from a cast in the Museum of the Royal College of Surgeons, the latter from the photograph of the cast of a Chimpanzee's skull, which illustrates the paper by Mr. Marshall "On the Brain of the Chimpanzee" in the *Natural History Review* for July, 1861. The sharper definition of the lower edge of the cast of the cerebral chamber in the Chimpanzee arises from the circumstance that the tentorium remained in that skull and not in the Man's. The cast more accurately represents the brain in the Champanzee than in the Man; and the great backward projection of the posterior lobes of the cerebrum of the former, beyond the cerebellum, is conspicuous.

in the lower mammals, the line is much more inclined in the same direction, and the cerebellar chamber projects considerably beyond the cerebral.

When the gravest errors respecting points so easily settled as this question respecting the posterior lobes, can be authoritatively propounded, it is no wonder that matters of observation, of no very complex character, but still requiring a certain amount of care, should have fared worse. Any one who cannot see the posterior lobe in an ape's brain is not likely to give a very valuable opinion respecting the posterior cornu or the hippocampus minor. If a man cannot see a church, it is preposterous to take his opinion about its altar-piece or painted window—so that I do not feel bound to enter upon any discussion of these points, but content myself with assuring the reader that the posterior cornu and the hippocampus minor, have now been seen— usually, at least as well developed as in man, and often better—not only in the

Chimpanzee, the Orang, and the Gibbon, but in all the genera of the old world baboons and monkeys, and in most of the new world forms, including the Marmosets.

In fact, all the abundant and trustworthy evidence (consisting of the results of careful investigations directed to the determination of these very questions, by skilled anatomists) which we now possess, leads to the conviction that, so far from the posterior lobe, the posterior cornu, and the hippocampus minor, being structures peculiar to and characteristic of man, as they have been over and over again asserted to be, even after the publication of the clearest demonstration of the reverse, it is precisely these structures which are the most marked cerebral characters common to man with the apes. They are among the most distinctly Simian peculiarities which the human organism exhibits.

As to the convolutions, the brains of the apes exhibit every stage of progress, from the almost smooth brain of the Marmoset, to the Orang and the Chimpanzee, which fall but little below Man. And it is most remarkable that, as soon as all the principal sulci appear, the pattern according to which they are arranged is identical with that of the corresponding sulci of man. The surface of the brain of a monkey exhibits a sort of skeleton map of man's, and in the man-like apes the details become more and more filled in, until it is only in minor characters, such as the greater excavation of the anterior lobes, the constant presence of fissures usually absent in man, and the different disposition and proportions of some convolutions, that the Chimpanzee's or the Orang's brain can be structurally distinguished from Man's.

So far as cerebral structure goes, therefore, it is clear that Man differs less from the Chimpanzee or the Orang, than these do even from the Monkeys, and that the difference between the brains of the Chimpanzee and of Man is almost insignificant, when compared with that between the Chimpanzee brain and that of a Lemur.

It must not be overlooked, however, that there is a very striking difference in absolute mass and weight between the lowest human brain and that of the highest ape—a difference which is all the more remarkable when we recollect that a full-grown Gorilla is probably pretty nearly twice as heavy as a Bosjesman, or as many an European woman. It may be doubted whether a healthy human adult brain ever weighed less than thirty-one or two ounces, or that the heaviest Gorilla brain has exceeded twenty ounces.

This is a very noteworthy circumstance, and doubtless will one day help to furnish an explanation of the great gulf which intervenes between the lowest man and the highest ape in intellectual power; but it has little systematic value, for the simple reason that, as may be concluded from what has been already said respecting cranial capacity, the difference in weight of brain

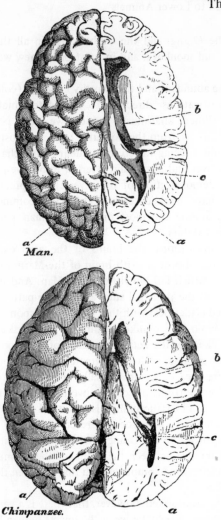

Man.

Chimpanzee.

Fig. 7. Drawing of the cerebral hemispheres of a Man, and of a Chimpanzee of the same length, in order to show the relative proportions of the parts: the former taken from a specimen, which Mr. Flower, Conservator of the Museum of the Royal College of Surgeons, was good enough to dissect for me; the latter, from the photograph of a similarly dissected Chimpanzee's brain, given in Mr. Marshall's paper above referred to. *a*, posterior lobe; *b*, lateral ventricle; *c*, posterior cornu; *x*, the hippocampus minor.

between the highest and the lowest men is far greater, both relatively and absolutely, than that between the lowest man and the highest ape. The latter, as has been seen, is represented by, say twelve, ounces of cerebral substance absolutely or by 32:20 relatively; but as the largest recorded human brain weighed between 65 and 66 ounces, the former difference is represented by more than 33 ounces absolutely, or by 65:32 relatively. Regarded systematically, the cerebral differences of man and apes, are not of more than generic value; his Family distinction resting chiefly on his dentition, his pelvis, and his lower limbs.

Thus, whatever system of organs be studied, the comparison of their modifications in the ape series leads to one and the same result—that the structural differences which separate Man from the Gorilla and the Chimpanzee are not so great as those which separate the Gorilla from the lower apes.

But in enunciating this important truth I must guard myself against a form of misunderstanding, which is very prevalent. I find, in fact, that those who endeavour to teach what nature so clearly shows us in this matter, are liable to have their opinions misrepresented and their phraseology garbled, until they seem to say that the structural differences between man and even the highest apes are small and insignificant. Let me take this opportunity then of distinctly asserting, on the contrary, they they are great and significant; that every bone of a Gorilla bears marks by which it might be distinguished from the corresponding bone of a Man; and that, in the present creation, at any rate, no intermediate link bridges over the gap between *Homo* and *Troglodytes*.

It would be no less wrong than absurd to deny the existence of this chasm; but it is at least equally wrong and absurd to exaggerate its magnitude and, resting on the admitted fact of its existence, to refuse to inquire whether it is wide or narrow. Remember, if you will, that there is no existing link between Man and the Gorilla, but do not forget that there is a no less sharp line of demarcation, a no less complete absence of any transitional form, between the Gorilla and the Orang, or the Orang and the Gibbon. I say, not less sharp, though it is somewhat narrower. The structural differences between Man and the Manlike apes certainly justify our regarding him as constituting a family apart from them; though, inasmuch as he differs less from them than they do from other families of the same order, there can be no justification for placing him in a distinct order.

Perhaps no order of mammals presents us with so extraordinary a series of gradations as this—leading us insensibly from the crown and summit of the animal creation down to creatures, from which there is but a step, as it seems, to the lowest, smallest, and least intelligent of the placental Mammalia. It is as if nature herself had foreseen the arrogance of man, and with Roman severity had provided that his intellect, by its very triumphs, should call into prominence the slaves, admonishing the conqueror that he is but dust.

These are the chief facts, this the immediate conclusion from them to which I adverted in the commencement of this Essay. The facts, I believe, cannot be disputed; and if so, the conclusion appears to me to be inevitable.

But if Man be separated by no greater structural barrier from the brutes than they are from one another—then it seems to follow that if any process of physical causation can be discovered by which the genera and families of ordinary animals have been produced, that process of causation is amply sufficient to account for the origin of Man. In other words, if it could be shown that the Marmosets, for example, have arisen by gradual modification of the ordinary Platyrhini, or that both Marmosets and Platyrhini are modified ramifications of a primitive stock—then, there would be no rational ground for doubting that man might have originated, in the one case, by the gradual modification of a man-like ape; or, in the other case, as a ramification of the same primitive stock as those apes.

On the Human Skeleton from
the Neander Valley

D. Schaaffhausen
with certain remarks by T. H. Huxley*

The history of the Human remains from the cavern in the Neanderthal may best be given in the words of their original describer, Dr. Schaaffhausen, as translated by Mr. Busk:

In the early part of the year 1857, a human skeleton was discovered in a limestone cave in the Neanderthal, near Hochdal, between Dusseldorf and Elberfeld. Of this, however, I was unable to procure more than a plaster case of the cranium, taken at Elberfeld, from which I drew up an account of its remarkable conformation, which was, in the first instance, read on the 4th of February, 1857, at the meeting of the Lower Rhine Medical and Natural History Society, at Bonn.† Subsequently Dr. Fuhlrott, to whom science is indebted for the preservation of these bones, which were not at first regarded as human, and into whose possession they afterwards came, brought the cranium from Elberfeld to Bonn, and entrusted it to me for more accurate anatomical examination. At the General Meeting of the Natural History Society of Prussian Rhineland and Westphalia, at Bonn, on the 2nd of June, 1857,‡ Dr. Fuhlrott himself gave a full account of the locality, and of the circumstances under which the discovery was made. He was of opinion that the bones might be regarded as fossil; and in coming to this conclusion, he laid especial stress upon the existence of dendritic deposits, with which their surface was covered, and which were first noticed

*1858 (from D. Schaaffhausen, *On the Crania of the most Ancient Races of Man*; translated by George Busk) as it appeared in T. H. Huxley, *Man's Place in Nature*.

†*Verhandl. D. Naturhist. Vereins der preuss. Rheinlande und Westphalens.*, xiv.–Bonn, 1857.

‡*Ib.* Correspondenzblatt. No. 2.

upon them by Professor Mayer. To this communication I appended a brief report on the results of my anatomical examination of the bones. The conclusions at which I arrived were: 1st. That the extraordinary form of the skull was due to a natural conformation hitherto not known to exist, even in the most barbarous races. 2nd. That these remarkable human remains belonged to a period antecedent to the time of the Celts and Germans, and were in all probability derived from one of the wild races of North-western Europe, spoken of by Latin writers; and which were encountered as autochthones by the German immigrants. And 3rdly. That it was beyond doubt that these human relics were traceable to a period at which the latest animals of the diluvium still existed; but that no proof of this assumption, nor consequently of their so-termed *fossil* condition, was afforded by the circumstances under which the bones were discovered.

As Dr. Fuhlrott has not yet published his description of these circumstances, I borrow the following account of them from one of his letters. 'A small cave or grotto, high enough to admit a man, and about 15 feet deep from the entrance, which is 7 or 8 feet wide, exists in the southern wall of the gorge of the Neanderthal, as it is termed, at a distance of about 100 feet from the Düssel, and about 60 feet above the bottom of the valley. In its earlier and uninjured condition, this cavern opened upon a narrow plateau lying in front of it, and from which the rocky wall descended almost perpendicularly into the river. It could be reached, though with difficulty, from above. The uneven floor was covered to a thickness of 4 or 5 feet with a deposit of mud, sparingly intermixed with rounded fragments of chert. In the removing of this deposit, the bones were discovered. The skull was first noticed, placed nearest to the entrance of the cavern; and further in, the other bones, lying in the same horizontal plane. Of this I was assured, in the most positive terms, by two labourers who were employed to clear out the grotto, and who were questioned by me on the spot. At first no idea was entertained of the bones being human; and it was not till several weeks after their discovery that they were recognised as such by me, and placed in security.

'But, as the importance of the discovery was not at the time perceived, the labourers were very careless in the collecting, and secured chiefly only the larger bones; and to this circumstance it may be attributed that fragments merely of the probably perfect skeleton came into my possession.'

My anatomical examination of these bones afforded the following results: —

The cranium is of unusual size, and of a long-elliptical form. A most remarkable peculiarity is at once obvious in the extraordinary development of the frontal sinuses, owing to which the superciliary ridges, which coalesce completely in the middle, are rendered so prominent, that the frontal bone exhibits a considerable hollow or depression above, or rather behind them, whilst a deep depression is also formed in the situation of the root of the nose. The forehead is narrow and low, though the middle and hinder portions of the cranial arch are well developed. Unfortunately, the fragment of the skull that has been preserved consists only of the portion situated above the roof of the orbits and the superior occipital ridges, which are greatly developed, and almost conjoined so as to form a horizontal eminence. It includes almost the whole of the frontal bone, both parietals, a small part of the squamous and the upper-third of the occipital. The recently fractured surfaces show that the skull was broken at the time of its disinterment. The cavity holds 16,876 grains of water, whence its cubical contents may be estimated at 57.64 inches, or 1033.24 cubic centimetres. In making this estimation, the water is supposed to stand on a level with the orbital plate of the frontal, with the deepest notch in the squamous margin of the parietal, and with the superior semicircular ridges of the occipital. Estimated in dried millet-seed, the contents equalled 31 ounces, Prussian Apothecaries' weight. The semicircular line indicating the upper boundary of the attachment of the temporal muscle, though not very strongly marked, ascends nevertheless to more than half the height of the parietal bone.

Besides the cranium, the following bones have been secured:—

1. Both thigh-bones, perfect. These, like the skull, and all the other bones, are characterized by their unusual thickness, and the great development of all the elevations and depressions for the attachment of muscles. In the Anatomical Museum at Bonn, under the designation of 'Giant's bones,' are some recent thigh-bones, with which in thickness the foregoing pretty nearly correspond, although they are shorter.

2. A perfect right humerus, whose size shows that it belongs to the thigh-bones.

Also a perfect right radius of corresponding dimensions and the upper-third of a right ulna corresponding to the humerus and radius.

3. A left humerus, of which the upper-third is wanting, and which is so much slenderer than the right as apparently to belong to a distinct individual; a left *ulna*, which, though complete, is pathologically deformed, the coronoid process being so much enlarged by bony growth, that flexure of the elbow beyond a right angle must have been impossible; the anterior fossa of the humerus for the reception of the coronoid process being also filled up with a similar bony growth. At the same time, the olecranon is curved strongly downwards. As the bone presents no sign of rachitic degeneration, it may be supposed that an injury sustained during life was the cause of the anchylosis. When the left ulna is compared with the right radius, it might at first sight be concluded that the bones respectively belonged to different individuals, the ulna being more than half an inch too short for

articulation with a corresponding radius. But it is clear that this shortening, as well as the attenuation of the left humerus, are both consequent upon the pathological condition above described.

4. A left *ilium*, almost perfect, and belonging to the femur; a fragment of the right *scapula*; the anterior extremity of a rib of the right side; and the same part of a rib of the left side; the hinder part of a rib of the right side; and, lastly, two hinder portions and one middle portion of ribs which, from their unusually rounded shape, and abrupt curvature, more resemble the ribs of a carniverous animal than those of a man. Dr. H. v. Meyer, however, to whose judgment I defer, will not venture to declare them to be ribs of any animal; and it only remains to suppose that this abnormal condition has arisen from an unusually powerful development of the thoracic muscles.

But the human bones and cranium from the Neanderthal exceed all the rest in those peculiarities of conformation which lead to the conclusion of their belonging to a barbarous and savage race. Whether the cavern in which they were found, unaccompanied with any trace of human art, were the place of their interment, or whether, like the bones of extinct animals elsewhere, they had been washed into it, they may still be regarded as the most ancient memorial of the early inhabitants of Europe.

Mr. Busk, the translator of Dr. Schaaffhausen's paper, has enabled us to form a very vivid conception of the degraded character of the Neanderthal skull, by placing side by side with its outline, that of the skull of a Chimpanzee, drawn to the same absolute size.

Some time after the publication of the translation of Professor Schaaffhausen's Memoir, I was led to study the cast of the Neanderthal cranium with more attention than I had previously bestowed upon it, in consequence of wishing to supply Sir Charles Lyell with a diagram, exhibiting the special peculiarities of this skull, as compared with other human skulls.

In truth, the Neanderthal cranium has most extraordinary characters. It has an extreme length of 8 inches, while its breadth is only 5.75 inches, or, in other words, its length is to its breadth as 100:72. It is exceedingly depressed, measuring only about 3.4 inches from the glabello-occipital line to the vertex. The longitudinal arc, measured in the same way as in the Engis skull, is 12 inches; the transverse arc cannot be exactly ascertained, in consequence of the absence of the temporal bones, but was probably about the same, and certainly exceeded 10¼ inches. The horizontal circumference is 23 inches. But this great circumference arises largely from the vast development of the supraciliary ridges, though the perimeter of the brain case itself is not small. The large supraciliary ridges give the forehead a far more retreating appearance than its internal contour would bear out.

HUMAN FOSSILS

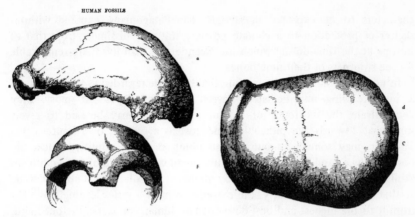

Fig. 1. The skull from the Neanderthal cavern. A, side, B, front, and C, top view. One-half the natural size. The outlines from camera lucida drawings, one-half the natural size, by Mr. Busk: the details from the case and from Dr. Fuhlrott's photographs. *a* glabella; *b* occipital protuberance; *d* lambdoidal suture.

To an anatomical eye, the posterior part of the skull is even more striking than the anterior. The occipital protuberance occupies the extreme posterior end of the skull, when the glabello-occipital line is made horizontal, and so far from any part of the occipital region extending beyond it, this region of the skull slopes obliquely upward and forward, so that the lambdoidal suture is situated well upon the upper surface of the cranium.

Under whatever aspect we view this cranium, whether we regard its vertical depression, the enormous thickness of its supraciliary ridges, its sloping occiput, or its long and straight squamosal suture, we meet with ape-like characters, stamping it as the most pithecoid of human crania yet discovered. But Professor Schaaffhausen states that the cranium, in its present condition, holds 1033.24 cubic centimetres of water, or about 63 cubic inches, and as the entire skull could hardly have held less than an additional 12 cubic inches, its capacity may be estimated at about 75 cubic inches, which is the average capacity given by Morton for Polynesian and Hottentot skulls.

So large a mass of brain as this, would alone suggest that the pithecoid tendencies, indicated by this skull, did not extend deep into the organization; and this conclusion is borne out by the dimensions of the other bones of the skeleton given by Professor Schaaffhausen, which show that the absolute height and relative proportions of the limbs, were quite those of an European of middle stature. The bones are indeed stouter, but this and the great development of the muscular ridges noted by Dr. Schaaffhausen, are characters to be expected in savages. The Patagonians, exposed without shelter or protection to a climate possibly not very dissimilar from that of Europe at the time during which the Neanderthal man lived, are remarkable for the stoutness of their limb bones.

In no sense, then, can the Neanderthal bones be regarded as the remains of a human being intermediate between Men and Apes. At most, they demonstrate the existence of a Man whose skull may be said to revert somewhat towards the pithecoid type—just as a Carrier, or a Pouter, or a Tumbler, may sometimes put on the plumage of its primitive stock, the *Columba livia*. And indeed, though truly the most pithecoid of known human skulls, the Neanderthal cranium is by no means so isolated as it appears to be at first, but forms, in reality, the extreme term of a series leading gradually from it to the highest and best developed of human crania. On the one hand, it is closely approached by the flattened Australian skulls, of which I have spoken, from which other Australian forms lead us gradually up to skulls having very much the type of the Engis cranium. And, on the other hand, it is even more closely affined to the skulls of certain ancient people who inhabited Denmark during the "stone period," and were probably either contemporaneous with, or later than, the makers of the "refuse heaps," or "Kjokkenmödings" of that country.

In conclusion, I may say, that the fossil remains of Man hitherto discovered do not seem to me to take us appreciably nearer to that lower pithecoid form, by the modification of which he has, probably, become what he is. And considering what is now known of the most ancient Races of men; seeing that they fashioned flint axes and flint knives and bone-skewers, of much the same pattern as those fabricated by the lowest savages at the present day, and that we have every reason to believe the habits and modes of living of such people to have remained the same from the time of the Mammoth and the tichorhine Rhinoceros till now, I do not know that this result is other than might be expected.

Where, then, must we look for primaeval Man? Was the oldest *Homo sapiens* pliocene or miocene, or yet more ancient? In still older strata do the fossilized bones of an ape more anthropoid, or a Man more pithecoid, than any yet known await the researches of some unborn paleontologist?

Time will show. But, in the meanwhile, if any form of the doctrine of progressive development is correct, we must extend by long epochs the most liberal estimate that has yet been made of the antiquity of Man.

Pithecanthropus erectus –
a Form from the
Ancestral Stock of Mankind

Eugene Dubois*

The fossil remains upon which I have founded this new species consist of a calvarium, or skullcap, two upper molars, and a femur. With the exception of one tooth, the second upper molar on the left side, they have already been described by me in a paper published in Batavia in 1894. It now seems desirable to give some special details.

It is well known that a not inconsiderable number of anatomists and zoologists hold diametrically opposite views regarding the significance of these remains. For instance, as to the skull, a few have believed that it is human, although of much more apelike appearance than hitherto known, while others have considered it the skull of an ape far more human in character than any previously discovered. It is remarkable that only a few have believed in a third possibility, intermediate between these two views, viz, that we have before us here a transition form between apes and men that is neither man nor ape. Recently this intermediate view has made quite significant progress, and a considerable number have accepted it. As to the anthropists and pithecists, as the upholders of the extreme views may be called, the former find their fossil Java man more apelike than they at first did, while the latter have placed their most anthropoid of apes still a few steps higher on the ladder of ascent toward man. These views now tend to coincide still more, because in the meantime it has been possible to test them by an exhibition of the objects themselves, and I have been able to give further particulars, especially as to the circumstances under which the remains were found.

*1896 (from the Smithsonian translation for 1898).

166   The Fossil Record

For the proper interpretation of these osseous remains the circumstances under which they were found is quite as important a factor as the anatomical considerations. I will therefore first give some particulars regarding their situation when discovered.

Near the remains that are the subject of this paper I have collected in Java, at Trinil, in the Ngawa district of the Madiun Residency, a great number of fossil skeletal parts of other vertebrate animals belonging to the same species

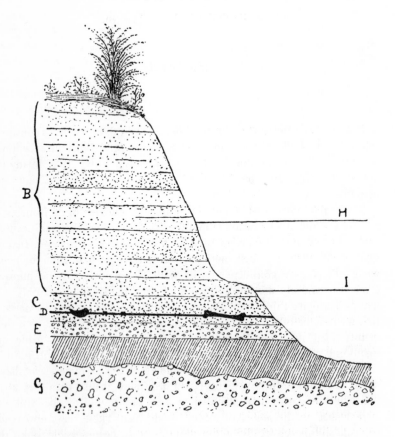

Fig. 1.   Section of the ossiferous strata at Trinil. A, area of growing plants; B, soft sandstone; C, lapilli stratum; D, level at which the skeletal remains were found; E, conglomerate; F, argillaceous layer; G, marine breccia; H, wet-season level of the river; I, dry-season level of the river.

as those found by me during five years of researches at many other places in the same strata, which lie exposed over some hundreds of square kilometers.

The four fragments of the skeleton of *Pithecanthropus* were found in different years, because, on account of the rise in the river during every rainy season, the excavations were necessarily suspended and could not be resumed until the next dry season. Besides, in the same working season one fragment was found later than the other, because the stone had to be removed cautiously in layers and by marked-off areas.

The four fragments were, however, found at exactly the same level in the entirely untouched lapilli stratum (Fig. 1). They were therefore deposited at the same time; that is to say, they are of the same age. The teeth were distant from the skull from 1 to, at most, 3 meters; the femur was 15 meters away. The quite sharp relief of their surface does not support the theory that they have been washed out from some older layer and then embedded for a second time. They were found at the place of their original deposit. Besides they all show exactly the same state of preservation and of petrefaction as do all other bones that have been taken from this particular stratum at Trinil. Their specific gravity (sp. gr. of compact tissue = 2.456) is much greater than that of unpetrified bones (sp. gr. of compact tissue = 1.930). The femur weighs 1 kilogram, therefore considerably more than double the weight of a recent human femur of the same size; the medullary cavity is partly filled with a stony mass. The eroded upper surface which the skullcap and not the femur shows occurred in the bed where it was found, appearing on many bones excavated near the skullcap, and is caused by infiltration of water through the cliff at that place.

A few anatomists hold that the fragments are parts of a human skeleton; according to others there is no doubt that they belonged to individuals of the same race. Others, again, consider the femur to be quite human, while they think that the skullcap and the teeth must have belonged to the most anthropoid of all anthropoid apes. A few anatomists, however, agree with me in the opinion that a femur entirely human in character might nevertheless belong to the same individual as this apelike skull, because a similar function would entail a similar form. Besides, this femur has certain peculiarities that I have not been able to find in a single one of some hundreds of thigh bones, so that it is not human in the usual sense of the word.

If we adopt the view that the skullcap is that of an ape, and, indeed, as must be acknowledged, that of the most manlike of all, but that the femur is that of a man, then both of these fragments must have been deposited at the same time in what was very probably an early Tertiary bed. We would then have in this case two specially important, but wholly unknown, closely related forms found together. Now, on the one hand, human bones have never been recognized below the Middle Pleistocene, much less as low as the Tertiary, and, on the other, but few remains of apes have been found, and these are much smaller, more significant, and by no means as human in character as the skullcap in question. There is therefore little probability that this view is correct. The view that these fragments were derived from different individuals of one and the same race has also very little to support it. After explorations which have been extended for five years over hundreds of square kilometers of exposed strata more than 350 meters thick and containing everywhere a numerous and homogeneous fauna, I have found, with but one possible exception, nothing which could be referred to this or any similar race.

According to all paleontological experience, the parts must have belonged to a single skeleton in case their anatomical configuration does not contradict such unity of origin. This is, however, not the case. The considerations advanced by many anatomists on this subject lead, when taken together, really to no other conclusion than that the fragments were derived from one individual. The more I myself have studied these fragments the more firmly I have been convinced of this unity of origin; and at the same time it has become ever clearer to me that they are really parts of a form intermediate between men and apes, which was the ancestral stock from which man was derived. They all show, though in somewhat different degree, intermingled human and apelike characters.

I. The Skullcap

In the form of the skullcap similitude to that of the ape is undoubtedly predominant. Never yet has there been seen so flat and low a human skull, never yet, outside of the true apes, has so strong a projection of the orbital region been found. The skulls of Neanderthal and Spy and all microcephalic skulls are more highly vaulted, especially in the parietal region; the ratio between the central portion of the skull and the orbital part lying in front of the temporal fossa is quite the same as in the apes, differing widely from that of the lowest human skulls, even that of Neanderthal and those of microcephali. Virchow has referred especially to this. It can be seen only on the left side, the right having suffered a notable loss of substance. The part of the wall of the orbit that lies in front of the deepest portion of the temporal fossa and belongs to the zygomatic process (external angular process) of the frontal bone is, in its antero-posterior dimension, about twice as large as that of the most apelike human skulls. Further, it would be difficult to find in a human skull so strongly developed a torus occipitalis transversus as that of the Javanese skull, and the lower part of the squama temporalis of that specimen retreats outwardly, as it does in the apes.

Those who have followed the history of the Neanderthal skull are aware that there has never existed regarding it such divergence of opinion as to its man- or apelike qualities as has arisen concerning the *Pithecanthropus*. The two opposed views in that case were: Apelike man or diseased man; the native of the Neanderthal has from the very first always been considered as an undoubted, real man. The human character of the *Pithecanthropus* is, however, very questionable. The skull of the gibbon almost doubled in size would not be very different from it in external appearance.

Its considerably greater size constitutes a significant difference between it and all other skulls of apes. In the length and breadth measurements of the skull the chimpanzee is exactly a mean between it and the largest gibbon. Its cranial capacity I estimated in my above-mentioned description, according to a comparison of the external lineal dimensions, as about 1,000 c. cm. Estimating now upon a more recent comparison of the internal lineal dimensions with those of gibbons' skulls makes it but little more than 900 c.

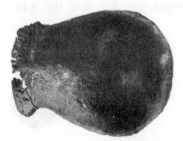

Fig. 2a. *Pithecanthropus erectus*, Dubois, skullcap, from above, after photograph. One-half natural size.

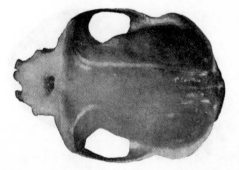

Fig. 2b. *Anthropopithecus troglodytes*, Gmelin, adult female, skull from above, after photograph. Two-thirds natural size.

cm. A Capacity of 900 c. cm. is, however, far above anything we know in the skull of apes. The largest skulls of anthropoid apes have, on the average, no greater capacity than about 500 c. cm., and it is very seldom that they have been found to attain the capacity of 600 c. cm.

If, then, the former possessor of this cranium was not an ape, and if he possibly walked erect, must he then have been a man?

I think that the apelike form of the skullcap and its capacity, too small for a man, cannot be brought to harmonize with such a conception. Even Cunningham, who has examined the skull, and is convinced that it is human, finds that its apelike characters greatly predominate, and that there is nothing human about it except its excessive size for an ape. Virchow has also, after a personal examination of the skullcap, very clearly adjudged it, in Leyden and Berlin, as the skull of an ape. So experienced a craniologist as Hamy, in Paris, said, after examining the same, that he never would have supposed it to be human. On the contrary, the most apelike human skulls that are anywhere known, the Neanderthal, the Spy, and the Australian skulls, were not

Fig. 3a. *Pithecanthropus erectus*, Dubois, skullcap, from left side, after a photograph. One-half natural size.

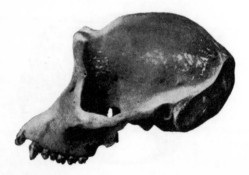

Fig. 3b. *Anthropopithecus troglodytes*, Gmelin, skull, from left side, after a photograph. Two-thirds natural size.

considered by any as apes. It was only questioned concerning these skulls whether or not their resemblance to the pithecoids should lead us to give to that race a higher phylogenetic significance.

According to the conception which we have of the human skull, the Java skullcap is certainly not a human relic.

But the size also is not adapted to that of the human skull. For it is quite inadmissible to suppose that we are here dealing with a microcephalous skull, not only on account of the great improbability of such a view, but also because its form is quite different. We are certainly acquainted with normal human skulls of an equally small capacity; but these appear less "bestial" the smaller they get, while, on the contrary, the very "bestial" Neanderthal and Spy skulls are very large. The smaller the absolute size of a cranium is, within the same species of mammals, the more significant is its relative size as compared with the rest of the body, and the more reduced are those features of the cranium that have directly to do with the size of the body and are especially related to the skeleton of the face. It is exactly these features that constitute the bestial marks of any skull.

A skull that in comparison with that of normal man is so small and so apelike in its form that it is declared by not a few experienced anatomists to be the skull of an ape, cannot be human!

II. Teeth

The teeth, a left second upper molar and a third right upper molar, belong, if we may judge from the circumstances of their discovery, to each other and to the skullcap. They are also modeled in a very similar manner and are in the same state of preservation and of petrifaction. The unequal wear of their crowns and the considerable difference in their size are appearances that can often be seen both in the skulls of men and of apes. Both have very strongly diverging roots, such as others as well as myself acknowledge never to have seen in human molars. Only exceptionally are there found in man upper molars with a crown of such great size. I measured on a skull from New South Wales, in Virchow's laboratory, the transverse and sagittal diameters of a left second upper molar, finding it 15.5 by 12.5 mm., and those of a third left upper molar, finding it 15 by 10.5 mm. The same dimensions of the fossil molars from Java are 14 by 12 mm. for the second upper molar, and 15.3 by 11.3 mm. for the third upper molar. A second upper molar from the cave of Spy I found to be of exactly the same dimensions as the molar from Java.

In the form of the crown the Javanese molars show a marked apelike type; that is to say, in the relative development of their cusps. As in anthropoid apes, the posterior buccal cusp is in both teeth the smallest, so that the cusps of both are smallest on the outer side. In man the reverse is the case. Only in the third molar is an exception to this rule rarely found.

An exhaustive comparison has, however, convinced me that the teeth are in no closer relation to those of any of the living anthropoids.

In spite of all their simian characters, both, especially in the third molar, show a strong retrogression of the crown, such as is more frequently found in man than in the anthropoid apes. According to this the general arrangement of the dental arch must have been widely different from that which obtains with the great anthropoid apes. Comparing the size of the teeth with that of the skull, the proportion is found to be the same as that in the gibbon, but somewhat less than that which prevails with the anthropoid apes. They therefore agree very well with the smooth, crestless skullcap.

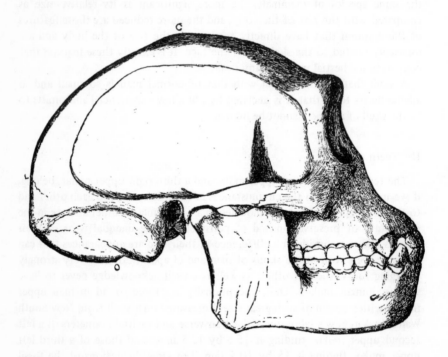

Fig. 4.   Attempt at a restoration of the skull of the *Pithecanthropus erectus* half the natural size. C, coronal suture; O, foramen magnum.

The following corrections should be made in this figure: The point O (posterior border of the foramen magnum) is about 3 mm. (in the half-sized figure; in nature, therefore, 6 mm.) too high. Also the posterior part of the Linea temporalis is about 3 mm. (in natural size about 6 mm.) too low.

III. Femur

The femur was quite generally declared to be human by authors who had closely examined either the actual specimen or drawings of it. It has, as before mentioned, a very deceptive resemblance to the human femur. It differs from the latter, however, and that difference is as great as that between bones of the same name in different but somewhat related species of mammals having a similar locomotion, as, for instance, *Colobus* and *Semnopithecus, Cervus* and *Antilope*. The most important difference concerns the form of the diaphyses in the popliteal region. It is much rounder than in man. The planum popliteum is therefore less extensive and more convex, so that exactly in its middle a kind of swelling extends as far as the neighborhood of the condyles. In the human femur the most projecting portion of the popliteal region is in the neighborhood of the lateral lip of the linea aspera. In the fossil femur, on the contrary, that lip is situated more on the lateral surface of the shaft.

The exostosis of the fossil bone—considered by me as the result of a traumatic periostitis, and by Virchow as caused by a psoas abscess that had descended from along the spinal column—appears as a so-called tendinous or aponeurotic deposit of osseous tissue, such as occurs not very infrequently in man and is also to be seen, though in a less degree, on the humerus of the skeleton of an orang-outang in the Dresden Museum. This pathological formation has no significance as regards the systematic determination of the bones.

It has been generally allowed by everyone that the femur must have belonged to an animal that walked erect. The circumstances under which it was found, in the neighborhood of the skullcap, make it very highly probable that both belonged to the same individual; and now, since we have shown that the anthropoid skullcap may not have belonged to an ape, but possibly to a being that walked upright, this probability increases quite to certainty, for this reduces the deficiency in human characters which the skullcap showed when compared with the femur. The femur is not human in the usual sense, for it, as we have seen, shows features that occur only very seldom in human femora. Besides, the similarity of form may, as before stated, be sufficiently explained by a similarity of function, so that an entirely human form of femur need not necessarily have belonged to a man, but be found likewise in some other genus. Only an examination of the entire skeleton could give a complete solution to this question.

According to the relative proportions of these parts they cannot both have belonged to an ape. For an ape with such a cranial capacity would, as we have seen, have been a giant, whose femur would certainly have been much larger

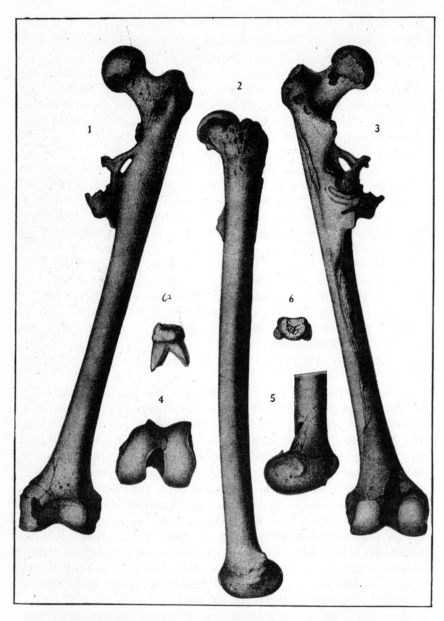

Fig. 5. *Pithecanthropus erectus*: left femur—1, from before; 2, from side; 3, from behind; 4, from below; 5, lower end from median side. 6, Right third upper molar, from below; 6a, from behind.

than twice the size of that of a siamang. But a man with a cranial capacity of 900 c. cm. would have a shorter femur; for all men, except microcephali, that have so low a capacity as this have a much smaller stature than that of 165 to 170 cm., which is the height of the individual as calculated from the length of this femur according to human proportions. This is again an evidence that the individual in question was, in the anatomical sense, neither an ape nor a man.

With the length and breadth measurements of the skull, however, the length of the femur agrees very well, both from a human and anthropoid point of view. A man with a skullcap of these dimensions could well have had a femur of that size, and if we conceive the proportions of a siamang to be doubled, the length and breadth of the femur will exactly correspond with that of *Pithecanthropus*.

Nothing contradicts the view that the possessor of this cranium had a body to which this femur belonged. The skull requires exactly such a femur and no other.

As, therefore, from different points of view, probability speaks most strongly in favor of the common origin of these fragments, it is carrying skepticism too far to doubt longer that both of them, and the teeth as well, belonged to one skeleton.

I believe that it now hardly admits of a doubt that this upright-walking ape-man, as I have called him, and as he is really shown to be after the most searching examination, represents a so-called transition form between men and apes, such as paleontology has often taught us to recognize between other families of mammals; and I do not hesitate now, any more than I formerly did, to regard this *Pithecanthropus erectus* as the immediate progenitor of the human race. This is my conviction after the most careful testing of the matter, and has only become stronger after having submitted the specimens to many anatomists.

The Discovery of a Human Mousterian Skeleton
at La Chapelle-aux-Saints (Correze)

A. Bouyssonie, J. Bouyssonie,
and L. Bardon*

Mr. Boule has presented at the meeting of the 14th of December, 1908, the remains of a human skeleton from the Middle Pleistocene, which we had the good fortune to find recently. Here summarized in a few words are the circumstances of this discovery.

"It dates from the 3rd of August, 1908. It was found in a *bouffia* (the colloquial name for *grotto*), situated in the commune of La Chapelle-aux-Saints (Correze), in the valley of a little tributary of the Dordogne. This grotto is a very low and winding corridor which penetrates a crumbly marine limestone. It contains a Mousterian archeological stratum, discovered in 1905 by us and excavated entirely by our hands, which was exposed largely on the slope in front of the excavation and which penetrated almost 6 meters into the interior. There, covered over by light soil and modern debris, the bed is directly on the soil of the grotto, intact from all alteration. It has a thickness in general of 30 cm to 40 cm, but reaching almost double that at the location of the trench."

In fact, a trench had been hollowed out in the ground about 3 meters from the entrance, towards the middle of the corridor. Nearly rectangular in form, it had the following dimensions: 1 meter 40 by about 0 meters 85 across, with a depth of 0 meters 30.

It is there that the human skeleton lay, stretched on its back, oriented from East to West, the head to the West raised against the edge of the trench and propped up by several stones, the right arm folded in an attitude of bringing the hand towards the face, the left arm a little more extended, the

*1908 (A note by the authors to the French Academy of Sciences on the 21st of December, presented by Edmond Perrier) translated by Jack and Stephanie Prost.

177

legs bent. Other peculiarities that we noticed were that above the head there were several large pieces of bone laid flat, and nearby, the extremity of a hind foot of a large Bovid with several connecting bones.

Above and around, the archeological layer was rich in broken bones as well as in tools of jasper silex and quartz.

There were no hearths properly speaking.

The craftsmanship of the tools is fine and pure Mousterian, characterized by abundant scrapers, and by points in lesser number than other varied tools. The almost total absence of amygdaloid [almond-shaped] pieces (*coups de poing*), the presence of the beginnings of Aurignacian forms indicates the Upper Mousterian. There was not a single worked bone (as those from La Quina or from Petit-Puymoyen, in the Charente).

The fauna which accompanied the tool industry is comprised of the reindeer, *Cervus tarandus*, very numerous; a large Bovid, numerous; the horse, *Equus caballus*, rare; some debris of badger, fox, sheep or goats, birds.

Outside of the bones which we ourselves have studied, the determination of species for the most delicate pieces has been made by the Reverend Breuil and especially by Mr. Harle.

The Fossil Man
of La Chapelle-aux-Saints (Correze)

Marcellin Boule*

Several weeks ago, the Reverends J. Bouyssonie, A. Bouyssonie and L. Bardon sent me a crate of human remains which they found on August 3rd, 1908, in the course of archeological excavations in a grotto near La Chapelle-aux-Saints (Correze).

The competance of my correspondents in prehistoric archeology is recognized by all authorities. The result from the geological section to which they have called attention, just as from the examination of the animal remains and from the dressed flints gathered with the human remains is that these remains date from the Middle Pleistocene (archeologically Mousterian). Besides, their state of fossilization and their morphological characteristics are sufficient cause in the absence of all other indications to attribute to them a very great antiquity.

These human bony remains comprise: a skull broken into numerous fragments (cranium and mandible), several vertebrae and several limb bones. These last show a certain number of peculiarities which I shall indicate in a more detailed work. I am satisfied to say today that they denote an individual of masculine sex and of a stature of barely 1 meter 60.

The reconstruction of the skull, a long and precise work, has been carried out under my direction by my able assistant Mr. Papoint. As many of the fragments were large and the edges of the breakage well intact, the joining of these pieces could be made exactly, and, on the whole, their reconstruction is very satisfactory; you may assure yourselves by examining the precious fossil which I have had the honor of placing before the eyes of the Academy.

*1908 (A note by the author to the French Academy of Sciences on the 14th of December, 1908, presented by Edmond Perrier) translated by Jack and Stephanie Prost.

The state of the cranial sutures and of the dentition proves that this skull is that of an elderly man. It strikes one first by its very considerable dimensions, keeping in mind meanwhile the small stature of its ancient possessor. Next it strikes us with its bestial appearance, or, to put it better, by the general collection of simian or pithecoid characteristics.

The cranium, an elongated shape (dolichocephalic; cephalic index = 75), is remarkable in fact for the thickness of its bones; the flattening of the cerebral vault; the lack of forehead; the enormous development of the brow ridges, as projecting as on the famous cranium of Neanderthal, and topped by a large groove spreading from one orbital process to the other; the strong projection of the occipital area, which is very depressed; the receding position of the occipital hole [foramen magnum]; the flattened form of the occipital condyles; the small size of the mastoid processes, etc.

The face is no less extraordinary; it displays a very considerable facial prognathism; the orbits, which project, are large; the nose, separated from the forehead by a deep depression, is short and very large. The superior maxillary, instead of growing hollow beneath the orbits because of a canine fossa, as in all living human races, projects forward, straight up and down, so as to form, in the elongation of the molar bones, a sort of muzzle, without any depression. The teeth are missing, but the roof of the mouth is very long; the lateral borders of the alveolar arcade are almost parallel, as in the anthropoid apes.

The lower jaw is remarkable for the great size of the condyle, the shallow depth of the sygmoid notch, the heavy thickening of the body of the bone, the angle of the symphysis and the absence of a chin. The genial processes are very well developed.

The skull of La Chapelle-aux-Saints presents, in an exaggerated form, all the characteristics of the skull caps of Neanderthal and Spy, so that these diverse bony pieces, found at places in Western Europe which are very remote from each other, but very similar in geological levels, belong certainly to the same morphological type. Our mandible shows also the traits of true fossil mandibles of the same age which are known today; La Nauletter, Spy, Malarnaud, etc. When one had only the skull cap of Neanderthal, scientists such as Virchow and Carl Vogt, in opposition moreover to men no less eminent, such as Quatrefages and Hamy, could declare that this specimen of a skull must have belonged to an idiot or to a sick person. Later, the fortunate finds at Spy put a quick end to this hypothesis, which could not have resisted, I believe, the discovery which I am announcing today.

I will add that a Swiss excavator, Mr. Hauser, who made periodical excavations of all our marvelous burials at La Vezere, found at Le Moustier a human skull also showing Neanderthaloid characteristics. This skull has been taken to Germany.

This allows the formulation of several important conclusions:

The human type, called Neanderthal, must be considered as a normal type, characteristic for a certain area of Europe of the Middle Pleistocene and not, as is sometimes said, of the Lower Pleistocene.

This human type, fossil, differs from living types and is placed below them, for, in any living race, one does not find altogether the inferior characteristics which are seen in the skull of La Chapelle-aux-Saints. Can one create a species or even a genus? The skeletons of Neanderthal, of Spy, of La Chapelle-aux-Saints do not justify a generic distinction. As to the question of a species, this will be of real interest only when we know really what is meant by the word *species*. But it is very necessary to say that if it was a question of a monkey, or of a carnivore, or of a ruminant, etc., one would not hesitate to distinguish, by a specific name, the skull of La Chapelle-aux-Saints from skulls of the other human groups, fossils or living.

It seems to me no less certain that, from the collection of its characteristics, the group of Neanderthal-Spy-La Chappelle-aux-Saints represents an inferior type closer to the Apes than to any other human group. Morphologically it appears to be placed exactly between the Pithecanthropus of Java and the more primitive living races, which, I hasten to say, does not imply, in my opinion, the existence of direct genetic descent.

Finally, I will point out that the human group of the Middle Pleistocene, so primitive from the point of view of physical characteristics, is very primitive from an intellectual point of view. When, during the Upper Pleistocene, we are in the presence of individual manifestations of a higher order of veritable works of art, the human skulls (Cro-Magnon race) have acquired the principle characteristics of a true *Homo sapiens*, that is to say, of high foreheads, large brains and a prominent face.

On the Discovery of a Palaeolithic Human Skull
and Mandible in Flint-Bearing Gravel
Overlying the Wealden (Hastings Beds)
at Piltdown, Fletching (Sussex)

Charles Dawson
and
Arthur Smith Woodward*

I. Geology and Flint-Implements
(Dawson)

Several years ago I was walking along a farm-road close to Piltdown
Common, Fletching (Sussex), when I noticed that the road had been mended
with some peculiar brown flints not usual in the district. On enquiry I was
astonished to learn that they were dug from a gravel-bed on the farm, and
shortly afterwards I visited the place, where two labourers were at work
digging the gravel for small repairs to the roads. As this excavation was
situated about 4 miles north of the limit where the occurrence of flints
overlying the Wealden strata is recorded, I was much interested, and made a
close examination of the bed. I asked the workmen if they had found bones
or other fossils there. As they did not appear to have noticed anything of the
sort, I urged them to preserve anything that they might find. Upon one of my
subsequent visits to the pit, one of the men handed to me a small portion of
an unusually thick human parietal bone. I immediately made a search, but
could find nothing more, nor had the men noticed anything else. The bed is
full of tabular pieces of ironstone closely resembling this piece of skull in
colour and thickness; and, although I made many subsequent searches, I
could not hear of any further find nor discover anything—in fact, the bed
seemed to be quite unfossiliferous.

*1913 (fron the "Quarterly Journal of the Geological Society," March, 1913, Vol. lxix.)

It was not until some years later, in the autumn of 1911, on a visit to the spot, that I picked up, among the rain-washed spoil-heaps of the gravel-pit, another and larger piece belonging to the frontal region of the same skull, including a portion of the left superciliary ridge. As I had examined a cast of the Heidelberg jaw, it occurred to me that the proportions of this skull were similar to those of that specimen. I accordingly took it to Dr. A. Smith Woodward at the British Museum (Natural History) for comparison and determination. He was immediately impressed with the importance of the discovery, and we decided to employ labour and to make a systematic search among the spoil-heaps and gravel, as soon as the floods had abated; for the gravel-pit is more or less under water during five or six months of the year. We accordingly gave up as much time as we could spare since last spring (1912), and completely turned over and sifted what spoil-material remained; we also dug up and sifted such portions of the gravel as had been left undisturbed by the workmen.

For many years the harder layers of this gravel-bed have been intermittently worked for farm-road material, as shown by old excavations which are now overgrown, but are traceable over the adjoining fields; and there is known to exist a gravel-bed of appreciable thickness extending over several neighbouring acres. Where the beds have been naturally denuded, a large number of the brown and red flints and the ironstone gravel are to be seen overlying the plough-lands in all directions.

Considering the amount of material excavated and sifted by us, the specimens discovered were numerically small and localized.

Apparently the whole or greater portion of the human skull had been shattered by the workmen, who had thrown away the pieces unnoticed. Of these we recovered, from the spoil-heaps, as many fragments as possible. In a somewhat deeper depression of the undisturbed gravel I found the right half of a human mandible. So far as I could judge, guiding myself by the position of a tree 3 or 4 yards away, the spot was identical with that upon which the men were at work when the first portion of the cranium was found several years ago. Dr. Woodward also dug up a small portion of the occipital bone of the skull from within a yard of the point where the jaw was discovered, and at precisely the same level. The jaw appeared to have been broken at the symphysis and abraded, perhaps when it lay fixed in the gravel, and before its complete deposition. The fragments of cranium show little or no sign of rolling or other abrasion, save an incision at the back of the parietal, probably caused by a workman's pick.

A small fragment of the skull has been weighed and tested by Mr. S. A. Woodhead, M.Sc., F.I.C., Public Analyst for East Sussex & Hove, and Agricultural Analyst for East Sussex. He reports that the specific gravity of the bone (powdered) is 2.115 (water at 5°C. as standard). No gelatine or organic matter is present. There is a large proportion of phosphates (originally present in the bone) and a considerable proportion of iron. Silica is absent.

Besides the human remains, we found two small broken pieces of a molar tooth of a rather early Pliocene type of elephant, also a much-rolled cusp of a molar of *Mastodon*, portions of two teeth of *Hippopotamus*, and two molar teeth of a Pleistocene beaver. In the adjacent field to the west, on the surface close to the hedge dividing it from the gravel-bed, we found portions of a red deer's antler and the tooth of a Pleistocene horse. These may have been thrown away by the workmen, or may have been turned up by a plough

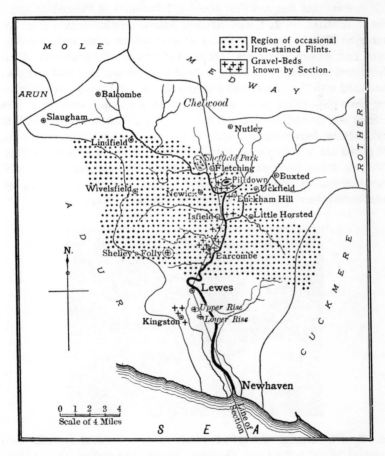

Fig. 1. Plan of the basin of the Sussex Ouse, showing the distribution of iron-stained flints and flint-bearing gravels.

which traversed the upper strata of the continuation of this gravel-bed. Among the fragments of bone found in the spoil-heaps occurred part of a deer's metatarsal, split longitudinally. This bone bears upon its surface certain small cuts and scratches, which appear to have been made by man. All the specimens are highly mineralized with iron oxide.

Conclusions

In conclusion, we may briefly consider the age of the human skull and mandible.

It is clear that this stratified gravel at Piltdown is of Pleistocene age, but that it contains, in its lowest stratum, animal remains derived from some destroyed Pliocene deposit probably situated not far away, and consisting of worn and broken fragments. These were mixed with fragments of early Pleistocene mammalia in a better state of preservation, and both forms were associated with the human skull and mandible, which show no more wear and tear than they might have received *in situ*. Associated with these animal remains are 'Eoliths,' both in a rolled and an unrolled condition; the former are doubtless derived from an older drift, and the latter in their present form are of the age of the existing deposit. In the same bed, in only a very slightly higher stratum, occurred a flint-implement, the workmanship of which resembles that of implements found at Chelles; and among the spoil-heaps were found others of a similar, though perhaps earlier, stage.

Fig. 2. Flint-bearing gravel-bed overlying the Tunbridge Wells Sands (Hastings Beds), at Piltdown, Fletching, Sussex. The darkest stratum resting on the bed-rock in the section is that from which the skull and mandible were obtained.

From these facts it appears probable that the skull and mandible cannot safely be described as being of earlier date than the first half of the Pleistocene Epoch. The individual probably lived during a warm cycle in that age.

II. Description of the Human Skull and Mandible and the Associated Mammalian Remains.
(Smith Woodward)

The Human Skull and Mandible

The human remains comprise the greater part of a brain-case and one ramus of the mandible, with lower molars 1 and 2. All the bones are normal, with no traces of disease, and they have not been distorted during mineralization.

Of the brain-case there are four pieces (reconstructed from nine fragments) sufficiently well preserved to exhibit the shape and natural relations of the frontal, parietal, occipital, and temporal bones, and to justify the reconstruction of some other elements by inference. These bones are particularly noteworthy for their thickness, and for the depth of the branching grooves which are impressed on their cerebral face by the meningeal vessels. The thickening is due to the great development of the finely cancellated diploe, the outer and inner tables of the bone being everywhere comparatively thin. The thickest point is at the internal occipital protuberance, where the measurement is 20 millimetres. A thickness of 11 or 12 mm. is attained at the postero-lateral angle of the left parietal and at the horizontal ridges of the occipital; while a thickness of 10 mm. is observable along the greater part of the fractures of the parietals and frontals. Compared with the corresponding portion on the opposite side, the postero-lateral region of the right parietal is rather thin, its thickness at the lambdoid suture being 8 to 9 mm. It is interesting to add that the average thickness of modern European skulls varies between 5 and 6 mm.; while that of the Australian skulls and of the Mousterian skull from La Chapelle-aux-Saints (France) is from 6 to 8 mm.

The capacity of the brain-case cannot, of course, be exactly determined; but measurements both by millet-seed and by water show that it must have been at least 1070 c.c., while a consideration of the missing parts suggests that it may have been a little more. It therefore agrees closely with the capacity of the brain-case of the Gibraltar skull, as determined by Prof. Keith, and equals that of some of the lowest skulls of the existing Australians. It is much below that of the Mousterian skulls from Spy and La Chapelle-aux-

Saints, which have a brain-case larger than that of the average modern civilized man.

A detailed examination of the several bones of the skull is interesting, as proving the typically human character of nearly all the features that they exhibit. The only noteworthy reminiscences of the ape are met with in the upward extension of the temporal fossae, and in the low and broad shape of the occipital region.

The right mandibular ramus (Fig. 3, parts 2, 2a, 2b, & 2c) is in the same mineralized condition as the skull, and corresponds sufficiently well in size to be referred to the same specimen without any hesitation. It lacks the articular condyle and the upper part of the bone in advance of the molars; but it is otherwise well preserved, and still exhibits the first two molars in their sockets. Its outer face is sufficiently disintegrated to show the direction of the constituent fibres of the bony tissue. The ascending portion, as in the mandibles from Heidelberg and La Chappelle-aux-Saints, is relatively broad, its width just below the sigmoid notch being 45 mm.; while its depth at the coronoid process (cor.) is about 70 mm. As in the same jaws, its hinder margin makes an angle of 110° with the inferior margin, its sigmoid notch is comparatively shallow, and the neck of its articular condyle (cd.) must have been short. The bone itself is thin, and its outer face is deeply impressed with irregular hollows for the insertion of a powerful masseter muscle.

Fig. 3. *Eoanthropus dawsoni*, gen. et sp. nov.; from a gravel near Piltdown Common, Fletching (Sussex).

Part 1. Imperfect occipital in outer view; (1a) inner view and (1b) broken vertical section, left side.

cb.=cerebellar fossa; cer.=cerebral fossa; e.o.c.=external occipital crest; e.o.p.=external occipital protuberance; f.mag.=foramen magnum; i.o.c.=internal occipital crest; lamb.=portion of lambdoid suture; l.c.l.=lower curved line; l.s.=linea suprema; si.=groove for lateral sinus; u.c.l.=upper curved line.

Part 2. Right mandibular ramus, imperfect at the symphysis, in outer view; (2a) inner view, (2b) lower view, and (2c) upper view.

b.=ridge below origin of buccinator muscle; cd.=neck of condyle; cor.=coronoid process; d.=inferior dental foramen; i.pt.=area of insertion of internal pterygoid muscle; m.1,m.2=first and second molars; m.3=socket for third molar; m.g.=mylohyoid groove; ma.=area of insertion of masseter muscle; s.=incurved bony flange of symphysis; t.=area of insertion of temporal muscle.

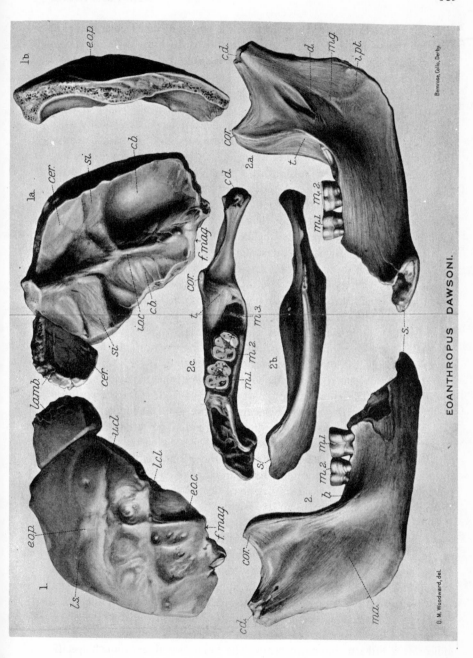

EOANTHROPUS DAWSONI.

Bemrose, Collo, Derby.

G. M. Woodward, del.

If this restoration prove to be correct, the length of the alveolar border in front of the molars is 60 mm., instead of 30 to 40 mm., as in all known human jaws; and it seems difficult to fill this space without assuming that a relatively large canine was present.

That the canine in any case cannot have been very prominent, seems to be proved by the remarkable flatness of the worn surface of the molar teeth (Fig. 3, part 2c: m. 1, m. 2). Enamel and dentine have been equally worn down by very free movements in mastication, and such a marked regular flattening has never been observed among apes, though it is occasionally met with in low types of men. Although the cusps have been worn down to the plane of the central area in each tooth, very little dentine is exposed—much less, in fact, than is seen in the similarly worn teeth of apes. Both the first and second molars are noteworthy for their considerable length in proportion to their width, each being provided behind with a large fifth cusp. They are constricted in the ordinary manner at the base of the crown (parts 2 & 2a, m. 1, 2), and in each tooth the two divergent roots are completely separate to their upper end. They are thus very different from some human teeth with fused roots which are claimed to be of Palaeolithic age. The first molar measures 11.5 mm. in length by 9.5 mm. in width; while the second molar is larger by 0.5 mm. in each direction. The third molar, which is situated almost completely on the inner side of the ascending portion of the jaw, is represented only by its well-preserved socket (part 2c, m. 3), which shows that its two divergent roots resembled those of the other molars in not being fused together. The anterior root must have been wider than the posterior root, and impressed by a vertical median groove along its hinder face. The posterior root is shown to have been the thicker antero-posteriorly. The tooth must have been relatively large, not less than 11 mm. in length, and inclined a little inwards. The molar teeth, therefore, although distinctly human, are of the most primitive type, and must be regarded as reminiscent of the apes in their narrowness. The first molar may be compared with a detached specimen already known from Taubach, in Saxe-Weimar.

While the skull, indeed, is essentially human, only approaching a lower grade in certain characters of the brain, in the attachment for the neck, the extent of the temporal muscles, and in the probably large size of the face, the mandible appears to be almost precisely that of an ape, with nothing human except the molar teeth. Even these approach the ape-pattern in their well-developed fifth cusp and elongated shape. The specimen, therefore, represents an annectant type, and the question arises as to whether it shall be referred to a new species of *Homo* itself, or whether it shall be considered as indicating a hitherto unknown genus. The brain-case alone, though specifically distinghished from all known human crania of equally low brain-capacity, by the characters of its supraorbital border, and the upward extension of its temporal muscles, could scarcely be removed from the genus *Homo*; the bone of the mandible so far as preserved, however, is so completely distinct from that of *Homo* in the shape of the symphysis and the parallelism of the molar-premolar series on the two sides, that the facial parts of the skull almost certainly differed in fundamental characters from those of any typically human skull. I therefore propose that the Piltdown specimen be regarded as the type of a new genus of the family Hominidae, to be named *Eoanthropus* and defined by its ape-like mandibular symphysis, parallel molar-premolar series, and narrow lower molars which do not decrease in size backwards; to which diagnostic characters may probably be added the steep frontal eminence and slight development of brow-ridges. The species of which the skull and mandible have now been described in detail may be named *Eoanthropus dawsoni*, in honour of its discoverer.

The skull is equally remarkable when compared with the other undoubtedly ancient human skulls hitherto known, and suggests generalizations

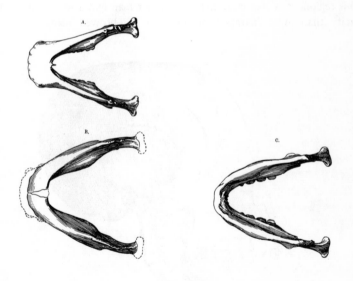

Fig. 4. Restoration of the Piltdown mandible (B), compared with that of man (C) and the young chimpanzee (A), in left side view; two-thirds of the natural size.

of even wider import. The discoveries of the brain-case of *Pithecanthropus* and several skulls of the Mousterian (Neanderthal) type have led to the very general belief that early man was characterized by a low, flattened forehead and a prominent bony brow, like the corresponding parts in the adult existing apes. The only opinions to the contrary have been based on discoveries of very doubtful authenticity, or on theoretical considerations which still need to be tested by more facts. Now, the Piltdown specimen, which is certainly the oldest typically-human brain-case hitherto found, exhibits no anterior flattening, but has the frontal eminence as steep as in modern man, without any prominent supraorbital ridge. The small development of this ridge may possibly be due in some degree to the circumstance that the new specimen represents a female, as suggested by the small backward extent of the temporal muscles, the weakness of the mandible, and the relative small size of the mastiod processes. Even so, however, a full-grown male of the same race could not have developed a supraorbital prominence approaching that of Mousterian man. The conclusion seems therefore inevitable, that at least one type of man with a high forehead was already in existence in Western Europe long before Mousterian man, with a low and prominent brow, spread widely in this region. It is also clear that this earlier man had a much lower cranial capacity than most examples of the later low-browed man. We are thus

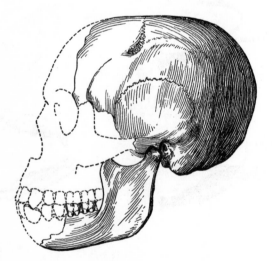

Fig. 5. Outline (left lateral view) of the skull and mandible of *Eoanthropus dawsoni*, with the bones of the face and the symphysis of the mandible in dotted outline. (1/3 nat. size.)

reminded of the interesting fact that, during the post-natal life of all the existing apes, the skull has at first the curiously rounded shape of the Piltdown specimen, with a high frontal eminence and scarcely any brow-ridge; while as growth proceeds a postorbital constriction begins, the bony brow grows forwards, the forehead becomes flattened, and the familiar well-marked ape-skull is the result. Our knowledge of the principles of palaeontology compels us to suppose that the full-grown skull in the ancestral mid-Tertiary apes was of the immature rounded shape just mentioned, although we have not yet been fortunate enough to discover an example; and, during the lapes of Upper Tertiary time, the skull-type in the whole race of apes has gradually undergone changes which are more or less exactly recapitulated in the life-history of each individual recent ape. Hence, it seems reasonable to interpret the Piltdown skull as exhibiting a closer resemblance to the skulls of the truly ancestral mid-Tertiary apes than any fossil human skull hitherto found. If this view be accepted, the Piltdown type (Fig. 5, p. 192) has gradually become modified into the later Mousterian type (Fig. 6, below) by a series of changes similar to those passed through by the early apes as they evolved into the typical modern apes, and corresponding with the stages in the development of the skull in an existing ape-individual. It tends to support the theory that Mousterian man was a degenerate offshoot of early man, and

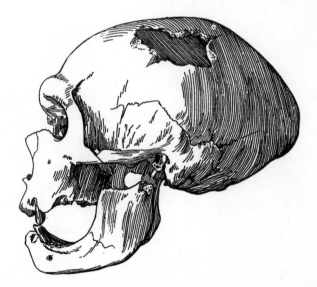

Fig. 6. Outline (left lateral view) of the human skull and mandible from La Chapelle-aux-Saints, after M. Boule. (1/3 nat. size.)

probably became extinct; while surviving man may have arisen directly from
the primitive source of which the Piltdown skull provides the first discovered
evidence.

For much valuable help in studying these human remains I wish especially
to thank Mr. W. P. Pycraft, A.L.S., and Mr. Arthur S. Underwood, M.R.C.S.

Supplementary Note on the Discovery of
a Palaeolithic Human Skull and Mandible
at Piltdown (Sussex)

Charles Dawson
and
Arthur Smith Woodward*

I. Geology and Flint-Implements
(Dawson)

Since reading our paper on December 18th, 1912, we have continued our researches in the Piltdown gravel.

Our first work this year was to clear away completely all debris overlying the floor of the dark gravel-bed from the vicinity of the spot where the mandible and piece of occipital bone were found last year, so that the irregularities of its level might be fully exposed. We found that the floor was full of depressions, often measuring 2 to 7 feet across and 1 to 2 feet in depth. Into these depressions had been drifted the dark ferruginous gravel, and in places there yet remained small undisturbed patches. The area so exposed by us measured about 20 feet square.

Following a small rift or channel in the floor which was yet filled with undisturbed gravel, we discovered another fragment of a tooth of *Stegodon* bearing three cusps. This specimen was worked out very carefully, and preserved in the gravel matrix. It seems probable, from its general appearance and condition, that this fragment is a portion of the same molar as that to which the two fragments found last year belonged: like them, it is shattered, and shows little sign of rolling. If so, it must have been broken before its original deposition, and not by the workmen. The other portions were found about 10 yards away, in debris composed of the dark gravel.

*1914 (from "The Quarterly Review of the Geological Society," April, 1914, Vol. lxx.)

In a depression adjoining that in which a portion of the human mandible occurred, was found what appears to be a flint-flake roughly worked on one face and stained dark brown; also a triangular flint of Palaeolithic outline, but having 'Eolithic' 'edge-chipping' about the apex, the colour and patination resembling those of the 'Eolithic' forms found in the pit generally. Among some of the disturbed gravel in the pit Dr. Smith Woodward found a flint worked on one face and simply flaked on the other face, and similar to the Palaeolithic flints described in our last paper.

The whole of the work was perforce carried on very slowly, and we found it impossible to employ more than one labourer, for the actual excavation had to be closely watched, and each spadeful carefully examined. The gravel was then either washed with a sieve, or strewn on specially-prepared ground for the rain to wash it; after which the layer thus spread was mapped out in squares, and minutely examined section by section.

While our labourer was digging the disturbed gravel within 2 or 3 feet from the spot where the mandible was found, I saw two human nasal bones lying together with the remains of a turbinated bone beneath them *in situ*. The turbinal, however, was in such bad condition that it fell apart on being touched, and had to be recovered in fragments by the sieve; but it has been pieced together satisfactorily by Mrs. Smith Woodward.

All the gravel *in situ* excavated within a radius of 5 yards of the spot where the mandible was found, was set apart and searched with especial care, and was finally washed and strewn as before mentioned. It was in this spread that Father Teilhard de Chardin, who worked with us three days last summer, on August 30th, 1913, discovered the canine tooth of *Eoanthropus*, hereafter described. In this way also Dr. Smith Woodward recovered a small fragment of a tooth of *Rhinoceros*, in the same state of mineralization as the fragments of teeth of *Stegodon* and *Mastodon*.

There now remains little excavation to be done in the immediate vicinity of the site of these remains. Other excavations which we have made in the pit have so far proved unproductive of fossils; but we have opened up some trial-holes which give evidence of a continuation of the bedded gravel to the west, under the plough-land there, and across the small valley on the east near Moon's Farm House.

II. Description of Lower Canine Tooth of Eoanthropus dawsoni, and some Associated Mammalian Remains.
(Smith Woodward)

The remarkable new canine tooth is certainly that of a Primate Mammal, and may therefore be referred without hesitation to *Eoanthropus*. As it belongs to the right side of the mandible, corresponds in size with the jaw already found at the same spot, and agrees with the molar teeth in having been considerably worn by mastication, it may almost certainly be regarded as part of the specimen previously described. No trace of the socket for the tooth is seen in the bone preserved at the symphysial end of the fragmentary mandible, but its position can be determined approximately by reference to the corresponding tooth in the Apes.

The crown of the tooth is conical in shape, but much laterally compressed, so that its inner (lingual) face is concave, while its outer (labial) face is only gently convex. The extreme apex is missing, but whether by wear or by accidental fracture cannot be decided. In the upper half of the outer face the thin layer of enamel is shown, marked by the usual faint transverse striations (or imbrications); but below this the tooth is encrusted with a film of hydrated oxide of iron, which has broken away at the base of the crown, removing the enamel with it. The darkly-stained dentine is thus exposed here, and the only mark of the lower limit of the crown is a faintly-impressed transverse line just above the constricted neck of the tooth. The enamel on the inner face of the crown has been completely removed by mastication, while that of the outer face, showing its prismatic structure, is exposed in worn section along the edges of the apical portion. The surface of wear forms a simple gently-curved concavity, evidently produced by a single opposing tooth; and it extends to the basal edge of the crown, as indicated by the clear ending of the cement along its lower margin. It is probably almost parallel with the original inner face of the crown, and the wear has been sufficient near the apex to expose the secondary dentine at the upper end of the pulp-cavity. The extent of this pulp-cavity, which is widely open at the lower end of the root, is well shown in two radiographs prepared by Mr. Archibald D. Reid. It is filled with grains of ironstone or sand. The anterior (median-interstitial) edge of the crown widens below to a triangular tumid area, which is sharply bounded by the outer face, the inner worn face, and the constricted neck of the tooth. Whether or not this area was originally covered to any extent by enamel is uncertain: appearances rather suggest that it is invested, instead of enamel, with a direct continuation of the cement-layer of the root. The posterior (lateral interstitial) edge of the crown is sharp, and is not produced below into any inner (lingual) protuberance or heel.

The degree of wear of this newly-discovered canine tooth is of especial interest, when considered in connexion with the worn condition of the first and second molars in the mandible to which it apparently belongs. As already described, both these molars are flattened by mastication down to the level of the middle area of their crown, while the third molar (known only by its socket) must have been fully in place. The permanent canine should therefore be completely extruded and in use, whether the order of appearance of the teeth corresponded with that in Man or with that in the Apes. As, however, the enamel of its inner face is not merely worn, but entirely removed by

A.

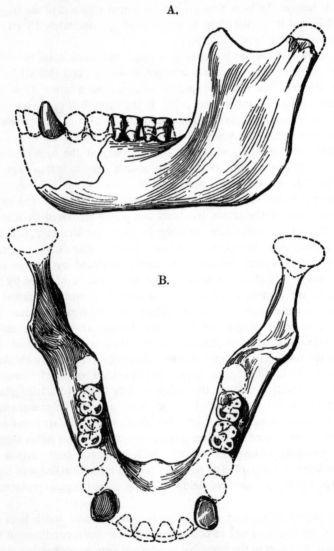

B.

Fig. 1. Restoration of the mandible of *Eoanthropus dawsoni*, in left side view (A) and upper view (B); two-thirds of the natural size.

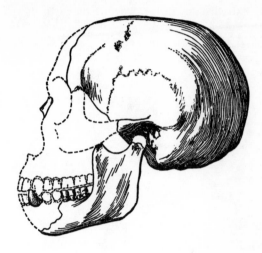

Fig. 2. Restoration of the skull and mandible of *Eoanthropus dawsoni*, left lateral view; nearly a third of the natural size.

mastication, the tooth must have been well used for a considerable period. It probably, therefore, came into place before the second and third molars, as in Man—not after one or both of these teeth, as in the Apes.

It results, therefore, from these comparisons that, among known Upper Tertiary and Recent Anthropoids, the permanent lower canine of *Eoanthropus* agrees more closely in shape with the milk-canine both of Man and of the Apes than with the corresponding permanent tooth in either of these groups. It is also obvious that the resemblance is greater between *Eoanthropus* and *Homo* than between the former and any known genus of Apes. In other words, the permanent tooth of the extinct *Eoanthropus* is almost identical in shape with the temporary milk-tooth of the existing *Homo*. Hence it forms another illustration of the well-known law in mammalian palaeontology, that the permanent teeth of an ancestral race agree more closely in pattern with the milk-teeth than with the permanent teeth of its modified descendants.

In this connexion, it is interesting to add that even in *Homo sapiens*, if the base of the crown of the canine were raised in the gum to the same level as that of the adjacent teeth, its apex would frequently project well above the rest of the dental series. The relatively large size and depth in the milk-dentition is especially well seen in a preparation in the Central Hall of the British Museum (Natural History).

For valuable help in making these studies, I have again to thank Mr. W. P. Pycraft and Prof. Arthur S. Underwood.

Australopithecus africanus:
The Man-Ape of South Africa

by Prof. Raymond A. Dart*

Towards the close of 1924, Miss Josephine Salmons, student demonstrator of anatomy in the University of the Witwatersrand, brought to me the fossilised skull of a cercopithecid monkey which, through her instrumentality, was very generously loaned to the Department for description by its owner, Mr. E. G. Izod, of the Rand Mines Limited. I learned that this valuable fossil had been blasted out of the limestone cliff formation—at a vertical depth of 50 feet and a horizontal depth of 200 feet—at Taungs, which lies 80 miles north of Kimberley on the main line to Rhodesia, in Bechuanaland, by operatives of the Northern Lime Company. Important stratigraphical evidence has been forthcoming recently from this district concerning the succession of stone ages in South Africa (Neville Jones, Jour. Roy. Anthrop. Inst., 1920), and the feeling was entertained that this lime deposit, like that of Broken Hill in Rhodesia, might contain fossil remains of primitive man.

I immediately consulted Dr. R. B. Young, professor of geology in the University of the Witwatersrand, about the discovery, and he, by a fortunate coincidence, was called down to Taungs almost synchronously to investigate geologically the lime deposits of an adjacent farm. During his visit to Taungs, Prof. Young was enabled to inspect the site of the discovery and to select further samples of fossil material for me from the same formation. These included a natural cercopithecid endocranial cast, a second and larger cast, and some rock fragments disclosing portions of bone. Finally, Dr. Gordon D. Laing, senior lecturer in anatomy, obtained news, through his friend Mr. Ridley Hendry, of another primate skull from the same cliff. This cercopithecid skull, the possession of Mr. De Wet, of the Langlaagte Deep Mine, has also been liberally entrusted by him to the Department for scientific investigation.

*1925 (From "Nature," February, 1925, Vol. 115)

The cercopithecid remains placed at our disposal certainly represent more than one species of catarrhine ape. The discovery of Cercopithecidae in this area is not novel, for I have been informed that Mr. S. Haughton has in the press a paper discussing at least one species of baboon from this same spot (Royal Society of South Africa). It is of importance that, outside of the famous Fayüm area, primate deposits have been found on the African mainland at Oldaway (Hans Reck, *Sitzungsbericht der Gesellsch. Naturforsch. Freunde,* 1914), on the shores of Victoria Nyanza (C. W. Andrews, *Ann. Mag. Nat. Hist.,* 1916), and in Bechuanaland, for these discoveries lend promise to the expectation that a tolerably complete story of higher primate evolution in Africa will yet be wrested from our rocks.

In manipulating the pieces of rock brought back by Prof. Young, I found that the larger natural endocranial cast articulated exactly by its fractured frontal extremity with another piece of rock in which the broken lower and posterior margin of the left side of a mandible was visible. After cleaning the rock mass, the outline of the hinder and lower part of the facial skeleton came into view. Careful development of the solid limestone in which it was embedded finally revealed the almost entire face depicted in the accompanying photographs.

It was apparent when the larger endocranial cast was first observed that it was specially important, for its size and sulcal pattern revealed sufficient similarity with those of the chimpanzee and gorilla to demonstrate that one was handling in this instance an anthropoid and not a cercopithecid ape.

Fig. 1. Norma facialis of *Australopithecus africanus* aligned on the Frankfort horizontal.

Fossil anthropoids have not hitherto been recorded south of the Fayüm in Egypt, and living anthropoids have not been discovered in recent times south of Lake Kivu region in Belgian Congo, nearly 2000 miles to the north, as the crow flies.

All fossil anthropoids found hitherto have been known only from mandibular or maxillary fragments, so far as crania are concerned, and so the general appearance of the types they represented has been unknown; consequently, a condition of affairs where virtually the whole face and lower jaw, replete with teeth, together with the major portion of the brain pattern, have been preserved, constitutes a specimen of unusual value in fossil anthropoid discovery. Here, as in *Homo rhodesiensis,* Southern Africa has provided documents of higher primate evolution that are amongst the most complete extant.

Apart from this evidential completeness, the specimen is of importance because it exhibits an extinct race of apes *intermediate between living anthropoids and man.*

In the first place, the whole cranium displays *humanoid* rather than anthropoid lineaments. It is markedly dolichocephalic and leptoprosopic, and manifests in a striking degree the *harmonious relation* of calvaria to face emphasised by Pruner-Bey. As Topinard says, "A cranium elongated from before backwards, and at the same time elevated, is already in harmony by itself; but if the face, on the other hand, is elongated from above downwards, and narrows, the harmony is complete." I have assessed roughly the difference in the relationship of the glabella-gnathion facial length to the glabella-inion calvarial length in recent African anthropoids of an age comparable with that of this specimen (depicted in Duckworth's "Anthropology and Morphology," second edition, vol. i.), and find that, if the glabella-inion length be regarded in all three as 100, then the glabella-gnathion length in the young chimpanzee is approximately 88, in the young gorilla 80, and in this fossil 70, which proportion suitably demonstrates the enhanced relationship of cerebral length to facial length in the fossil (Fig. 2).

The glabella is tolerably pronounced, but any traces of the salient supra-orbital ridges, which are present even in immature living anthropoids, are here entirely absent. Thus the relatively increased glabella-inion measurement is due to brain and not to bone. Allowing 4 mm. for the bone thickness in the inion region, that measurement in the fossil is 127 mm.; *i.e.* 4 mm. less than the same measurement in an adult chimpanzee in the Anatomy Museum at the University of the Witwatersrand. The orbits are not in any sense detached from the forehead, which rises steadily from their margins in a fashion amazingly human. The interorbital width is very small (13 mm.) and the ethmoids are not blown out laterally as in modern African anthropoids.

This lack of ethmoidal expansion causes the lacrimal fossae to face posteriorly and to lie relatively far back in the orbits, as in man. The orbits, instead of being subquadrate as in anthropoids, are almost circular, furnishing an orbital index of 100, which is well within the range of human variation (Topinard, "Anthropology"). The malars, zygomatic arches, maxillae, and mandible all betray a delicate and humanoid character. The facial prognathism is relatively slight, the gnathic index of Flower giving a value of 109, which is scarcely greater than that of certain Bushmen (Strandloopers) examined by Shrubsall. The nasal bones are not prolonged below the level of the lower orbital margins, as in anthropoids, but end above these, as in man, and are incompletely fused together in their lower half. Their maximum length (17 mm.) is not so great as that of the nasals in *Eoanthropus dawsoni.* They are depressed in the median line, as in the chimpanzee, in their lower half, but it seems probable that this depression has occurred post-mortem, for the upper half of each bone is arched forwards (Fig. 1). The Nasal aperture is small and is just wider than it is high (17 mm. X 16 mm.). There is no nasal spine, the floor of the nasal cavity being continuous with the anterior aspect of the alveolar portions of the maxillae, after the fashion of the chimpanzee and of certain New Caledonians and negroes (Topinard, *loc. cit.*).

In the second place, the dentition is *humanoid* rather than anthropoid. The specimen is juvenile, for the first permanent molar tooth only has erupted in both jaws on both sides of the face; *i.e.* it corresponds anatomically with a human child of six years of age. Observations upon the milk dentition of living primates are few, and only one molar tooth of the deciduous dentition in one fossil anthropoid is known (Gregory, "The Origin and Evolution of the Human Dentition," 1920). Hence the data for the necessary comparisons are meagre, but certain striking features of the milk dentition of this creature may be mentioned. The tips of the canine teeth transgress very slightly (0.5–0.75 mm.) the general margin of the teeth in

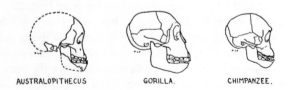

AUSTRALOPITHECUS   GORILLA.   CHIMPANZEE.

Fig. 2. Cranial form in living anthropoids of similar age (after Duckworth) and in the new fossil. For this comparison, the fossil is regarded as having the same calvarial length as the gorilla.

each jaw, *i.e.* very little more than does the human milk canine. There is no diastema whatever between the premolars and canines on either side of the lower jaw, such as is present in the deciduous dentition of living anthropoids; but the canines in this jaw come, as in the human jaw, into alignment with the incisors (Gregory, *loc. cit.*). There is a diastema (2 mm. on the right side, and 3 mm. on the left side) between the canines and lateral incisors of the upper jaw; but seeing, first, that the incisors are narrow, and, secondly, that diastemata (1 mm.–1.5 mm.) occur between the central incisors of the upper jaw and between the medial and lateral incisors of both sides in the lower jaw, and, thirdly, that some separation of the milk teeth takes place even in mankind (Tomes, "Dental Anatomy," seventh edition) during the establishment of the permanent dentition, it is evident that the diastemata which occur in the upper jaw are small. The lower canines, nevertheless show wearing facets both for the upper canines and for the upper lateral incisors.

The incisors as a group are irregular in size, tend to overlap one another, and are almost vertical, as in man; they are not symmetrical and well spaced, and do not project forwards markedly, as in anthropoids. The upper lateral incisors do project forwards to some extent and perhaps also do the upper central incisors very slightly, but the lateral lower incisors betray no evidence of forward projection, and the central lower incisors are not even vertical as in most races of mankind, but are directed slightly backwards, as *sometimes* occurs in man. Owing to these remarkably human characters displayed by the deciduous dentition, when contour tracings of the upper jaw are made, it is found that the jaw and the teeth, as a whole, take up a parabolic arrangement

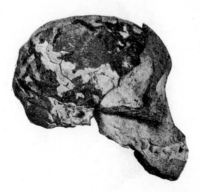

Fig. 3. Norma lateralis of *Australopithecus africanus* aligned on the Frankfort horizontal.

comparable only with that presented by mankind amongst the higher primates. These facts, together with the more minute anatomy of the teeth, will be illustrated and discussed in the memoir which is in the process of elaboration concerning the fossil remains.

In the third place, the mandible itself is *humanoid* rather than anthropoid. Its ramus is, on the whole, short and slender as compared with that of anthropoids, but the bone itself is more massive than that of a human being of the same age. Its symphyseal region is virtually complete and reveals anteriorly a more vertical outline than is found in anthropoids or even in the jaw of Piltdown man. The anterior symphyseal surface is scarcely less vertical than that of Heidelberg man. The posterior symphyseal surface in living anthropoids differs from that of modern man in possessing a pronounced posterior prolongation of the lower border, which joins together the two halves of the mandible, and so forms the well-known *simian shelf* and above it a deep genial impression for the attachment of the tongue musculature. In this character, *Eoanthropus dawsoni* scarcely differs from the anthropoids, expecially the chimpanzee; but this new fossil betrays no evidence of such a shelf, the lower border of the mandible having been massive and rounded after the fashion of the mandible of *Homo heidelbergensis*.

That hominid characters were not restricted to the face in this extinct primate group is borne out by the relatively forward situation of the foramen magnum. The position of the basion can be assessed within a few millimetres of error, because a portion of the right exoccipital is present alongside the

Fig. 4. Norma basalis of *Australopithecus africanus* aligned on the Frankfort horizontal.

cast of the basal aspect of the cerebellum. Its position is such that the basi-prosthion measurement is 89 mm., while the basi-inion measurement is at least 54 mm. This relationship may be expressed in the form of a "head-balancing" index of 60.7. The same index in a baboon provides a value of 41.3, in an adult chimpanzee 50.7, in Rhodesian man 83.7, in a dolichocephalic European 90.9, and in a brachycephalic European 105.8. It is significant that this index, which indicates in a measure the poise of the skull upon the vertebral column, points to the assumption by this fossil group of an attitude appreciably more erect than that of modern anthropoids. The improved poise of the head, and the better posture of the whole body framework which accompanied this alteration in the angle at which its dominant member was supported, is of great significance. It means that a greater reliance was being placed by this group upon the feet as organs of progression, and that the hands were being freed from their more primitive function of accessory organs of locomotion. Bipedal animals, their hands were assuming a higher evolutionary role not only as delicate tactual, examining organs which were adding copiously to the animal's knowledge of its physical environment, but also as instruments of the growing intelligence in carrying out more elaborate, purposeful, and skilled movements, and as organs of offence and defence. The latter is rendered the more probable, in view, first, of their failure to develop massive canines and hideous features, and, secondly, of the fact that even living baboons and anthropoid apes can and do use sticks and stones as implements and as weapons of offence ("Descent of Man," p. 81 *et seq.*).

The cranial capacity of the specimen may best be appreciated by the statement that the length of the cavity could not have been less than 114 mm., which is 3 mm. greater than that of an adult chimpanzee in the Museum of the Anatomy Department in the University of the Witwatersrand, and only 14 mm. less than the greatest length of the cast of the endocranium of a gorilla chosen for casting on account of its great size. Few data are available concerning the expansion of brain matter which takes place in the living anthropoid brain between the time of eruption of the first permanent molars and the time of their becoming adult. So far as man is concerned, Owen ("Anatomy of Vertebrates," vol. iii.) tells us that "The brain has advanced to near its term of size at about ten years, but it does not usually obtain its full development till between twenty and thirty years of age." R. Boyd (1860) discovered an increase in weight of nearly 250 grams in the brains of male human beings after they had reached the age of seven years. It is therefore reasonable to believe that the adult forms typified by our present specimen possessed brains which were larger than that of this juvenile specimen, and equalled, if they did not actually supersede, that of the gorilla in absolute size.

Whether our present fossil is to be correlated with the discoveries made in India is not yet apparent; that question can only be solved by a careful comparison of the permanent molar teeth from both localities. It is obvious, meanwhile, that it represents a fossil group distinctly advanced beyond living anthropoids in those two dominantly human characters of facial and dental recession on one hand, and improved quality of the brain on the other. Unlike Pithecanthropus, it does not represent an ape-like man, a caricature of precocious hominid failure, but a creature well advanced beyond modern anthropoids in just those characters, facial and cerebral, which are to be anticipated in an extinct link between man and his simian ancestor. At the same time, it is equally evident that a creature with anthropoid brain capacity, and lacking the distinctive, localised temporal expansions which appear to be concomitant with and necessary to articulate man, is no true man. It is therefore logically regarded as a man-like ape. I propose tentatively, then, that a new family of *Homo-simiadae* be created for the reception of the group of individuals which it represents, and that the first known species of the group be designated *Australopithecus africanus,* in commemoration, first, of the extreme southern and unexpected horizon of its discovery, and secondly, of the continent in which so many new and important discoveries connected with the early history of man have recently been made, thus vindicating the Darwinian claim that Africa would prove to be the cradle of mankind.

It will appear to many a remarkable fact that an ultra-simian and pre-human stock should be discovered, in the first place, at this extreme southern point in Africa, and, secondly, in Bechuanaland, for one does not associate with the present climatic conditions obtaining on the eastern fringe of the Kalahari desert an environment favourable to higher primate life. It is generally believed by geologists (*vide* A. W. Rogers, "Post-Cretaceous Climates of South Africa," *South African Journal of Science,* vol. xix., 1922) that the climate has fluctuated within exceedingly narrow limits in this country since Cretaceous times. We must therefore conclude that it was only the enhanced cerebral powers possessed by this group which made their existence possible in this untoward environment.

In anticipating the discovery of the true links between the apes and man in tropical countries, there has been a tendency to overlook the fact that, in the luxuriant forests of the tropical belts, Nature was supplying with profligate and lavish hand an easy and sluggish solution, by adaptive specialisation, of the problem of existence in creatures so well equipped mentally as living anthropoids are. For the production of man a different apprenticeship was needed to sharpen the wits and quicken the higher manifestations of intellect—a more open veldt country where competition was keener between swiftness and stealth, and where adroitness of thinking and movement played a preponderating role in the preservation of the species. Darwin has said, "no country in the world abounds in a greater degree with dangerous beasts than Southern Africa," and, in my opinion, Southern Africa, by providing a vast open country with occasional wooded belts and a relative scarcity of water, together with a fierce and bitter mammalian competition, furnished a laboratory such as was essential to this penultimate phase of human evolution.

In Southern Africa, where climatic conditions appear to have fluctuated little since Cretaceous times, and where ample dolomitic formations have provided innumerable refuges during life, and burial-places after death, for our troglodytic forefathers, we may confidently anticipate many complementary discoveries concerning this period in our evolution.

The Rhodesian Find of 1921

Ales Hrdlička*

The success of the writer's visit to Northern Rhodesia was due largely to the aid of Professor Dart of Johannesburg, and to the fine men in charge of the "Rhodesia Broken Hill Development Company." The efficient and high-minded officials of the mine deserve the thanks of the whole scientific world, for it was due only to them that the Rhodesian skull was preserved and brought in safety to the British Museum.

Upon his arrival at Broken Hill the writer was rather astonished to find the whole region for many miles in every direction to be a great, loosely forested plateau, perfectly level except for a small "kopje" situated near the railway tracks as one nears the Broken Hill mine and settlement. This little hill, only about 90 feet high, is said to resemble closely the former "broken" hill which gave us the Rhodesian man and which has now been removed through mining operations.[1]

The plateau of the town of Broken Hill is 3,874 feet above sea level. Up to the time of the commencement of mining operations it was a part of a vast, featureless, more or less openly forested region. But the minerals in the two kopjes—lead and zinc—may have been known to the natives in earlier times. At all events, in digging ditches and in other surface excavations about the mines and in the town, there are being found, buried as deep as 8 feet below the present surface, old primitive native smelters, with here and there some negro pottery indicating probably former burials.

The "broken" kopje consisted of hard dolomitic limestone impregnated with lead, zinc salts, and vanadium. It was originally full of crevices and holes, and had, as shown in the course of mining, at least two large caves leading

---

*1930 (from his book, *The Skeletal Remains of Early Man*).

[1]In one of the accounts to be quoted later mention is made of several such small hills, but only one and the remains of the one that gave the skull were seen by the writer.

211

deep into the interior. The cave of special interest became known as the bone cave. In the course of time it had become filled with sand, soil, bones of animals, and detritus of various kinds, which in turn were impregnated by seepage carrying in solution mineral salts and lime. The salts formed incrustations on the walls, here and there new ore deposits, and in general consolidated most of the contents, bones included, into "pay ore."

The kopje that yielded the "Rhodesian skull" was situated approximately northwest to west of the present railroad station, and was about 50 feet high by 250 feet in its longer diameter. This entire elevation has now disappeared and where once was a hill is now a deep hole, in and about which mining operations are still energetically conducted (1925).

Mining by white men is said to have begun at Broken Hill in 1895. Information about these times is hazy. The tradition is that the "broken hill" before mining looked much like the kopje now remaining; that its weathered and irregular surface was, as already said, honey-combed with holes and crevices; but that apparently none of the openings led to the great cave filled with bones, debris, and ore, which in 1921 gave the Rhodesian man.

The main part of the bone cave appears to have been entered by the miners accidentally in the course of their operations; it was partly excavated and found to contain large quantities of more or less mineralized animal bones, with some stone implements. Of this occurrence there are reliable records.

So much for the earilier information about the Broken Hill cave, and nothing further appears to have been said in print about it until the latter part of 1921, when the Bulawayo and other South African papers brought news about the discovery of the "Rhodesian skull."

These earlier reports of which the writer saw copies at the office of the Broken Hill Development Company, are of the usual newspaper style and, beyond signalling the discovery, give little of value. The first more detailed notices of the find appeared on November 8, 9, 10, and 11, 1921, in the London "Times." Shortly after that, on November 17, the first brief scientific report of the find was published in "Nature" by Dr. A. Smith Woodward; and on November 19, a comprehensive and gorgeously illustrated report by W. E. Harris, as well as a description of the skull itself by Sir Arthur Keith, was carried by the "Illustrated London News," with the addition of an ingenious restoration of the race of men represented by the specimen.

Four years (1925) have elapsed since then. In their course at least eight further brief scientific contributions on the subject of the "Rhodesian Man" have seen light. And the skull, with the type and age of the human form to which it belonged, remains still largely a puzzle. Moreover, errors of a serious nature have crept into the accounts of the circumstances of the discovery, and these have already materially affected important conclusions.

What one learns definitely from the early notices of Broken Hill, by one of the chief officials of the mine, is that about 1907 the bone cave was found accidentally in tunneling operations; that it was not known to have any outward opening; that it was nearly filled with large quantities—many tons—of more of less mineralized bones, clay, degris, and ore; and that with the bones were fairly numerous quartz and chert implements, resembling in general those of Bushmen and perhaps other African natives of protohistoric and prehistoric times.

Some of the implements and bones were saved and donated to the Bulawayo Museum. They were later studied by Mennell and Chubb. Still later the bones came to the British Museum and were examined by Andrews. They were diagnosed, with one probable exception, as belonging to recent forms of Rhodesian mammals. There were no human bones in the collection. The archeological objects were noted but the find was not followed up.

Then came the accidental great discovery of 1921. Again there was no scientific expert on the spot and none came after. The details were not noted in writing. The news circulated in the South African papers, but there was no authoritative account; the reports differed among themselves and included inaccuracies.

Five months after the discovery, the skull and a number of human as well as other bones were brought to England by Mr. Macartney, the manager of the mine, and were generously donated by the company to the British Museum (Natural History). No written statement accompanied the donation. But from the oral account of Mr. Macartney, and above all from the good illustrated article by William W. Harris, an official of the mine, in "The Illustrated London News," November 19, 1921, there became established a notion of the details of the find which was gradually adopted by all writers on the skull and which is responsible for serious uncertainties. Above all it became an accepted idea that several human bones brought to England with the skull were found with the cranium and belong to the same individual or the same people, and from the characteristics of these bones deductions were made as to the morphological and even chronological status of the Rhodesian man. Some measurements of the skull and bones were published, also a few observations and thoughts on the endocranial cast which represents the brain; a tacit expectation was reached that a complete report on the case was being prepared by Doctor Smith Woodward; and active interest was gradually transferred to new discoveries.

These were the data and such was the state of affairs when the opportunity to visit the Broken Hill locality came to the writer during the summer of 1925. . . .

As good fortune would have it, before the writer's departure from Broken Hill he was able to locate and interview five of the men concerned from the beginning in the discovery, including Mr. Zwigelaar who actually found the skull; and a sixth one was reached later by a letter. Each of these men was most willing to tell all he knew; but their memories regrettably were no longer clear as to the particulars. However, what was obtained is not without importance.

The most noteworthy information is that of the discoverer of the specimen, Mr. Zwigelaar. He was found to be a serious middle-aged man, not highly educated but of good common sense, and he tried hard to give the main facts of the find as he remembered them. The gist of his statements, repeated and reasserted, follows:

> It was about 10 a.m. one day. We were working back from the incline at its lower part. I had a colored boy (young man) with me and we were "hand picking" in a pocket where there was much lead ore. The digging was not hard, not like stone, more loose. After one of the strokes of the pick some of the stuff fell off, and there was the skull looking at me. It was very strange and with some of the matter adhering to it looked so unlike an ordinary human skull that I thought it was a big gorilla. I took it out carefully, showed it to the officials of the mine and others, and later that day brought it in to Mr. Macartney who in turn sent it to Dr. Wallace. Soon after the find was made Mr. against the place where it came from. Macartney (I believe) took a photograph of me holding the skull.
>
> The skull was at some depth under the pure lead ore and, as far as I can recall, about 10 feet below what seemed to be the floor of the bone cave further away. Where we were then I could see no connection between the material about the skull or the pocket it was in and the bone cave, though it may have been [and later was shown to be] the same old crevice. They were separated by the lead ore and the stuff in which the skull lay. That ore was very rich; it was not hard though necessitating the use of a pick. There was much of it further in and above.
>
> There were no other bones close to or near the skull, and no other objects that aroused attention. But a little later and not far below the skull we came on a sort of a bundle which looked like a flattened roll of hide standing nearly upright; the "hide" was thick and was of ore; it showed no remains of a real hide but looked somewhat like it. Pieces of it were removed and shown about, the rest was smelted. There was nothing within the "roll"—no bones nor any other object.
>
> The skull was surrounded by softer stuff. There was something like bat bones. There were hard and soft spots in the digging. Next day we looked for the lower jaw but nothing was found.

Some time afterwards, but on the same day, we found outside of where the bundle was and to one side of it, about three feet away as near as I can remember, the leg bone of a man. There were no other bones. Later and lower was found a skull said to be that of a lion; but that was not found by me.

The skull was taken first to the manager's office and from there to the doctor's. That's all I know.

Critical Remarks

The Rhodesian find of 1921 is more complex than has been generally appreciated. Due to the absence on the spot of any scientific man exact details of the find have not been ascertained. Of what was learned but little was recorded, and of the rest much has since become confused. The precise circumstances of the discovery are therefore, and must remain, deficient.

The main part of the bone cavern was evidently for a long time a habitat or feasting place of late Africans, bushmen or negro. The larger bones were none of them brought in by animals, but were the remains of the repasts of the black man. A very large majority were broken for the marrow. Similarly broken human bones suggest cannibalism. There were apparently no human burials in the cave. How the strange Rhodesian skull got in is inexplainable.

The skull was found alone in the lowest and most remote part of the cave, some distance beneath considerable accumulations of soft pure lead ore. There was neither lower jaw nor skeleton. One human bone, the tibia, and parts of a lion's skull, it is well established, lay from a few to about ten feet from and at a lower level than the skull.

As to the other human bones deposited at the British Museum with the skull, and those now added, all that may be said is that they proceed from several skeletons of modern size and form; that some of them, at least, probably came from other parts of the cave; and that there is no proof, and but a remote possibility, of any of them belonging to the skull.

The skull itself is positively not the skull of any now known African types of man or their normal variants. Neither is it any known pathological monstrosity, such as gigantism or leontiasis. It is a most remarkable specimen of which the age, provenience, history, and nature are still anthropological puzzles.

Morphologically the skull is frequently associated now with the Neanderthal type of Europe. This may be fundamentally correct, but only to that extent. In its detailed characteristics the specimen in some respects is inferior, in others superior to anything known as yet of the Neanderthal man.

Meanwhile mining operations at Broken Hill are proceeding. They will gradually do away with what may still remain of the former bone crevice; and they will soon, if they have not already, involve the second kopje with its crevices. All this work should be intently watched, for any day it may uncover new evidence of much importance.

Description of the Skull

The skull is monstrous; its frontal and most of the facial parts exceed in primitiveness every other known specimen of early man. The skullcap, on the other hand, from behind the frontal ridges is of a decidedly higher grade equalling in many respects and in some even exceeding those of the more typical Neanderthal crania.

The subject was plainly a very powerful male, probably over 40 years of age. The skull is in no way pathological, though showing some diseased conditions; and it cannot be diagnosed as a reversion. It represents a distinct crude variety of man, which strangely combines many ancient, even pre-Neanderthal conditions with others that are relatively modern. It could represent, conceivably, a very brutish individual development of the upper Neanderthal or the post-Neanderthal period.

The most striking features of the skull are its huge supraorbital ridges. They are not far from twice as stout as in the Neanderthalers. Moreover, they are stouter in their middle third, especially in the region corresponding to that of the supraorbital foramen. They measure near glabella, 21 mm.; in the region of the supraorbital foramen, R. 23, L. 24 mm.; and above the outer third of the orbit, R. 21, L. 20 mm.; maximum transverse diameter, 14 cm. The external biorbital diameter, between the outermost parts of the fronto-malar sutures, is only 13.4 cm., showing the amount by which the tori bulge over these articulations. No such huge welts have ever been seen in any other human specimen, nor even, if their thickness alone is considered, in the anthropoid apes. They constitute a huge exaggeration of this ancient primate masculine character.

Yet these ridges are already human rather than anthropoid in character. They do not form such a transverse promontory above the orbits with but a moderate median depression, as they do in the chimpanzee or the gorilla, but show a very marked dip downward at the glabella, approaching thus somewhat nearer to the condition seen in adult male orangs. Moreover while the surface of this supraorbital promontory faces forward or nearly so in the Rhodesian skull passing from the interorbital process outward, it becomes more and more everted until in its distal portion it looks considerably upward. In this respect it differs from the ridges of both the apes and the Neanderthalers, where such eversion is not present.

The palate is very high, spacious, broad in front and close to U-shaped. The alveolar process is strong, yet not excessively stout; it could be matched in

Fig. 1.   Rhodesian skull, front view.

Fig. 2.   Rhodesian skull, side view. (After Pycraft, 1928.)

Fig. 3.   Rhodesian skull, top view. (After Pycraft, 1928.)

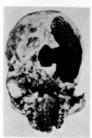

Fig. 4.   Rhodesian skull, basal view. (After Pycraft, 1928.)

strong male modern skulls. The teeth were 16 in number, regularly disposed; but their condition, both morphologically and as to preservation, is most interesting. The teeth are moderately macrodont by our present scale. The rear teeth are moderately, the frontal teeth markedly, worn. The canines were evidently as in modern man—their roots are but little stouter than those of the adjacent pre-molars. The molars show a marked diminution of both M_3 as in more recent crania.

Pathologically, the teeth show a unique condition for primitive skulls, viz., extensive caries. At least nine of the teeth had advanced decay, in half of the cases nothing remaining but a small shell of the tooth. The destruction is such that there is no other explanation. In addition there were some root abscesses and probably some pyorrhea. On both sides externally in the molar region there are irregular hyperostoses which, with some on the lingual side, may be of the ordinary strengthening variety, but may in part also be pathological.

Comment.—The study of the specimen leaves an impression of anamorphism. It is a combination of pre-Neanderthaloid, Neanderthaloid, and recent characters. It is not a Neanderthaler; it represents a different race, a different variety. The specimen does not fit with its surroundings. It does not fit at all with the fine, long, essentially modern-negro-like tibia. It does not fit with any of the other human remains saved from the cave, skeletal or cultural. It does not fit with anything, the negro in particular, found thus far in Africa.

It seems impossible to conceive the specimen as a reversion. Reversions tend as a rule to manifest themselves in individual characters or in small association. The primitive conditions of the Rhodesian skull greatly surpass all this. It seems equally impossible to regard the strain of man represented by the skull as a survival to recent time. There is nothing in anthropoligical knowledge that would support such an assumption. Yet the diminishing third molars, the shape and size of the other teeth, the extensive caries, and other points, speak strongly against hoary antiquity.

The Rhodesian skull is a tantalizing specimen to the student, who is wholly at a loss as to just where it belongs taxonomically or chronologically. It is a comet of man's prehistory.

Tertiary Man in Asia:
the Chou Kou Tien Discovery

Davidson Black*

A rich fossiliferous deposit at Chou Kou Tien, 70 li [about 40 kilometres] to the south-west of Peking, was first discovered in the summer of 1921 by Dr. J. G. Andersson and later surveyed and partially excavated by Dr. O. Zdansky. A preliminary report on the site was published by Dr. Andersson in March 1923, followed in October of that year by a brief description of his survey by Dr. Zdansky. The material recovered from the Chou Kou Tien cave deposit has been prepared in Prof. Wiman's laboratory in Upsala and afterwards studied there by Dr. Zdansky. As a result of this research, Dr. Andersson has now announced that in addition to the mammalian groups already known from this site, there have also been identified representatives of the Cheiroptera, one cynopithecid, and finally two specimens of extraordinary interest, namely, one premolar and one molar tooth of a species which cannot otherwise be named than *Homo? sp.*

Judging from the presence of a true horse and the absence of Hipparion, Dr. Andersson in his preliminary report considered that the Chou Kou Tien fauna was possibly of Upper Pliocene age, an opinion also expressed by Dr. Zdansky. It is possible, however, in the light of recent research, that the horizon represented by this site may be of Lower Pleistocene age. Whether it be of late Tertiary or of early Quaternary age, the outstanding fact remains that, for the first time on the Asiatic continent north of the Himalayas, archaic hominid fossil material has been recovered, accompanied by complete and certain geological data. The actual presence of early man in eastern Asia is therefore now no longer a matter of conjecture.

*1926 (from "Nature," November, vol. 118)

While a complete description of these very important specimens may shortly be expected in *Palaeontologia Sinica*, the following brief notes may be of interest here. One of the teeth recovered is a right upper molar, probably the third, the relatively unworn crown of which presents characters appearing from the photographs to be essentially human. The posterior moiety of the crown is narrow and the roots appear to be fused. The other tooth is probably a lower anterior premolar, of which the crown only is preserved. The latter also is practically unworn, and appears in the photograph to be essentially bicuspid in character, a condition usually to be correlated with a reduction of the upper canine.

The Chou Kou Tien molar tooth, though unworn, would seem to resemble in general features the specimen purchased by Haberer in a Peking native drug shop and afterwards described in 1903 by Schlosser. The latter tooth was a left upper third molar having a very much worn crown, extensively fused lateral roots, and from the nature of its fossilisation considered by Schlosser to be in all probability Tertiary in age. It was provisionally designated as *Homo? Anthropoide?* It is of more than passing interest to recall that Schlosser, in concluding his description of the tooth, pointed out that future investigators might expect to find in China a new fossil anthropoid, Tertiary man or ancient Pleistocene man. The Chou Kou Tien discovery thus constitutes a striking confirmation of that prediction.

It is now evident that at the close of Tertiary or the beginning of Quaternary time man or a very closely related anthropoid actually did exist in eastern Asia. This knowledge is of fundamental importance in the field of prehistoric anthropology; for about this time there also lived in Java, *Pithecanthropus*; at Piltdown, *Eoanthropus*; and, but very shortly after, at Mauer, the man of Heidelberg. All these forms were thus practically contemporaneous with one another and occupied regions equally far removed respectively to the east, to the south-east, and to the west from the central Asiatic plateau which, it has been shown elsewhere, most probably coincides with their common dispersal centre. The Chou Kou Tien discovery therefore furnishes one more link in the already strong chain of evidence supporting the hypothesis of the central Asiatic origin of the Hominidae.

On an Adolescent Skull of *Sinanthropus pekinensis*

Davidson Black*

The adolescent *Sinanthropus* skull specimen upon which the following report is chiefly based, was discovered by Mr. W. C. Pei of the staff of the Cenozoic Research Laboratory of the Geological Survey of China on the second of December 1929 while excavating a sheltered recess of the main fossiliferous deposit (Locality I) at Chou Kou Tien. The circumstances attending this discovery have elsewhere been fully reported. It is of interest to note in this connection that the specimen since it was first carefully extricated from its original resting place by Mr. Pei himself, has at no time been out of the custody of responsible members of the scientific staff of the Geological Survey. Its individual history is thus completely known and since it is further fully documented by extensive and accurate geological and palaeontological evidence no question as to its geological antiquity can arise.

Two short preliminary papers briefly describing this specimen at different stages of its preparation have already been published. In these preliminary notes particular attention was drawn to the fact that the few measurements given in each represented but reasonable approximations which would be subject to subsequent correction. In the present report this has been done, the earlier tentative and the corrected values appearing together in the section below devoted to the subject of measurements. Similarly the preliminary views earlier expressed on the subject of the ontogenetic age and sex of the specimen have here been reviewed and revised.

It was noted in Mr. Pei's report cited above that in the latter part of October 1929 he had discovered a new *Sinanthropus* locus in the main deposit at Chou Kou Tien, the locus being recognized by the recovery *in situ* of a worn adult tooth, and subsequently from the sieves of four additional adult teeth referable to the genus. The site of this find has been designated

*1930 (from "Palaeontologia Sinica," vol. vii)

221

Locus D in the preliminary geological and palaeontological report by P. Teilhard de Chardin and C. C. Young, that in which occurred the adolescent *Sinanthropus* skull found in December being termed Locus E.

From the Locus D site a considerable amount of material embedded in blocks of various size was brought in field wrappings to Peking there to be developed. During the spring of 1930 preparation work on these blocks was begun by technicians in the Cenozoic Laboratory and early in the summer numerous uncrushed skull fragments were recovered from them which, when pieced together by the simple method of matching broken edges, developed into a second *Sinanthropus* skull of definitely adult age. This specimen will be referred to throughout the present report as the *Locus D* skull in contrast to the *Locus E* specimen. The descriptions below lacking a Locus designation are intended to refer only to the latter skull.

Only a very brief preliminary note on the Locus D skull has so far been published. For this reason, though the specimen is not yet restored to the extent that will eventually be possible, advantage is taken of the present report to include in it as much information concerning the morphology and size of the Locus D skull as its present state of preparation permits.

[Here follows a long, detailed report on the external morphology of the skull, which is omitted in this reprinting.]

The primary object of the present report has been devoted to the detailed descriptive morphology, craniometry and craniography of the two *Sinanthropus* specimens. To the latter descriptions there have been added two brief sections in which comparisons have been made between the *Sinanthropus* crania and those of other hominids and anthropoids, the chief results of which are summarized below.

There are general resemblances in outline, though not in size and proportions, to be observed between the *Sinanthropus* contours and those of certain of the Neanderthaloid skulls, over special regions of the median sagittal and glabella horizontal craniograms. However these minor resemblances are such as to modify in no essential the foregoing general statement. In certain other respects (e.g., glenoid contour, cranial length-bicondylar index, horizontal occipital arc outline, relative levels of interporial and nasion gamma planes, etc.) the *Sinanthropus* specimens are suggestively modern in their character, the skull type which they represent being that of a very generalized though quite archaic hominid.

It early became apparent that the skull of *Sinanthropus* resembled that of *Pithecanthropus* much more closely than it did any of the Neanderthaloid, Rhodesian or modern types. For this reason a section of the report has been devoted to a detailed metric and craniographic comparison of the two *Sinanthropus* specimens and the *Pithecanthropus* skull. As a result of this comparison it is clearly evident that the crania of *Sinanthropus* and *Pithecanthropus* resemble one another much more closely than they do any other known hominid type. Further it is equally apparent that they differ from one another in points of size, proportions and detail to a degree amply sufficient to proclaim their generic distinction.

It is a remarkable fact that in all its cranial parts as they are at present known, *Pithecanthropus* shows evidences of an archaic specialization in marked contrast to the evidences of archaic generalization so abundantly preserved in the crania and teeth of *Sinanthropus*. The latter form, aside from its massive supraorbital torus and reduced third molar teeth, presents no highly specialized skull features. On the contrary, the general proportions of its calvaria proper, its dental morphology and that of the tympanic and other individual skull elements, all give evidence that *Sinanthropus* was a generalized and quite progressive type, even the unusual thickness of some of its skull bones being subject to an extraordinary degree of variability. On account of these peculiarities *Sinanthropus* provides a morphological type admirably suited to serve as a starting point for phylogenetic speculation.

Since this report deals with but a part of the rich material still awaiting further preparation, study and description, the present would be an unfortunate time to select for indulgence in such speculation, tempting though the material may be. However the opinion offered as to the probable phylogenetic status of *Sinanthropus* in my preliminary note on the Locus E skull would seem to be amply sustained by further study of that specimen and of the Locus D skull. The latter opinion may therefore here be re-stated as follows:— Its cranial and dental characters are such as to imply that *Sinanthropus* could not have been far removed from the type of hominid from which evolved both the extinct Neanderthaloid and Rhodesian forms and the modern *Homo sapiens*.

Preliminary Notice of
New Man-Like Apes from India

G. Edward Lewis*

As indicated by the title, the present paper is a preliminary one. A more adequate memoir on the Yale North India Expedition primates will be submitted in the future. The material was all collected by the author in 1932.

Systematic Description

Order PRIMATES.
  Suborder ANTHROPOIDEA.
    Series CATARRHINI.
      Family SIMIIDAE (HOMINIDAE?).
        Genus RAMAPITHECUS†, gen. nov.

Generic Characters.—Simiidae (Hominidae?) in which the dentition parallels the hominid type in its broader aspects. The dental arcade of the upper jaw is parabolic, rather than U-shaped as in recent Simiidae, and hence the palate broadens posteriorly. The cheek-teeth of opposite sides of the jaw are more widely separated posteriorly than anteriorly, rather than approximately equidistant from M^2 to P^3. The face is very slightly prognathous, as contrasted with recent Simiidae. There are no diastemata in the dental series. The canine is small, not an antero-posteriorly elongated trenchant tusk but a hominid type with a transverse dimension exceeding the antero-posterior dimension.

Genotype.—*Ramapithecus brevirostris*, sp. nov.

*1934 (from "American Journal of Science," March, Vol. XXVII).
†After *Rama* (prince of Ayodhya, deified protagonist of the Sanskrit epic *Ramayana* of the poet Valmiki) + πιθηκος (ape).

225

Ramapithecus brevirostris, gen. et sp. nov. (Figure 1, parts 1a and 1b)

Holotype.—The right maxilla and premaxilla with M^2, M^1, P^4, P^3, the alveolus of the canine, the root of I^2, and the alveolus of I^1 (Y.P.M. No. 13799).

Locality.—¼ mile east of Chakrana, 4 miles east of Hari Talyangar village in northwestern Bilaspur Kehloor State, Simla Hills; Yale North India Expedition paleontological locality number 39, *Survey of India Map* No. 53 A/NE, C-6.

Horizon.—Pliocene. Either latest *Middle Siwalik* or basal *Upper Siwalik*.

As in the Hominidae, there are no diastemata. The dental arch is very much compressed. The nearest approach to a diastema occurs between the alveoli of the canine and second incisor, which are separated by a scant 2 mm.—no more than in many human specimens, and insufficient to produce a diastema between the crowns. The palate is relatively high. The premolars are strikingly bicuspid types with a marked antero-posterior sulcus, and represent a stage considerably advanced beyond that of the maxilla referred by Pilgrim to *Dryopithecus punjabicus.* The molars are also of a more human type.

Hopwood has pointed out the differences and similarities between the upper dentition of *Proconsul* and *Dryopithecus.* The African genus has little in common with *Ramapithecus,* although the former shows several points of approach to *D. rhenanus. Proconsul* has cheek teeth of relatively short antero-posterior diameter which in this respect parallel *Ramapithecus,* but the very strong cingula are reminiscent of *D. rhenanus,* which represents a decidedly primitive stage of superior molar development as compared to the other dryopithecoids.

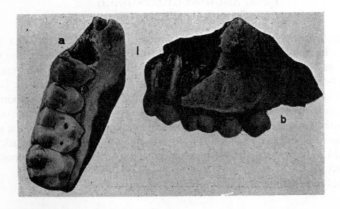

Fig. 1. *Ramapithecus brevirostris,* gen. et sp. nov. Holotype Y.P.M. No. 13799. (a) Occlusal aspect of right maxilla and premaxilla. (b) Buccal aspect of right maxilla and premaxilla. Natural size.

D. germanicus is apparently close to *D. punjabicus*, but not to *Ramapithecus*. By far the nearest approach to *Ramapithecus* is the superior molar—which I believe to be correctly designated by the author as the second—assigned by Glaessner to *D. darwini*. From *Sivapithecus*, *Ramapithecus* is distinguished by the more crowded dentition, and by the more hominid and less ape-like canine and incisors.

The high breadth indices, low and rounded cusps, and simple structure of the molar crowns; the extremely bicuspid premolars, the man-like canine and incisors; and the divergent dental arcade and very slight prognathism are characteristic of *Ramapithecus*.

Genus *Bramapithecus*, gen. nov.

Generic Characters.—Simiidae in which there has been an extreme reduction in the length of the lower molars as related to the width. Characterized by the fact that the molars of the mandible have been very much compressed antero-posteriorly, have rather high crowns, and a peculiar relief made up of the usual furrows complicated by numerous coarse grooves.

Genotype.—*Bramapithecus thorpei*, sp. nov.

Bramapithecus thorpei, gen. et sp. nov.

Holotype.—The left ramus bearing M_3, M_2, the alveolus and roots of M_1, and a portion of the alveolus and root of P_4 (Y.P.M. No. 13814).

Locality.—1.5 miles SE of Hasnot, 3 furlongs NW of Gulial, on the Andar Kas; District Jhelum, Tahsil Jhelum, in the Punjab; Yale North India Expedition paleontological locality number 81, *Survey of India Map No.* 43 H/5, B-3.

Horizon.—Upper *Chinji, Lower Siwalik*.

Bramapithecus exhibits several primitive features. On the other hand, the sculpture of the crowns is highly suggestive of many human molars. The deep folds, persistent in spite of severe wear, are notable features. The author is not prepared to embark on an extended study of the relationships of *Bramapithecus* at this time, but believes that the genus has affinities with *Dryopithecus*, and was probably derived from a common stock. It may very well lie near to the stem which led to the Hominidae proper.

The Palaeanthropi in Italy:
The Fossil Men of Saccopastore and Circeo

Sergio Sergi*

The earliest traces of man in Italy are denoted by the presence of Abbevillian and Acheulian handaxes in Lower Pleistocene formations. The discoveries of an Abbevillian handaxe by G. A. Blanc on the Via Flaminia, near the Ponte Milvio, and of a flake of Clactonian technique by A. C. Blanc also close to the Via Flaminia, at one of the gates of Rome itself, have shown that Latium was inhabited during the most ancient phases of the Quaternary. We are ignorant of the physical features of the men of that time, since we possess none of their skeletal remains. They may have been the Protanthropi of Italy, but we are unable to say whether or not they were similar to the other European Protanthropi, e.g. Heidelberg, of whom we still lack precise and detailed knowledge.

The Mousterian industry had a wide distribution over the Italian peninsula in the Middle Pleistocene. Just a century ago, in 1846, the occurrence of Mousterian flint implements accompanying the remains of large extinct mammals in alluvial deposits along the Tiber was recorded by Ceselli of Rome. His claims were rejected, however, until the finds at Saccopastore indicated that the Palaeanthropi[1] of Latium were the makers of Mousterian implements. In 1929 a cranium (Saccopastore I) was excavated in a gravel pit near the Ponte Nomentano, three kilometres from the Porta Pia. In 1935 the fragments of a second skull (Saccopastore II) were brought to light at the

*1948 (from "MAN, A Monthly Record of Anthropological Science," June, Vol xlviii)

[1]By the term 'Palaeanthropi' I mean the completely extinct Old World forms that constituted a polymorphous stage of humanity dominant in the Middle Pleistocene, viz. the Neanderthalians of Europe and the men of Rhodesia, Palestine and Ngandong. By 'Protanthropi' are designated the extinct fossil hominids of the Lower Pleistocene and by 'Phaneranthropi' (from φανερός, manifest, visible) all representatives of Homo sapiens, past and present.

same place by A. C. Blanc and the Abbé Breuil. In 1939 A. C. Blanc discovered a cranium (Circeo I) in a cave on Monte Circeo,[2] and later a mandible belonging to another individual (Circeo II) was found there.

Saccopastore I was found with bones of *Hippopotamus major, Rhinoceros mercki, Elephas antiquus* and other mammals, some of which bore signs of intentional fracture. The site is characterized by gravel and sand of fluvio-lacustrine origin, rich in volcanic elements and dating from the period when the lower Tiber valley was in process of assuming its present appearance. Thus stratigraphically the specimen may be assigned to the Riss-Würm interglacial. Apart from the absence of the lower jaw, the skull (see Figure 1, *a*) was recovered in a relatively complete state, though the orbital margins and the supraorbital region are damaged and the zygomatic arches destroyed. Judging from the degree of sutural ossification and the dentition, I assign it to a subject aged about thirty and of the female sex.

The cranial capacity is small, certainly less than 1200 c.c., and the form mesocephalic, bordering on the limit of brachycephaly. The basi-bregmatic height (109 mm.) is one of the lowest so far known. The frontal torus is very prominent at the sides but appears to have been little marked towards the centre. There is a cluster of supernumerary ossicles at the lambda. The depression on the internal surface corresponding to the third frontal convolution is greatly accentuated on the left-hand side, which suggests a particular development of the cerebral region associated with articulate speech. The position and slope of the foramen magnum are such that the head must have been held erect as it is in present-day man. As the result of his faulty reconstruction of the base of the La Chapelle skull, Boule has affirmed that the Neanderthalians had their heads slightly thrust forward. In respect of the foramen magnum, however, Saccopastore I bears a close resemblance to the La Ferrassie and Gibraltar specimens, which I have been able to study, thanks to the kindness of the late Professor Boule and Sir Arthur Keith, respectively. The face is large and high and the orbits are of considerable size. The nasal aperture is wide and low, the maxillae project in the form of a wedge and the extensive alveolar arcade is shaped like a horseshoe. Of the Neanderthalian skulls, that from Gibraltar, found in 1848, most nearly approaches Saccopastore I in its dimensions and general and special morphology.

Saccopastore II (see Figures 2 and 3) was collected in fragments embedded in rock. As reconstructed by me, it comprises part of the left and almost all the right half of the upper facial skeleton, together with the zygomatic arch, the supraorbital torus, the temporal and a portion of the sphenoid on the

---

[2]The legendary meeting place of Ulysses and the enchantress Circe, at the foot of which stands the village of San Felice Circeo, about 100 km. south of Rome.—Ed.

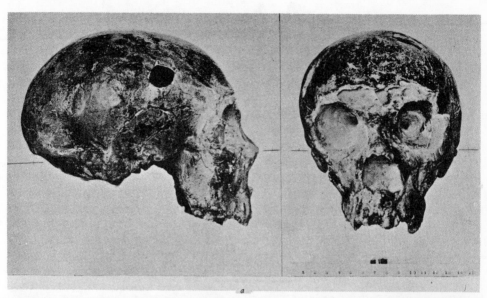

a

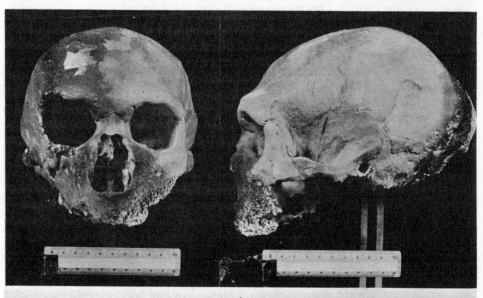

b

Fig. 1. (*a*) The Saccopastore I skull; (*b*) the Circeo I skull. Photographs by Sergio Sergi.

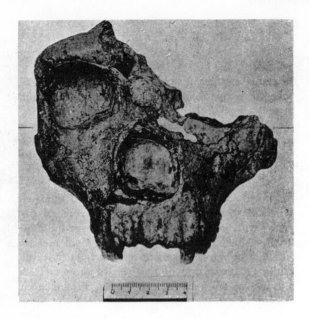

Fig. 2.   The Saccopastore II skull (frontal view).

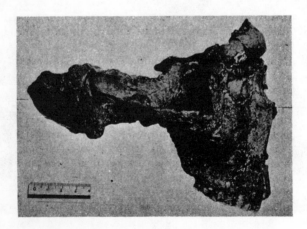

Fig. 3.   The Saccopastore II skull (profile).

more complete side. From a comparison with Saccopastore I, we can accept it as belonging to an adult male. It is markedly narrower than Circeo in the lower temporo-occipital region, and at this level the transverse diameters are close to those of Saccopastore I and Gibraltar. The capacity may be taken as not more than 1300 c.c. In the totality of its characters Saccopastore II bears a strong resemblance to Saccopastore I. As regards the flexion of the base, the form of the alveolar arch, the pronounced height of the palatine vault and the orbital index, the two specimens are extremely similar. The face of Saccopastore II is leptoprosopic and orthognathous and the nasal breadth slightly larger than that of Saccopastore I.

In the spring of 1936, on the initiative of the Italian Institute of Human Palaeontology and with the co-operation of the Institute of Anthropology of the University of Rome, an excavation was started in the Saccopastore gravel pit. At the level where the second skull was found there occurred flint and jasper implements of typical Mousterian technique, together with fossil fauna and flora indicating a terminal phase of the last interglacial. At that remote period the men of Saccopastore were sheltering in caves at the foot of the mountains facing the valley of the Tiber, where a hundred thousand years later Rome was to rise.

The first Circeo specimen (Figure 1, b) was discovered in a cave whose entrance had been closed by a landslip in Mousterian times. The cave floor was in the same state as it had been when the skull was deposited there. The skull itself lay on stones distributed in a circle with stag and horse bones. Under it were the metacarpals of a deer and an ox, intentionally fractured. Among the other bones, in which those of bovids, equids, and cervids predominated, were the remains of elephant, leopard, lion and hyena. A. C. Blanc is of the opinion that the skull belongs to the Tyrrhenian regression of the last glacial period, when the warm fauna still survived and man had the particular Mousterian industry which from its local characteristics this author has called 'Pontinian.' The Pontinian differs from the Levalloiso-Mousterian of Western Europe as well as from the so-called Alpine Mousterian, but resembles the Mousterian of the Castillo cave and is perhaps represented at Devil's Tower, Gibraltar. Applying Milankovitch's oscillation curve of solar radiations, A. C. Blanc considers that Circeo man lived about seventy thousand years ago. The men of Saccopastore, who belong to the Pleistocene low terrace of the Anio River, appear to have existed at a time when the cave in which the Circeo skull was found was still invaded by the sea.

Circeo I consists of an almost complete cranium with the base and the right temporo-orbital region mutilated. The base has a large trapeze-shaped aperture, which involves the nuchal and the condylar portions of the occipital, but only slightly the anterior margin of the foramen magnum, and seems to have been made artificially at the time of death in order to extract the brain. A similar opening in the right temporo-orbital region which exposes the cranial cavity appears to have been caused by a sharp instrument. The state of ossification indicates an age between forty and fifty years. Supernumerary ossicles occur in all the fontanelle regions. The general form resembles other typical Neanderthalian skulls, especially La Chapelle, as they are both male and of nearly the same age. The differences are due to posthumous deformation or defects of reconstruction of the La Chapelle skull, which has been elongated excessively at the base with some advancement of the face, producing a degree of prognathism which does not appear in any of the other Neanderthalian skulls. The position of the foramen magnum of the Circeo skull, close to that of Saccopastore I and rather more forward than that of La Chapelle, confirms that the reconstruction of the latter was defective and also the fact that Neanderthal man had an erect posture like modern man.

The frontal curve of the Circeo skull is almost exactly similar to that of the Neanderthal calotte. The cranial capacity is about 1550 c.c., and consequently the skull falls into the group of the most typical Neanderthalian skulls: La Chapelle, Neanderthal, La Ferrassie and the two from Spy. The skull is the lowest of the capacious Neanderthalian skulls. The face is very large, orthognathous, extremely narrow in relation to the height and narrower than in La Chapelle; the inclination of the plane of the large, low orbit to the sagittal plane is 70 degrees, as in La Chapelle, where the orbits are inclined to each other at 140 degrees. The nose is the highest and widest among known Neanderthalian skulls; the nasal index is notably chamaerrhine, as in La Chapelle. The alveolar arch also has the U-form of the La Chapelle specimen.

The mandible discovered in the Circeo cave (Circeo II) is incomplete. The left ramus is totally destroyed and the right partially. It has Neanderthalian characteristics, but does not belong to the Circeo I cranium. The alveolar region is partially destroyed, with vestiges of the alveolus still present; the last right molar remains in place; the region of the chin is 'neutral' (mesogeneiotic).

The Saccopastore and Circeo skulls thus have some characters in common with the European Palaeanthropi of the Middle Pleistocene, which are generally called Neanderthalians. The distinctions of the Neanderthalian type are based on a complex of morphological characters of the skeleton and, more particularly, of the skull. With larger or narrower attribution of the finds to the group, agreement on such characters is not absolute, some including in it the Rhodesian cranium and the Asiatic ones of Ngandong (Java) and Palestine, others excluding even some of the European forms of the same geological period. Reasons for such differences are found either in theoretical presuppositions or in the limits of variation of the type. It is now possible to affirm that the Palaeanthropi of the European (Neanderthalian) series are distinct morphologically from the Palaeanthropi of Asia and Africa. The separation of the Rhodesian skull from the Neanderthalians is necessary at first sight, even without the aid of metrical characters, on account of its cerebral and facial morphology, on which I shall·not dwell. The cerebral cavity, in the Rhodesian, expands in the direction of the vault, as opposed to the Neanderthalians, in whose skulls the cavity enlarges in the occipital region; so that the two types, Rhodesian and Neanderthalian, should be considered quite different in the direction of their evolution. The whole occipital sector is characteristically very much more expanded in the La Chapelle, Circeo and Saccopastore skulls. Occipital expansion and platy-cephaly are common to all Neanderthalian skulls, in which the point of maximum posterior extension falls somewhat above the inion, while in the Rhodesian the opisthocranion is coincident with the occipital protuberance as in the anthropomorphous ape and *Sinanthropus*, so that the occipital region does not expand above the inion. Moreover, while the whole occipital sector in the Rhodesian skull is limited in height, the contrary happens in the Neanderthalian skull, whose vault is more expanded towards the fronto-parietal region. The Neanderthalian parietal bones have a special form of the curve from bregma to asterion; the curve is different in the Rhodesian skull.

The morphological evolution of the human skull, which is already realized in *Sinanthropus* (the Asiatic Protanthropus), develops among the higher Hominidae (namely the Palaeanthropi) in various directions which show their decisive expression in different architectural types. The Palaeanthropi of Ngandong, too, are distinguished from the Neanderthalian type by different skull architecture. They resemble the Rhodesian skull in the inclination of the nuchal plane and the position of the opisthocranion, but are also dissimilar from it, particularly in the morphology, inclination and lowness of the frontal bone. The various forms of European, Asiatic and African Palaeanthropi, which have so many likenesses in the convergence of some characters, are indeed distinct, because their architecture develops on different planes. Their simultaneous occurrence in very different places makes it possible that they individually represent a stage of an independent evolution of the Middle Pleistocene Hominidae, during which the brain increases in volume and power.

These various Palaeanthropi are therefore parallel in evolution and constitute a polymorphous stage of mankind. The Palestinian Palaeanthropi are separate from all the others in the height of the skull, the form of the face and the presence of a chin, so that they have in general a phaneranthropic appearance, some calling to mind Neanderthalian and others hinting at

Australian or Negroid characters. But the European Palaeanthropi, more commonly called Neanderthalians, are not all alike. Saccopastore I resembles Gibraltar, but differs from the Neanderthalians, including Circeo, so that I regard the skulls of Saccopastore and Gibraltar as Mediterranean variants of the group.

The cranial capacity of Circeo is large and that of the Saccopastore skulls small. The basi-bregmatic height is smallest in Saccopastore I (109 mm.), while in Circeo it is 123 mm. Both Saccopastore skulls have the clivus set more upright and the sphenoidal plane bent more forward. In Saccopastore I the frontal angle is larger; the outline of the occipital region, in the median plane, is rounded, and it does not show the bulge observed in Circeo and La Chapelle. In Saccopastore I the fundamental facial triangle (nasion-basion-prosthion) is notable for the size and relative position of its sides; with the orthognathism of the lateral profile of the face is associated a notably high gnathic index, owing to the great predominance of the basion-prosthion length over the basion-nasion length, and an exceptional inclination of such diameters to the orbito-auricular plane. The maxillary segments of the horizontal craniograms of Saccopastore are not so rectilinear as are those of La Chapelle and Circeo, but they are rather concave forward and converge with a wider angle, i.e. they present a greater 'frontalization' with signs of backward folding. The anterior surface of the maxillary bone has a tendency to curve following the transverse planes, and to fold in oblique sagittal sections, while La Chapelle and Circeo display some flatness in the horizontal and frontal profiles. The nasal aperture of Saccopastore I is wide and low. The *dorsum nasi* of Circeo is quite different from that of Saccopastore. The alveolar region is particularly characteristic in the incisor-canine section, which is very high and lightly arched. The alveolar ridges of the canine teeth of Saccopastore I are strongly developed, the canines deviating downwards from their alignment with the alveolar incisor plane; the great bicanine distance relative to the bimolar distance, associated with sphenoprosopy, constitutes a characteristic theriomorphism of the whole gnathic-facial region, in contrast to the reduction of the strength of the set of teeth, which cannot be traced in any other human type. In Saccopastore the alveolar arch has a horseshoe form, while La Chapelle and Circeo have a U-shape.

Saccopastore I and II possess some fundamental characteristics in common; in the first place, the particular flexion of the base, which in both is a strong folding-forward of the sphenoidal plane; also similar in both is the morphology of the tympanic bone and the articulation of the temporo-mandibular region. The features of the face are of the same morphological order for the naso-maxillary and alveolar regions, e.g. the naso-maxillary curves at the height of the various planes; in the horizontal profile the folding of the frontal process of the maxillary bone at various levels; the folding of the anterior face of the central part of the maxilla; the form of the nasal bones; the form of the alveolar arch; the relative position of the canine and molar teeth, etc. But there are also differences between Saccopastore I and Saccopastore II that, in part, are of small significance, because some of them are due to sex, the first skull being female, the second male; others could be considered dissimilar or of a higher order or with a positive significance. Among the sexual differences are the general size of the face, the cranial capacity (conjectured for Saccopastore II) and the development of the frontal torus. Among the individual differences are the various degrees of the folding of the anterior surface of the maxilla, of the straight elevation of the anterior alveolar region and of the alignment of the canine-incisor teeth. There are also differences whose value is disputable, e.g. the different degree of inclination of the orbits and the value of the gnathic index, which in Saccopastore I is very high (112.3), while in II it is 103.4. This is due in the former to the great size of the basion-prosthion relative to the basion-nasion tract, while the enormous face assumes the same degree of orthognathism in relation to the orbito-auricular plane. If we admit another gnathic index based on the relation between the projected porion-nasion-porion-prosthion distances, the difference of the value of this new index is small: Saccopastore I, 119; Saccopastore II, 116. This proves that the great difference in the gnathic index (basion-nasion-basion-prosthion) in both depends on the different height of the basion, namely, the distances of the basion from the porion.

A New Fossil Anthropoid Skull
from South Africa

Robert Broom*

It is nearly twelve years ago since Prof. R. A. Dart startled the world by the announcement of the discovery of a new type of fossil anthropoid found in a limestone cave at Taungs in Bechuanaland, South Africa. The specimen consists of most of the brain cast and the practically perfect face of a very young ape. The functional teeth are all of the milk set, though the first upper and lower molars have cut the gum but do not yet meet. Though the ape was only very young, Dart estimated the cranial capacity at more than 500 c.c., and considered that in an adult it might exceed 700 c.c. He believed that this little fossil ape is not very closely allied to either the chimpanzee or the gorilla, and that it is probably nearer to the ape from which man has been descended and thus to be practically the long sought for missing link.

Many European and American men of science considered that Dart had made a mistake, and that if he had had a series of young chimpanzee skulls for comparison he would have recognized that the Taungs ape is only a variety of chimpanzee. When after some years the lower jaw was detached from the upper and the crowns of the teeth could be examined fully, it was found that the milk teeth are not in the least like those of either the chimpanzee or gorilla, and that they agree entirely with those of man, though larger. In the gorilla and chimpanzee the first upper milk molars have each two cusps: in man and in *Australopithecus* there are three well-marked cusps in each. In the first lower milk molar of the gorilla there is only one large cusp; in the chimpanzee there is one large cusp and a second rudimentary cusp. In man and in *Australopithecus* there are four well-developed cusps.

*1936 (from "Nature," September)

239

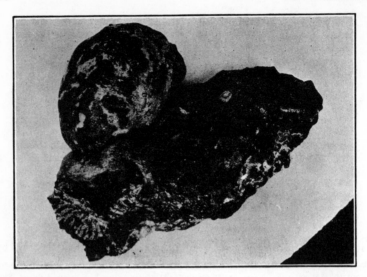

Fig. 1.   Half side view of the brain cast resting on the imperfect base. The
brow ridges are shown with parts of the frontal sinuses exposed. Part of
the left cheek bone is also shown. About 1/3 natural size. Photograph by
Mr. Herbert Lang.

I have constantly maintained since I first examined the skull in 1925
that Dart was essentially right in holding *Australopithecus* is not closely
allied to either the gorilla or chimpanzee, and is on or near the line by
which man has arisen.

I do not know what is at present the opinion in Europe as to where
Australopithecus ought to be placed. Gregory of New York regards it as
fairly near to the origin of the human line; and Romer of Harvard says it
is "clearly not a chimpanzee or a gorilla". But the most important thing
to do seemed to be to get an adult skull. For the last three months, I have
been busy working on the bone breccia of the limestone caves of the
Transvaal largely in the hope of getting either a new 'missing link' or a
type of primitive man. I have so far found no trace of man, though I have
discovered more than a dozen new species of fossil mammals, a number of
which belong to new genera.

Two weeks ago [Dr. Broom's covering letter is dated August 8.—Ed.] ,
when visiting the caves at Sterkfontein near Krugersdorp, Mr. G. W.
Barlow, the very understanding manager of the lime works there and on
whom I had impressed the importance of keeping his eyes open for a
Taungs ape, handed me the brain cast of what appeared to be a large
anthropoid (Figure 1). It had been blasted out of the side of the cave a

Fig. 2. Side view of right upper maxilla with the 2nd premolar and the 1st and 2nd molars. Parts of the roots of the canine and 1st premolar are shown. Slightly enlarged. Photograph by Mr. Herbert Lang.

couple of days before. A search for some hours failed to find any other part of the skull, but we found the cast of the top of the head in the cave wall. A more extensive search on the following day with a large party of workers resulted in the discovery of most of the base of the skull, with the upper part of the face (Figure 2). In the same matrix was found the detached right maxilla with three teeth, and the third upper molar was also found, though detached. The lower part of the face had been removed before fossilization; and so far no mandible or lower teeth have been found, though parts may yet be discovered in a mass of crushed and broken bones near the side of the head. As the bones are very friable, no attempt has as yet been made to remove them from the much harder matrix.

Much of the cranial vault has been destroyed by the blast, but a large part of each parietal is preserved and a considerable part of the occiput. Unfortunately, the back of the brain cast is missing, and though the base of the skull is complete to the back of the foramen magnum, the contacts of the occipital fragment are lost.

The brain cast is perfect in its anterior two thirds. When complete it probably measured in length about 120 mm. and in breadth about 90 mm.; and the brain capacity was probably about 600 c.c. The skull probably measured from the glabella to the occiput about 145 mm., and the greatest parietal width was probably about 96 mm.

The brow ridges are moderately developed and there are fairly large frontal sinuses. The auditory meatus is 73 mm. behind the brow. It will be possible to make out much of the detailed structure of the base of the skull, but as yet no attempt has been made to clean it out as the bone is very friable and the investigation cannot be done in a hurry.

In the maxilla there are three well preserved teeth, the 2nd premolar and the 1st and 2nd molars (Figure 3). The canine and 1st premolar are lost but the sockets are preserved. The canine has been relatively small. At its base it probably measured about 10 mm. by 8 mm. The 2nd premolar is somewhat worn. Its crown measured 11 mm. by 9 mm. Its pattern is well seen in Figure 3.

The 1st molar is moderately large. Antero-posteriorly it measures 12 mm. and transversely 13 mm. It is of the typical Dryopithecid pattern—four well-developed cusps with a little posterior ridge and a well-marked posterior fovea. The tooth agrees fairly closely with that of the first molar of *Dryopithecus rhenanus*. The 2nd molar is exceptionally large. It measures 14.5 mm. in antero-posterior length and is 16 mm. across. It has four large cusps with a well-marked posterior fovea. The 3rd molar has been detached from the bone but it is preserved in perfect condition and unworn. It has three well-developed cusps, but the hypocone is relatively small owing to the invasion of the large fovea. The tooth measures antero-posteriorly 13.7 mm. and transversely 15.5 mm. The crown in this unworn condition is extremely wrinkled.

The whole premolar and molar series measures 59 mm.

This newly-found primate probably agrees fairly closely with the Taungs ape, but the only parts that we can compare are the brain casts and the 1st upper molars. The brain cast of the new form is considerably wider, especially in the frontal region, and the molar teeth differ in a number of important details. Further, the associated animals found at Taungs are all different from those found at Sterkfontein. I think the Taungs deposit will probably prove to be Lower or Middle Pleistocene, while the Sterkfontein deposit is most probably Upper Pleistocene. I therefore think it advisable to place the new form in a distinct species, though provisionally it may be put in the same genus as the Taungs ape.

This discovery shows that we had in South Africa during Pleistocene times large non-forest living anthropoids—not very closely allied to either the chimpanzee or the gorilla but showing distinct relationships to the Miocene and especially to the Pliocene species of *Dryopithecus*. They also show a number of typical human characters not met with in any of the living anthropoids.

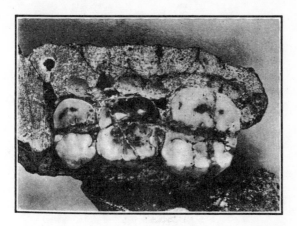

Fig. 3. Crowns of right upper 2nd premolar and 1st and 2nd molars. X about ¾. Photograph by Mr. Herbert Lang.

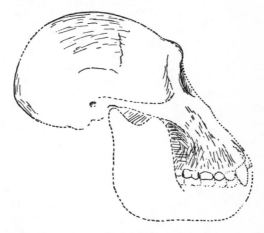

Fig. 4. Attempted restoration of skull of *Australopithecus transvaalensis* Broom. 1/3 natural size. Sufficient of the cranium is preserved to show its shape with certainty. Most of the right maxilla is preserved, but it is not in contact with the upper part of the skull, and there is thus a little doubt as to the relations.

The Pleistocene Anthropoïd Apes
of South Africa

Robert Broom*

Dart's discovery in 1924 of the fossil ape of Taungs, which he named *Australopithecus africanus*, opened a new chapter in the history of the origin of man. The type skull, which unfortunately is the only one known from that locality, is that of a five-year-old child, and though there seems little doubt that Dart was right in regarding it as an ape much nearer to man than either the chimpanzee or the gorilla, some European men of science still seem to believe that it is a variety of chimpanzee or a dwarf gorilla, in spite of the fact that the milk teeth are entirely different in structure from those of the living anthropoids, and closely similar to those of man.

In 1936 I discovered, at Sterkfontein, much of an adult skull which I described as *Australopithecus transvaalensis*. It is clearly allied to the Taungs ape, but there are few points in which a comparison can be made between the two, and I provisionally placed it in the same genus. In the last two years almost continuous exploration has been going on at Sterkfontein, and many interesting further remains have been found, notices of some of which have been published in "Nature."

Until this year, nothing was known of the lower jaw except a beautifully preserved 3rd molar. We still do not know much of the mandible, but we now have a well-preserved 2nd premolar, much of what I regard as a female canine, and the incisor portion of the jaw of a young male, corresponding to a human boy of nine years, with the perfectly preserved crown of an unworn canine. This canine is unlike that of any ape at present known, but there seems little doubt that it is rightly identified as that of the male *A. transvaalensis*, from the resemblance it bears in a number of respects to the canine, which I regard as the lower canine of the female. Though little more than the incisor portion

*1938 (from "Nature," August)

of the symphysis is preserved, it shows the sockets of the incisors, and reveals the interesting fact that the lateral incisors are considerably larger than the central ones. The shape of the symphysis is so different from that of the Taungs ape that it seems advisable to place *A. transvaalensis* in a distinct genus, for which the name *Plesianthropus* is proposed.

In June of this year a most important new discovery was made. A schoolboy, Gert Terblanche, found in an outcrop of bone breccia near the top of a hill, a couple of miles from the Sterkfontein caves, much of the skull and lower jaw of a new type of anthropoid. Not realizing the value of the find, he damaged the specimen considerably in hammering it out of the rock. The palate with one molar tooth he gave to Mr. Barlow at Sterkfontein, from whom I obtained it. Recognizing that some of the teeth had recently been broken off, and that there must be other parts of the skull where the palate was found, I had to hunt up the schoolboy. I went to his home two miles off and found that he was at school another two miles away, and his mother told me that he had four beautiful teeth with him. I naturally went to the school, and found the boy with four of what are perhaps the most valuable teeth in the world in his trouser pocket. He told me that there were more bits of the skull on the hillside. After school he took me to the place and I gathered every scrap I could find; and when these were later examined and cleaned and joined up, I found I had not only the nearly perfect palate with most of the teeth, but also practically the whole of the left side of the lower half of the skull and the nearly complete right lower jaw. The only missing parts of importance are the halves of two molars, the crown of the left 1st upper premolar and the crown of the right lower canine. Those I still hope to discover. As, however, we have impressions in the matrix of some of the missing teeth and parts, we know nearly the complete dentition.

The skull is that of a large ape, larger than most male chimpanzees and nearly as large as most female gorillas; but it differs very greatly from both the living African anthropoids. Much of the palate is preserved in perfect condition. The whole of the left side of the sphenoid bone is also preserved; while the zygomatic arch is nearly complete. The glenoid cavity and the tympanic bone are in perfect preservation, and much of the mastoid region, and part of the occiput with a portion of the left condyle.

The glenoid cavity and the relations to the tympanic bone are of exceptional interest. In the gorilla, the chimpanzee, the orang and the gibbon, the outer part of the tympanic is situated behind the posterior glenoid process. In man, the tympanic is situated mainly below the glenoid process, and even at its outer part it forms the posterior nonarticular part of the glenoid cavity. In the new fossil ape, the condition of the glenoid and tympanic is almost exactly as in man, though the parts are very much larger.

Fig. 1. Palatal view of skull of *Paranthropus robustus* Broom, about ½ natural size. The teeth of the left side have been weathered off, but are replaced in what must have been nearly their original position. Part of the socket of left m^3 is preserved.

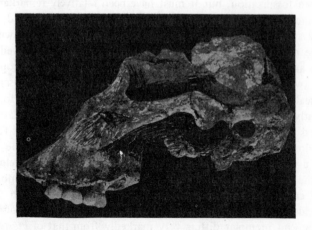

Fig. 2. Side view of skull of *Paranthropus robustus* Broom. About ½ natural size.

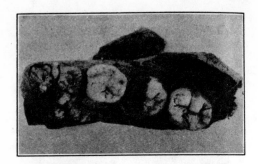

Fig. 3. Occlusal view of molars, with roots of premolars, of right mandible of *Paranthropus robustus* Broom.

The occipital condyle is in practically the same plane as the external auditory meatus and thus farther forward than in the gorilla and the chimpanzee; which appears to indicate that the ape walked somewhat more erect than the living anthropoids.

From the portion of the brain case preserved, I estimate the volume of the brain to have been about 600 c.c. The face is remarkably flat and much shorter than in the gorilla. A curious bony ridge runs down from the inner border of the large infraorbital foramen.

The molar teeth, as will be seen from the illustrations, differ considerably in shape from those in *Plesianthropus transvaalensis* and the 2nd premolar is about half as large again as in Sterkfontein ape. The upper canine had been lost before fossilization, but it must have been relatively remarkably small, and the incisors, of which we have much of the sockets preserved, were also relatively small. The palate is relatively short and broad, and owing to the small size of the incisors and canines the anterior part is narrowed, and the teeth are arranged more as in man than in any of the living anthropoids. The anterior two-thirds of the right mandible are satisfactorily preserved. The symphyseal region has been broken off behind the canine before fossilization and slightly displaced. The incisors which are lost have been relatively very small, and the lateral ones are scarcely larger than the central. The canine crown is lost, but the impression of its outer side is preserved in the matrix. It is quite a small tooth, and remarkably human in shape. It is clearly very unlike the canine of *Plesianthropus transvaalensis*. The premolars have rounded crowns without any high well-developed cusps as in the living anthropoids, and are thus fairly similar to those of man, but about twice as large. The 2nd premolar differs very markedly from that of *Plesianthropus transvaalensis*, and we may thus confidently place the new skull in a new genus and species.

The deposit in which the skull was found is the floor of an old cave the walls of which have probably been weathered away thousands of years ago. We may therefore suspect that the deposit is very much older than that in the Sterkfontein caves, and this is confirmed by the associated fauna. It contains a jackal, a baboon, a horse and a hyrax, which are all of different species from those at Sterkfontein, and are most probably all older. The skull may be referred to as the Kromdraai (pronounced 'Kromdry') skull, and may be given the name *Paranthropus robustus*.

It seems probable that the Sterkfontein skull is of Upper Pleistocene age, the Kromdraai skull of Middle Pleistocene and the Taungs skull probably of Lower Pleistocene; though of course more work will have to be done before the geological ages of any of these skulls can be determined with more than probability.

Clearly, during the Pleistocene there lived in South Africa a number of large-brained anthropoids which resemble man in the shape of their premolars and in having relatively small canines, and in having the glenoid region, in at least some forms, remarkably human in structure. These Pleistocene apes are probably the modified descendants of forms that may have been widely distributed over Africa in Pliocene times, and it is probably from one of the Pliocene members of the group that man arose.

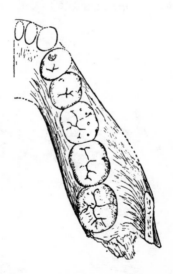

Fig. 4. Occlusal view of right mandible of *Paranthropus robustus* Broom. ¾ natural size. The portion of the jaw with canine and incisor sockets was detached and is placed in what was probably its actual relationship.

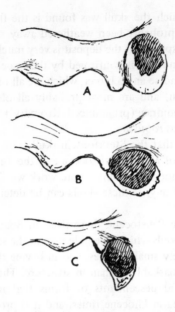

Fig. 5. The glenoid and the external auditory meatus in (A) a large male
gorilla; (B) *Paranthropus robustus*; and (C) a large Korana male. ¾ natural
size.

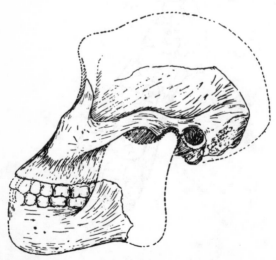

Fig. 6. Side view of skull of *Paranthropus robustus* Broom. 3/8 natural size.
Restored. The parts in line are known.

Quite certainly the conditions in Pleistocene times in South Africa were not unlike those of to-day. The apes lived on the plains and among the rocky krantzes. At Taungs most probably the apes lived in the caves. The associated animal remains seem to be the kitchen midden of *Australopithecus*.

At Sterkfontein and Kromdraai the larger bones in the caves seem all to have been introduced by carnivorous animals and the small bones by owls. Nearly every bone of the larger animals has been broken in pieces. No perfect limb bone has been found, and most teeth are detached from the jaws and many of the teeth have also been broken before fossilization.

We have now a fairly good knowledge of the faunas associated with the apes. We know about a dozen fossil mammals from the Taungs caves, all extinct; about thirty mammals from Sterkfontein, nearly all extinct; and we know about a dozen from Kromdraai, all extinct except one—the living porcupine.

Preliminary Note on a New Fossil
Human Skull from Swanscombe, Kent

Alvan T. Marston*

In June 1935, a fossilized human occipital bone was found *in situ* at a depth of 24 ft. below the surface, in the middle gravels of the Thames 100-ft. terrace at Swanscombe, Kent, in association with implements of the Acheulean culture phase. A note on the discovery appeared in "Nature" of October 19, 1935, p. 637.

In March 1936, at the same depth, and in the same seam of gravel, the left parietal bone of the same skull was discovered, and this was witnessed and photographed while still embedded in the gravels, by an independent observer.

Both of the bones are in a remarkable state of preservation. The occipital bone is unique among the earlier specimens of fossil man in preserving the basilar process, the foramen magnum and the condyles, and both bones are complete in all their margins. They thus furnish the important positions for cranial measurements of the bregma, lambda, asterion, opisthion, inion, pterion and basion, and the completeness of the two bones permits of the most precise measurements being taken without resort to speculation.

In its relation to other fossil types, the Swanscombe skull is to be regarded definitely as a precursor of the Piltdown type. The comparison of the Swanscombe and the Piltdown skulls may be summarized as follows.

(1) The anatomical features of the two skulls points to a definitely more primitive status for the Swanscombe skull than for Piltdown. The features of the Swanscombe are those of a specialized type less advanced than Piltdown but of the same general type, rather than a variant due to either the difference in sex or in age between two individuals of the same contemporaneous type. Both skulls are almost brachycephalic.

*1936 (from "Nature," August, Letters to the Editor)

The main features in which the Swanscombe shows greater primitiveness are:

(a) Lower vault measured by the bregma-opisthion chord. Swanscombe is smaller than the lowest of the three British reconstructions of Piltdown (after Sir Grafton Elliot Smith).

(b) Flat ruggedness and non-filled out contours.

(c) Lower height and greater outward and downward slope of the parietal vault.

(d) The parietal eminence is not developed to the upward and backward position of Piltdown, but occupies the centre of the parietal bone.

(e) Lower frontal development at the coronal suture, with greater incurvature of the antero-inferior parietal angle.

(f) The parietal bone covers more of the frontal and the temporal regions of the brain than in Piltdown.

(g) An extensive obelion depression marks the sagittal border, and two peculiar depressions or pits, an anterior pit above the temporal line near the anterior border, and a posterior pit near the postero-superior angle are present.

(2) The comparison of the endocranial casts of the two skulls shows a definitely more primitive stage for Swanscombe than for Piltdown.

(a) The visual territories on the occipital region extend over the greater part of the cerebral hemispheres covered by the occipital bone. On the left side, the sulcus lunatus crosses the line of the lambdoid suture.

(b) In the parietal region, the orbital, fronto-parietal and temporal opercula have not approximated at the anterior end of the horizontal limb of the fissure of Sylvius, and a large fossa lateralis measuring about 2.5 cm. from above downwards, and 1.0—2.0 cm. from before backwards is present.

(c) The parietal lobule, and the temporal lobe stand out in high relief as exuberant masses of neopallial growth, and the central and the intraparietal sulci occur in primitive form.

(d) The Sylvian fissure runs obliquely upwards and backwards.

(e) Low development of the parietal association area.

(f) The distribution of the middle meningeal arteries on the endocranial cast is more primitive in form than Piltdown.

(g) The shallow depth from above downwards of the cerebellar fossae is more primitive in form in Swanscombe.

Consideration of the above is sufficient to invite an inquiry into the status of the Piltdown skull. While the geological horizon of Swanscombe as the fossil of the middle gravels of the 100-ft. terrace is authenticated and recognized by the Geological Survey, the Piltdown horizon has been referred to the 80-ft. terrace, the 50-ft. terrace, and the 100-ft. terrace. The presence of the 'eoliths' or of the 'bone implement' is not reliable evidence of a Pliocene or Early Pleistocene status for Piltdown. The acquisition of a brain is a process of slow growth, and the differences between the actual anatomical features of the two skulls overwhelmingly favours the view that the geological horizon of Piltdown should be considered as later than that of the Swanscombe horizon in the middle gravels of the 100-ft. terrace.

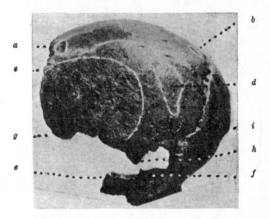

Fig. 1. Left lateral view of the Swanscombe skull. *a*, anterior oval depression, *b*, posterior round depression; *c*, temporal line; *d*, muscle attachment above and behind temporal line, perhaps for origin of functional ear muscle; *e*, basilar process; *f*, foramen magnum, filled with plasticene to support skull; *g*, inverted antero-inferior angle of parietal bone; *h*, everted postero-inferior angle; *i*, external occipital protuberance.

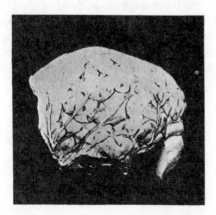

Fig. 2. Left lateral view of Swanscombe endocranial cast.

The Swanscombe associated implements and flakes have been examined by the Abbé Breuil, who classes them as belonging to the St. Acheul 1 and 3 divisions of his nomenclature. The Swanscombe skull may therefore be referred to the St. Acheul 3 culture phase of Breuil.

The Swanscombe associated fauna is being examined separately by Mr. M. A. C. Hinton.

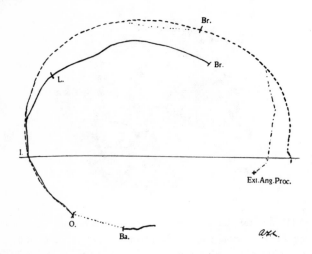

Fig. 3. Sagittal contours of Piltdown (Elliot Smith) and Swanscombe superimposed so that the inion and opisthion coincide. The Piltdown basion does not exist, but the opisthion is represented on the occipital fragment. The difference between the bregma-opisthion chord of the two specimens is not the result of the faulty reconstruction of the Piltdown skull, for if the bones of the two skulls be examined and angulated separately apart from the skull restorations as a whole, the Piltdown bones show an advanced developmental stage over the Swanscombe bones. (Swanscombe: full line. Piltdown: interrupted line.)

Excerpts from
"The Stone Age of Mount Carmel"

Dorothy A. E. Garrod et al*

Foreword

By George Grant MacCurdy

Palestine had been for a long time one of the richest fields for the historian. Until recently no one seems to have suspected it of being an equally rich field for the prehistorian. Geographically it is the keystone of an arch of land enclosing the Mediterranean, except for Gibraltar. It is the meeting-place of three great land masses, in one of which man first appeared. Since the cumulative evidence points more and more to Asia as man's birthplace, he would have arrived in Palestine before reaching Africa and western Europe. Thus, in so far as the western part of the Old World is concerned, the original spread of culture in prehistoric times was from east to west; on the other hand, the spread of our knowledge of pre-history has been from west to east. Even as late as the 60's, when Lartet and Christy entered upon their record-making discoveries in the Dordogne, Palestine was still a *terra incognita* from the viewpoint of pre-history.

Before the end of the century Palestine seemed in a fair way to profit by the example of prehistoric research in western Europe. From 1900 to 1925 progress continued to be rather slow. In the spring of the latter year F. Turville-Petre, for the British School of Archaeology in Jerusalem, began the excavation of Mugharet ez-Zuttiyeh, near Tabgha on the Sea of Galilee, where he unearthed portions of a cranium of a young adult Neandertalian, associated with a Mousterian culture. This discovery, together with the

*1937 (Oxford, Clarendon Press)

257

sessions of the International Congress of Archaeology at Jersualem and Beirut in 1926, inaugurated a new era of prehistoric research in Palestine. It was my good fortune to be able to attend this Congress as well as to see the Galilee skull and the site from which it came. I also did enough reconnaissance to satisfy myself that excavations in Palestine would yield rich results. I followed with much interest Miss Dorothy A. E. Garrod's excavation (spring of 1928) of the Shukbah cave in the Wady en-Natuf, some 27 km. north-west of Jerusalem. Two years earlier she had unearthed the skull of a five-year-old Neanderthal child from a rock shelter at Gibraltar.

In the autumn of 1928 the American School of Prehistoric Research and the Sladen Fund sent an expedition to Iraq, under the direction of Miss Garrod. Shortly after the return of the Iraq Expedition to Jerusalem soundings made by the Department of Antiquities in a cave in the Wady el-Mughara led to a series of seven joint expeditions by the British School of Archaeology in Jerusalem and the American School of Prehistoric Research, the results of which now appear in two memoirs, this being one. The joint excavations were begun under Miss Garrod's direction in the spring of 1929, and she has been ably assisted by Theodore D. McCown, Fellow of the American School of Prehistoric Research.

The group of caves is only 3.5 km. from the Mediterranean shore and has proved to be richer in results than any other Mediterranean coastal group, not even excepting Grimaldi. That the harvesting of these incomparable prehistoric results has been so complete and satisfactory is due to the able and liberal policy of the Department of Antiquities of Palestine; and especially to Miss Garrod, whose training, experience, and skill in directing have fitted her pre-eminently for the task.

Introduction

The excavations at the Wady el-Mughara were carried out by a Joint Expedition of the American School of Prehistoric Research and the British School of Archaeology in Jerusalem. The Expedition staff was composed of students and representatives of both Schools, who proved themselves enthusiastic and competent collaborators. In the spring season of 1932 Mr. Theodore D. McCown, of the American School, acted as Director in my absence; I greatly regret that his arduous work on the preparation of the skeletons from the Mugharet es-Skhul deprived me of his help in the field during the last three seasons. Dr. George Grant MacCurdy, Director of the American School of Prehistoric Research, was unfortunately never able to visit the excavations in person, but his interest and encouragement were unfailing, and during the six years in which the Expedition was at work I was in close touch by correspondence both with him and with Professor J. L. Myres, Chairman of the Council of the British School.

The two Schools have to express their sincere gratitude to the following institutions whose generous financial support has made it possible to carry out the work of excavation and study of material:

The American Council of Learned Societies.
The British Association for the Advancement of Science.
The University of California.
The Davenport Public Museum (Davenport, Iowa).
Harvard University.
The University of Michigan.
Mount Holyoke College.
The Department of Anthropology, University of Oxford.
The University of Pennsylvania.
The Royal College of Surgeons.
The Royal Society.
The Percy Sladen Memorial Fund.
The Stuart Research Fund (Newnham College).
Wellesley College.
The Wesleyan University.
The Anthony Wilkins Fund (University of Cambridge).
The Wörts Fund (University of Cambridge).
Yale University.

Mount Carmel, which has played so notable a part in the history of Palestine, is one of the outstanding landmarks of the northern half of the country. It stands up from the western side of the Kishon valley as a precipitous wall of dolomitic limestone, 20 km. long, running NNW.–SSE., and rising throughout its length from 209 m. to 482 m. above sea-level. Its northern end, on which is built the Carmelite monastery of St. Elias, projects into the sea to form the western arm of the Bay of Acre, and its southern extremity, the Deir el-Mihirqa (Place of Sacrifice), dominates the foot-hills spreading southwards to Jenin and the great expanse of the Plain of Esdraelon.

The western side of the mountain is less impressive than the eastern, because it spreads out into foot-hills which fall rather gradually from the central ridge to the coastal plain, which here has an average width of 3 km. These hills are dissected by a number of valleys with a general E.–W. direction, which for the most part have a rather rapid fall until they reach the limit of the mountain, and then cross the plain as mere stream-beds, dry for the greater part of the year.

The Wady el-Mughara, which is one of these valleys, opens on to the plain towards the southern end of the mountain, 18 km. south of the monastery of St. Elias, and 10 km. due west of the Place of Sacrifice. It differs from the wadis which lie to the north in that it does not originate high up on the hill-side, but in a small "hill-locked" plain, which lies at only 80 m. above sea-level, 2½ km. inward from the western edge of the mountain. The Wady el-Mughara begins its course as an opening in the hills which bound this basin to the west, and pursues a rather devious way, first northward, then westward, to the borders of the mountain, after which its stream-bed runs nearly due west across the plain and cuts through the coastal ridge, reaching the sea 4 km. to the south of the Crusaders' Castle at Athlit. Like the majority of Palestinian river-valleys, it is quite dry for the greater part of the year, but during the winter rains it is occasionally filled by a broad and swift-running stream.

The name Wady el-Mughara means Valley of the Caves, and it is so called from a conspicuous group of caves which lie at the point where it joins the coastal plain. The mouth of the valley is here flanked by two bluffs of crystalline limestone, and in the imposing cliff-face of the southern one lie three openings, two of which, the Mugharet el-Wad (Cave of the Valley) and Mugharet ej-Jamal (Cave of the Camel), were visible for miles before excavation began, while the third, et-Tābun (the Oven) was completely masked by carob trees.

In 1928 the cliffs of the Wady el-Mughara were threatened by quarrying operations for the construction of the new harbour at Haifa, and it was mainly through the energetic action of Mr. E. T. Richmond, Director of Antiquities in Palestine, that the site was saved. While negotiations were being carried on with the Department of Public Works, the late Mr. Charles Lambert was deputed to make soundings on behalf of the Department of Antiquities in order to test the value of the site. Mr. Lambert dug three trenches at the Mugharet el-Wad, one in the outer chamber and two on the terrace, and although he never reached a completely undisturbed layer he was able to demonstrate the great importance of the cave as a prehistoric site. His most notable find was the carving in bone of Natufian date, which was the first example of Stone Age art to be discovered in the Near East.

Meanwhile the British School of Archaeology in Jerusalem had entered into an alliance with the American School of Prehistoric Research for the purpose of exploring Stone Age sites in Palestine, and the two schools had planned to continue work in the cave of Shukba, in western Judaea, during the spring season of 1928. In view of the importance of Mr. Lambert's discoveries, the Director of Antiquities asked the schools to postpone the completion of Shukba and to undertake instead the excavation of the Wady el-Mughara caves. To this we agreed, and at the beginning of April 1929 I set up my first camp at the mouth of the valley. The work was carried out in seven seasons of excavation between this date and the end of August 1934, the actual time spent in digging being twenty-one months and two weeks.

In this time extensive excavations were carried out in the Mugharet el-Wad, in the Tabūn, and in the Mugharet es-Skhūl (Cave of the Kids), a small rock-shelter which lies a little way up the valley on its southern side, 120 m. to the east of the Mugharet el-Wad. The Mugharet ej-Jamal was tested, but was found to be practically empty of deposit; only a skin of breccia, apparently of Mousterian age, remained in patches on the rock, and a few Early Bronze Age sherds and flints were found in a depression in the floor.

et-Tabūn – Description and Excavations

The cave known as et-Tabūn (the Oven) lies approximately 70 m. to the SW. of the Mugharet el-Wad, in a semicircular bay of the same stretch of cliff, but at a higher level. The surface of the deposits in the mouth of the cave before excavation stood at 63.10 m. above sea-level, 31.10 m. above the level of the plain at the opening of the Wady el-Mughara, and 18.70 m. above the level of the rock-floor in the mouth of the Mugharet el-Wad.

The entrance of the cave before excavation was a pointed arch approximately 4.50 m. in height and 4.60 m. in breadth, facing north. This gave access to an outer chamber, measuring roughly 5.70 X 5.70 m., with a floor of red earth rising steeply (approximately 1 in 5) towards the back. On the SE. side of the chamber a wide archway was blocked with red earth and fallen masses of rock. It was possible to climb upwards through the archway by means of two shafts running through the deposit at either end, and to emerge in an inner chamber of irregular shape measuring 7 X 7 m. and open to the sky. This was filled with sticky red earth to a maximum height of 5.40 m. above the highest point in the outer chamber. The SE. wall of the inner chamber ran back into a roughly semicircular apse (SE. apse) and from this point the deposit fell in a slope of approximately 1 in 3 to the mass of fallen rock blocking the opening to the outer chamber, which was piled up to a height of 1.50 m. above the top of the archway. The latter would have been completely hidden from the inner side but for the presence of the two shafts described above, which were probably the work of burrowing animals. This inner chamber is really a great well or chimney, the opening in the cliff-top, which lay 6.50 m. above the highest point of the deposit, measuring 4.30 X 5 m.

Outside the Tabūn the deposit fell in a steep, very stony talus, tailing off finally far down on the rocky surface of the hill-side. At the top of this talus was a small grove of carob trees, which masked the cave-mouth, rendering it invisible from below.

The excavation of the Tabūn covered five seasons (1929 and 1931–4). During this time the deposit in the inner chamber was lowered to a maximum depth of 8.30 m. below its highest point, and a large trench was dug in the outer chamber and talus. This covered a maximum area of 18.50 × 23 m. and had a maximum depth of 15.50 m., the bedrock being reached over an area of approximately 100 sq. m. It is very difficult to make these measurements exact, as the walls of the cave opened out as we went down, and were at the same time very irregular, so that the ground-plan was constantly changing, and the lower levels covered a much wider area than the surface of the deposit. The maximum thickness of the deposits from the highest point in the inner chamber to the lowest point of the bedrock was 24.50 m., but owing to the steep slope, both of the surface and of the bedrock, this thickness was nowhere present in a single vertical section.

By the end of the last season of excavation (August 1934) the Tabūn presented a very different appearance from the modest cave which was visible in 1929. The small pointed archway had widened into a vast irregular opening filled with a totally unsuspected thickness of archaeological deposit. In the back of the inner chamber this deposit had been excavated to a depth of 6.80 m. below its greatest height, and from this point downwards a control section was left in place, cut into wide steps to prevent collapse and make inspection possible. The full extent of the excavation is hidden by a large buttress of deposit left in place to support a dangerous piece of the cliff-face. Owing to the shortage of time and funds the lowest archaeological layers have been left unexcavated in this western area. In the eastern area, on the other hand, the rock-wall has been completely exposed, and can be seen to open out abruptly from the base of the original archway, and then curve in again so as to form a steeply sloping floor. At the angle where the east wall joins the cliff-face there is a kind of natural buttress which finally curves round to form a rock-barrier across the cave-mouth. This runs in a westerly direction and passes under the deposits left in place on the west side, and there is little doubt that if these deposits were excavated completely the barrier would be found to connect at some point with the west rock-wall.

The lowest archaeological layers on the east side fall in a kind of cascade over the sloping bedrock, but the bottom of the trench is hidden by the rock-barrier. The rock-floor slopes abruptly down to within 2 m. of the west wall of the trench, excavation being impracticable beyond this point owing to restricted space. If it had been possible to carry the trench down another metre it is practically certain that the rock would have been found to run obliquely into the west wall of deposit. The whole appearance of this area makes it clear that the bottom of the excavation is occupied by a large swallow-hole of which the eastern rock-floor and the barrier form one side, the centre lying somewhere in the western area, underneath the deposits left in place. If the semicircular bay of rock in which the Tabūn is situated were completed into a circle on the west side, it would be seen that this pot-hole lies approximately in its centre. This suggests that the cave originally consisted of two wells open to the sky of which one only, the present inner chamber, remains intact. The present outer chamber would be merely a passage way between the two. Before the human occupation of the cave began the northern wall of the outer and larger well had broken down, leaving the site as we see it to-day. If this theory be correct, a second pot-hole must lie at the base of the deposits in the inner chamber, with a sill of rock separating it from the outer pot-hole.

One more point must be dealt with in order to complete the description of the site as it appears to-day. After the removal of Layer A (Bronze Age to Modern), the palaeolithic deposits were found to spread out from the cave in a fan-shaped talus, the lower part of which was hardened into a tough breccia. At its north edge this rested on a mass of rock projecting outward from the cliff-face and forming an outer barrier, the top of which lies 3.70 m. above that of the inner one which bounds the pot-hole. Although the junction of this rock with the cliff is masked by the deposit left in place on this side, there can be little doubt that it is bedrock. It dips fairly steeply from east to west and on the west side passes under Layer A, which has not been removed below this line. This mass of rock is probably the base of the vanished rock-wall which I suppose to have bounded the outer well on the north side.

The palaeolithic talus was excavated completely down to a level slightly below the surface of Layer E*b* (Upper Acheulean); after this it became necessary to limit the area of excavation, and the remainder of the work was carried on in a trench whose outer boundary was drawn 8 m. to the south of the edge of the fan.

The layers met with in the course of excavation were as follows (from above downwards):

A. Bronze Age to Modern.
    Chimney I and II. Upper Levalloiso-Mousterian.
B. Upper Levalloiso-Mousterian.
C. Lower Levalloiso-Mousterian.
D. Lower Levalloiso-Mousterian.

$$\left.\begin{array}{l} \mathrm{E}a. \\ \mathrm{E}b. \\ \mathrm{E}c. \\ \mathrm{E}d. \end{array}\right\} \text{Upper Acheulean (Micoquian).}$$

F. Upper Acheulean.

G. Tayacian.

Mugharet es-Skhūl –
Description and Excavations

By T. D. McCown

The smallest and the least impressive of the prehistoric sites of the Wady el-Mughara is the Mugharet es-Skhūl (Cave of the Kids). It is situated a little way up the valley on the south side, 100 m. to the east of the Mugharet el-Wad. The oval opening of the cave penetrates the steeply rising valley wall about a fourth of the way to the top of the cliff, while the rock-floor of the cave lies about 11 m. above the valley bed. The Skhūl is, strictly speaking, a rock shelter or *abri*; the cave from which the site takes its name is of small size, occupying about a fourth of the total area of the site and containing a relatively small part of the total archaeological deposit.

Before excavation the site appeared as a shallow bay in the limestone cliff, with a small arched chamber extending a short distance (6 m.) into the back wall of the bay near its centre. Blasting operations, carried out in 1928 in connexion with tests for a suitable quarry site for the Haifa breakwater and harbour works, destroyed the NW. corner of the shelter wall; this broken area is visible as a white scar to the left of the cave-mouth. Some hundreds of tons of broken rock ultimately had to be moved to reach the eastern third of the archaeological deposit, but apart from a small amount of surface disturbance, the deposit in this part of the terrace seems to have been little affected.

The eastern side of the shelter wall appears to have curved sharply northwards in its original form, with the outlook from the terrace directed NW. Now, with the NE. angle of the wall destroyed, the site is definitely more open and the main axis of both cave and terrace lies north and south. The western wall of the terrace curves away from the cave-mouth in a smooth, flat arc.

The deposit, as the excavation showed subsequently, filled the cave portion of the site to about half its height. When excavation had been completed and the site stripped of its deposit, both the cave and the shelter bore little resemblance to their original appearance. Behind the oval cave-mouth with its pronounced sill is a circular chamber. To the rear of this the inner half of the cave takes the form of a narrow and irregular recess, the floor of which is a metre above that of the outer chamber. The rock-floor of the terrace in front of the cave slopes gently away from the sill at the entrance. It is more or less level in its eastern half, but its western half consists of two parts: a gradually deepening, narrowing, and downward sloping channel which follows the outward curving shelter wall, and a flat-topped elevated area which forms the north or outer boundary of the channel. The top of this promontory of rock lies 25–30 cm. higher than the east portion of the terrace floor. The eastern half of the terrace extends outwards 6 m. from the shelter wall, then slopes gradually downwards; the western half is 7 m. at its widest part, but drops abruptly at its northern or outer edge.

Various recesses and alcoves in the walls, both of the cave and the shelter, were revealed as the deposit was removed. The two largest are situated in the east wall of the main chamber of the cave and at the SE. corner of the terrace respectively. (The latter contained the fragments of a human burial of Levalloiso-Mousterian age.) The other recesses were in the west wall of the shelter. All had served either as seepage channels for ground-water or as the openings of springs.* The alcove in the SE. corner undoubtedly was the opening of a former spring, and a similar condition may have prevailed formerly at the rear of the cave.

The site was first investigated in 1929, when Miss Mary Kitson Clark made a small trial sounding just inside the mouth of the cave. This sounding confirmed the scanty surface indications; the industry proved to be Levalloiso-Mousterian and the state of preservation of the fossil fauna was found to be excellent. Complete and definitive excavation was reserved until a later time, and no further work was done then or during 1930. In 1931 Miss Garrod generously allotted to the writer the sole responsibility for the excavation of the site. Eight weeks of work—from the 4th of April to the 3rd of June—were devoted to the exploration of the site and its deposit. The results exceeded all expectations, indicating at the same time that a further season of excavation would be required to determine fully the character of the cave and rock-shelter and the nature of their contents.

Work was begun in 1931 with the clearance of the vegetation and loose rock covering the terrace. The site was then planned, using a plane table, the main axes of the cave and terrace laid out, and a zero point established to

---

*Some of the recesses on the west shelter wall bear on their sides a series of smooth groves of varying length, depth, and direction. Some were above, others below, the original level of the deposit. They do not seem to be cracks in the limestone, but whether they are of natural or of artificial origin is obscure.

make levelling a constant factor. Some of the human burials discovered in 1932 lay well out on the terrace where the top of the deposit dipped valley-wards, and in the present account these depths are given in relation both to the surface immediately above them and to datum.

The first step in actual excavation was to make a clearance across the cave-mouth and over part of the terrace. The south wall of the 1929 sounding formed the southern limit of this clearance, the area excavated measuring roughly 4 × 4 m. (Area A). It was carried to a depth of −1.50 m. No indication of the rock-floor was found at this depth, and except for the greater quantity of humus in the uppermost 20–50 cm., and the increasing consolidation and hardening of the deeper portions of the cut, no stratification was apparent.

Attention was next directed to the deposit lying behind the 1929 sounding which filled the interior of the cave. The topmost 10–50 cm. was easily removed, but below this was hard grey breccia. The rear third of this area was excavated to a depth of −0.50 m., while the front portion was cleared downwards to meet the bottom level of the 4 m. trench. The work was then extended to the unexcavated parts of the terrace east and west of area A, these being removed to a depth of −1.50 m. There was still no indication of the possible total depth of the deposit, so a deepening within the original limits of the 4 m. trench was begun and in the course of this the mandible and the skull of a child were discovered. The skull lay at a depth of 1.80 m. below the surface, very nearly in the centre of the terrace.

Two preliminary tasks were necessary at the beginning of the 1932 season. The first of these was the removal of the upper 2 m. of the tip-head to allow the excavation to be extended northward and down the slope. The second was the removal of the remainder of the rock debris left from the Public Works Department quarry explorations. Both of these tasks were acomplished and excavation was resumed.

The area lying to the north of the 1931 excavation was divided into two parts and the innermost was reduced to the same level as the areas immediately behind it. Later the remaining portion was excavated during the period when the cleaning and removal of the human remains made impossible any extensive excavation of the terrace itself. This area became increasingly barren of artifacts both near the rock and at its outer limits. The high proportion of rough flakes and waste flint and the absence of any trace of hearths indicated clearly that the northern boundary of the deposit had been reached.

The abundance of flint and of animal bones, and the discovery of the infant's skeleton and skull during the previous year within the level area enclosed by the curving walls of the rock shelter, showed plainly that the intensive occupation of the site had been on the terrace fronting the cave. The areas to the east, west, and north of the deep 1931 trench were attacked and the breccia slowly removed with picks, mauls, and wedges.

On the last day of April human bones were discovered at three places on the east side of the terrace. Human remains had been recovered previously from the deposit, but always as isolated and incomplete specimens—portions of the shafts of long bones, a patella, and some isolated teeth. On this occasion it appeared that we were concerned with something more than fragments, and this new series of remains was numbered, the initial figure being allotted to the infant's skull and skeleton found in the previous year. Skhūl II, III, and IV were found on April 30th. The top of another adult cranium was uncovered on May 2nd, while on the day following the incomplete remains of a sixth individual came to light. Ten days followed without any further finds of human remains. During this time the removal of the breccia from the specimens already located showed that Nos. IV and V were in a most gratifying state of completeness. Then, on the 13th of May, two more individuals were found, this time in the western half of the terrace. The locations were suitably marked and the exploration of the surrounding areas left until such time as the work could be finished on the individuals already in hand. The scattered condition of the human bones belonging to individual No. VI led to the excavation of the breccia over a gradually increasing area in the centre of the terrace, and as a result, on the 19th of May, the exceedingly thick skull of a ninth fossil human was found in the hard breccia just above the rock-floor. This proved to be the last of the individuals in this most ancient prehistoric necropolis.

The general procedure in excavating the deposit was the systematic removal of 10—15 cm. layers over a predetermined area. The 4 m. trench of the 1931 season was dug in this manner, and as neither a study of the artifacts nor a careful inspection of the walls of this cutting revealed any apparent stratification there seemed to be no reason for altering this technique. With the upper parts of the deposit the level of each strip could be consistently maintained, but in the underlying portions the breccia proved too intractable to make systematic stripping of any significance. A variety of methods was tried to make the breccia removal easier and quicker, but the only effective way was to hack it out with heavy picks in as large 'chunks' as might be obtained. These were then carefully broken up by hand with small hammers and the flint and bone saved. With the less heavily consolidated material screening was difficult because of the many lumps; the most productive method was to sort the loosened material, pick out all the archaeological material, and break up the lumps.

The deposit as a whole was remarkably free from broken rock and small stones. This was particularly true of the underlying heavily brecciated portions. Medium-sized blocks of limestone were found buried in the upper parts of the terrace and the greatest concentration of these was in the western half, near the northern margin. There was no convincing evidence from the amount of buried rock debris that the shelter wall had receded to any appreciable extent. Such fragments as did occur might well have fallen on to the site from the steep hill-side lying above it.

The absence of clearly defined hearths in the whole of the deposit was a feature which distinguished the Levalloiso-Mousterian of the Skhūl from the same layers in et-Tabūn. The flints and the animal bones were scattered in an even manner throughout the deposit in the cave and upon the terrace. In only two instances was there a local concentration of cultural or faunal material which might have been hearth-sites, but in neither instance was the evidence conclusive. Flints showing thermal pitting and various degrees of discoloration due to fire, aa well as charred or calcined animal remains, were met with in all parts of the deposit. The same was true of small fragments of charcoal.

The general nature of the deposit may be summarized as follows. The superficial soft layer covered the whole of the site. Underneath this the material became increasingly harder as one approached the rock, either the floor or the walls, and changed from brown to grey and dark grey in colour. Exceptions to this general condition were the thin sheets of stalagmite which were localized in extent and played no considerable part in the structure of the deposit. On the floor of the main chamber of the cave was a thin layer of abraded flints, and without, on the terrace, was a similar layer restricted to a small area near the west wall. At the rear of the cave, lying on the floor, was a sandy pocket, another was situated just outside the entrance, and a third occurred under the western layer of rolled flints.

The occupation of the site in Levalloiso-Mousterian times was of considerable duration, and if it was abandoned at any moment of this occupation the period was too brief to leave any sign. The condition and the nature of the fauna adds point to this conclusion (see Part II).

The human remains recovered during the excavation of this site make it one of the most important yet discovered. The unequivocal character of the deposit, combined with the large number and remarkable completeness of the human individuals, is without a parallel for sites of comparable age. In a separate memoir the writer and Sir Arthur Keith consider in detail the anatomy of these fossil people. Here it is proposed to describe minutely their relations to the deposit in which they were buried or embedded, and to each other.

The first of the 1932 discoveries (No. II) consists of the fragmentary remains of an adult, probably female, and aged about 30 years. The remains were found in the partly hardened earth at the outer margin of the east half of the terrace. The fragments lay at a depth of 1.40 m. below the surface (2.3 m. below datum), and consisted of about two dozen pieces of the skull, ten very worn teeth, and the symphyseal part of the mandible bearing the sockets of the incisor, canine, pre-molar, and the first molar teeth. The right humerus is represented by the lower two-thirds of the shaft, the left humerus by the distal third of the shaft and by part of the head and neck. All that remain of the forearms are the incomplete proximal ends of both ulnae and a part of the head and neck of the right radius. No other bones were found although the surrounding area was both searched and screened. The portions recovered lay in no sort of order or position; their appearance might well be ascribed to their having been dropped in a small heap, to be gradually buried by the accumulating terrace. They have not been gnawed by animals, and the fractures are old, the exposed cancellous parts being filled with matrix. The bone is quite hard but not heavily mineralized.

The remains of another adult (No. III) were found in the alcove at the SE. corner of the terrace. Under several medium-sized stones were the fragments of a left human leg. The parts preserved consist of the lower third of the shaft of the femur, a fragment bearing the trochanter minor, a dozen fragments of the badly crushed tibia, and the incomplete end of the fibula with about half of the adjoining shaft. The relationship of the fragments preserved shows that we have to do with a contracted left leg, the knee directed towards the deepest part of the recess. The body must have lain partly in the alcove, but the greater part undoubtedly lay outside and had been disturbed and destroyed. The lack of any lower limb fragments for No. II raises the possibility that Nos. II and III may be widely separated (3.60 m.) portions of the same individual. No. II was covered to a depth of 2.35 m., but relative to the base-point for levelling was 20 cm. lower (2.50 m. below datum) than No. II. The principal objections to this theory are the robustness of these bones in contrast with the slight character of the humeri of Skhūl II, their greater degree of mineralization, and their inclusion in the hard breccia just above the floor of the alcove. None of these difficulties is insuperable, but there are no positive considerations for not believing this to be a distinct individual.

Almost at the same time as the puzzling fragments of No. III were brought to light, one of the workmen uncovered the skull of Skhūl IV; in so doing he broke part of the already fissured parietals, but the greater number of these fragments were recovered. A day's work of careful chipping around the edges of the oval section thus created showed that more than just a fragment of the skull was to be obtained. In clearing the surrounding area during the third day, the right ankle and some of the adjacent metatarsal bones came to light at the same level as the skull, but some 70 cm. distant from it to the west. The direction and extent, and the fact that we were concerned with something more than a skull, being thus determined, the process of chipping away the breccia was pushed forward.

The individual lay on its right side, the skull inclined sharply towards the left shoulder and lying directly above the position once occupied by the right scapula and the head of the right humerus. The left arm was tightly flexed; the hand lay with the palm directed upwards, while the thumb is in opposition and lies obliquely across the palmar surfaces of the metacarpals. The phalanges extended under the mandible. The right hand lay slightly above and in front of the left one; the volar surfaces of the radius and ulna lay uppermost, the wrist and fingers were in a supine position, with the back of the hand directed towards the floor of the grave. Lying between the two hands, but nearer to the right than to the left one, was a quite ordinary flint racloir.

As seen from above, the legs appear to be tightly flexed; such was doubtless the intention of those making the interment. The knees, of which the left was in advance of and a little above the right one, were 20 cm. higher than the level of the top of the pelvis. Both femora sloped upwards from the pelvis, but the left tibia and fibula ran downwards again with the calcaneus touching the trochanter major of the thigh bone. The right leg was inclined at a moderate angle upwards; its ankle and foot, which were situated 10 cm. higher than the knees, lay immediately over the left foot and toes, and were at the same level as the base of the skull.

We have to do with a deliberate, if carelessly made burial. At the side of the shelter a shallow, concave hole must have been scooped out of the then soft deposit and the body placed in it, the head resting on the downward curving eastern side and directed in such a way that it looked up the valley. The arms were folded, the hands placed in front of the face, and the legs folded back upon the buttocks. The knees rested against the sloping north face of the pit, and the right foot was caught against the western lip of the grave. That such must have been the case is proved by the position of the left foot. This lay directly underneath the right foot with the heel against the right buttock, but the ankle has been twisted so that the dorsal aspect lies towards the pelvis and is directed upwards—the sole of the foot must have pressed against the side of the grave.

All the bones show a natural articular relationship with respect to each other; such would not have been the case if there had been any later disturbance or if the corpse had come to rest at this spot by accident. The nature of the hard matrix made it impossible to detect the original outline of the grave, but the position of the bones can leave no doubt regarding its size or shape. There were no stones or rocks covering the body and no traces of grave furniture, if the single scraper found near the hands be excluded. Its occurrence in this place may well be fortuitous.

The fourth specimen to be discovered in 1932 (No. V) lay a few centimetres above the rock-floor, 2.30 m. west of I–II and 2.15 m. north of III–IV. The surface of the deposit originally began its downward slope towards the valley floor a metre or so behind and above the skeleton; the accumulation above the interment amounted to only 1.25 m. (2.40 m. below datum), but the matrix surrounding the bones was of the same brown colour and degree of hardness as that which contained No. IV.

Again we have no chance assemblage of human bones. The body lay on its back, slightly inclining towards the right side; the head was tilted through an angle of 90° and the chin pressed deeply into the thoracic cavity. The right clavicle had been displaced and lay in front of, and at the same level as, the mouth. The left arm lay across the body, slightly bent at the elbow and with the hand just below the right elbow. The right arm was directed a little away from the body, the humerus being nearly parallel with the left bone, but the forearm was flexed sharply backwards and directed outwards and upwards. The position of the right wrist and hand must have been level with the right ear of the skull. The right clavicle lay parallel with the right cheek, with its dorsal aspect turned uppermost. Some of the ribs of the left side lay underneath the humerus and in correct relation to the fragmentary dorsal vertebrae.

The lower part of the skeleton showed signs of an ancient disturbance and much crushing. There remain, however, enough of the pelvis and the legs to make certain what was the original position. The lower dorsal vertebrae were missing; only fragments of the lumbar ones remained, and a small piece of the sacral element of the pelvis. This was attached to the right ilium, which lay with its lateral surface directed downwards. Cemented into the acetabulum was the crushed head of the right femur; below, the latter was continued in the neck and proximal half of the shaft of that bone. Lying at a right angle to the main axis of the torso, above and across the obliquely placed right femur, was the shaft and incomplete distal end of the left femur. The corresponding tibia and fibula lay parallel with this thigh bone—the leg had been tightly flexed with the heel pressed against the hip.

It was clear that we were dealing with a deliberate burial. The body of this 45-year-old male lay on its back, head bent upon the chest, the right arm tightly flexed with the left arm lying across the body; the legs were tightly flexed with feet against buttocks and the hips twisted laterally so that the right one lay deepest in the grave. Here, too, it would seem that the deceased had been crowded into a grave of inadequate size.

One fact yet to be mentioned is sufficiently remarkable to deserve close attention. In the angle formed by the left forearm and the right humerus was the mandible of a very large pig. The ascending rami on both sides had been broken away, but the dental arcade with the roots of the tusks was preserved. The jaw lay parallel with the right humerus of the skeleton, with its symphyseal aspect directed towards the right shoulder. There can be no doubt, from its position, and from the fact that the left forearm rests upon the broken, hinder ends of the mandible, that its inclusion in the grave was deliberate. Its presence is a subject for speculation rather than explanation. Perhaps it represents a trophy acquired during life, a magical or religious symbol, or a food offering.

It was impossible to determine the exact limits of the grave, as was likewise the case with No. IV, or the level from which the interment was made. There had been no attempt at protecting the remains with a covering of rocks or stones. The grave was probably a shallow hole with the body laid upon the rock-floor. The head looks up the valley in an easterly direction, as did that of No. IV, and both show evidence of deliberate arrangement of the arms and legs. Here the resemblance ends: No. IV was placed with head to the east and the body lies SE.–NW.; No. V lies with the head to the west, while the other parts of the skeleton lie along an axis directed 12° north of east.

In the account which has been presented above the facts show that the human remains found in the Skhūl represent no chance assemblage of skulls and skeletal parts. The site was not only a place of habitation; it was a cemetery as well. The bones of seven of the ten individuals bear witness to a normal or articulated relationship to each other. That fact alone is perhaps not enough to warrant the assertion that they were buried by other than natural agencies, but if we take it in conjunction with the unequivocal evidence of Nos. I, IV, V, and VII, no doubt can remain that the positions in which we found these ancient people are the result of deliberate interment.

The form, arrangement, and orientation of the individual burials varies so considerably that it is evident that these practices had not become systematized as they were in later times. The one character which all the better preserved burials had in common was contraction of the limbs. The lowest limbs, with the exception of those of No. VIII, are always acutely flexed. Greater variation is found in the positions taken by the arms, but these, too, are usually flexed. There was a preference for burial on the right side in three cases (Nos. IV, VII, IX), No. V lay on its back but with the right hip the deeper of the two and the knees directed to the right, while No. I was buried in a squatting position, leaning forward and to the left. In three instances the head lay to the east (Nos. IV, VII, IX), to the west in No. V although the skull faced east up the valley, and in No. I the skull lay in a southerly direction and must have looked towards the cave.

The only object found with the skeletons, concerning which there can be no doubt that it was buried with the corpse, was the mandible of an extinct species of wild boar, clasped in the arms of No. V. The ox skull found with No. IX must certainly be regarded as a later intrusion. Buried in and covered by the normal midden deposit, bone fragments, artifacts, flint flakes, and cores naturally did occur among and around the human bones, but never in sufficient concentration to differ significantly from conditions elsewhere in the site. None of the burials were protected with stones or rock fragments, with the doubtful exception of No. III, and if there was an underlying, specially prepared hearth upon which the body was laid it has long ago become indistinguishable from the normal breccia.

The western European parallels of Mousterian age to the burial conditions described above are restricted to two instances: the adult male from the cave of La Chapelle-aux-Saints and the male skeleton from the rock shelter of La Ferrassie. There is little reasonable doubt that the Le Moustier youth and the two individuals from Spy were buried intentionally, but the descriptions of the positions and the circumstances of these remains are inadequate for comparative purposes.

The position of the La Chapelle skeleton is nearly identical with that of Skhūl V. The head was to the west, resting on its base with the chin pressed into the chest, the body lay on its back, the right arm flexed and the hand placed by the right ear. The legs were contracted, with the knees directed to the right. The left arm was extended beside the body; the latter is the only significant difference in the positions of these two fossils.

The La Ferrassie male exhibited the same general burial attitude as that of the La Chapelle individual. The major exception was found to be the position of the head; this lay on its left side and was turned as though it were looking over the left shoulder. The female skeleton from La Ferrassie is of interest in another connexion: the remains were less complete than those of the man, but were buried with the head directed towards the head of the male, the body lying on its right side with the legs contracted. In western Europe as well as in Palestine, it would seem that these early people were alike in burying their dead with the limbs flexed, but that custom had not become fixed with regard either to the details of the arrangement of the limbs or to the direction in which the body was placed. At Le Moustier, at La Chapelle-aux-Saints, and La Ferrassie the excavators discovered a considerable amount of rude grave furniture; numerous flints, complete animal bones, slabs of rock lying over the head and shoulders of La Ferrassie I. This state of affairs was noticeably absent in the Skhūl, the exception being the boar's jaw placed with No. V.

The chronology of the separate burials within the period represented by the deposit can only be stated in relative terms. One face is clear; all the burials are contemporaneous with the deposit, and do not represent post-Levalloiso-Mousterian intrusions. When we turn to a consideration of which were the earliest made interments the evidence is less sure. On Sections I–II and III-IV the respective depths below datum are shown in projection. Relative depths of interment are never a sure guide to the chronology of burials, but it will be observed that Nos. VI, VII, VIII, IX, and X are lower than IV and V, which are at the same level, and No. I which is higher than these latter. The colour, the mineralization, and the state of preservation of the fossil human bones, combined with a corresponding similarity in colour and density of the surrounding matrix, also lead to the conclusion that as a group these individuals are more ancient than Nos. I, IV, and V. No. III may also belong to this older series.

The preceding paragraphs have been concerned mainly with the presentation of facts and observations; these facts largely fit together and the conclusions to be drawn from them are, in the main, straightforward. The cave and rock shelter were first inhabited by people making and using implements of a Levalloiso-Mousterian facies. There are no indications that the site had any earlier occupants; the long sequence represented by the Acheulean layers of et-Tabūn is absent, and neither on the site nor near it were discovered any rolled or abraded specimens which might represent the eroded remnants of an earlier occupation.

The sandy floor pockets and the two small layers of abraded flints are perhaps best explained as having been caused by water action during the earliest period of the site's use. The sheets of stalagmite found at a higher level, and the irregular hardness of the deposit in the cave and along the shelter walls, leave no doubts that springs issuing from the fissures in the limestone were intermittently active. It seems unlikely that one of these, or even a combination of several, would create a flow of water sufficient to abrade the flints to the degree existing. The remaining inference to be drawn is that the valley bottom was higher at a given moment, more nearly on a level with the terrace, and that the deposit was partially affected for a limited time by stream action.

Structurally and industrially the remainder of the deposit shows no signs of other than a continuous occupation. The animal remains show no signs of gnawing by carnivores. The carnivore remains were not abundant, and the burials, where disturbed, seem to have been affected by the later human occupants of the site, not by foraging animals. The burials certainly do not contradict the theory of a continuous occupation of the site. It would appear that there were no scruples against using the terrace simultaneously as a home and as a burial ground. If the spot was deserted following a death and burial, the period was too short to leave any mark upon the site.

Anatomically the inhabitants were a curious combination of Neanderthal and Neanthropic man: perhaps it is more accurate to say a form of Palaeoanthropic man with many physical characters hitherto most commonly met with in *Homo sapiens*. In a separate memoir the writer and Sir Arthur Keith set forth the facts, and their considered opinion that these people represent a branch of the extinct Palaeoanthropic family of mankind. Among the individuals in the Skhūl the variation is large both in kind and degree of development of physical characters, but not so great as to raise any question that we have to do with differing races. The fossil human remains from Layer C of et-Tabūn, the woman's skeleton and the male mandible, present an interesting and instructive series of problems of a related but differing order from those which concern the inhabitants of the Mugharet es-Skhul.

There are some slight indications that the filling of the cave and terrace of the Skhūl may once have been of greater depth; the pockets of hard breccia left on the walls above the surface-level are like the breccia of the main deposit. The abandonment of the site in post-Levalloiso-Mousterian times prevented any increase due to human agency, and purely natural increments carried by the wind, or washed on to the site from the hill slope above, seem to have been equalled by the normal forces of denudation and erosion. The surface of the terrace has shrunk downwards—enough at any rate to leave pockets of hard material above the existing surface. The principal cause has been the tendency of the whole deposit to settle and become consolidated; the vegetation cover was sufficient to prevent excessive erosion.

The Mugharet es-Skhūl is one of the most remarkable of prehistoric sites by virtue of the cemetery it contained. The archaeological problems presented by it are comparatively easy of explanation. The industry is correlated with fair exactitude with part of the long and full sequence of Palaeolithic cultures discovered in the Mugharet el-Wad and et-Tabūn. This increases enormously the importance of the human remains, inasmuch as their chronological position is made certain both with regard to the prehistory of western Asia and of Europe. At the same time the abundance and the excellent preservation of the fossil skeletons presents an unexampled opportunity for amplifying our knowledge of the middle Palaeolithic people of Palestine and the Near East and especially for studying the course taken by human evolution at what may ultimately prove to be a critical moment in the biological development of mankind.

The Fossil Remains

An Enumeration of the Individuals With a Résumé
of the Evidence Bearing on Their Antiquity

The fossil human skulls and skeletons which form the subject of this study were found in caves on the western slope of Mount Carmel in Palestine.

The assemblage of fossil human material which it has been our good fortune to study is both exceptionally complete and well preserved. There are individuals of both sexes, children as well as adults.

With the exception of certain specimens from the Mugharet el-Wad and et-Tabūn which are specially noted below, the human remains come from the Levalloiso-Mousterian layers of et-Tabūn and of the Mugharet es-Skhūl.

From the Mugharet es-Skhūl

Skhūl I.   Contracted burial of an infant, about four to four and a half years of age. Sex probably male. Bone moderately mineralized, with surface parchment brown in colour.

Skhūl II.   Adult, age 30–40 years; female.

Skhūl III.   Adult, male. This individual is represented by parts of the left leg. The femur is represented by the middle and distal part of the shaft and another fragment representing the trochanter minor. The tibia is represented by the middle half of the shaft. The fibula consists of the defective distal end and about half of the shaft.

Skhūl IV.   Adult, 40–50 years; male.

Skhūl V.   Adult, about 30–40 years; male.

Skhūl VI.   Adult, 30–35 years; male.

Skhūl VII.   Adult, 35–40 years; female.

Skhūl VIII.   Child, 8–10 years; probably male. Shaft of the right femur; shaft with distal epiphysis of the right tibia, with the right talus and the medial half of the right calcaneus; the right navicular (incomplete). The left tibia is represented by the shaft and the distal epiphysis and with this is articulated the tarsus and metatarsals. The proximal phalanx of the first metatarsal and the proximal of the second are also present. None of these bones is complete. The left fibula is represented by four segments of the shaft as well as the proximal end and the distal end with its epiphysis.

Skhūl IX.   Adult, about 50 years; male.

Skhūl X.   Infant, about 5–5½ years; probably male. Represented by the symphysial part of the mandible containing three milk incisors, the unerupted crown of the left canine, four incisors, as well as the crown of the right canine. There is a fragment of the corpus containing first and second milk molars, and in addition to this there are the crowns of both upper permanent first molars. The crown of the upper permanent canine is also present. Of the skeleton there is only the lower half of the shaft and the distal end of the right humerus.

From Mugharet et-Tabūn

Tabūn I. A partially extended burial, about 30 years, female.

Tabūn II. About 30–35 years; male. Represented by an isolated mandible. The specimen is intact with the exception of the left condyle and the left medial incisor.

Serial Specimens from Mugharet et-Tabūn.

Tabūn Series I: Fragment of an adolescent maxilla with alveoli for right incisors and canine. Belonging to this are the upper right teeth, I–2; C, Pm–1; Pm–2; M–1; M–2. This specimen came from Layer B.

Tabūn Series II: Unworn miscellaneous teeth, including upper left I–2; lower right I–2; upper right Pm–1; upper left M–1; the crown of upper right M–1. All of the specimens except the lower right I–2 (Layer B) came from Chimney II.

Tabūn Series III: Teeth showing various degrees of wear, consisting of an upper left I–2; upper left I–1; lower left M–1; lower right M–3. All of the specimens came from Layer B.

Tabūn Series IV: Milk-teeth; upper right i–1 (Chimney II); upper right and left m–2 (Layer B); a lower left m–2 (Chimney II).

Tabūn Series V: Miscellaneous teeth from Tabun found in the superficial deposits of the terrace and probably not Palaeoanthropic.

Tabūn E*a*: Fragment of a heavily mineralized, adult, right femur shaft extending from just below the neck to a point a little above the lower end of the shaft (from Layer E*a*, upper Acheulean).

Tabūn E*b*: Lower right M–1 or M–2, very worn with defective roots (from Layer E*b*, upper Acheulean).

The Skhūl individuals were associated with a characteristic Levalloiso-Mousterian industry in a homogeneous deposit which filled the cave and terrace of the Mugharet es-Skhūl. The Tabūn woman and the man (Tabūn II) were found in an archaeological layer in et-Tabūn which yielded implements almost indistinguishable in type and in proportions from those of the Skhūl stratum. The maxillary fragment (Series I) and the isolated teeth (Series II, III, IV) come from Layer B, lying above Tabūn I and Tabūn II; while the industry is also Levalloiso-Mousterian it shows certain developments which have led Miss Garrod (1937) to attribute to it a somewhat lesser age than that of Layer C.

Miss Bate's (1937) studies of the fauna from the Skhūl cave and from the long Tabūn prehistoric sequence are significant in two important respects as regards the fossil human remains. In et-Tabūn there is a sharp change in the character of the faunal census between Layers C and B. Not only are the proportions of the animal forms altered, but Layer B lacks certain species which are characteristic of Layer C and of the yet older strata (Layers D–F). As we have mentioned above, the flint industry shows an orderly change, and as far as our evidence goes, the human types which occupied the Tabūn remained essentially the same. Whatever were the factors that were responsible for the changes in the Palestinian fauna, they seem not to have affected the human population which dwelt in the Oven Cave.

Just as the artifacts indicate an identity of culture between the Skhūl deposit and the prehistoric layer in which were found the Tabūn man and woman, so the Skhul fauna shows that this site was occupied before the time of the big faunistic change which is recorded in the history of the Tabūn cave. The Skhūl animals include species which are notable for their absence in Layer B of et-Tabūn and which are characteristic of Layer C. The outstanding difference between the faunas of the Skhul and of the Tabūn is that in the former the most abundant of the animal remains consisted of the bones of wild oxen, while in the latter the most numerous were the bones of gazelles. There were ox remains in Layer C of et-Tabūn, just as there were gazelle bones in the Skhūl deposit. We have no ready explanation for this difference; what is convincingly clear is that we may speak of the Skhūl specimens as being contemporaneous in a moderately narrow sense with Tabūn I and II. Further, both the archaeological and the palaeontological evidence now at our disposal make it plain that the Skhūl people were antecedent to the various fragmentary individuals recovered from Layer B of the Tabūn cave. On anatomical grounds, the latter appear to be later members of the human type which we know from our study of the skeleton of the Tabūn woman and of the massive male mandible.

The Relationship of
the Fossil People of Mount Carmel
to Prehistoric and Modern Types

Before our readers proceed to study the detailed description of the remains of the fossil people from Mount Carmel which we have given in this work, it will be advantageous for them to know the chief conclusions to which we have come as a result of our prolonged investigation. These conclusions refer (1) to the relationship of one individual to another, and (2) to their relationships to other prehistoric peoples and to the living races of mankind.

In the earlier stages of our investigations we were inclined to believe we had before us the remains of two distinct types or kinds of humanity, the Tabūn and the Skhūl. The Tabūn type, represented by the complete skeleton of a woman (Tabūn I), the mandible of a man (Tabūn II), and some other fossil fragments, comes from the Mugharet et-Tabūn. The Skhūl type is represented by the complete skeletons of two adult males, the complete skeleton of a child, the incomplete skeletons of a male and a female, and the fragmentary remains of five other individuals. We are persuaded that all the complete and the imperfect skeletons represent deliberate burials. As our investigations proceeded we encountered so many characters which linked the Skhūl to the Tabūn type that we were ultimately obliged to presume that we had before us the remains of a single people, the Skhūl and the Tabūn types being but the extremes of the same series. Yet the range in form, from that represented by Skhūl IV (male) to Tabūn I (female), is unexpectedly great. The Tabūn type possesses many features which link it to the Neanderthal type of Europe while the extreme Skhūl type passes towards a Neanthropic form such as that found at Cromagnon. Between these extremes are intermediate forms. All the members of the group possess certain characters in common, a list of which is given in our final chapter.

The chief consideration which moves us to regard all the specimens from both sites as members of the same species or race are: (1) their dental characters are uniform; we can draw no sharp line between the dentitions of the Tabūn and of the Skhūl people; (2) their cultures are very nearly identical; (3) they lived in the same locality at approximately the same period of time. On strictly anatomical grounds one would presume that the Skhūl was the later type. There is the same difference between the robust mandible of the Tabūn male and that of Skhūl IV or V as there is between the Cromagnon mandible and that of a modern Englishman—almost as great as between the Heidelberg mandible and that of the La Chapelle man. In size of palate the Skhūl men rivalled Neanderthal man, but in the form of their jaws, particularly of the mandible, there is evidence of certain retrograde changes. Miss Dorothea Bate has observed that the fauna represented in the Skhūl cave differs in certain details from that recorded for the Tabūn cave.

Relationship to Galilee Man

Our knowledge of the Galilean fossil people is based on part of a skull unearthed in 1925 by Mr. Turville-Petre during excavations at the Mugharet ez-Zutteiyeh, about thirty-five miles distant from the Wady Mughara. All that was found of the Galilee man were three bones of his skull, the frontal, the right malar, and part of the sphenoid.* A close comparison of these parts with the corresponding bones from Mount Carmel has convinced us that the Galilee and the Mount Carmel specimens should be regarded as members of the same group. His place is apparently towards the Tabūn extreme of this group.

The evidence which led us to this conclusion is worth considering by all who are concerned in the classification of extinct races, when only fragmentary fossil remains are available. The Galilean frontal, malar, and sphenoid bones were similar in their chief characters to the same bones of Neanderthal man. There were minor differences—the narrowness of the forehead and the height of the cranial vault. The fossil Galilean was regarded as a member of the species which is represented by Neanderthal man in Europe.

Now our investigations of the Mount Carmel people have shown us that in them it is just the bones found by Mr. Turville-Petre, the frontal, malar, and sphenoid, that are most Neanderthaloid in their characterization. In the frontal of the Mount Carmel people we meet with the same narrowness and height as in the Galilee frontal, and we infer that had the rest of his skull and skeleton been found these parts would have possessed a series of characters similar to those of our Tabūn type. We may presume, provisionally at least, that in mid-Pleistocene times the people of Palestine were of the type or types described in this work.

Variability

We are of the opinion that the variability found amongst the fossil people of Mount Carmel is greater in degree and in kind than is to be observed in any local community of modern times. Had the Mount Carmel people been discovered—not collectively, in one place, but separately, in diverse localities, each excavator would have been convinced that a new and separate form of humanity had been unearthed, so great does one Carmelite individual differ from another.

How are we to explain the structural instability of the Mount Carmel people? Do they represent a people in the throes of an evolutionary transition and therefore unstable and plastic in their genetic constitution? Or is the variability due to hybridity, a mingling of two diverse people or races? We shall see that the Mount Carmel people represent a series which can be arranged between a Neanderthal form at one end and a Cromagnon form at

---

*A fuller knowledge of the sex differences in Palaeoanthropic races has led us to ascribe the skull to a man, not to a woman. Hrdlicka came to this conclusion in 1930.

the other. Is it possible that Neanderthal and Cromagnon—Palaeoanthropic and Neanthropic—stocks had met on the flanks of Mount Carmel in mid-Pleistocene times and that the fossil bones described here represent the progeny of their union?

We have given the supposition of hybridity our serious consideration and have rejected it. To win support for such a theory we should have to produce the fossil remains of a Neanthropic form of a man in Palestine from a level as old, or older, than the Levalloiso-Mousterian of Mount Carmel, as well as the remains of a fully evolved Neanderthal form. We have no such evidence. All who believe in evolution are agreed that Neanderthal man and modern man are descendants of a common human stock. There must have been a time in history of that ancestral stock when individuals were undergoing differentiation along, at the least, two directions—towards the purely Palaeoanthropic (Neanderthal) type and towards a Neanthropic type represented by the early people of Cromagnon. We regard the tendency of the Mount Carmel people to diverge into two types as being due not to miscegenation but to an evolutionary divergence. We suppose that the Mount Carmel people were in the throes of evolutionary change.

Relationship to Other Prehistoric Types

Readers must not think that we look upon the Mount Carmel people as the actual stock which gave the world its Neanthropic or modern races on the one hand, and its Palaeoanthropic or Neanderthal races on the other. This is not our opinion. We can make our position clear by discussing the place which must be assigned to the Mount Carmel people among the prehistoric peoples of the Old World. Their relationship to the prehistoric peoples of the East—Sinanthropus and Pithecanthropus—is distant both in space and in time. Between them lies the whole width of Asia. It will be time to discuss how the peoples of the West stand to those of the East when the Pleistocene deposits which lie between Palestine and China have been explored and the cultural history of the intervening peoples has been unravelled. But in the Western world itself we know of at least five groups of prehistoric peoples with whom the Mount Carmel people may claim an evolutionary relationship. These five groups are (1) that found at Krapina in Croatia and so well described by Dr. Karl Gorjanovic-Kramberger (1906); (2) that found near Weimar in Germany and described by Prof. Franz Weidenreich (1928) and by Dr. Hans Virchow (1920). To this group we would add the type described by Dr. H. Weinert (1936) from Steinheim-am-Murr in Württemberg; (3) the western Neanderthal group, found in France and the surrounding countries; the classical monograph on this group is Prof. Marcelin Boule's study of the La Chapelle skeleton (1911); it is probable that this widely spread group was broken up into local types; (4) the Predmost people described by Prof. J. Matiegka (1925, 1929), (5) the Cromagnon people of France described by Dr. René Verneau (1906). The Cromagnon and the Predmost groups are Neanthropic in type and are the earliest representatives of the European, white or Caucasian races which have been discovered as yet.

Relationship to the Krapina Group

The Mount Carmel people find their nearest affinities among the extinct groups of humanity available for comparison at Krapina. Both peoples—Mount Carmel and Krapina—are assigned to the same geological period, the latter part of the Riss-Würm interglacial epoch. The habitat of the Krapina people is nearer to that of the Palestinians than are the homelands of the other four types. Croatia is 1,400 miles from Palestine as the crow flies. At Krapina no complete skeletons were found, only fragments, but valuable fragments and in great number. There were no people at Krapina of the tall Skhūl type; all are small people, strong in jaw but relatively short and weak in limb. Indeed, in form of limb-bone there is much resemblance between the smaller specimens from Mount Carmel and those of Krapina. Neither at Mount Carmel nor at Krapina were the thick massive femora and tibiae of western Neanderthal man represented. Nor do we find molar teeth of the taurodont type at Mount Carmel, a type so prevalent among the Krapina people, yet both people possess the same pattern in the crowns of their molar teeth. The crowns of the other teeth, too, are similar if we exclude certain individuals of the Skhūl type. The Krapina people had low-vaulted skulls, whereas the vault in the Mount Carmel people is of medium, even of great, height. The chin was developed to a variable extent in both the Krapina and the Mount Carmel people, but among the former never to the maximum degree shown by some of the Carmel specimens. It is our Tabūn type which makes the nearest approach to that of Krapina. In brief, the Krapina people, although they serve to bridge the gap between the ancient Palestinians and the Neanderthalians of western Europe, have their chief affinities with the latter group.

Relationship to the Ehringsdorf People

The Ehringsdorf group, like that of Mount Carmel and Krapina, is assigned to the Riss-Würm interglacial period and is therefore earlier in date than most members of the Neanderthal group of western Europe. Our knowledge of the group is limited to a skull and two mandibles. The skull is frankly Neanderthal but has three peculiar features which are worthy of note because they are met with in the Mount Carmel people: a relatively high vault, a neanthropic mastoid process, and an incipient external occipital protuberance. Apparently the Ehringsdorf type will find its closest resemblances with the Neanderthal people of western Europe.

Of the Neanderthaloid skulls of central Europe, that which bears the closest resemblance to the Palestinian type is the Steinheim cranium described by Weinert (1936, 1937). That writer ascribes this fossil specimen, which is one of the most complete of the mid-Pleistocene series yet discovered, to post-Riss times or to an early phase of the Riss-Würm interglacial. It is the skull of a woman and in many points resembles the skull of the Tabūn woman. In the meantime it may be included in the Ehringsdorf group, for it may well be the female form of this group. The molar teeth differ from those of the Tabūn woman. It is a remarkable fact that the Steinheim skull, which seems to be the earliest representative of the Neanderthal type so far discovered in Europe, should show so little of the occipital characterization found in specimens of later date, and should, in its occipital characters, make an approach to the Palestinian type.

Relationship to the Neanderthal Group of Western Europe

Our conception, hitherto, of the Neanderthal type or species has been based upon the fossil remains found in central and south-western Europe. The man of Düsseldorf and the man of La Chapelle-aux-Saints best represent the male form of this group. They were squat, strongly built men who differed from living types of mankind in almost every detail of bodily structure. Many points in their anatomy recall those found in the anthropoid apes, particularly in the gorilla. This type—the Neanderthal of Europe—is not found among the Mount Carmel people. Our Skhūl men are tall; their lower limbs were long and straight; the long, straight, heavily pilastred Skhūl femur differs altogether from the short, bowed Neanderthal femur, with its massive articular extremities. The feet of the Mount Carmel people were moulded and used as ours are. Like Neanderthal man, the Skhūl men were big-brained, but the moulding of their head and jaws was modern. And yet, through the anatomy of the Mount Carmel people there runs a substratum of characters which link them to the Neanderthal type. We have mentioned that the individuals described in this study can be arranged in a series with the Tabūn type, plainly Neanderthaloid, at one extreme and the Skhūl type at the other. Similarly the groups of fossil man just enumerated can be arranged in a series with the Neanderthal group of western Europe at one extreme and the Mount Carmel group at the opposite extreme. It does now seem probable that western Europe, in the middle phases of the Pleistocene period, had become an evolutionary backwater so far as humanity was concerned and that the centres of active evolutionary progress lay much farther to the east, probably in western Asia.

Relationship to the Predmost People

The Predmost people are the earliest representatives of the Neanthropic type of man that have been discovered in central Europe. The men have certain primitive characters, such as their prominent supra-orbital ridges, but in general structural characterization they are Caucasian. There are resemblances between them and the Skhūl men which deserve mention. The Predmost man (No. 3) has supra-orbital ridges which, although falling short of the development seen in Skhūl IV, serve as a link between that of Skhūl and of the development found in some modern Europeans. In shape, size, and characterization of their skulls, the Predmost and the Mount Carmel people had many points in common. But the Predmost people are of medium or short stature and are devoid of the Neanderthaloid features of the Skhūl people. Their relationship to the Mount Carmel people is more remote than that of the Neanthropic group we are now to discuss.

Relationship to the Cromagnon Group

If only the limb-bones of the Skhūl people had been discovered at the Wady Mughara, we have no doubt of the verdict that anatomists would have passed on them. They would have declared that they were the fossil remains of a Neanthropic race, near akin to the Cromagnon people, the people who appeared in Europe towards the end of the Pleistocene period. Because of their crude characters and seeing how much the Skhūl people antedate the Cromagnons of Europe, these fossil limb-bones would have been accepted as evidence of the existence of proto-Cromagnons in mid-Pleistocene times. Or let us suppose that only hands, or feet, or the hinder part of the skull, or the auricular region carrying the joint for the mandible, or the lower jaw itself had come to light; the verdict would have been the same. These parts would have been accepted as evidence of the existence of a Neanthropic race. On the other hand, if it had happened, as it did in the case of the Galilee discovery, that only the anterior part of the skull of the Mount Carmel people had been recovered, then the verdict would have been Neanderthal. Most of the teeth, a study of the vertebrae, or of the ribs would have led to the same conclusion: that they must be ascribed to a Neanderthaloid race. Even in the case of the ribs the evidence would have been equivocal for both forms of ribs occur at Mount Carmel, the rounded Neanderthal form and the wide-bladed ribs of Neanthropic man.

Of the early Neanthropic types known to us, there can be no doubt as to the one which comes nearest that of our Skhūl people. It is the Cromagnon type of southern France, the cave-dwellers of the Aurignacian. The Skhūl men, like the male Cromagnons, were tall; their stature ranged from 5 ft. 6.7 in. (1,700 mm.) to 5 ft. 10.3 in. (1,787 mm.). The bones of their lower extremities, from hip-joint to toes, are very similar to those of the Cromagnon men. So it is as regards the bones of the upper extremity, save that those of the Cromagnon males are more robust. But although what we have said of the bones of the upper and lower extremities is true of most of the Skhūl men, it is not true of all. Some have bones exhibiting certain Neanderthal characters to a greater or less degree.

A critical survey of the bones of the pelvis, shoulder, and trunk of the Skhūl males yields a mixed list of characters, Neanderthal, modern, and some which are neither; the latter appear to be peculiar to the Skhūl type. These features of the pelvis and the clavicle are duly described in their respective chapters. An examination of the skull gives the same mixed result. On the whole, characters of a Neanthropic nature are dominant to those of a Neanderthal kind. The Skhūl men had more rugged faces than the Cromagnons. Their brow-ridges formed continuous, prominent, bony ledges above the orbits; their noses were wide, their jaws large, and their chins under-developed to a varying degree. Certainly in the extreme Skhūl form (represented by Skhūl IV) the Cromagnon predominates over the Neanderthal characters.

Dr. Ales Hrdlicka may now claim that the presence of a proto-Cromagnon type among the cave-dwellers of Mount Carmel is a confirmation of the theory he advocated in his Huxley Lecture of 1927, namely, that the Neanderthalians of Europe did not become extinct, but in the course of a rapid evolution became transmuted into modern man. Dr. Hrdlicka believes that evolution was speeded up under the pressure of a growing arctic environment. Palestine lay beyond the ice-sheet and we cannot invoke glacial conditions to account for the evolutionary state of the Mount Carmel people.

It might be asserted that the right interpretation of the state of affairs found among the Mount Carmel people is very simple: that Neanderthal man is there being transformed into modern man of the Cromagnon type. This certainly is a simple explanation and a possible one, yet it does not seem to us to be the most probable.

In the first place, it is to be noted that the Neanthropic type which is making its appearance amongst the Skhūl people is a very particular form of modern man, one of the white or European type, for concerning the racial status of Cromagnon man there should be no doubt. All his features are European, Caucasian, or white. Our belief is that at Mount Carmel we have reached a transitional zone which leads from one ancient area of racial differentiation (the Neanderthal or Palaeoanthropic) to another ancient area lying farther to the east, a Neanthropic area where the proto-Caucasian (or proto-Cromagnon) type of man was being evolved. The evidence is now convincing that in mid-Pleistocene times the inhabitants of Europe—of the continent at least—were all Neanderthal in type, but we have seen that the type becomes modified as we proceed from west to east and that in Palestine we find a transitional type leading towards the Neanthropic type. It seems logical to us to assume that when the wide tracts of western Asia of mid-Pleistocene times are entered we shall find ourselves in the homeland of the proto-Caucasian. Eastern Asia we regard as the evolutionary cradle of the proto-Mongols. Our theory therefore assumes that the Mount Carmel people are not the actual ancestors of the Cromagnons but Neanderthaloid collaterals or cousins of the ancestors of that type. We expect that the fossil remains of the real proto-Cromagnons will be discovered still farther to the east.

Our hypothesis helps us to explain many events in the history of mankind in the western part of the Old World. If we assume that a progressive and conquering type of humanity was being evolved in western Asia in the remote times at which the Mount Carmel peoples lived, and that as their tribes increased in numbers and in strength they pushed continually westwards, replacing and extinguishing the native Neanderthalians, then we can give a reasonable explanation of the discoveries made by prehistorians and anthropologists in the late Pleistocene burials of Europe. Before the dawn of history western Asia served as a nursery for Europe, sending out peoples, cultures, and tongues. If our theory is well founded, then we must assume that this relationship between the two continents goes back to the remote times in which the Mount Carmel people lived. In brief, our theory assumes that Europe became the 'Australia' of the ancient world after mid-Pleistocene times and that the people who colonized it and extinguished its Neanderthal inhabitants, as the whites are now ousting the 'blacks' of Australia, were Caucasians evolved in western Asia.

An Analysis of the Structural Characters
of the Mount Carmel People

With a Note on Their Diseases,
Injuries, and Longevity

Marcellin Boule, in his monograph on *L'Homme fossile de la Chapelle-aux-Saints* (1911), has laid a foundation upon which other workers must build. He gives a list of characters which distinguish the Neanderthal species of man. We shall enumerate these characters in one column—altering his arrangement only in minor points; side by side with it we shall set a second column in which the corresponding characters of the Mount Carmel people are listed and agreements as well as differences noted. Then, in a third column, we shall give the corresponding characters of early Neanthropic peoples, selecting the Cromagnon described by Dr. René Verneau (1906) as a basis for our statements:

Analysis of the Diagnostic Characters of the Type or Species Represented by:

Neanderthal Man	*Mount Carmel Man*	*Cromagnon Man*
1. Stature, short but stocky.	Men tall, women short or of medium stature.	Men tall, women of medium stature or small.
2. Head massive with the facial parts large relatively to the brain-containing part.	Head massive, but face not excessively developed.	Head massive, but face not excessively developed.
3. Skull dolichocephalic or mesaticephalic.	Most are strongly dolichocephalic but one—Tabūn woman—has an index of 77.	Most are strongly dolichocephalic.
4. The vault is very low (platycephalic).	Vault of medium, or even above medium height.	Vault high.
5. Eyebrow ridges assume form of continuous torus.	Torus, but with a tendency to separate into medial and lateral parts.	Separation into medial and lateral parts is complete.
6. Forehead very receding.	Forehead moderately full.	Moderately or fully developed.
7. Occiput 'en bourrelet', compressed vertically; does not project behind attachment of neck.	Not compressed vertically. Projects slightly beyond attachment of neck.	Compressed laterally. Projects well behind attachment of neck.
8. Face—particularly the upper face—very long.	Face of moderate—or above moderate—length.	Face of moderate length.
9. Face prognathous.	Face usually orthognathous.	Face orthognathous.
10. Malar bone has the flat form seen in anthropoid apes.	Malar is flat and anthropoid-like, but with a decided tendency in some individuals towards a Neanthropic form.	Malar is Neanthropic.
11. Superior maxilae are devoid of canine fossae and are snout-like in form.	Superior maxillae, although devoid of fossae, are flattened in front but are usually not snouted.	Neanthropic.

Neanderthal Man	*Mount Carmel Man*	*Cromagnon Man*
12. Orbits are large and rounded in form.	Orbits wide but not high.	Orbits wide but not high.
13. Nose very large, projecting and wide, its lateral margins not demarcated from face.	Nose variable in projection and width. Laterally it is partially demarcated.	Nose variable in projection, usually narrow; laterally sharply demarcated.
14. Subnasal part of face is deep and wide.	Subnasal area wide, but not deep.	Subnasal area moderate in width and depth.
15. Mandible robust.	Variable – some robust, others if large yet not robust, some small, but stoutly built.	Moderate in development both in size and in strength.
16. Chin absent or rudimentary.	Chin absent or of moderate development.	Chin moderate or well developed.
17. Ascending mandibular ramus very wide.	Width varies – in some very wide, others of moderate width.	Width varies; some very wide.
18. Mandible, in the region of the angle, truncated or flattened.	Angle moderately developed.	Angle moderately or well developed.
19. Teeth are big.	Teeth are moderate in size or large.	Teeth moderate in size.
20. Molars retain certain primitive characters.	Molars retain certain primitive characters.	Molars are Neanthropic in characterization.
21. Spinal column and its vertebrae present pithecoid characters.	Spine and vertebrae possess certain Neanderthaloid features; others are Neanthropic.	Spine and vertebrae are Neanthropic.
22. Adaptation to the upright posture and to bipedal progression less perfect than in Neanthropic man.	Adaptation to bipedal progression apparently as perfect as in modern man; cervical curvature probably less developed than in Neanthropic man.	As in Neanthropic man.
23. Lower limbs short.	Lower limbs long.	Lower limbs long.
24. Mean cranial capacity about 1,400 c.c.	Capacity in three adult males ranges from 1,518 c.c. to 1,587 c.c.; one woman (Tabūn) 1,271 c.c.; one woman (Skhūl) about 1,300 or 1,350 c.c.	Capacity large.
25. In form the brain shows primitive or simian features, particularly in the small size of frontal lobes and in convolutionary pattern.	Neither in size nor in form of lobes is there a decided difference from brain of Neanthropic man. Convolutionary pattern – so far as our evidence goes – was simple.	Lobes large and well convoluted.

When we analyse the twenty-five characters tabulated above we find only three in which the Mount Carmel people answer to M. Boule's definition—in the frontal torus, in the form of malar, and in the pattern of molar teeth. In eight they agree with the Cromagnon type. In twelve they are intermediate; three characters are common in all there—namely, dolichocephaly, a wide ascending mandibular ramus and a moderate or large cranial capacity. If we base our conclusions solely on these diagnostic characters then we must regard the Mount Carmel as an intermediate people in which Cromagnon (Neanthropic) characters predominate over those which are Neanderthal (Palaeoanthropic).

If we are to be guided entirely by this census of characters then we must count the Mount Carmel people to have a greater resemblance—to be much more akin—to an early Neanthropic people—the Cromagnons—than to the Neanderthal people of western Europe. For our table shows that Neanderthal characters, and *quasi*-Neanderthal characters, make up only 55.8 per cent of the total, while Neanthropic, and *quasi*-Neanthropic features, amount to 70.2 per cent of the total. This must be our final conclusion if we regard every character in our list as of equal value. We do not believe that characters are of equal value when we come to adjudicate on the genetic relationship of one human race to another. A very large proportion of the Neanthropic characters of the Mount Carmel people lies in the conformation of their limb bones. Such characters form a functional group which must undergo correlated changes—all directed towards the fulfilment of the purposes for which limbs are used. By counting each character as of equal value we give the minor correlated or plastic features an unfair representation. We feel that dental characters—such as the cusp arrangement of the incisors, premolars, and molars—have a greater taxonomic value than the anatomical features of the femur. So, too, with the supra-orbital torus, the form of the malar, the width of the great wing of the sphenoid, and certain features of the carpal bones; these seem to us to be the more reliable 'sign-posts'

Two other considerations weigh with us in placing the Mount Carmel people in the Palaeoanthropic genus and not in the Neanthropic. The first is the great number of their characters which are intermediate, namely, 41.4 per cent. The second is this: we feel certain that when the limb bones of the Krapina people—certainly a Palaeoanthropic people—are better known, they will show many more resemblances to those of the Mount Carmel people than to the Neanderthalians of Western Europe.

There is, too, an important matter to be mentioned about the characters we have classified as intermediate. First, there are those of a true transitional kind—such as the size and shape of the squama of the temporal, the nuchal impressions of the occipital, the spines of the cervical vertebrae, characters at the upper end of the femur, and in the characterization of the calcaneus. But in the same group we have also included such features as the mastoid process—which is Neanderthal in form and size in the Tabūn woman and in a Skhūl woman (VII), but is purely Neanthropic in the Skhūl men, particularly in Skhūl VI. Or take the chin: it is absent in the Tabūn woman and every grade in its earlier evolution is found in the other mandibles. A great number of our intermediate characters are intermediate in that they form units of an intermediate series. The Mount Carmel people collectively possess intermediate states which bridge the structural hiatus lying between the Neanderthal and Neanthropic types.

We have already given it as our opinion that Mount Carmel man has come by his Neanthropic characters—not by hybridization—but by a natural and separate evolutionary history. The abundance of Neanthropic characters in Mount Carmel man is an indication, we think, that he broke away from the stem of mankind emerging in western Asia during early Pleistocene times, at a date later than did the ancestral stock of the Neanderthals of western Europe. Being later in his separation, Mount Carmel man has thereby come to have a larger share of Neanthropic characters of the stock which ultimately produced the Cromagnon and other Neanthropic types.

We have not drawn up a list of the points in which the Tabūn woman differs from the Skhūl people. In every chapter we have discussed their differences. There are, however, two anatomical features of the Tabūn woman which demand particular consideration. These are the peculiar form taken by the pubic part of her pelvis and the strange shape given to her pisiform. We find it very difficult to believe that these are mere individual anomalies; they have all the appearance of intrinsic structures of morphological value. Only future discoveries can resolve the problem of her position—whether an individual sport, or a representative of a distinct race.

One point more remains to be mentioned. We have presumed—whenever we have discussed the Tabūn and Skhūl types—that the Tabūn was the more primitive and therefore the earlier. Is this assumption justified? Miss Garrod draws attention to the possibility of the Tabūn woman being later than the stratum in which her remains were found. She might therefore be later in date than the Skhūl people. The teeth and jaws of the child found in the upper stratum (B) of the Tabūn cave have all the characters of the Tabūn type but the deposit in which they were found is later than that in which the Tabūn woman was interred.

In rejecting the idea that the Tabūn people came after those of the Skhūl type we are guided by the very primitive features of the mandible known as Tabūn II and the similarity of its teeth to those of the Tabūn woman; it is hard to believe that the mandible of the Tabūn man could represent people which lived later than the Skhūl people. Miss Garrod found fragments of the people who lived in the Tabūn cave at a very early period—towards the close of the Acheulean. These fragments—a shaft of a femur and a worn molar—indicate a people of the Tabūn—not of the Skhūl type. This fact also supports the idea that the Tabūn type is the older.

Injuries and Diseases of the Mount Carmel People

Discussing the industry of the Neanderthalians of Europe, Boule has written, 'L'utilisation d'une seule matière première (en dehors du bois et peut-être de l'os), l'uniformité, la simplicité et la grossièreté de son outillage lithique . . . s'accordent bien avec l'aspect brutal de ce corps vigoureux et lourd.'* The Mount Carmel People. assigned to an earlier geological period than the Neanderthalians of Europe, were better equipped. A wound of the left hip joint of the strong Skhūl man (IX) gives unequivocal testimony to their possession of spear-like weapons of great penetrating power. The injury was caused at death or soon after death. The weapon pierced and shivered the whole thickness of the head of the femur, the floor of the acetabulum, and entered the pelvic cavity. After the matrix had been cleaned out of the track of the weapon it was possible to obtain a cast which reproduces the shape and the size of the bony cavity formed by the implement. The penetrating part of the weapon evidently became broken from the shaft; at least this part remained embedded in the wound and became surrounded by a coating of stalagmite. Had the head of the weapon been made of stone or bone it would have persisted, just as the bone around it has been preserved. We infer that it was made of hard wood, perhaps fire-hardened. To cause such an injury the weapon must have had a hard and resistant point and the man who used it must have had great strength.

The skull of the same man shows an extensive injury. A close examination of the margins of the injury leads us to think that it was caused by a glancing blow at, or soon after, death. The evidence in this case in not unequivocal.

The body of the child, Skhūl I, shows three injuries which were inflicted at death, or not unlikely at some time soon after death, but before the bones had become mineralized. The injuries affect the forehead, the right temporo-mandibular region, and the lower dorsal region of the spinal column.

The distal halves of metatarsals II and III of the left foot of Skhūl IV show evidence of having been broken obliquely, followed by good union. From the

*"The use of a single raw material (besides wood and perhaps bone), the uniformity, simplicity, and crudeness of his lithic tool suits well the brutal aspect of his vigorous and heavy body."

site of fracture on each side of the second space there has been a bony outgrowth. These outgrowths come into contact but have not united.

There is no trace of caries in any of the teeth from the Tabūn or from the Skhūl caves, there are few signs of alveolar abscesses and very few teeth have been lost during life.

The roots of the lower molar teeth of Skhūl IV are exposed owing to a depression of the alveolar bone which surrounds them. This seems to have been due to a 'packing' of food rather than to pyorrhea alveolaris. Indeed, there is no certain evidence of the latter disease.

The crowns of the teeth show varying degrees of wear, but none manifests the degree of erosion often met with in the dentitions of modern native peoples. When we regard their probable age, the teeth of the Skhūl men are remarkably little worn.

The second premolars in Skhūl IV, both upper and lower, are malposed, an anomaly which occurs in modern races. In a lower jaw found at Krapina the first premolar shows a similar malposition.

The absence of rheumatiod changes in the joints is quite remarkable. Only two joints are the seat of such changes: the left temporo-mandibular joint of Skhūl VII (female) and the same joint on the right side in Skhūl V. It will be remembered that the large Krapina mandible (I) was the subject of this disease. It is not uncommon in the skulls of native peoples in which the teeth are deeply worn.

Longevity

Recently Professor H. Vallois (1937) has drawn attention to the high rate of mortality amongst races of the Pleistocene period. Relying on the degree to which cranial sutures had closed and the extent of wear of the teeth as guides to age, he came to the conclusion that old age, as we know it, was never reached by Palaeolithic man. The evidence from Mount Carmel has led us to a similar conclusion. We have grounds for assessing the age at which twelve individuals of the Mount Carmel population died. Four died in childhood (Skhūl I, VIII, X, Tabūn Series I) ranging from 4 to 10 years. One was under thirty (Tabūn I); five were between 30 and 40 (Tabūn II, Skhūl II, V, VI, VII), one was over 40 and under 50 (Skhūl IV), and only one (Skhūl IX) was over 50. We leave to statisticians the task of calculating the expectation of life, and the birth-rate that was needed to maintain even a stationary population in this Palestinian community of the last or Riss-Würm interglacial period.

Observations on the Anatomy of the
Fossil Australopithecinae

W. E. Le Gros Clark*

The Australopithecinae, a sub-family of the Hominoidea originally created by Gregory & Hellman (1939), include all those fossil ape-like creatures whose remains have been recovered from limestone deposits in South Africa and which are at present allocated to the three genera *Australopithecus* (Dart), *Plesianthropus* (Broom) and *Paranthropus* (Broom). The present writer has recently had the opportunity and privilege of seeing this material during a short visit to Johannesburg and Pretoria and, owing to the generous facilities provided by those who were concerned with its actual discovery, Prof. Raymond Dart and Dr Robert Broom, he has been able to study it in some detail. In the present paper, some of the results of this examination are presented. In view of the numerous publications which have already appeared in reference to the Australopithecinae, and particularly the comprehensive monographic study recently published by Broom & Schepers (1946), it might be deemed superfluous to submit a further report. However, this appears justifiable for two reasons. In the first place, it has now become apparent that the fossils are of quite paramount importance in relation to problems of human phylogeny, and it is, therefore, hardly possible to overemphasize their significance. Secondly, it has to be admitted that, in the past, several anatomists of recognized distinction have, by their misinterpretation of the evidence, tended to belittle their importance. Even in some recent publications dealing with human palaeontology, e.g. the latest edition of Boule's '*Les Hommes Fossiles*' edited by Vallois (1946), their significance is evidently understated. The observations recorded in this paper are partly supplementary to those of Dart and Broom, and partly a re-emphasis of details which

*1947 ("The Journal of Anatomy," Vol. 81, Part 3, October)

293

have already been mentioned by those authorities and which seem to the present writer of such special significance as to merit renewed attention.

As is now well known, the first representative of the Australopithecinae to be discovered was *Australopithecus*. This genus is represented by the skull and natural endocranial cast of a young individual which were discovered at Taungs in Bechuanaland and described by Dart in 1925. In 1936 and during subsequent years, remains of adult Australopithecines were found by Broom at Sterkfontein and Kromdraai, two places close to Krugersdorp and only two miles from each other. These remains, which include portions of skulls, natural endocranial casts, jaws, teeth and fragments of limb bones have been allocated by Broom to two separate genera, *Plesianthropus* (from Sterkfontein) and *Paranthropus* (from Kromdraai).

For convenience of reference, the following list is given of the parts of Australopithecine skulls found by Dr Broom.* The type specimen of *Plesianthropus* consists of the whole of the base of the skull (with a natural endocranial cast in position), a considerable part of the facial skeleton and palate, a portion of the cranial roof (including a negative cast of the latter in the limestone matrix), and a fragment of the squamous portion of the occipital bone. Other material from Sterkfontein includes an excellently preserved right maxilla with some of the teeth *in situ*, a much crushed left maxilla with a portion of the zygomatic bone attached, the symphysial part of an immature mandible, and the angular region of the mandible of an adult individual. The type skull of *Paranthropus* consists of the left maxilla and zygomatic bone, a considerable part of the palate, the temporal and sphenoidal regions of the skull wall, the zygomatic arch, the glenoid fossa, the external auditory meatus, and part of the occipital bone. The type mandible includes the body of the right side with the molar and premolar teeth, the lower end of the vertical ramus, and a (separated) symphysial fragment. In addition, the mandible of a young individual with the milk dentition excellently preserved was found embedded in the limestone matrix not more than 4 ft. from the type skull.

A systematic account of all the fossil Australopithecine remains has been given by Broom & Schepers in their recent monograph. From this account, the following main points emerge. The Australopithecinae had quite small brains, approximating in size to those of the gorilla and chimpanzee, and massive jaws with large molar and premolar teeth but relatively small incisors and canines. The dental arch is evenly curved in parabolic form (thus contrasting very strongly with the recent anthropoid apes), and the molar

*Since this was written Dr Broom has announced further important discoveries of *Plesianthropus* material.

teeth show a type of wear due to attrition apparently identical with that characteristic of man. In the construction of the supra-orbital region, the details of temporo-mandibular articulation, and the disposition of the foramen magnum (as well as several other cranial characters), the Australopithecine skull shows a definite approach to the human skull. Lastly, the limb-bone fragments, particularly the lower end of the humerus of *Paranthropus*, and the lower end of the femur of *Plesianthropus*, seem to indicate a limb structure which evidently approximated very closely indeed to that of *Homo sapiens*. This evidence of the limb bones is sufficiently startling in character to raise a doubt as to whether they actually belonged to the same creatures as the skulls of *Plesianthropus* and *Paranthropus*. That the association is entirely correct, however, seems quite well assured as will be seen in a later section. On the basis of the evidence presented by the first announcement of the discoveries of the Australopithecine fossils, there seemed at first sight to be several possible interpretations. The Australopithecinae might be nothing more than extinct varieties of ape closely akin to the chimpanzee and gorilla, but with certain modifications which in some minor respects show a spurious resemblance to the Hominidae. Secondly, they might have no special relationship to the gorilla and chimpanzee, but, nevertheless, represent a collateral group of anthropoid apes showing certain human characters developed as the result of a parallel evolution but not necessarily indicative of any real affinity with the Hominidae. Lastly, the Australopithecinae could be regarded as extinct hominoids which, while still at (or, at least, close to) the simian level in their cerebral development, were early representatives of the human branch of evolution and thus quite distinct from the Pongidae. This last interpretation has for a number of years been reiterated by Dart and Broom. On the other hand, other anatomists and palaeontologists (particularly those who have not had the advantage of examining the original fossil material) have, either by direct statement or by implication, favoured one of the first two interpretations. As the result of his personal studies, the present writer has come to the firm conclusions (1) that the Australopithecinae have no special relationship to the recent anthropoid apes except so far as they are large hominoids of comparable size, and (2) that the human resemblances in the skull, dentition and limb bones are so numerous, detailed and intimate as virtually to preclude the introduction of the idea of 'parallel evolution' in order to explain them. In other words, there must be a real zoological relationship between the Australopithecinae and the Hominidae.

For the main descriptive details of the Australopithecine material, the reader is referred to the many publications of Dart and Broom (see the bibliography in the monograph by Broom & Schepers, 1946). As already mentioned, the present communication is concerned not with a systematic account of these fossils (which would be unnecessary), but with certain points which appear to be of special significance.

The Skull of the Australopithecinae

The general character of the Australopithecine skull. The facial part of the skull of *Australopithecus* is excellently preserved, and the natural endocranial cast permits a satisfactory reconstruction of the general contour of the calvarium, including certain features of the skull base. The type skull of *Plesianthropus* is sufficiently complete (except for the mandible) to justify a reconstruction of the intact skull with reasonable accuracy. The skull fragments of *Paranthropus* include the facial and temporal regions, some important components of the basis cranii, and most of the mandible. It is thus possible, from this material, to enumerate with considerable confidence all the outstanding features of the Australopithecine skull. In general appearance the combination of massive jaws with a small brain case comparable in size with that of a large chimpanzee or of a gorilla suggests to the inexperienced or uncritical eye a creature closely related to the modern large apes. However, those who are well acquainted with primate anatomy will recognize some highly significant differences. These are to be seen in the degree of alveolar prognathism (conditioned by the relative size of the incisor and canine teeth), the contour of the supra-orbital and frontal regions, the appearance in lateral view of the orbits (particularly the recession of the lateral margin), the forward position of the auditory meatus, temporo-mandibular joint and foramen magnum, the shape and disposition of the zygomatic bone (including the level of its temporal process), the details of the glenoid cavity, the contour of the aveolar borders of the maxilla and mandible, the late closure of the sutures of the cranial vault, and the relatively weak development of muscular ridges. In all these features, the Australopithecinae show a very definite approach to *Homo*, and in many of them the detailed resemblances seem to be sufficiently remarkable to exclude the idea of parallelism as a possible explanation.

The Dentition

The anatomical characters of the Australopithecine dentition have been discussed in great detail by Dart (1943), Broom & Schepers (1946), and Gregory & Hellman (1939) as the result of studies of the original fossil material, and also by Adloff (1932), Abel (1931), Senyürek (1941) and Montandon (1939) on the basis of casts and photographs. There is little that can be added to the information already published. The present writer was able to confirm all the descriptive details reported by Broom and Dart, and was much impressed with the remarkably human characters apparent in the milk dentition and in the attritional wear of the permanent premolars and molars. There is no doubt that these human appearances obtrude themselves much more forcibly on the eye in the examination of the original teeth than in the examination of plaster casts (however excellent and accurate the latter may be). The special importance of the milk dentition lies in the consideration that, if the human characters of the adult Australopithecine dentition are after all merely secondary developments, i.e. the result of a convergent evolution from a more typically simian dentition of the Dryopithecine type, then the 'primitive' simian features might at least be expected to manifest themselves in the milk dentition. However, this is by no means the case, as was first demonstrated by Dart in *Australopithecus*. The milk dentition of *Paranthropus* is now also known in the greatest detail from the beautifully preserved teeth which Dr Broom discovered on the Kromdraai site not more than 4 ft. from the spot where the adult *Paranthropus* skull was obtained. These teeth reproduce the same general features (but with some differences in detail) already described in the milk dentition of *Australopithecus*. The incisors and canine teeth are, in their diminutive size, beyond the range of variation recorded for the corresponding deciduous teeth of the modern large apes (Remane, 1921), and the first deciduous molar appears to be entirely human in its shape, proportions and cusp pattern. The *Australopithecus* jaw belongs to a relatively older child than the immature *Paranthropus* jaw, for in the former the first molar had almost completed its eruption. A point of some considerable interest lies in the extent to which the deciduous molars in the *Australopithecus* specimen have been worn down by attrition. It would be difficult to express such a feature quantitatively, but such an exposure of the dentine by wear has not been observed by the present writer in the milk molars of modern anthropoid apes of a corresponding age. According to the information at present available (see Schultz, 1935), in the chimpanzee the milk molars have completed their eruption by the seventeenth month and the first permanent molars come into position as early as the end of the third year. Thus, there is a comparatively short interval of about 19 months between the two periods of eruption during which the milk molars are exposed to attrition. In man the milk molars have usually erupted before the end of the second year, while the first permanent molar does not come into position till the sixth year. In this case, therefore, the interval between the two events is much longer (perhaps as much as 4 years). The degree of attrition of the milk molars in *Australopithecus* suggests rather strongly that in this extinct genus the eruption time of the first permanent molar may have been delayed as it is in man. If this inference is sound, it serves to confirm the implication of the delayed closure of the sutures of the cranial vault in *Plesianthropus* (vide supra), i.e. that the growth period of the Australopithecinae was prolonged beyond that of the modern large apes. Such a conclusion is of considerable significance, for the prolongation of the growth period is highly characteristic of the human family.

That the dental anatomy of the Australopithecinae as a whole is far more human than simian is sufficiently attested by the conclusions of all those authorities who have made a serious study of the fossil teeth. It is instructive to record these conclusions in summary form. Dart (1934) stated that there is no really significant feature in the dentition of *Australopithecus* that can be termed simian, and that 'if any single tooth in this dentition had been found separately, it would unquestionably have been called a human tooth'. Broom (Broom & Schepers, 1946) sums up his comprehensive survey of all the available Australopithecine teeth by saying that 'the dentition of both the milk and the permanent sets agrees remarkably closely with the dentition of man, and only differs in retaining a few more primitive characters and in being a little larger in most cases'. Gregory (1930), in a comparative study of the teeth of *Australopithecus*, drew up a list of resemblances to, or differences from, other hominoids; out of twenty-six characters he found that in twenty the *Australopithecus* teeth are transitional to, or nearer to, primitive man, while in only three characters are they nearer to the chimpanzee or gorilla. In a subsequent intensive study of all the Australopithecine teeth then available, Gregory & Hellman (1939) were led to agree with Broom that 'in South Africa there once lived apes which had almost become men'. Abel (1931), in a critical examination of the Australopithecine dentition, thought the teeth showed some signs of specialization, but he recognized many of the remarkable hominoid features. For example, he noted that little difference is to be found in the comparison of the first milk molar with that of recent hominoids. Adloff (1932) was more definite in his conclusions, for he emphatically affirms: 'The bite of the Australopithecine however is purely human and leads to the conclusion that the Australopithecine is not an anthropoid but a hominoid.' Senyürek (1941) concluded from his studies of the teeth that the Australopithecines 'are nearer to the primitive hominoids than to the apes', and Montandon (1939) expressed exactly the same opinion. As the result of his study of the original material, the present writer is able to add his support to all these conclusions by expressing the opinion that, on the basis of the dentition alone, there can be no question of any close affinity of the Australopithecinae with the modern anthropoid apes, or even with the Dryopithecinae. In other words, if only the evidence of the teeth were to be taken into account, the allocation of these fossil creatures to the Hominidae rather than to the Pongidae would seem a logical necessity.

The Limb Bones

At Sterkfontein and Kromdraai some important fragments of limb bones have been found which have been ascribed to *Plesianthropus* and *Paranthropus*. Those which we shall consider in this section include the lower end of a left femur and a right os capitatum from Sterkfontein, and the lower end of a right humerus, upper end of a right ulna and a right talus from Kromdraai. The striking fact which has emerged from Dr Broom's studies is that all these bones show remarkably human characteristics; indeed, the lower end of the humerus and the femoral fragment, if considered alone and without reference to the circumstances of their recovery, would probably be classified as belonging to *Homo sapiens*. It may be questioned, therefore, whether the limb bones are correctly to be associated with the skulls and teeth of *Plesianthropus* and *Paranthropus*. Are they, for example, the limb bones of some hominid form which lived contemporaneously with the Australopithecinae, or which, though found in the same kind of bone breccia and on the same site, are really derived from a geological horizon of later date? The available evidence is against such suppositions. They are all heavily mineralized like the skull bones. Dr Broom has affirmed that the humeral and ulnar fragments and the talus were found close together in the same bone breccia which contained the type skull of *Paranthropus* and within 1 ft. of it. The ulnar and humeral fragments articulate in close conformity with each other and thus almost certainly represent the component parts of the right elbow joint of the same individual. The talus also belongs to the right side. All these bones are identifiable as the bones of a large hominoid, and no remains of a large hominoid have been found at the site apart from *Paranthropus*. Also, no other remains of any large limb bones have been discovered at the Kromdraai site which could be attributed to *Paranthropus*. Lastly, in spite of an extensive search through great quantities of breccia, during which many skulls, teeth and bones of lower mammals have been found, no trace has been seen of human skulls and teeth, nor any signs of human habitation. The intrinsic evidence of the limb bones themselves provides the final justification for their association with *Paranthropus*, for, though predominantly human in their general appearance, they have quite special characteristics of their own. As will be seen below, the humerus and the talus both present exceptional features, and in the case of the talus there is an interesting combination of simian and human characters which harmonizes well with the same sort of combination provided by the skull, brain and teeth of *Paranthropus*.

The capitate bone and lower end of the femur ascribed to *Plesianthropus* were not found in direct association with the remains of the skull and teeth, but were derived from the limestone matrix at the Sterkfontein site where (as Broom states) the remains of not less than three separate skulls of *Plesianthropus* have been discovered. As with the Kromdraai specimens, they are both clearly bones of a large hominoid, and no remains of any fossil hominoids apart from *Plesianthropus* have been found at the Sterkfontein site. There is certainly no trace of human skulls and teeth, or of human occupation. The capitate bone shows a combination of human and simian characters which is in harmony with the skull and brain of *Plesianthropus*. The lower end of the femur is adapted for a completely erect posture as in man, but also shows peculiarities of its own. Thus, although the human appearance of these two bones, particularly the femur, might raise a doubt as to the correctness of their association with skulls and brains which are so simian in their general proportions, the available evidence is entirely in favour of this association. The climatological evidence is also pertinent to this question, for it indicates that the Australopithecinae were certainly not forest-living creatures like the recent anthropoid apes. They must, therefore, have been adapted to a completely terrestrial life, which would have required the type of lower limb indicated by the femoral fragment discovered at Sterkfontein. Lastly, as at Kromdraai, many skulls, teeth and bones of lower mammals have been exposed in the breccia from the Sterkfontein site, but among this mass of material there is no sign of other types of hominoid limb bones which could belong to *Plesianthropus* excepting these. Taking all this evidence into careful account, the present writer finds no reason to doubt the

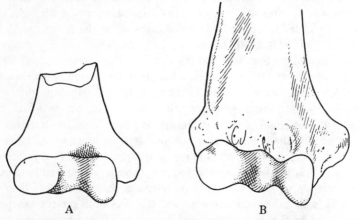

Fig. 1. The lower end of the right humerus of *Paranthropus* (A) seen from in front, compared with that of an adult male chimpanzee (B). X 2/3.

Australopithecine nature of the large limb bones so far discovered at Kromdraai and Sterkfontein and ascribed to *Paranthropus* and *Plesianthropus* by Dr Broom.

The humerus. The lower end of the right humerus of *Paranthropus* is quite well preserved except for a small flake off the anterior surface of the capitulum. It shows a very close resemblance to the humerus of *Homo sapiens* and none of the distinctive features found in the recent anthropoid apes (Figure 1). The triceps and brachialis surfaces of the lower end of the shaft of the humerus are smooth, and their contours are quite similar to those of man. Broom suggests that the curvature of the articular surface of the capitulum shows certain features which may distinguish it from the humerus of modern man, but, if this should prove to be the case, they are probably too slight to be of great significance. On the other hand, the position of the capitulum in relation to the axis of the lower end of the shaft of the humerus (particularly as seen in lateral view) is not set quite so far forward as it normally is in *Homo sapiens*. This relation of the lower articular end to the shaft of the humerus is much more pronounced in the trochlear surface, as seen both from the lateral and medial views of the humerus (Figures 2 and 3). In the human (and more so in the simian) humerus, the trochlea is set well forward in relation to the shaft, and especially in relation to the medial epicondyle. In *Paranthropus*, on the other hand, the transverse central axis of the trochlea lies approximately within the line of the long axis of the lower end of the shaft of the humerus. The significance of this alinement of the trochlea is not at all clear. Mechanically it must mean some limitation of the power of flexion (since the leverage in the flexor action of the biceps and brachialis muscles would be somewhat diminished) and a capacity for hyper-extension at the elbow joint to a degree not usually possible in recent anthropoid apes or man. The only other feature of the humeral fragment which calls for mention is the presence of a deep pit about 2 mm. in diameter, evidently a vascular foramen, behind the lateral epicondyle. Around this foramen the bone is slightly roughened. It is suggested that this is the result of a mild localized periostitis (probably due to trauma) which has led to increased vascularization and the enlargement of one of the vascular foramina which are usually found in this position.

The ulna. The upper end of the right ulna (which consists of little more than the olecranon process and the upper two-thirds of the trochear notch) was found in close proximity to the lower end of the right humerus of *Paranthropus*, and since they articulate together in close conformity, there is no doubt (as Broom has also stated) that they belong to the same individual. Like the humeral fragment, the ulnar fragment appears to correspond in all its main features to the human bone. The curvature of the trochlear notch and the prominence of the 'beak' of the olecranon process (so far as this is preserved) are not quite so marked as they usually are in *Homo*. On the upper aspect of the olecranon process the rim of the articular surface (for the attachment of the joint capsule) is preserved in its lateral third and is separated by a narrow well-defined groove from a smooth bursal area which closely corresponds in its extent with that of the human ulna. The area for the attachment of the triceps is relatively small and but slightly roughened. In

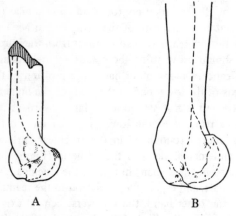

Fig. 2. The lower end of the right humerus of *Paranthropus* (A) seen from the lateral aspect, compared with that of an adult male chimpanzee (B). X 2/3.

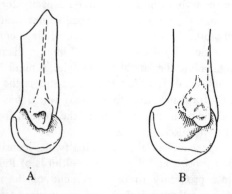

Fig. 3. The lower end of the right humerus of *Paranthropus* (A) seen from the medial aspect, compared with that of an adult male chimpanzee (B). X 2/3.

all these characters, the *Paranthropus* ulna contrasts strongly with that of the anthropoid apes, which shows a massive development of the olecranon process with particularly prominent ridges on its medial and lateral aspects demarcating the surfaces for the attachment of the flexor digitorum profundus and anconeus muscles. These features are, of course, related to the powerful development of the arms in the recent anthropoid apes for use in brachiation.

The talus. The talus of *Paranthropus* presents a number of remarkable features which together appear to indicate a general construction of the bone somewhat intermediate between that of man and the lower hominoids. The whole bone is very small, as is evident from the size of the superior articular surface (for articulation with the lower end of the timia). The width of this at its anterior margin is 20.5 mm., which corresponds closely with that of an adult chimpanzee foot. In Europeans the same dimension is stated to have a range of 31–37 mm., and in female Japanese 28–30 mm. (Adachi, 1905). In two Bushman skeletons which have been examined, the measurements were 23 and 25 mm. It may also be of interest to record that in the talus of a European child aged 12 years in this department, the width is 23 mm.

The superior articular facet of the *Paranthropus* talus resembles man in being relatively broad and also in its even curvature from side to side (Figures 4 and 5). In the gorilla and chimpanzee, the surface in transverse section is somewhat flattened medially, and laterally slopes gradually upwards to the lateral border. This asymmetrical contour is related to a different orientation of the subtalar articular facets (see Morton, 1926), and is possibly associated with the fact that the load line of the femur and tibia passes through their medial condyles and presumably is transmitted rather to the medial side of the body of the talus. In man (as also in *Paranthropus*) the shape of the superior surface evidently indicates a more even distribution in the transmission of body weight. The lateral fibular facet is somewhat less strongly curved than in the recent anthropoid apes, and is also less extensive. In the fossil talus, it should be noted, the lower margin of this facet at its apex can be made out close to the lower fractured surface of the bone. In the chimpanzee and gorilla, the maximum vertical extent of the fibular facet is always greater than the width of the superior articular surface taken at a level midway between its anterior and posterior borders. In the *Paranthropus* talus, as in man, it is less. The medial facet (for the medial malleolus) is quite similar in contour and extent to that of man, and its articular surface is approximately vertical. In the gorilla and chimpanzee this surface slopes medially to a marked extent (Figure 6), and in the chimpanzee it is excavated anteriorly to form a conspicuous cup-shaped socket which engages and locks with the anterior margin of the medial malleolus, so limiting movement at full

dorsiflexion. The neck of the fossil talus is rather short, but its unusual
relative width tends to give this character a somewhat exaggerated appearance. The wide neck of the talus is associated with an extent of the articular
surface (for the navicular bone) on the 'head' of the bone which is remarkable
(particularly when it is considered in relation to the size of the bone as a
whole). Medially this navicular surface projects to a distance of at least 8 mm.
beyond the level of the plane of the medial tibial articular facet (when the
talus is oriented with the central axis of the superior facet in a sagittal plane),
and in this character it reproduces the condition found in the gorilla and
chimpanzee and differs strongly from the modern human talus. In its lateral
extent, however, the articular head of the fossil talus reaches towards the
level of the lateral border of the superior articular surface, well beyond the

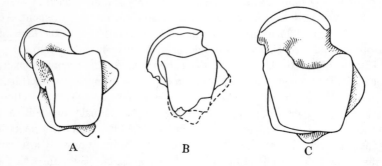

Fig. 4. The dorsal aspect of the right talus of a male chimpanzee (A),
Paranthropus (B) and a female Japanese (C). × 2/3.

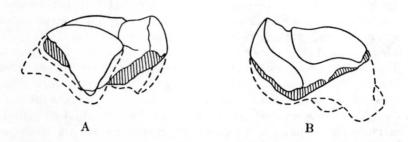

Fig. 5. Lateral (A) and medial (B) views of the right talus of *Paranthropus*.
The reconstructed portions are indicated by interrupted lines. Natural size.

central axis of the latter, as in man, and thus contrasts with the typical simian condition in which it hardly extends laterally beyond the level of the central axis. Lastly, it will be noted from the accompanying figures that in the fossil bone the type of curvature of the head corresponds with the human and not with the chimpanzee talus. In the latter the head is of much more hemispherical form and permits of greater freedom of movement at the subtalar joints in eversion and inversion. In the gorilla where, in adaptation to a heavier body weight and more terrestrial habits, greater stability is required, the articular surface of the head is more broadly curved as in man.

From a consideration of these anatomical details, it may be inferred that in *Paranthropus* the body of the talus was constructed for stability in weight bearing, as shown by the contour and relative width of the superior articular facet, and for the rapid alternating movements of flexion and extension of the ankle joint required for walking, and particularly for running. This is evidenced by the contour and orientation of the facets for the malleoli, which with the superior articular surface form a composite 'trochlear' articulation of much greater efficiency as a pure hinge-joint mechanism than in the modern anthropoid apes. On the other hand, the slope and contour of the lateral and

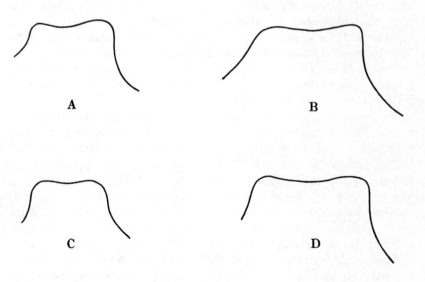

Fig. 6. The contours of transverse sections through the talus in the plane of the maximum extension of the medial and lateral facets. A, chimpanzee; B, gorilla; C, *Paranthropus*; D, man. Natural size.

medial facets in the gorilla and chimpanzee, together with the relative narrowness of the superior articular facet, clearly provide for more complex movements (involving some degree of side-to-side deflection) and at the same time limit the weight-bearing stability of the ankle joint, particularly during attempted movements of walking and running. The broad curvature of the head of the *Paranthropus* talus evidently provides for stability in the transmission of the body weight to the fore part of the foot in standing. Its remarkable extent medially and laterally would presumably permit the transference of a major component of the body weight directly forwards as in man or would permit it to be deflected medially to the extent which is found in the modern anthropoid apes with their divergent great toes. It is thus perhaps permissible to suggest that in *Paranthropus* the hallux may have been capable of some degree of divergence which would allow of its use for grasping purposes, and that it could also be brought into close alinement with the other toes for use in the human posture of standing and walking.

The femur. The distal extremity of a left femur discovered in the lower cave at Sterkfontein has been ascribed by Broom to *Plesianthropus*. There can be little doubt that this allocation is correct. The femoral fragment is clearly that of a large hominoid, and intensive and prolonged searches in the Sterkfontein deposits have failed to reveal the remains of any large hominoid other than *Plesianthropus*. Moreover, the small size of the femur is in harmony with the small size of the capitate bone which was also found in the Sterkfontein matrix and which, as already indicated, is almost certainly to be referred to *Plesianthropus*. In its anatomical details, however, the bone shows a resemblance to the femur of *Homo* which is so close as to amount to practical identity.

The size of the bone is remarkably small. The bicondylar width (measured by the method described by Parsons, 1913–14) is 56.5 mm., which is considerably below the lowest measurement recorded by Parsons for adult English femora of either sex. On the other hand, it corresponds to the bicondylar width of a European child of 12 years (as shown by a comparison with material in this department) or to that of an adult male chimpanzee. In four Bushman skeletons examined, the measurement was found to range from 53 to 63.5 mm. The lower end of the shaft of the femur, however, is relatively to the bicondylar width more robust than in the chimpanzee, European child, or Bushman. The width of the shaft can be estimated with reasonable accuracy to be 32 mm. at a distance of 6.5 cm. from the level of the tibial articular surfaces. In an adult chimpanzee the corresponding measurement was found to be 26 mm., and in the only Bushman skeleton in which the bicondylar width did not exceed that of the *Plesianthropus* femur, 24.5 mm. The obliquity of the shaft of the fossil bone, that is to say the angle between the axis of the shaft and the vertical axis in the standing position, makes a strong contrast with that of the femora of modern anthropoid apes. The angle can be approximately estimated by placing the tibial articular surfaces on a flat surface and measuring the angle of inclination of the axial line extending from the centre of the preserved part of the shaft to the mid-point of the anterior end of the intercondylar notch. By this method, it can be shown (Figure 7) that the angle of obliquity is at least 7°. This compares with an average of 10° recorded by Parsons for normal male English femora (with a range of 4–17°). In the African anthropoid apes, the obliquity of the femoral shaft is very slight, the average for the gorilla being (according to Pearson & Bell, 1919) 1.8° and for the chimpanzee–0.1°. It may be inferred, therefore, that in the erect standing position adopted by *Plesianthropus* the femur sloped downwards and medially as in man. The contour of the patellar surface is in conformity with this conclusion. For while in the anthropoid apes this surface is broad, shallow, and evenly curved, thus permitting considerable freedom of lateral movement between the patella and the femur, in *Plesianthropus* it is relatively deeper, and laterally slopes rather abruptly into a prominent lip. It should be mentioned that the summit of this lip is actually missing in the fossil bone, but its position can be reconstructed with fair accuracy. If the condyles are viewed from below and compared with those of the modern anthropoid apes (Figure 9), the contrast is striking. The shape and disposition of the condyles are again typically human, and are separated by a relatively narrow intercondyloid notch. The

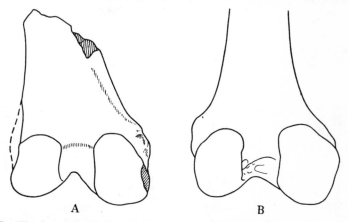

A   B

Fig. 7. The lower end of the left femur of *Plesianthropus* (A) seen from in front, compared with that of an adult chimpanzee (B). × 2/3. Note the marked obliquity of the shaft in *Plesianthropus*, and also the relatively greater robustness of the shaft.

latter is prolonged forwards to an unusual extent, and at its anterior end presents a notch which is an exaggeration of a similar notch often to be observed in human femora. This notch, as pointed out by Siddiqi (1934), is related to the pressure of the anterior cruciate ligament of the knee joint in full extension, and appears to indicate, therefore, that the joint could be habitually sustained in this typically human position in *Plesianthropus*. A comparison of views of the posterior aspect of the fossil femur and that of the chimpanzee serves to emphasize another interesting point. In the modern anthropoid apes, the load line of the body in the standing position passes through or medial to the medial condyle of the femur (Walmsley, 1933). In relation to this fact the medial condyle presents a much larger articular

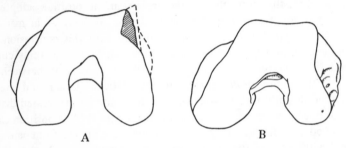

A   B

Fig. 8. The lower end of the left femur of *Plesianthropus* (A) seen from behind, compared with that of an adult chimpanzee (B). X 2/3. Note the relatively larger size of the medial condyle in the chimpanzee.

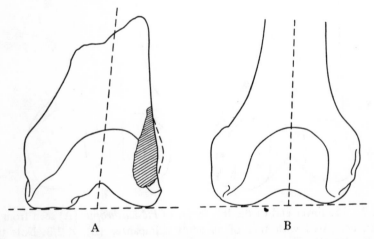

A   B

Fig. 9. The lower end of the left femur of *Plesianthropus* (A) seen from below, compared with that of an adult chimpanzee (B). X 2/3.

surface than the lateral condyle. In modern man, the load line in the erect standing position (with the knees together) passes through the lateral condyle which thus becomes more important for weight bearing; in the human femur, therefore, the medial condylar articular surface is relatively less strongly developed. In the *Plesianthropus* femur, the proportionate sizes of the two condyles are quite similar to those of *Homo*.

In addition to the observations just recorded, the following descriptive points may also be referred to. The lateral epicondyle is almost entirely missing from the femoral fragment. However, near the lateral margin of the lateral condyle a portion of the posterior half of the groove for the popliteus tendon remains. The medial epicondyle is well preserved, and shows a distinct facet for the medial head of the gastrocnemius muscle. The adductor tubercle is small, but forms quite a well-defined pointed process, and leading down to it is a rather strongly developed supracondylar ridge. The popliteal surface is smooth and slightly concave. About 14 mm. above the posterior extremity of the lateral condyle, and extending laterally across the lateral supracondylar ridge, is a low rough eminence which presumably marks the attachment of the plantaris muscle. A strong rounded ridge separates the intercondylar fossa from the popliteal surface, which in its definition and general appearance is quite similar to that of *Homo sapiens*. The lateral and medial walls of the intercondylar fossa are hollowed out but show no definite impressions of the attachment of the cruciate ligaments. It has been mentioned above that the intercondylar notch is prolonged forwards to an unusual extent, in association with the exaggerated development of the impression related to the anterior cruciate ligament. Broom has already referred to this forward extension and states that he has been unable to match it in femurs of Kafirs, Europeans, Bushmen, Amerindians and Australian natives. A further examination of large numbers of femora in this department and elsewhere has also failed to demonstrate a precise parallel in modern man.

A survey of the anatomical details of the *Plesianthropus* femur, and a critical examination of the accompanying diagrams, will make it quite clear that the bone is constructed almost entirely on the human plan. In other words it is mechanically adapted for standing, walking and running in the erect position. It thus offers a complete contrast to the femur of the modern anthropoid apes. In the latter, the hind-limbs may be used as temporary struts on which these animals can occasionally balance themselves in an approximately upright position, but they do not permit of progression in the fully erect position characteristic of man.

Conclusions

Those who are acquainted with the previous accounts of the Australo-pithecinae which have been published from time to time by Dart and Broom will recognize that much of the present communication has been concerned with 'underlining' and amplifying statements already made by these South African authorities. Such additional information as may have been presented only serves to reinforce their general conclusions that the Australopithecinae represent by far the most important discoveries which have so far been made in the field of human palaeontology. These fossil creatures were at a simian level of evolution in regard to the size of the brain and the general proportions of the skull, but in the details of their anatomical structure they present no evidence of any close affinity to the recent anthropoid apes. On the other hand, the resemblances which they show to man in the morphological features of the skull, dentition and limb bones are so remarkable that their zoological relationship to the Hominidae can hardly be doubted. It is particularly interesting to note that the evidence derived from the study of different parts of the skeleton is reciprocally confirmatory. Thus, the nature of the wear of the permanent teeth leads to the inference that the temporo-mandibular joint was constructed on the human pattern, and this is borne out by an examination of the skull. The position of the occipital condyles indicates a poise of the head and a bodily posture which approximates to that of man, and this is confirmed by an examination of the limb bones. Further, the climatological evidence leads to the inference that the Australopithecinae were well adapted for terrestrial (and not for arboreal) life, and this is reflected in the conformation of the lower end of the femur. Lastly, the size and proportion of the brain, as well as the massive jaws, the large size of the molar and premolar teeth, and certain features of the reduced canine teeth, are definitely ape-like characters which, in combination with the more advanced characters of the skull and dentition, indicate a morphological status in some degree intermediate between the simian and human levels of evolution. In conformity with this is the remarkable combination of simian and human characters presented by the talus and os capitatum.

The anatomical study of the Australopithecine fossils necessarily raises the question whether their hominid characters betoken an ancestral relationship to man, or only a collateral relationship. So far as purely morphological criteria are concerned, there seems to be no serious objection to the conception of an ancestral relationship, for the fossil material so far available shows no evidence of any gross specialization which would necessarily preclude this. Indeed, the major importance of these fossils lies in the fact that they conform so closely in their anatomical structure to theoretical postulates for an intermediate phase of human evolution, such as had been based on the indirect evidence of comparative anatomy. However, the place occupied by the Australopithecinae in human phylogenesis will be precisely determined only when more adequate palaeontological and geological data are available. At present the evidence for assessing the antiquity of the limestone deposits in which the South African fossils were found is based on faunal associations and is still inconclusive. We may, however, note Dr Broom's tentative estimate (Broom & Schepers, 1946) that the Sterkfontein deposits are of upper Pliocene date (or earlier) and that the Taungs deposits may even be attributed to the middle Pliocene. If it should be established, as the result of further systematic excavations, that the Australopithecine fossil material is no older than the early Pleistocene or late Pliocene, it must probably be assumed that, at the most, these extinct hominoids represent the little modified survivors of the ancestral stock from which, at a still earlier date, the line of human evolution originated.

Certain inferences of a general nature may be drawn from a consideration of the morphological features of the Australopithecinae. In the first place, it now seems clear that in human phylogenesis the evolution of the limb structure proceeded at a more rapid rate than that of the brain, since in these fossils the limb skeleton approximates to that of *Homo* while the brain volume hardly surpasses the simian level. This conclusion fits in well with the evidence provided by the remains in Java and China of *Pithecanthropus*, for in this early fossil hominid the limb bones appear to be quite similar to those of modern man while the skull, teeth and brain still show very primitive characters. The Australopithecine material also supports inferences drawn from the indirect evidence of comparative anatomy that many of the diagnostic characters of the recent large anthropoid apes such as the powerful canines and the large incisors, the sectorial form of the first lower premolar, the exaggerated development of the supra-orbital torus, and the construction of the powerful brachiating arms, are to be regarded as aberrant specializations peculiar to these apes and not as primitive features to be sought for in human ancestry. If such reasoning is sound, however, it must also apply (at least in part) to the extinct dryopithecine apes, for these had already to some degree developed the typical simian specializations of the dentition. Hence, it appears very doubtful whether the conception of a 'dryopithecine phase' in human evolution is any longer tenable. Finally, the more detailed knowledge of Australopithecine anatomy which is now available demands a careful reconsideration of the taxonomic status of these extinct hominoids. It seems clear that while in their cerebral development, and therefore in the *general* proportions of the skull, they represent a level of evolution corresponding to that of the large anthropoid apes, they show no structural evidence of close relationship to the latter. On the contrary, the advanced characters which are already very evident in their skull dentition and limb bones indicate their position in the phylogenetic radiation of the Hominidae rather than the Pongidae.

I wish to express my gratitude to my friends Prof. Raymond Dart and Dr Robert Broom for the very generous hospitality which they gave me during my visit to their laboratories. They placed their valuable fossil material completely at my disposal, with every facility for its study, and they also provided special arrangements for visiting the sites of their outstanding discoveries.

Fig. 10. Occlusal view of the left maxillary teeth of the type specimen of *Plesianthropus*. X 5/4 approx. Note the type and degree of wear shown in the premolar teeth. Photograph lent by Dr R. Broom.

Fig. 11. Natural endocranial cast of the type specimen of *Plesianthropus* lying in contact with the base of the skull. ✕ 1/2 approx. After this photograph was taken, some of the facial skeleton was exposed by removal of the limestone matrix. In the photograph can be seen the supra-orbital ridges (*a*), the natural casts of the frontal air sinuses (*b*), and the lateral margin of the left orbit (*c*). Photograph lent by Dr R. Broom.

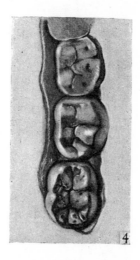

Fig. 12. Occlusal view of the right lower molar teeth of *Paranthropus*, drawn from a cast. ✕ 10/9 approx. Note the degree of differential attrition in the three molars.

Fig. 13. Photographs (natural size) of a cast of the deciduous lower dentition of the right side (and the incompletely erupted first permanent molar) of *Paranthropus*. *a*, occlusal view; *b*, lateral view. Note particularly the relatively small size of the lateral incisor and the canine, and the human appearance of the first deciduous molar.

The Saldanha Skull
From Hopefield, South Africa

Ronald Singer*

Introduction

The site. During the past 25 years a number of fossilized animal skeletal remains had been submitted by farmers and District Surgeons of the south-western coastal area of the Cape Province to the Cape Town Museum and the above department, but no scientist had subsequently investigated those sites. In May, 1951, I was instrumental in locating an extensive fossil site on the farm "Elandsfontein" about 10 miles from Hopefield, which is a small village situated 90 miles north of Cape Town and about 15 miles east of Saldanha Bay. Here, in the middle of the sandy veld, situated 300 feet above sea level, is a veritable Solutrean-like accumulation of fossilized material lying on the floors of wind-scoured kloofs or depressions between stationary vegetated or moving sand-dunes. Ridges of ferricrete cut diagonally across the length of the site, and, in places, the dunes are capped by massive calcrete mounds or flat boulders of partly silicified surface limestone. Softer, cellular calcretes are found in certain places at the lowest parts of the depressions. The tortuous courses of the ferricrete ridges indicate that they are the indurated lower flanks of old sand-dunes now stripped bare of the sand walls. This ferruginisation is usually associated with moist ground conditions, a fairly high and stable water-table and an abundance of vegetable acids in the soil. It seems that this fossil site may at one time have been a large vlei or lagoon continuous or contiguous with one of the mouths of the large rivers that open into the sea 12 miles away. The site at "Elandsfontein" which extends over an area of approximately two square miles is not an isolated one, as I have already explored two similar fossil-bearing locations, one on

*1954 ("American Journal of Physical Anthropology," Vol. 12).

each side of this farm, lying in series with it parallel to the coastline. It may yet be shown that all these sites are segments of one massive geographical fossil area.

On numerous subsequent visits, various members of the University of Cape Town staff, Doctors M. R. Drennan, J. A. Keen (later replaced by E. N. Keen), Messrs. J. A. Mabbutt and K. Jolly, and I have collected highly fossilized bones and stone implements from the surface of the site.

Stone implements. The rich collection of stone implements indicate the presence of Man on the site from the period of a late stage of the Chelles-Acheul (Stellenbosch V) Culture until the period when the Bush races were developing their culture. This occupation was certainly not a continuous one. The most striking elements of the archaeological collection are the tool types of the Chelles-Acheul, namely, hand-axes (large and pygmy), cleavers, unconventional cutting tools, pebble choppers and bola-like stones. In addition, there are examples of the Middle Stone Age Still Bay Culture, but it is not mixed with implements of the Howieson's Poort Development, which is a more developed stage. Furthermore, some unique specimens of worked bone tools have been removed by us. Drennan stated that the Saldanha skull (described below) belonged to the "palaeoanthropic Man who practised the last stages of the hand-axe culture in South Africa." There is, however, no stratigraphical or direct proof of this yet.

Fossil fauna. The large amount of palaeontological material collected thus far is in the early stages of identification and general description by Dr. E. N. Keen and myself. Already established is a good series of suid teeth which is diagnosed as being almost identical to *Mesochoerus olduvaiensis* Leakey

Fig. 1. Map of South Africa, showing sites described.

(except in size) and we have a detailed description awaiting publication. There is an impressive collection of the teeth of various species of horse, among which are many specimens of the extinct *Equus capensis* and allied types. Our classification of the equid dentitions would indicate a wider variability within a species than has hitherto been accepted in this country, and will probably allow the merging of several described species. The 8 giraffid teeth thus far discovered appear to be indistinguishable from the extinct *Sivatherium* (from the Siwalik Hills, India) and also resemble the extinct South African *Griquatherium*. There are numerous teeth and long bones of *Palaeoloxodon*, both the black and white rhinoceros, and *Hippopotamus amphibius*. A large variety of *Bovidae*, extinct and existing, have also been identified by us (to be published in the Indian Journal of Palaeontology). Especially important are complete dentitions, skulls, horn cores and long bones of a long-horned buffalo, *Bubalus* or *Homoioceras*, definitely different from those few specimens previously described from Southern Africa. Generally speaking, in this fossil collection of existing and extinct mammals, the proportions indicate an Upper Pleistocene period, probably from the later part of the Middle Pleistocene onwards, in terms of current African chronology (which is based mainly on the beds at Oldoway in Tanganyika and the Vaal River beds in South Africa). True stratification has not yet been found at Elandsfontein, and it is debatable whether the same mode of dating is to be applied at a site 2000 miles away. Consequently, it has not been decided whether the profusion of extinct species at this one site may suggest an early part of the Upper Pleistocene. Such factors as the tropical climate at Oldoway and the temperate coastal climate at Cape Town will have to be taken into account in making these decisions. Fluorine tests, carried out through the courtesy of Dr. Oakley of the British Museum on a wide range of specimens, do not support the idea that specimens of a widely differing age have been mingled in the collection. Dr. Leakey recently informed us that none of the *Mesochoerus* specimens in East Africa have been recovered from Upper Pleistocene deposits, but that his specimens were found in Middle Pleistocene layers, namely, Beds I and II at Oldoway. Thus if one tends to be conservative about the dating at Elandsfontein, the presence of *Mesochoerus olduvaiensis* represents the survival of an isolated species which had become extinct further north. However, our *Mesochoerus* teeth are slightly longer, narrower and higher-crowned than the mean of the few recorded specimens of *M. olduvaiensis* Leakey. Thus if our specimens prove to be definitely beyond the range of variation of *M. olduvaiensis* Leakey, then these differences in dental development can best be interpreted as later stages and suggestive of our specimens being offshoots of *M. olduvaiensis*. Fluorine tests also revealed that the *Mesochoerus* and *Paleoloxodon* lived contemporaneously with Saldanha Man at Elandsfontein.

The Saldanha Skull

On the first field trip after my return from the U.S.A. on January 8, 1953, Keith Jolly, a young archaeologist, then employed as a field research assistant at Hopefield, and I discovered and identified 11 fragments of human fossilized cranial bones on the main site. They were lying loose on the sandy surface over an area of about 16 square feet, some with the endocranial surface uppermost and some with the exocranial surface uppermost. One fragment was later discarded as it was not human. The fragment which drew our attention to the others was part of a right frontal bone with a massive supraorbital torus (extending almost to the median line) from which a marked temporal ridge extended back to bifurcate almost immediately into two less distinct temporal lines. Posteriorly this fragment tapered to a narrow base of about 1 inch, the border of which was the edge of the coronal suture in the region of the pars pterica. On the endocranial aspect part of the orbital roof was present while the orbital plate had an irregular broken edge, and a portion of the frontal sinus extended into the plate. Another key fragment consisted of most of the occipital squama in the lambdoid suture region, thus providing the posterior occipital curve and opisthocranion (coincident with inion here). Fortunately the remaining fragments (numbered 1.B. through 1.J. on the endocranial part of the reconstruction) had distinct landmarks, and, by making full use of sutural markings, most of the vault in the region of the major sutures could be juxtaposed, and it was possible to reconstruct accurately the maximal height and length of the skull.

On two subsequent visits in January and February, Jolly and I retrieved additional fragments within a radius of 10 yards of the initial site of the discovery which, when added to the reconstruction completed most of the frontal bone. These fragments were classified 2.A., 3.A. (these two not being found at the original site—vide infra) and 16 fragments were marked "3." Five of the latter fragments have not yet been included in the reconstruction. On a field trip in July, Jolly recovered a left frontal supraorbital torus which appeared to fit the right side and complete the curve of the frontal bone above the orbits. However, the left is not quite symmetrical with the right, as the ophryonic groove bulges on the left, but this may be a normal variation. On our third visit I recovered two fragments about 500 yards away from the original place of discovery.

Thus the Saldanha skull (so styled because Hopefield lies within the greater Saldanha Bay area), reconstructed from 27 fragments by Professor M. R. Drennan, assisted by Dr. E. N. Keen and myself, at present consists of a fairly complete "cap" or vault. There is a striking resemblance between it and the Rhodesian (Broken Hill) skull in general outline and measurements (fig. 2). On the other hand, there are also features of similarity between it and the

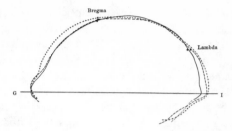

Fig. 2. Sagittal dioptographs, orientated in glabella-inion plane, using glabella (G) as fixed point, indicate relationships between Saldanha Skull
————; Rhodesian Skull —————; and Florisbad Skull +++. (### indicates
plaster reconstruction in Florisbad Skull; ————— indicates plaster reconstruction in Saldanha Skull.)

Sinanthropus-Pithecanthropus-Homo soloensis group, especially the latter
(fig. 3). It is not necessary in this short paper to repeat what has been said
before, because Weidenreich's discussion in his masterly monograph on the
skull of Sinanthropus, where he dealt with the relationships between the Far
East fossil group and Rhodesian man holds good, by and large, for the
incomplete Saldanha skull. The latter is characterized by a moderately low
braincase (but higher than any skull in the Far East group) with its greatest
breadth apparently near its base (fig. 9), and a relatively flat forehead
separated from massive supraorbital ridges by a distinct ophryonic groove.
The occipital crest is prominent and has a downward tilt. The supreme nuchal
line is also obvious. The sulcus supratoralis is fairly well marked. However,
the torus occipitalis does not seem to have the typically undermined edge
which is seen above the nuchal plane of the Ngandong skulls. The fracture

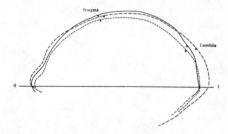

Fig. 3. Sagittal dioptographs orientated in glabella-inion plane, indicating
relationships between Saldanha Skull ————; La Chapelle-aux-Saints Skull
—————; and Sinanthropus XII (Skull I, Locus D) ————— (after Weidenreich).

just below the protuberant torus prevents any conclusive opinion as regards the position of the foramen magnum or as regards the appearance of the nuchal plane, but there should be little reason to believe that it differs markedly from that in the Rhodesian skull: a different view is expressed by Drennan who stated that he considered that the nuchal plane would have been directed posteriorly and that "indications from the attachments of the muscles of the nape of Saldanha man's neck point to his having had the crouching posture of Neanderthal Man, whereas the Rhodesian skull shows that he held his head erect like sapient man." Weidenreich stated that in the Rhodesian skull the occipital foramen has a distinct central position which is a specific hominid character. Furthermore, Sergi and others indicated that Neanderthalians did not crouch or walk with a "simian stoop," and Schultz proved that, in the balance of their heads, the Neanderthalians also behave as does modern man and do not approach conditions of the anthropoids. Mainly on the above supposition, Drennan bases his view that "Saldanha man is anatomically a more primitive variety of the Rhodesian race."

Fig. 4. Norma verticalis. Note parietal bossing, and great anterior projection of supraorbital tori with a distinct central "sulcus."

The general thickness of the Saldanha skull is interesting, though not nearly as impressive as that of the Sinanthropus adolescent skull (discovered on December 2, 1929). The average thickness of the Saldanha frontal bone is 10 mm centrally and 6 mm laterally; the parietal bone averages 10.5 mm parasagitally and 7 mm near the temporo-parietal suture; the occipital squama is very thick, averaging 8 mm in each superior cerebellar fossa and 12 mm opposite the internal crest between the fossae. The supramastoid bulge of bone has a maximal thickness of 13 mm.

The maximal thickness of the supraorbital torus is 20 mm medially and 16 mm laterally, as compared with 21 mm and 15 mm respectively in the Florisbad skull; 19.6 mm and 11.2 mm respectively in Sinanthropus II (Weidenreich, '43); and 20 mm and 20 mm respectively in the Rhodesian skull. In the latter there is a bulge over the center of the orbit which gives a thickness of 23 mm. The shape and curvature of the tori differ in the Saldanha and Rhodesian skulls. In the former, the anterior surface curves evenly outward (with the convexity upward) in the same vertical plane, while in the Rhodesian the convexity is less accentuated and the anterior surface has a tortuous appearance, so that medially it is in a vertical plane while laterally it is in a semi-horizontal plane with the anterior surface looking

Fig. 5. Endocranial aspect. Note orbital plate with erosion into right frontal sinus.

Fig. 6.   Right oblique view. This view emphasizes the "vertical plane" of the anterior surface of the supraorbital torus, and also the ophryonic groove.

Fig. 7.   Norma lateralis, right.

Fig. 8.   Norma facialis. There is a slight flattening out of the left ophryonic groove.

upwards and outwards. The maximum breadth of the supraorbital ridges is 122 mm in the Saldanha (though a small piece is broken off), 136 mm in the Florisbad, and 139 mm in the Rhodesian skull. The left frontal sinus is compartmented and occupies the whole of the supraorbital torus, while the right sinus is very small, loculated and rounded (as seen on X-ray photographs).

The inclination of the frontal bone differs markedly between the Saldanha and Florisbad skulls, but the calvarial height is approximated in them, though the highest point is slightly nearer the bregma in the Florisbad skull. The highest point in the Rhodesian skull is just behind bregma, well ahead of the

Fig. 9. Norma occipitalis. Central area of nuchal plane is plaster reconstruction.

Fig. 10. Cranial fragments not incorporated in reconstruction with a part of ramus of mandible on the right (lingual aspect).

same point in the other two skulls. The inclination in the Rhodesian and Saldanha frontal bones is almost identical.

A modified frontal chord, using glabella instead of nasion, reads 116 mm for the Saldanha skull, while it is 121 mm in the Rhodesian; and the median frontal ridge in the latter is more angular and prominent. The parietal chord is 109.5 mm in the former and 113 mm in the latter, and the occipital chord is 54.5 mm in the former and 59.5 mm in the latter. The figures for the occipital chord are particularly interesting because, despite the fact that this is greater in the Rhodesian, the latter also subtends a larger angle at the lambda between the right and left lambdoid suture lines, namely, 160° compared with 130° in the Saldanha. The lengths of the lambdoid sutures in Saldanha, though incomplete, are estimated to approximate those in the Rhodesian, namely 91 mm on the left and 90 mm on the right. Thus the "surface area" of the Rhodesian occipital bone, above the torus occipitalis, is the greater of the two. In norma lateralis, the "bun-like" bulge in this region below lambda is far more marked in the Rhodesian skull (fig. 2), but this does not account for the apparent discrepancy in the surface areas. Moreover, this bulge is a variable feature and noticeable in many modern skulls, and its significance is as yet doubtful. Drennan considers this difference in occipital bulging a feature in favor of "the Saldanha skull diverging morphologically from the Rhodesian type." Furthermore, in norma occipitalis, there is a marked difference in appearance between the two skulls. The Saldanha appears to have a degree of parietal bossing which tends to flatten the horizontal plane of the skull in a line taken across vertex (fig. 9), while in the Rhodesian there is a marked sloping or falling away of this plane towards the mastoids. Despite these features, the maximum breadth in the two skulls appears to be in a line across the supramastoid regions and is approximately equal. A true torus angularis is not visible.

In the Saldanha skull the anterior ends of the temporal lines, arising as a bifurcation of the temporal crest or ridge behind the supraorbital tori, are prominent. The left superior temporal line kinks upwards at stephanion producing a high temporal arc which soon fades out. On the right side, the kinking is not obvious. The bregma-stephanion chord is 47.5 mm on each side in the Saldanha skull, while in the Rhodesian the reading is 58 mm on each side. However, though this figure is conventionally recorded, I have found so much variation in it in series of hundreds of skulls of "known racial" groups that these slightly variable figures here cannot be taken to be of much significance other than to record the position of the two points.

I feel that it is unnecessary at this stage to compare the Saldanha skull with the various Neanderthalians recorded, as only the protuberant supraorbital ridges definitely indicate the Neanderthal "streak" in this specimen. It is considered more logical at this stage to compare the "local" African fossil types, namely Rhodesian and Florisbad. The latter has been dealt with in greater detail in another paper (to appear in the Indian Journal of Palaeontology). The Eyasi skull (misnamed *Africanthropus njarasensis* by Weinert in 1939) has not been compared in this paper as a cast is not available here. Leakey ('47) assigned it to the East African Upper Pleistocene (Gamblian pluvial) period.

A detailed description of the endocranial cast of the Saldanha skull is yet to be completed.

Conclusions

The importance of the discovery of this incomplete skull may be stated as:

1. It confirms that the Rhodesian skull is no isolated, abnormal or pathological type of primitive man.

2. The Saldanha skull is akin to a similar region of the Rhodesian skull; such differences as have been mentioned in this paper may be regarded to fall within the limits of individual variation. It thus establishes an African Neanderthalian quite different in many respects from the European variety and resembling to some extent the larger specimens of the Asiatic Neanderthalian, Homo soloensis (as far as can be determined from the incomplete material available).

3. It provides a probable South African hand-axe man who was perfecting a transitional stage between the coastal South African Earlier and Middle Stone Age Cultures. This appears to have taken place during an Upper Pleistocene period, probably an early part, if one accepts the relationship between the fluorine dating of the Saldanha skull and the extinct fossil fauna.

It appears that Weidenreich's original classification (1928 and 1943) of the Neanderthal group into *Homo primigenius europaeus, Homo primigenius asiaticus* and *Homo primigenius africanus* is beginning to bear more weight. In this respect, I would like to quote two appropriate sentences of Franz Weidenreich's ('40) with which I readily concur:

> ". . . for it proves that the so-called Neanderthal Man of Europe, notwithstanding his uniformity when compared with the Rhodesian Man of South Africa or the *Homo soloenis* of Java, has produced certain regional variations which are equivalent to racial differences of today,"

and in similar vein,

> "while Man was passing through different phases, each of which was characterized by certain features common to all individuals of the same stage, there existed, nevertheless, within such

community different types deviating from each other with regard to secondary features. These secondary divergencies have to be rated as regional differentiations and, therefore, as correspondent to the racial dissimilarities of present Man."

Excerpts from
"The Piltdown Forgery"

J. S. Weiner*

On 18 December 1912 Arthur Smith Woodward and Charles Dawson announced to a great and expectant scientific audience the epoch-making discovery of a remote ancestral form of man—The Dawn Man of Piltdown. The news had been made public by the *Manchester Guardian* about three weeks before, and the lecture room of the Geological Society at Burlington House was crowded as it has never been before or since. There was great excitement and enthusiasm which is still remembered by those who were there; for, in Piltdown man, here in England, was at last tangible, well-nigh incontrovertible proof of Man's ape-like ancestry; here was evidence, in a form long predicted, of a creature which could be regarded as a veritable confirmation of evolutionary theory.

Twenty years had elapsed since Dubois had found the fragmentary remains of the Java ape-man, but by now in 1912 its exact evolutionary significance had come to be invested with some uncertainty and the recent attempt to find more material by the expensive and elaborate expedition under Mme. Selenka had proved entirely unsuccessful. Piltdown man provided a far more complete and certain story. The man from Java, whose geological age was unclear, was represented by a skull cap, two teeth, and a disputed femur. Anatomically there was a good deal of the Piltdown skull and, though the face was missing, there was most of one side of the lower jaw. The stratigraphical evidence was quite sufficient to attest the antiquity of the remains; and to support this antiquity there were the animals which had lived in the remote time of Piltdown man; there was even evidence of the tool-making abilities of Piltdown man. In every way Piltdown man provided a fuller picture of the stage of ancestry which man had reached perhaps some 500,000 years ago. . . .

*1955 (Oxford University Press)

327

Arthur Keith, Conservator of the Hunterian Museum of the Royal College of Surgeons, drew attention to a crucial point: there was no eye-tooth in the jaw, for most of the chin region had been broken away. What sort of canine would such a creature possess? On this point he did not agree with Smith Woodward's opinion. But Smith Woodward was quite definite. If his interpretation was correct, the tooth when found would certainly be somewhat like that of the chimpanzee, but not projecting sensibly above the level of the other teeth, and its mode of wear would also be utterly different from that of an ape. Like the wear on the molars, the canine tooth would be worn down in a way expected from a freely moving jaw such as the Piltdown man must clearly have possessed in view of its association with so human a cranium. The sort of canine he expected could be discerned in the plaster cast which was before the meeting.

It was very clear to those present how much the missing canine would help to decide the issue of the incipient humanity of the jaw.

Throughout that next long season of digging and sieving of 1913, the oft-discussed canine remained the principal objective. Little indeed came to light that season, but on Saturday 30 August, at the end of a day which again had so far proved fruitless, the young prient, Teilhard de Chardin, found the canine, 'close to the spot whence the lower jaw itself had been disinterred'.[1] There was jubilation. The Kenwards, tenants of Barkham Manor (Dawson was the Steward) who had followed the fortunes of the search with unfailing enthusiasm, were appraised of the triumph. It was indeed a triumph. The eye-tooth was just what they had hoped for and closely fulfilled Smith Woodward's prediction of its shape, size, and above all of the nature of its wear. As Dawson wrote in 1915,[2] 'the tooth is almost identical in form with that shown in the restored cast'. Dr. Underwood in 1913 also pointed out this remarkable resemblance, in an article in which, for the first time, X-rays of all the teeth were provided. 'The tooth', wrote Dr. Underwood,[3] 'is absolutely as modelled at the British Museum.'

The new facts further strengthened Woodward's position. Piltdown man could now be said with confidence to possess a dentition in a number of different respects human rather than ape-like, and in the X-ray appearance Keith[4] discovered that the roots of the molar tooth were inserted in the bone in the human and not the ape manner.

The next year's excavation at Barkham Manor yielded what Keith called 'the most amazing of all the Piltdown revelations'. Digging a few feet from the place where the Piltdown skull had first been found, the workman with Woodward and Dawson exposed a fossil slab of elephant bone which had been artificially shaped to form a club-like implement. It was found in two pieces 'about a foot below the surface, in dark vegetable soil beneath the hedge which bounds the gravel pit'. The clay encrusting the object enabled Woodward to settle its contemporaneity with Piltdown man, to whose kit of stone tools there was added this, the earliest known bone implement.

The finding of the canine convinced many of the sceptics of the rightness of Woodward's interpretation, but not Waterston, whose opinion remained unchanged till his death in 1921. The two camps persisted. Like Waterston, Gerrit Miller,[5] Curator of Mammals at the United States National Museum, preferred to believe that two fossil creatures were really represented in the Piltdown remains and introduced the new name *Pan vetus* for what seemed to him a new fossil form of chimpanzee. His arguments were met by the zoologists of the British Museum,[6] but Miller continued in his disbelief.[7] At this period Woodward's case was very strong and it had the benefit of Keith's powerful advocacy, presented in masterly fashion in the *Antiquity of Man*.

In 1915 the last, and in its way the most conclusive, of the Piltdown discoveries was announced, for Dawson found the remains of yet another individual two miles away.[8] To those who had been prepared to accept the theory (however far-fetched it might appear) that at Barkham Manor somehow two different creatures had become commingled, this new discovery came as a devastating refutation, for it was hard to conceive of so astonishing a coincidence happening yet again. At the second site at Sheffield Park there were, as before, parts of the brain-case and a molar tooth quite like those previously found. From that site came also another tooth of rhinoceros of, at least, lower Pleistocene age and perhaps older.

By 1915 the British anatomists and palaeontologists were generally of one mind and had accepted Woodward's views—though Waterston still stood out. A Royal Academy portrait[9] (Fig. 1) in oils of 1915 shows us the group of men concerned with the evolutionary study of Piltdown man, who now passed into the general histories and encyclopaedias as easily the best-known of the primal ancestors of the human species. In the centre, holding the reconstructed skull, is Keith, as if to symbolize the newly won harmony of view, with Woodward on one side and Elliot Smith on the other. Woodward's assistants, the zoologist Pycraft (he had been concerned in some interesting study of the jaw and refutation of Gerrit Miller) and Barlow, the skilful maker of the casts, are also of the group. The others depicted are Charles Dawson, Ray Lankester, who had been somewhat sceptical over the implements, and Dr. Underwood, who had advised on dental matters.

The season of excavation of 1916 proved completely unsuccessful. There were many helpers, but nothing was found, either human or animal. Dawson had fallen ill towards the end of 1915, and took no part, though Woodward kept in touch with him. His anaemia however led to septicaemia and his condition became steadily worse. He died on 10 September 1916.

Fig. 1. Personalities concerned with the Piltdown discovery. Back row: Mr. F. O. Barlow, Prof. G. Elliot Smith, Mr. C. Dawson and Dr. Arthur Smith Woodward. Front row: Dr. A. S. Underwood, Prof. Arthur Keith, Mr. W. P. Pycraft and Sir Ray Lankester. (From the Portrait painted by John Cooke, R. A., in 1915)

In 1917, after correspondence with Mrs. Dawson, Smith Woodward obtained from Dawson's home, before the auctioneers' sale, the fragments known as the Barcombe Mills skull, and these he deposited in the British Museum.

During the next few years Smith Woodward opened up a number of pits in the vicinity of the original excavation. He also watched closely the digging of some foundations near the farmhouse at Barkham Manor. Except for a flint which he took to be a 'pot-boiler' at the latter site and miscellaneous bone fragments of recent animals, nothing came to light. After his retirement Woodward went to live at Hayward's Heath, near Piltdown, in order to search the original site and the fields of Site II at Sheffield Park, but with no success whatever.[10] He occasionally employed one of the local labourers to do a little digging in these excursions. One such expedition, as late as 1931, yielded only a sheep's tooth.

The site of the first excavations was cleared under the auspices of the Nature Conservancy[11] in 1950 and a large new section of the gravel terrace opened up. Everything was carefully sieved and examined,[12] but the many tons of soil and gravel yielded nothing. This re-excavation made possible the exhibition of a demonstration section of the famous strata protected by a glass window. The cleared area was scheduled as a national monument. . . .

Towards the end of July 1953 a congress of palaeontologists was held in London under the auspices of the Wenner-Gren Foundation. The problems of fossil man were the subject of its deliberations. Java man, Neanderthal man, Rhodesian man, the South African prehumans—all these were given close attention. But Piltdown man was not discussed. Not surprisingly. He had lost his place in polite society. What more could one usefully say about him? Yet, unofficially, the Dawn Man did manage an appearance. Most of those present had not seen the original fossil specimens, so on a tour of the Natural History Museum these were shown along with others housed there. The sight of the actual fragments provoked the familiar tail-chasing discussion. As always there were those who could not feel that the famous jaw really harmonized with the rest, but there were others who took the opposite view. The enigma remained.

At the dinner that night Dr. Oakley remarked casually to Professor Washburn of Chicago and myself that owing to Dawson's early death in 1916 the Museum had no record of the exact spot where the remains of the second Piltdown had been found. They knew the place—Sheffield Park—but the actual spot or even the field had never been marked on a map. 'The fact is', said Oakley, 'that all we know about site II is on a postcard sent in July 1915 by Dawson to Woodward, and an earlier letter in that year, from neither of which can one identify the position of Piltdown II.' This was surprising. The second group of finds had done so much to convince many people that the first Piltdown man was by no means an isolated phenomenon. One had imagined that if it were ever thought worthwhile it would be possible to go and excavate the second site. Now it appeared that this had never been done because the second site could not be located, though Woodward had apparently visited it before the second find. This curious piece of information greatly puzzled me. I know that Dawson had died in 1916 and it seemed difficult to understand why he had not recorded so important a fact as the location of Piltdown II. Dawson had a reputation, I knew, for great conscientiousness and accuracy. Sir Arthur Keith had spoken in the highest terms of his qualities. Perhaps Woodward had been told verbally and somehow his own record had been mislaid? I did not know then that Dawson had been ill for nearly a year before his death.

This small puzzle turned my thoughts to the larger Piltdown conundrum. My own conclusion when reviewing the matter in 1950,[13] like that of others, was that Woodward's *Eoanthropus* had become a complete anomaly, that the only course was to wait till more material was dug up, and that it was really profitless to spend much time on choosing between possibilities, none of which was susceptible of final proof. Thinking it all over again, I realized with astonishment that while there were in fact only the two possible 'natural' theories, i.e. that Piltdown man was in fact the composite man-ape of Woodward's interpretation, or that two distinct creatures, fossil man and fossil ape, had been found side by side, neither of the 'natural' explanations was at all satisfactory. If the two 'natural' explanations failed in some way or another, what other possible explanation could there be? Was there any other way of resolving the whole disorder of fragments, dates, chronology? On evolutionary grounds alone a late Dawn Man stood out as an obvious incongruity. The riddle might be approached more simply (I argued) by accepting at once the extraordinary difficulties of regarding the fossil as an organically single individual and by concentrating entirely on the perplexities of the two-creature hypothesis. What were feasible alternative explanations of the coincidence of two distinct individuals? If the jaw and cranium had not come together by nature or by blind accident then could they have got there by human agency? This would mean that someone by mischance or error had dropped a fossil jaw in the pit (perhaps used as a rubbish dump) dug in gravel which happened to contain other fossil remnants.

But surely this could hardly have been repeated at the second site? Perhaps site II was after all of exaggerated significance or had been mistakenly interpreted. As Hrdlicka[14] and others had been saying all along, perhaps the single molar might not really be ape or have any affinity whatever with the first teeth, so that the Sheffield Park fragments, despite their other similarities to those at Piltdown, would simply be a quite ordinary set of human remains. Or could we dispose of Piltdown II by supposing that the bits had actually come from the Barkham Manor site two miles away, in gravel brought across for some reason or other. Even if one were prepared to accept them, this elaboration of ancillary hypotheses still avoided the main issue. For even if the jaw had been thrown on to the gravel, to meet with the cranium, it was still a *fossil* jaw and we had not in fact escaped the original dilemma: what fossil ape could it possibly be? Still, the idea of an accidental deposit or loss of a jaw could be pursued a stage further (still disregarding site II) if we postulated that the jaw was not a fossil, but really that of a *modern* ape. We might then accept the accidental coincidence. But could the jaw possibly be modern? Immediately strong objections loomed up. To say the jaw was modern implied that the fluorine analysis had been inaccurate or that the published results must be in some way compatible with modern bone recently buried. In effect this would imply that the most reasonable interpretation of the results had been in error. That difficulty was dwarfed at once by a far more serious objection. The teeth were almost unanimously acknowledged to possess features quite unprecedented in modern apes—the flat wear of the molars and the curious type of wear of the canine had never been matched in an ape's mandible.

A modern jaw with flat worn molars and uniquely worn-down eye tooth? That would mean only one thing: deliberately ground-down teeth. Immediately this summoned up a devastating corollary—the equally deliberate placing of the jaw in the pit. Even as a mere hypothesis this inference could at once dispose of two of the most intransigent Piltdown posers: how the jaw and teeth had ever got there and how the teeth had come by their remarkable wear. But the hypothesis of a deliberate 'salting' of the Piltdown gravels clearly carried much wider implications, and the idea was repellent indeed. Could one not find a fatal flaw at once, and quickly dismiss this as a solution of the Piltdown mystery? There would be no need to consider the idea any further or even to examine the specimens (or rather the casts) in the laboratory next day. (For this cogitation had occupied the small hours on my return to Oxford after the Wenner-Gren dinner.)

What then were the immediate points of weakness and strength of this theory? After further reflection, the only serious surviving objection seemed to be the figure for the fluorine analysis. It had to be admitted that a modern specimen was rather unlikely to exhibit a fluorine content quite so high as the published figures, even supposing that the ape had lived in a fluorine rich area. Yet even this objection could be countered. Oakley pointed out[15] that the probable error of the method of estimation used in 1949 was actually stated to be possibly as much as ±0.2 per cent.[16] Thus although recorded as

0.3 per cent, the fluorine content of the jaw might in fact be less than 0.1 per cent., as in recent bone. If the fluorine value was not a fatal objection, an *a priori* case for a deliberate hoax assumed some strength on a number of counts. Clearly, if the intention was to pass off as a fossil a modern jaw, it would still not have passed scrutiny, despite the abraded teeth, unless certain tell-tale features were first removed. And it was just such features that were missing. Nearly the whole chin region was lost and only the two molar teeth were left in place, and, more telling, the bony knob where the jaw articulates with the skull had been broken away. This knob (or condyle) would certainly have made it apparent that the jaw would not fit into the cranium. For there is often a marked difference between the human and ape-like articular condyle. Then there were the strange characters of the canine. Deliberate tampering with the tooth would easily explain this particular oddity.

This *a priori* case obtained added support from discussions with Professor Le Gros Clark and our examinations of the Piltdown casts in the Department of Anatomy at Oxford. Perhaps the most telling argument which could be marshalled at this stage lay in an extraordinary fact revealed by the anatomical reconsideration of the remains. It appeared to me that, despite the many claims advanced from time to time for the existence of a whole variety of human features in the jaw and of ape-like features in the cranium, the only completely acceptable and undoubted characteristic of a human kind in the jaw turned out to be the flat wear. Nothing else could unequivocally be said to be human. How strange, then, that this one feature should be present to link jaw and cranium and yet these were supposed to form a harmonious combination in a live animal. Surely a few other modifications should have been apparent in the jaw. Yet, as Woodward himself had often pointed out, such functional features of the jaw as its muscle attachments were entirely ape-like. The moment one attributed this flat wear to a deliberate abrasion of the teeth it became understandable.

It now appeared from our discussion that the canine was not merely peculiar in its mode of dental wear, but that it was itself paradoxical in that the wear was so heavy as to be quite out of keeping with the immaturity of the tooth. This was a fact first pointed out in 1916 by the dentist Mr. Lyne,[17] and never properly explained. Lyne's cogent arguments had been brushed aside by Woodward and Underwood.

Then we examined the plaster casts. These revealed features quite understandable as the outcome of artificial abrasion of the dental crowns. In particular we were struck by the extraordinary flatness of the second molar and the lack of a smooth continuity of biting surface from the one molar to the next. Next, a chimpanzee's molar, of about the same size as the Piltdown, was experimentally filed down. This proved easy enough to do and, even without any polishing of the surface, by staining with permanganate an appearance very like the Piltdown molars was obtained, as far as could be judged from the casts and from photographs.

Yet another piece of positive information emerged when one re-read Dr. Oakley's fluorine paper.[18] During the course of drilling to obtain his sample of dentine Dr. Oakley had made an observation which now assumed a special significance: 'Below the extremely thin ferruginous surface stain', he had written, 'the dentine was pure white, apparently no more altered than the dentine of recent teeth from the soil.' Re-reading of Dawson's and Woodward's papers further made it clear that they themselves had missed a chance of making what might have been a decisive comparison of jaw and cranium. It appeared that only on the cranium had chemical tests for organic matter and other constituents been made, and the cranium had been found to contain no organic matter. If the jaw was modern, its organic content would be high, but the analysis had not been done.[19]

Though all these points built up quite a strong *prima facie* case, new objections also appeared, to add to that provided by the rather anomalously high fluorine content already mentioned. There were two serious points of criticism. The dental wear of the canine had been pronounced to be indubitably natural by Dr. Underwood at that 1916 meeting, when he spoke in violent disagreement with Mr. Lyne's contention of the immaturity of the canine and its paradoxical nature. Dr. Underwood had pointed out that the X-ray showed clearly a patch of *secondary dentine* such as always is deposited progressively with natural wear. The other difficulty arose from the radiographs of the molars. The relatively short roots were not really ape-like, as Keith had pointed out. They furnished another near-human attribute on the jaw.

Our general hypothesis seemed sufficiently sound, however, to warrant an approach to the authorities at the British Museum for renewed investigations, anatomical, radiological, and chemical, of the Piltdown material. These investigations would be needed for three reasons if the hypothesis was to lead to proof: firstly, for confirmation (or otherwise) of the evidence already gleaned, secondly, to establish the validity (or otherwise) of the various objections to the hypothesis; thirdly, to apply any new tests which might be suggested at this stage.

To these lines of investigations others were added after the publication of the first report[20] and the results of these will be given their place in the narrative. But in August and September of 1953 we already had many critical tests to do. The fact that most of these were of quite independent characteristics, chemical, physical and biological, and on different specimens, meant that agreement between them would amount to overwhelming proof.

Equally clear and in view of the serious nature of the 'fraud' hypothesis, there would be every need for a complete and all round agreement in the tests.

The tests we had in mind at this stage turned simply on the issue of the modernity or otherwise of the jaw and teeth, but it was obvious that the implications extended to every aspect of the Piltdown discoveries.

At this time awaiting the outcome of our 'predictions' and repeatedly arguing and reviewing our case, and seeing no other possible solution to the problem, we could well appreciate Holmes's sage advice to Watson:

'How often have I said to you that when you have eliminated the impossible, whatever remains, *however improbable*, must be the truth.'[21] . . . (end of chapter)

On the basis of our preliminary arguments and our anatomical re-examination of the fragments, Mr. W. N. Edwards, the Keeper of Geology of the Natural History Museum, felt justified in allowing the specimens of mandible, cranium, and teeth to be drilled for much larger samples than could ever have been sanctioned hitherto. These larger samples and the use of improved chemical methods guaranteed a high degree of analytical reliability.

The drilling itself gave us an encouraging start. As the drilling proceeded, Dr. Oakley and his assistant perceived a distinct smell of 'burning horn' when the jaw was sampled, but they noticed nothing of the sort with any of the cranial borings. This subjective indication of some distinct difference between the constitution of jaw and cranium soon gained objective confirmation. The drilled sample from the jaw proved to be utterly unlike those from the cranium. In keeping with the belief in its fossil or semi-fossilized character, the latter produced a fine particulate granular powder, whereas the jaw yielded little shavings of bone, just as did a fresh bone sampled as a control. Here was the beginning of the series of findings which progressively widened the gulf between jaw and cranium.

Very soon Dr. Oakley obtained clear chemical evidence to justify fully the strong suspicion of the modernity of the jaw and of the totally distinct origin of the cranium. An improved technique for estimating small quantities of fluorine produced this decisive result. The cranial fragments of site I were found to contain fluorine in a concentration of 0.1 per cent., a value somewhat similar to that of specimens of known Late Ice Age. The jaw and the three teeth on the contrary gave much lower figures, at levels below 0.03 per cent., values well within the range of known modern and fresh specimens. Indeed, these values are on the borderline of the sensitivity of the method. The fluorine test gave its verdict twice over. For the two cranial fragments from the second Piltdown site contained a fluorine concentration of 0.1 per cent. and the isolated molar which went with these fragments contained less than 0.01 per cent. These fluorine results alone go far to settle the main issue. As the reader will recall, the method serves essentially to compare the dates of material from any one deposit, and the Piltdown fluorine values prove not only that the jaw and teeth do not belong to the crania but that they are of younger date, and the test shows this to be true at both Barkham Manor and Sheffield Park.

With this Dr. Oakley and his associates[22] now launched a whole battery of chemical and physical tests at the fragments, bringing to bear on the Piltdown problem an array of new techniques in the last few months of 1953 exceeding all endeavours of this kind in the whole history of palaeontology. In succession they tested and compared the fragments for iron, nitrogen, collagen, organic carbon, organic water, radio-activity and crystal structure. This list is an epitome of the resources which the chemist and physicist have in recent years put in the hands of the archaeologist and palaeontologist, and in the Piltdown problem these methods obtained a thorough trial.

The test for nitrogen content, greatly improved by Cooke and Heizer,[23] represented an independent approach for comparing the respective ages of the different fragments. Whereas the fluorine assay reflects the accumulation in bone of an extraneous element, the nitrogen content indicates the progressive loss of organic matter from the bone itself. Thus in fresh or recently buried bones and teeth, the fluorine content is low while the nitrogen is high with values of the order of 4 per cent. With the passage of time, as fluorine accumulates, nitrogen would tend to decrease.[24] The nitrogen results of the Piltdown specimens were quite clear: Piltdown jaw, 3.9 per cent.; Piltdown canine (dentine), 5.1 per cent.; molar tooth (dentine), 4.3 per cent. at site I, 4.2 per cent. at site II; fresh bone, 4.1 per cent,; modern chimpanzee molar, 3.2 per cent.; cranial fragments at site I, 1.4 per cent.; frontal bone at site II, 1.1 per cent.; occipital bone at site II, 0.6 per cent. The findings need little explanation. With the fluorine results, and independently, they prove that at both localities recent or modern jaw and teeth are in association with cranial bones of a different and much older constitution.

Here Dr. Oakley posed a serious objection. Could not these nitrogen values be vitiated by the possibility that in the making of plaster casts gelatine moulds might have been used or that the specimens had been sized? He answered this by pointing out that if such were the case the far more porous cranium would have absorbed as much and probably far more nitrogen than the denser dentine of the teeth, whereas the reverse is in fact what the analyses reveal. The point was settled by arranging with Professor Randall's Unit[25] for examinations (by means of the electron microscope) of the organic, nitrogenous fibrous material (collagen) itself. In keeping with the nitrogen values, an abundance of collagen with the characteristic banded appearance was revealed in the jaw and tooth, and an absence of the material from the cranium. Once again we have a separation into recent and older groups.

Another consideration had to be borne in mind in our investigations. Woodward (1948) said of the mandible: 'It had evidently been missed by the workmen because the little patch of gravel in which it occurred was covered with water at the time of the year when they reached it.' This raised the possibility that conditions in the Piltdown gravel were exceptional and perhaps, through being waterlogged, reducing conditions prevailed in the basal bed and had led to the preservation of the collagen. However, investigation[26] disproved this possibility, for the chemical state of the deposits in February 1951 was such that in fact oxidizing conditions were present.

Later on Dr. Oakley obtained estimations of the organic carbon and chemically-bound water and these, like the nitrogen, mirror the organic content. Like the nitrogen, they yield high values in the jaw and teeth, low values in the several cranial fragments.

The fluorine results confirmed by the nitrogen values, as has been shown, suffice to testify to the modernity of the jaw. But a modern ape's jaw would not be the brownish, slightly yellowish-tinged, colour of the Piltdown jaw unless it had been stained either by using chemicals or perhaps by being left for a sufficient time in iron-containing soil or mud such as the Ouse gravel in fact contains. The coloration of the skull fragments and the blackish brown coating of the canine tooth were investigated by a variety of means.

The tests made for iron early in the investigation yielded their own confirmation of what the fluorine and organic analyses had demonstrated. A distinct contrast was apparent in the iron-staining of jaw and cranium. The drill samples showed that the brown colour had penetrated uniformly and evenly through the porous and drier semi-fossilized pieces of skull-cap; in the jaw the staining was quite superficial and a few millimetres below the surface the bone became progressively lighter. There was 7 per cent. iron in the cranium. In the jaw it fell rapidly from about 8 per cent. to 3 per cent. below the surface. All this was, of course, consistent both with the separate identities of the jaw and cranium and the belief that the former represented only a recent burial in the Piltdown gravel. The result raised the suspicion that the staining might have been intentional.

Of deliberate staining we obtained a striking proof when the canine came to be examined. The tooth has a darkish brown outer coat, always taken to be an ordinary iron-stain, and it was under this 'ferruginous' layer that Dr. Oakley, it will be recalled, remarked with surprise the whiteness and freshness of the dentine. But there proved to be only minimal quantities of iron (oxide) in this stain, the nature of which eluded identification for some time. The layer was found to be a paint-like substance forming a flexible film. The possibility that it was a dried-out layer of Chatterton's compound[27] was ruled out, amongst other things, by its low solubility in organic solvents, but like this compound it contained bitumen. Finally, it turned out to be a bitumen earth containing iron oxide, in all probability the well-known paint—Vandyke brown. It might have been argued that bituminous earth could produce a natural incrustation were it not known that bituminous matter is entirely out of place in a highly oxidized gravel. Its artificiality is established beyond doubt by the finding by Dr. Claringbull of a minute spherule of an iron alloy embedded in the coating on the outer (labial) surface of the crown. The reddish brown stain on the occlusal or chewing surface (like that on the molars) is probably also a ferruginous earth pigment applied as an oil paint (e.g. red sienna).

Here we may mention briefly the two rather novel and up-to-date physical techniques which in the first instance were pressed into service in the examination of the skull. They were destined to lead us to findings as astonishing as the demonstration of the falsity of the jaw, and to clarify for us the significance of the colour of the specimens.

When the bones of *Eoanthropus* were tested with a Geiger counter the radio-activity was found to be almost indetectable in the jaw, which is a further confirmation of its modernity. The cranial fragments were slightly but appreciably radio-active, and this is attributable perhaps to different origin but more likely to the use of an oxidizing agent like potassium dichromate.

The other technique involved the X-ray examination of the crystal structure of bone. This crystallographic technique provides a clear identification of the mineral complex of calcium phosphate called apatite of which bone is composed. The bone is powdered and when the X-ray beam is played on the powder there is a characteristic absorption of some of the X-rays and reflection of the others. The resulting X-ray picture is quite specific. The apatite is clearly revealed in the jaw. But in the cranium it is aberrant. The crystallographic picture is that of a complex containing sulphate, and which is allied to gypsum. In other words the jaw contains no sulphate while the cranium does.

We may now put the results together in this simple table:

	Fluorine	Nitro-gen	Carbon	Water	Colla-gen	Radio-activity	Sulphate	Iron-stain
Piltdown *jaw* *(and teeth)*:	Negligible	Very high	High	High	Present	Negligible	Absent	Superficial
Piltdown *cranium*:	Present	Low	Low	Low	Absent	Slight	Present	Even

The divorce between mandible and skull cap is complete.

The chemical and physical tests had yielded overwhelming proof[28] of the primary contention that the jaw was modern and gave some clear evidence of fraudulent activity. Those tests had disposed of a major objection (the original fluorine values), confirmed the postulated expectations (in the new fluorine values, the nitrogen results, and the iron-staining) and added a whole new series of independent confirmatory evidence (the tests for organic carbon, bound water, radio-activity and the 'apatite-crystal'). The chemistry and physics had done all this virtually twice over, and even more, for the results were consistent at the two sites and on the different fragments at each site.

None of these findings was yet available on 5 August (1953) when Professor Le Gros Clark and I met Dr. Oakley at the British Museum to carry out the anatomical re-examination. The casts at Oxford, as already remarked, had provided some definite indications to favour the belief that the extraordinary occlusal wear of molars and canine represented nothing else but the results of deliberate abrasion.

The specimens had all been removed from the safe by Dr. Oakley, who, without a word as to his own verdict, handed them to us, the jaw to Professor Le Gros Clark, the canine to me. (In exchange I gave him the chimpanzee molar I had filed down and stained at Oxford.) The examination gave us evidence in plenty that the condition of the grinding surfaces of the teeth were fully consistent with the action of deliberate abrasion, as Dr. Oakley had concluded before our arrival. On the canine could be seen without any difficulty the very scratches of the abrasive; equally obvious were the scratchings on the isolated molar from site II. The two molars in the jaw were well polished over most of their biting surface, but on some of the cusps the tell-tale scratches could be seen. The polishing itself appeared artificial.

There was much more than this to provide detailed confirmation.

As we know from the casts, the occlusal surface of the molars was planed down to a flatness much more even than that seen in natural wear in apes' teeth. Indeed, flatness approaching that of the Piltdown molars is to be found only in aged apes with commonly the eye-tooth broken away, and at such a stage of attrition the tooth would be worn very far down. But on the 'fossils' the teeth are already flat at an early stage, altogether unusual for natural wear. In these originals we could see features completely obscured by the plaster casts. The borders of the flat, worn-down surfaces, instead of being bevelled as in natural wear, are sharp-cut, particularly on the outside edges. So too are the borders bounding the central depressed basins of the molar teeth. These edges are unnaturally sharp-cut while the floor of this basin is unworn, strange if the attrition was natural, but not surprising if a file had been applied over the tooth's surface. Another odd point is that the degree of wear of the two molars is almost identical. It is far more usual to find, at this stage of dental wear, that the first molar, erupting earlier, is more severely worn than the second.

The dental inspection tells us even more. At the points on the cusps where teeth wear away the enamel gets removed and the dentine becomes exposed. Now, in normal wear, as the dentine is softer, its level tends to be lower than that of the surrounding enamel and a little depression forms in it. But the Piltdown cusps exhibit (Fig. 2) dentine quite flat and flush with the

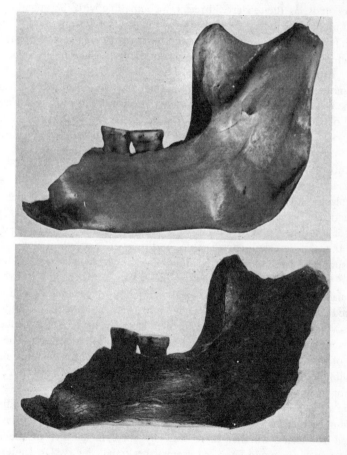

Fig. 2 The inner aspect of the Piltdown mandible (lower) is shown for comparison with a mandible from a female orang-utan (upper); the upper specimen has been broken and the teeth abraded to simulate the Piltdown specimen.

surrounding enamel, a state of affairs explicable only by rapid artificial rubbing down of the surface. Finally, the degree of wear on the different cusps departs from the normal sequence. Instead of greater wear and exposure of dentine on the outer cusps, as is invariable with this degree of wear, there is a complete reversal, with the inner cusps the more eroded.

As for the eye-tooth, the obvious scratches on it give good grounds for attributing its really extraordinary wear—an exposure of dentine over the entire surface from side to side—to the action of an abrasion. This severe and extensive wear is not only unlike anything found normally in ape or human canines; it is, as the reader will recall, incompatible with the immaturity of the tooth. This is judged from the X-ray picture, which shows that the tooth had only very recently erupted, for the inner cavity is large and open, quite characteristic of immature teeth of all kinds. Artificial abrasion would, of course, explain all these peculiarities of wear.

Remote from the anatomists' approach is the metal-shadowing technique for the electron microscopic examination of surfaces. In 1950[29] Dr. David B. Scott of the National Institute of Dental Research, Bethesda (Maryland), undertook to examine collodion replicas of the surfaces of the Piltdown teeth, using this metal-shadowing technique which he has developed with Wyckoff (1946). After examining replicas of the outer facial surfaces of the molars in the Piltdown mandible, Dr. Scott reported that 'they are not readily recognizable as ancient teeth, since they show very little evidence of post-mortem damage'. But, in contrast, replicas of the outer facial surfaces of the isolated molar, and of the outer facial surface of the crown of the canine near the tip, revealed considerable post-mortem damage. These findings correspond precisely with the results of the present detailed re-examination of the teeth, which have shown that the molars in the mandible have been artificially abraded only on the occlusal surfaces, whereas in the canine and isolated molar the facial surfaces have also been smoothed artificially. The water-worn appearance of the isolated molar may have been produced by treatment with a weak acid as well as by the use of an abrasive. The good state of preservation of the enamel on the facial surfaces of the molars in the mandible indicates that they were not in contact with an acid solution during the iron-staining of this bone.

The new X-rays of canine and molar brought to light some additional condemnatory pieces of evidence. In the first place, the new pictures were needed to decide whether there was any force in another of the initial objections which could be raised against the 'fraud' theory. Dr. Underwood had contended that the wear on the canine, for all its unusualness, was natural enough. The reader will recall that in opposing Lyne and as a supporter of Woodward he had claimed that 'secondary dentine', as was to be expected, could be seen in the X-rays. But our new and much clearer pictures showed no evidence whatever of such a deposition; there was no sign of the closing up of the cavity through secondarily deposited dentine which should have been very evident with so severe a degree of attrition. A little plaque of material which had been taken to denote some secondary dentine turned out to be a small mass of some plastic material at a point where the pulp cavity had actually come extremely close to the surface. In fact this material appears to plug an opening in the apex of the cavity to the outside—a wholly unnatural state of affairs and again only understandable as a consequence of artificial abrasion. Incidentally, in the X-ray picture of the canine the shadow of the tooth's outline does not appear at all firm. This fuzziness confirms what the chemical analyses of the surface coating already indicated, that the coating was not wholly iron oxide, for in this case it would have been more distinct. As it is we know that the coating is Vandyke brown, which is partly bituminous. Dr. Claringbull even found a minute spherule of a metallic alloy embedded in the coating on the labial surface of the crown.

The X-rays served to dispose also of the last of the three serious objections to our belief in the jaw as that of modern ape (orang or chimpanzee). In the old X-ray of the jaw first published by Dr. Underwood, at a time when dental radiography had not yet reached an invariable high standard, the roots of the molars presented a quite unape-like condition. They appeared rather short and stumpy, and suggestively human. Our recent radiographs disposed of this belief completely. The apparent shortness is due to the tip of the most forward root having been broken off. This broken off piece and the ends of the other specially short roots simply did not show up in the very poor original X-ray. One should add that the inked outlines of these roots were figured in various papers, so that even the original X-rays, bad as they are, were not examined as closely as they might have been.

The treatment which the mandible has received in order to 'fossilize' it explains very reasonably the presence of cracks on the surface of the bone. This pattern is very like the stress or split-line patterns produced in modern jaw bones which have been slightly decalcified and dried, as Dr. S. L. Washburn pointed out in July 1953. The treatment probably included not only drying, but possibly immersion in dilute acid to smooth fractured edges and thus simulate the wear due to abrasion in a river bed.

The objective testimony of the morphological and radiological examination furnishes a body of evidence quite as comprehensive as does the chemical and physical. As with the latter techniques, the fragments at both sites bear many different signs, ascertained by different methods, of the tampering to which the material has been subjected.

The anatomical, like the chemical and physical, investigations had disposed of postulated objections, confirmed the suggestions provided by the casts, and given unexpected confirmation in a number of different ways. The examinations had convinced us that the jaw was not that of a form of chimpanzee, as Woodward's first critics, Waterston in this country, Miller in the United States and Ramstrom of Sweden,[30] had maintained, but belonged to a fossil orang-utan, a view[31] first put forward in 1927 by Frassetto and by Friederichs in 1932, and supported by Weidenreich.

Of our reasons for this we may mention in particular that the height of the crown of the molar teeth and the shape of the pulp cavities seem to us quite unlike those of the chimpanzee. Friederichs advanced several good reasons for his views in his elaborate study of the detailed anatomy of the jaw.

Finally, we have been able to obtain a close similarity, anatomically and radiographically, to the Piltdown jaw in a female orang jaw by appropriate maltreatment (Figs. 2 and 3). This shows the finer points of detail on the exposed dentine of the abraded teeth very well. Particularly impressive is our artifically abraded canine. Apart from its somewhat greater size, it is almost an exact replica of the Piltdown original.

The completeness of the coherence between anatomical and chemical evidence can be easily illustrated. The independent evidence of the chemical tests is such that the extraordinary nature of the wear of the teeth cannot be other than fraudulent, since in a modern ape such characters cannot be matched; conversely, the independent anatomical evidence of the maltreatment of the teeth leads one to predict in detail (as we did) the very results of the chemical tests. When the reader recalls, in addition, that evolutionary and

Fig. 3 The cast of the Piltdown canine (left) is compared with a canine from a rather more mature orang; the latter tooth has been stained and abraded to simulate the Piltdown specimen.

chronological considerations make the real existence of *Eoanthropus dawsoni* in the highest degree incredible, then the exact correspondence between the anatomical and the other tests is altogether comprehensible. The Man of Piltdown was an artifact.

Before leaving, for the time being, the skull bones of 'Piltdown man', we must refer to the serious and disturbing matter of their chromium-stained condition. This is a complicated aspect of the whole affair and a complete evaluation of the significance of the use of chromium on the Piltdown material will be attempted later.

That some of the cranial bones had been treated with dichromate of potash was well known. Sir Arthur Keith knew for a long time that some such treatment had been employed. Smith Woodward recorded that 'the colour of the pieces which were first discovered was altered a little by Mr. Dawson when he dipped them in a solution of bichromate of potash in the mistaken idea that this would harden them'. Direct chemical analysis carried out by Drs. M. H. Hey and A. A. Moss in the Department of Minerals at the British Museum (Natural History), as well as the X-ray spectrographic method of Dr. E. T. Hall in the Clarendon Laboratory, Oxford University, confirmed that all the cranial fragments seen by Smith Woodward in the spring of 1912 (before he began systematic excavations) do contain chromate; on the other hand, there is no chromate in the cranial fragments subsequently collected that summer—either in the right parietal or in the small occipital fragment found *in situ* by Smith Woodward himself. This being so, it is not to be expected that the mandible (which was excavated later and in the presence of Smith Woodward) would be chromate-stained. In fact, as shown by direct chemical analysis carried out in the Department of Minerals of the British Museum, the jaw does contain chromate. It is clear from Smith Woodward's statement about the staining of the cranial fragments of Piltdown I (which we have verified), that a chromate-staining of the jaw could hardly have been carried out without his knowledge *after* excavation. The iron- and chromate-staining of the Piltdown jaw seemed to us to be explicable only as a necessary part of the deliberate matching of the jaw of a modern ape with the mineralized cranial fragments.

In the later stages of our investigation definite evidence was obtained, and this will be presented in due course, of the fraudulent nature of the iron-staining on many specimens said to have come from the Piltdown sites. By means of an intensive chemical and crystallographic study this was found to be true of the cranial fragments of both Piltdown men.

The creation of the composite man-ape, Piltdown man, was evidently an elaborate affair; much thought and work had gone into the preparation of the fraudulent jaw and in the provision of the other items of the deception. We

346 The Fossil Record

can discern in this elaboration the whole history of the successive discoveries, each new find adding to the whole case for the fossil man. Thus we see the discovery of an ancient gravel formation followed by the finding of a thick fossilized cranium, and this by the remarkable simian mandible, then comes the equally remarkable eye tooth and in due course the fragments of a second composite creature. And as if this was not persuasion enough, there is still the weighty ballast of the animal bones and the implements. As we are now aware beyond doubt of the spurious nature of some of these elements in the discovery, we naturally wonder about them all.

References

1. Woodward, A. S., 1915, *Guide to the Fossil Remains of Man*, British Museum (Natural History), p. 20.
2. Dawson, C., 1915, 'The Piltdown Skull', *The Hastings and East Sussex Naturalist*, 2, p. 182.
3. Underwood, A. S., 1913, 'The Piltdown Skull', *British Journal of Dental Science*, Vol. 56, pp. 650-2.
4. Keith, A., op. cit., p. 684.
5. Miller, G. S., 1915, 'The Jaw of Piltdown Man', *Smithsonian Miscellaneous Collection*, Vol. 65, pp. 1–31.
6. Woodward, A. S., 1917, 'Fourth note on the Piltdown gravel with evidence of a second skull of *Eoanthropus dawsoni*', *Quarterly Journal of the Geological Society*, Vol. 73, p. 9.
7. Miller, G. S., 1918, 'The Piltdown Jaw', *American Journal of Physical Anthropology*, Vol. 1, pp. 25–52.
8. Woodward, A. S., op. cit., pp. 1–7.
9. Painted by John Cooke, R.A., and presented to the Geological Society in 1924, by Dr. C. T. Trechmann, F.G.S.
10. Woodward, A. S., 1948, *The Earliest Englishman*, pp. 12–13, London, Watts.
11. Toombs, H. A., 1952, 'A New Section in the Piltdown gravel', *The South-Eastern Naturalist and Antiquary*, Vol. 67, pp. 31-3.
12. By Mr. Toombs, Dr. Oakley, and Mr. Rixon.
13. 'Physical Anthropology since 1935', in *A Hundred Years of Anthropology*, by T. K. Penniman, 1952, London, Duckworth.
14. Hrdlička, A., 1922, 'The Piltdown Jaw', *American Journal of Physical Anthropology*, Vol. 5, pp. 337-47.
15. Letter to Professor Le Gros Clark, 12 August 1953.
16. Oakley, K. P., and Hoskins, C. R., 1950, loc. cit., p. 380.
17. Lyne, C. W., 1916, 'The significance of the radiographs of the Piltdown teeth', *Proc. Roy. Soc. Med.*, Vol. 9, pp. 33–62.
18. Oakley and Hoskins, op. cit., p. 379.
19. The Moulin Quignon jaw was declared to be a deliberate intrusion on the evidence of the high nitrogen content, by Falconer and Busk in 1863. See Keith, A., 1925, *Antiquity of Man*, pp. 270-1.
20. Weiner, J. S., Oakley, K. P., and Le Gros Clark, W. E., 1953, 'The Solution of the Piltdown Problem', *Bulletin of the British Museum (Natural History) Geological Series*, Vol. 2, No. 3, pp. 139-46.
21. Conan Doyle, *The Sign of Four*.

22. Mr. C. F. M. Fryd and Mr. A. D. Baynes-Cope (Government Chemist's Dept.), Dr. G. F. Claringbull, Dr. M. H. Hey and Mrs. A. Foster (Mineral Dept., British Museum), Dr. A. V. M. Martin (King's College, London), Dr. G. Weiler and Dr. F. B. Strauss (Oxford), Mr. S. H. U. Bowie and Dr. C. F. Davidson (Geological Survey), Dr. A. E. A. Werner and Miss R. J. Plesters (National Gallery).

23. Cooke, S. F., and Heizer, R. F., 1947, 'The Quantitative Investigation of Aboriginal Sites: Analysis of Human Bone', *American Journal of Physical Anthropology*, Vol. 5, pp. 201-20.

24. The rate of decrease varies with local conditions. The fibrous substance collagen in bone and teeth from which much of the nitrogen comes is remarkably resistant and may decay quite slowly in Arctic regions and in anaerobic deposits. In the 'open' condition of the Piltdown gravel a fossil should lose its nitrogen readily.

25. Medical Research Council's Biophysics Research Unit, King's College, London.

26. By Dr. C. Bloomfield, through the courtesy of the Director of Soil Survey.

27. A bituminous compound used by jewellers for securing gems during polishing.

28. Still another indication of the modernity of the mandible is provided by the ash content. The specific gravity of the jaw, 2.05, also differs markedly from that of the cranial pieces of Piltdown I, 2.13. (For full details of all the tests see *Bulletin of the British Museum (Natural History) Geological Series*, 1955, Vol. 2, No. 6.

29. These findings by Dr. Scott are quoted verbatim from the reports in the *Bulletin of the British Museum (Natural History) Geological Series*, 1955, Vol. 2, No. 6.

30. Ramström, M., 1919, 'Der Piltdown-Fund', *Bulletin of the Geological Institute of the University of Uppsala*, Vol. 16, pp. 261-304.

31. Frassetto, F., 1927, 'New Views on the "Dawn Man" of Piltdown (Sussex)', *Man*, Vol. 27, p. 121. Friederichs, H. F., 1932, 'Schaedal und Unterkiefer von Piltdown (Eoanthropus dawsoni Woodward) in neuer untersuchung.' *Z. fur Anat. u Entwicklungsgeschichte*, Bd. 98, pp. 199-226. Weidenreich, F., 1943, 'The Skull of Sinanthropus pekinensis', *Palaeont. Sin.*, whole series No. 127.

A Further Fragment
of the Swanscombe Skull

J. Wymer*

The right parietal of a human skull, found in the Middle Gravels at
Swanscombe, Kent, on July 30 of this year, was discovered during
excavations under licence from the Nature Conservancy: a section was to be
cleared from near the top of the Upper Middle Gravel, through the Lower
Middle Gravel to the Lower Loam, for the purpose of studying the deposits
and their archaeological contents. The spot chosen was close to the site of Mr.
A. T. Marston's discoveries of 1935 and 1936, when he found the occipital
and left parietal of Swanscombe Man. It is one of the few places in the reserve
where undisturbed Middle Gravel deposits exist, although they are almost
completely buried beneath dump and scree. Previous work in the pit for five
years had proved the existence of this remaining piece.

The geology of the Swanscombe deposits is well known, having been
carefully studied during the years of commercial excavation, when large
exposures rendered the task more practical. Now there are only a few small
patches where any of the undisturbed deposits can be seen. All these terrace
deposits, except perhaps the topmost solifluxion layer, are of great
interglacial age, possibly 250,000 years old, and they fill a large channel cut
in the solid Thanet Sand and Chalk, almost a mile wide. When the River
Thames flowed at this level, it meandered across its flood plain, scouring out
new channels and filling in old. Such a channel remains 'fossilized' in the
Middle Gravels of Swanscombe, the Upper Middle Gravel representing a
channel cut into the Lower Middle Gravel and afterwards filled with gravels
and sand. It was near the base of this channel, not far from its banks, that the
Swanscombe Man fragments were found, in association with mammalian

*Nature, September 1955

remains and flint artifacts datable to the middle period of the Acheulian flint industry.

The channel of Upper Middle Gravel is obviously more recent than the Lower Middle Gravel below; but they both contain a flint industry of Middle Acheulian type. Some authorities consider the Upper Middle Gravel flint industry to be more evolved; but this is debatable. The surface level is 110 ft., and the bottom of the main channel attains a depth of 40 ft.

A thick capping of overburden and the lack of an existing face made it necessary for the excavation to be conducted downwards by horizontal planes in order to determine the lay of the strata. The current-bedded sand at the top of the excavation was recognized as part of the Upper Middle. It was devoid of bone or flint artifacts; but a thin seam of gravel running through it yielded numerous flint flakes, as did the thicker seam of gravel below which also contained a small hand-axe, two miniature cores and some bone fragments, as yet unidentified. The very loose sand with stones beneath contained few artifacts and no bone.

On the second day of the excavation, in the west-north-west end of the section, a thin band of very ochrous gravel was revealed with unstained gravel beneath it. This had a steep dip to the east-south-east and south-south-west. Immediately, several bone fragments and flint flakes were found. Further removal of material showed more inconsistent bands, also dipping but tending to converge upon the east-south-east. The gravel continued to be very rich in flint artifacts and bone fragments; many of the flint flakes were lustreless and sharp, as if freshly struck, others were slightly rolled. Excavation in this region was very difficult because of the proximity of thick, loose overlay, which tended to fall. A thicker band of dark, stained gravel was exposed beneath, and as this was being examined a small piece of bone showed through the lighter gravel at its base. The surrounding material was cleared away by the fingers and the new find, a right parietal, was exposed *in situ*, dome upwards. Its upper surface, at least, was seen to be in soft, soapy condition, and ancient cracks already existed. It was decided to cease all further work in order to decrease the probability of a fall of the disturbed material upon it, but to leave the bone *in situ*. Photographs were taken and a temporary protection of boards placed over the parietal in case of a dangerous fall; Mr. Marston arrived two hours later and confirmed the discovery. A protective covering of plaster was made over the bone; but the loose nature of the gravel and the existing cracks defied attempts to extricate the fragment complete. All the pieces, however, were retrieved without damage to them and packed carefully in a box that was not opened again until arrival at the British Museum (Natural History) on August 2, save for the placing of a saturated wad of cotton-wool above to prevent any serious drying out.

Mr. Marston confirmed that his occipital bone was found 51 ft. to the west-north-west of the new find and 49 ft. from the left parietal, the position of the three fragments forming a triangle with sides 51, 49 and 24 ft. In his report on the discoveries (*Journal of the Royal Anthropological Society*, Vol. 67, 350; 1937), his geological section agrees exactly with the new one figured, showing four oblique ochrous layers and, of great significance, the bottom one as the bone layer. The new fragment was barely one inch below this seam in the unstained sandy gravel, a difference of no importance in a river deposit.

A comparison of the two sections shows that there can be no doubt that the new right parietal was found in the same stratum as that in which Mr. Marston found an occipital and left parietal in 1935−36. This renders the fact that all three fragments fit each other perfectly, belonging to the skull of the same individual, a little less remarkable.

Numerous bone fragments were found in association with the right parietal, and these are now at the British Museum for purposes of hardening and identification. It is hoped that they may add to the list of fauna from this level. Almost three hundred primary and finishing flint flakes were found during the excavation, of which only twelve showed signs of possible utilization. Four small, primitive hand-axes were also found, typical of the Acheulian flint industry as represented at Swanscombe, as well as the point of a larger, finely finished hand-axe and a magnificent flake 'knife'. A full account of these artifacts will appear in the forthcoming report. Most of them were in a very sharp condition, with only a few minute chippings along the edge and a lustre from rolling in the water. Many, however, are lustreless and virtually in mint condition. Although separated, the skull fragments show very little abrasion from rolling and there can be no doubt that the flint industry is contemporary.

Inside the triangle formed by the position of the three skull fragments recovered remains a mound, part of which is definitely undisturbed gravel of the skull zone. This area is now efficiently protected, and is to be excavated in the near future.

A New Fossil Skull
from Olduvai

L. S. B. Leakey*

On July 17, 1959, at Olduvai Gorge in Tanganyika Territory, at Site *FLK*, my wife found a fossil hominid skull, at a depth of approximately 22 ft. below the upper limit of Bed I. The skull was in the process of being eroded out on the slopes, and it was only because this erosion had already exposed part of the specimen that the discovery was possible. Excavations were begun on the site the following day and continued until August 6. As a result, an almost complete skull of a hominid was discovered. This skull was found to be associated with a well-defined living floor of the Oldowan pre-Chelles-Acheul culture.

Upon the living floor, in addition to Oldowan tools and waste flakes, there were the fossilized broken and splintered bones of the animals that formed part of the diet of the makers of this most primitive stone-age culture. It has not yet been possible to study the fauna found on this living floor; but it can be said that it includes birds, amphibians, reptiles such as snakes and lizards, many rodents and also immature examples of two genera of extinct pigs, as well as antelope bones, jaws and teeth.

It is of special importance to note that whereas the bones of the larger animals have all been broken and scattered, the hominid skull was found as a single unit within the space of approximately one square foot by about six inches deep. Even fragile bones like the nasals are preserved. The expansion and contraction of the bentonitic clay, upon which the skull rested and in which it was partly embedded, had resulted, over the years, in its breaking up into small fragments which have had to be pieced together. The bones, however, are not in any way warped or distorted. A large number of fragments still remain to be pieced together.

Nature, August 1959.

This very great difference between the condition of the hominid skull and that of the animal bones on the same living floor (all of which had been deliberately broken up) seems to indicate clearly that this skull represents one of the hominids who occupied the living site; who made and used the tools and who ate the animals. There is no reason whatever, in this case, to believe that the skull represents the victim of a cannabalistic feast by some hypothetical more advanced type of man. Had we found only fragments of skull, or fragments of jaw, we should not have taken such a positive view of this.

It therefore seems that we have, in this skull, an actual representative of the type of 'man' who made the Oldowan pre-Chelles-Acheul culture.

This skull has a great many resemblances to the known members of the sub-family of Australopithecinae. Some scientists recognize only one genus, namely, *Australopithecus*, and treat Broom's *Paranthropus* as a synonym; others consider that the demonstrable differences are of such a nature that both genera are valid. Personally, having recently re-examined all the material of the two genera, in Johannesburg and Pretoria, I accept both as valid.

The Olduvai skull is patently a member of the sub-family Australopithecinae, and in certain respects it recalls the genus *Paranthropus*. In particular, this is the case in respect of the presence of the sagittal crest, the great reduction in the size of the canines and the incisors, the relatively straight line of these teeth at the front of the palate, the position of the nasal spines and the flatness of the forehead. In certain other characters, the new skull resembles more closely the genus *Australopithecus*, for example in respect of the high cranial vault, the deeper palate and the reduction of the upper third molars to a size smaller than the second, all of which are features to be found in *Australopithecus* but not in *Paranthropus*.

The very close examination and direct comparisons which I have personally made in South Africa have convinced me that, on the basis of our present state of knowledge, the new skull from Olduvai, while clearly a member of the Australopithecinae, differs from both *Australopithecus* and *Paranthropus* much more than these two genera differ from each other.

I am not in favour of creating too many new generic names among the Hominidae; but I believe that it is desirable to place the new find in a separate and distinct genus. I therefore propose to name the new skull *Zinjanthropus boisei*. This generic name derives from the word 'Zinj', which is the ancient name for East Africa as a whole, while the specific name is in honour of Mr. Charles Boise, whose constant encouragement and financial help ever since 1948 have made this and other important discoveries possible. I would also like to acknowledge the generous help received, from time to time, from the Wenner-Gren Foundation and the Wilkie Trust.

The following is the preliminary diagnosis of the new genus and the new species:

Zinjanthropus gen. nov.:

Genotype: a young male with third molars not yet in wear and sutures relatively open, from *FLK* I, Olduvai.

A new genus of the Hominidae, sub-family Australopithecinae, which exhibits the following major differences from the genera *Australopithecus* and *Paranthropus*:

(*a*) in males a nuchal crest is developed as a continuous ridge across the occipital bone;

(*b*) the inion, despite the great evidence of muscularity, is set lower (when the skull is in the Frankfurt plane) than in the other two genera;

(*c*) the posterior wall of the occipital bone rises more steeply to form, with the parietals, a very high-vaulted posterior region of the skull;

(*d*) the foramen magnum is less elongate and has a more horizontal position than in *Australopithecus* (in the crushed skulls of *Paranthropus* it is not possible to be quite sure of the plane of the foramen magnum);

(*e*) the presence of a very massive horizontal ridge or torus above the mastoids. This is much more marked than the normal type of supra-mastoid crest;

(*f*) the mastoids are more similar to those seen in present-day man, both in size and shape;

(*g*) the presence of a strong wide shelf above the external auditory meatus, posterior to the jugal element of the temporal bone;

(*h*) the shape and form of the tympanic plate, whether seen in *norma lateralis* or in *norma basalis*. In this character the new skull has similarities with the Far Eastern genus *Pithecanthropus*;

(*i*) the very great pneumatosis of the whole of the mastoid region of the temporal bones, which even invades the squamosal elements;

(*j*) the massiveness of the jugal element of the temporal bone relative to the total size of the temporal bone;

(*k*) the way in which the parietals rise almost vertically behind the squamous elements of the temporal before bending over to become a dome;

(*l*) the relative thinness of the parietals in comparison with the occipitals and the temporals;

(*m*) the very prominent and keeled anterior margin of the crests on the frontal bone for the anterior segment of the temporal muscles in the region of the post-orbital constriction (even the most muscular male *Paranthropus* exhibits nothing comparable);

(*n*) the very unusual position of the nasion, which is on the most anterior part of the skull, instead of being behind and below the glabella region;

(*p*) the very great absolute and also relative width of the inter-orbital area, with which may be associated the shape of the nasal bones, which are much wider at the top than at their inferior margin;

(*q*) the whole shape and position of the external orbital angle elements of the frontal bone;

(*r*) the very deep palate which is even more markedly like that of *Homo* than in *Australopithecus*, and is quite unlike the form seen in *Paranthropus*, except in respect of the more or less straight canine-incisor line which has already been commented on, as a character recalling *Paranthropus*;

(*s*) the conformation of the malar-maxillary area of the cheek. In all known members of the genera *Australopithecus* and *Paranthropus* there is a buttress of bone which runs down from the malar towards the alveolar margin of the maxilla in about the region of the fourth premolar; in *Zinjanthropus* this buttress is wholly absent and the form of architecture of this region is that which is found in *Homo*;

(*t*) the very great area of muscle attachment on the inferior margin of the malars;

(*u*) the relatively greater reduction of the canines in comparison with the molar—premolar series than is seen even in *Paranthropus*; where it is a marked character.

Zinjanthropus boisei sp. nov.

A special of *Zinjanthropus* in which the males are far more massive than the most massive male *Paranthropus*. The face is also excessively long. Males have a sagittal crest, at least posteriorly. Upper third molars smaller than the second.

The above is only a preliminary diagnosis of the genus *Zinjanthropus* species *boisei*. It is recognized that, if and when further material is found, the diagnosis will need both enlarging and possibly modifying.

The whole question of generic value is one which is relative. There are some who maintain that *Australopithecus* and *Paranthropus* are not generically distinct, and who will wish to treat *Zinjanthropus* as a third, but less specialized, species of a single genus; but the differences seem to be too great for this.

I must now turn to the absolute and relative geological age of the new skull. As stated earlier, *Zinjanthropus* comes from Olduvai Gorge, about 22 ft. below the upper limit of Bed I. It was found in association with tools of the Oldowan culture, on a living floor and with associated fauna.

In the past it has been customary to regard Olduvai Bed I as a part of the Middle Pleistocene, not differentiating it from Bed II. During the last few years, however, detailed excavations at sites *BK* II, *SHK* II and *HWK* II have shown that there is a constant and well-marked break between the top of Bed

I and the base of Bed II. It is incidentally on this clearly defined land surface that Chellean Stage I living sites are found.

There has also been found a great deal of new faunal evidence, and it is now clear that the fauna of Olduvai Bed I is the same as that of Omo, and that both are generally of the same age as that of Taungs. In other words, it is now necessary to regard Olduvai Bed I as representing the upper half of the Villafranchian and not the lower part of the Middle Pleistocene. So far as relative dating is concerned, it now seems clear that in the Far East the Djetis beds belong to the Middle, rather than to the Lower, Pleistocene, so that the new Olduvai skull would be older than the oldest *Pithecanthropus*.

In South Africa, the deposits at Taungs and Sterkfontein are now regarded as belonging to the upper part of the Lower Pleistocene; they must therefore be regarded as generally contemporary with Olduvai Bed I. The Makapan beds are a little younger, in all probability, while Swartkrans is of Middle Pleistocene age, as are the upper beds at Sterkfontein which are now yielding stone tools.

With the Taungs child, therefore, and the *Australopithecus* fossils from the lower beds at Sterkfontein, the new find represents one of the earliest Hominidae, with the Olduvai skull as the oldest yet discovered maker of stone tools.

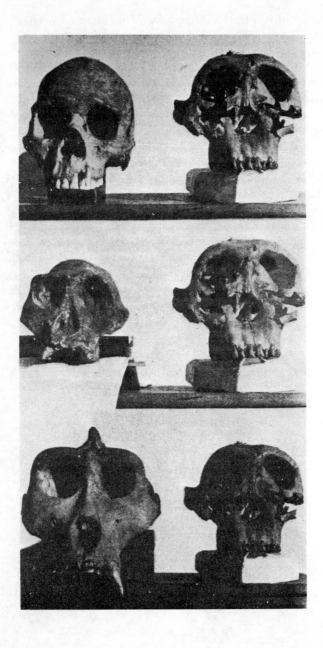

Des Bartlett–Armand Denis Productions

Fig. 2. The palate of the new skull compared with that of an East African native.

Fig. 1. *Above*: The new skull compared with the skull of an Australian aboriginal. Note the very long face, the architecture of the malar region, the unusual nasal bones, the torus above the mastoid, the sagittal and nuchal crests. *Middle*: The new skull compared with a cast of the most complete adult of *Australopithecus*. Note the difference in the size and shape of the face, the shape of the tympanic plate, the low position of the inion, the huge mastoid, as well as the difference in the shape of the malar region and the supra-orbital area. *Below*: The new skull seen next to that of a gorilla.

Age of Bed I,
Olduvai Gorge, Tanganyika

L. S. B. Leakey, J. F. Evernden
and
G. H. Curtis*

Olduvai Gorge is justly famous because of its unique geological sequence of Pleistocene deposits, which are exceedingly rich in fossil fauna, as well as a long sequence of stages of evolution of the earlier Stone Age cultures.[1]

In the monograph[1] published in 1951 the view was expressed that although Bed I differed from Bed II in faunal content, both belonged to the lower part of the Middle Pleistocene. This view was revised by one of us in 1959 as a result of reviewing the fauna collected in the series of detailed excavations during the period 1952–59 inclusive.

Leakey claimed that it was now apparent that the time-interval between Bed I and Bed II was greater than had been previously supposed, and he reverted to the view which he had published in 1935[2] that Bed I was of Lower Pleistocene age. In view of the extraordinary wealth of fossil and cultural material in the Olduvai deposits, it was not surprising when in 1959 a most important fossil hominid skull–*Zinjanthropus boisei*–was found in Bed I, at site *FLK* I, in association with faunal remains and Stone Age culture material of the Olduwan culture.[3] In 1960, thanks to the Research Committee of the National Geographic Society, the Wenner Gren Foundation and the Wilkie Trust, very extensive further work was carried out, resulting in the discovery of pre-*Zinjanthropus*[4] fossil hominid material at a lower geological level in Bed I.

Fortunately, many of the deposits at Olduvai Gorge are pure volcanic deposits, containing no derived material, and are therefore usable for the potassium-argon dating method. A preliminary examination of deposits in the

Nature, July, 1961

Gorge and collecting of material were carried out by two of us, Leakey and Evernden, in 1958 and additional material was collected at intervals and sent to Berkeley by Leakey in 1959 and 1960. In 1961, Curtis visited Olduvai Gorge with Leakey and Richard Leakey for further collecting and study. Although many of the samples collected have not yet been studied, we all three feel that a report on those specimens which have a direct bearing on the age of the fossil hominid remains in Bed I should be published, in view of the scientific importance of these early hominids.

The three sites which have yielded hominid remains in Bed I are: (a) *FLK* I, the site which yielded the skull of *Zinjanthropus boisei*; (b) *FLKNN* I, the site which yielded the remains of a 'child', representing a pre-*Zinjanthropus* hominid; and (c) *MK* I, which has not been referred to in the preliminary reports but which has yielded some teeth and parts of a skull of a hominid. All three sites have yielded an archaic fauna and tools of the Olduwan culture, and are regarded as of Lower Pleistocene (Villafranchian) age.

The Bed I samples which have been dated are as follows:

KA 412   Basal bed in the tuff and sediment sequence of Olduvai Gorge.
     437   Sample collected immediately west of third fault on south side of gorge at knife-edge descent. This horizon can be correlated with the series of tuffs in which hominid remains have been found by Leakey.

KA 846   Site *MK*, 18 in. below hominid remains. Buff coarse-grained tuff 13 in.–14 in. thick.

KA 847   Site *MK*, just above hominid layer. Light grey tuff, 20 ft. thick. Appears to be Pelean type ash. On every criterion, this must be considered an uncontaminated volcanic deposit.

KA 849   Site *FLK* I. 11-in. crystal tuff overlying *Zinjanthropus* layer.
KA 850   Site *FLKNN* I. 2-in. ash above very fine-grained 1-in. ash resting on pre-*Zinjanthropus* floor.

KA 851   Site *FLK* I. 12-in. tuff immediately under *Zinjanthropus* floor. Sample is rather weathered and soft with numerous Zinj-time root holes.

KA 664   Sample collected near top of Bed I, some distance from the
     664R hominid sites. At time of collection, it was thought that this horizon was older than the hominid sites and it is so described in a paper submitted for publication by the INQUA Congress, Warsaw, 1961. However, more careful field work has established unequivocally that this horizon is definitely younger than any of the hominid sites.

KA 861   19-in. soft lapilli tuff, near top of Bed I and definitely younger than any of the hominid sites.

In the area of the three hominid sites, between 25 and 30 individual tuffs and tuffaceous beds can be distinguished in Bed I. At these sites these aggregate 39 ft.—43 ft. in thickness. Most tuffs are approximately a foot in thickness, but at the *MK* site the tuff immediately overlying the hominid floor is 129 in. In order of abundance, the tuffs fall into the following categories: anorthoclase-bearing vitric-crystal tuffs; anorthoclase-bearing crystal vitric tuffs; oligoclase-bearing lapilli tuffs; and tuffaceous sandstones.

Within individual beds faint lines of stratification and evidence of size sorting may sometimes be seen. Some beds, however, show little or no sorting, vary tremendously in grain and lapilli size and exhibit characteristics of nuée ardente deposits. This is true of the tuff overlying the hominid remains at *MK* site. Some of the crystal vitric tuffs show marked crossbedding and have probably been re-worked. Most beds, however, appear to be primary ash falls.

Vitric shards in most of the tuffs have been more or less altered to clay, but the crystals appear fresh. Dark and strongly altered tops of some tuffs probably marked old soil zones. Numerous root casts below such zones strengthen this interpretation. Angular quartz and quartzite fragments are obvious in only a few of the tuffs. The nearest source of basement complex contaminants of this type is an inselberg of quartzite and gneiss approximately 1½ miles north of the hominid sites. More common visible contaminants are bone fragments. These are usually confined to thin strongly weathered layers; but in some cases, as in the tuff below *Zinjanthropus*, occur throughout the tuff.

Reck believed that the source of these tuffs was to the east, and the rapid thickening and coarsening of the strata in that direction is convincing proof that this is so.

At the *FLK* and *FLKNN* sites the hominid remains occur approximately 15 ft.—16 ft. above the basalt flow at the base of Bed I, while at the *MK* site, the hominid remains occur 9 ft. above the basalt. The samples dated, with the exception of *KA* 851 below the *Zinjanthropus boisei* floor which contained numerous bone fragments, showed no visible contaminants. In four of the six samples, the glass shards had been almost completely altered to clay. In one of these, *KA* 849, about 20 per cent of the glass shards were fresh, while in *KA* 847, from just above the hominid remains at *MK* site, most of the glass shards were fresh. Whether the more intense alteration of the four samples is the cause of their somewhat younger ages is not known, but it appears reasonable. . . .

These samples were critically selected and examined and there seems to be no chance of their being contaminated by older eroded debris. It is to be noted that the hominid-site dates fail to fall in the proper relative order but all are between 1.6 and 1.9 million years. At the present time, the best estimate that we can make of the age of these sites is the average of the several ages, that is, 1.75 million years. This figure is in excellent agreement with *KA* 412, which is at the same stratigraphic level, but which was sampled a few miles from the hominid sites. The two samples from the top of Bed I give an average age of 1.23 million years, that is, 0.5 million years younger than the hominid sites. It may be of interest to note that we have obtained[5] an age of 360,000 years on a post-Chellean II tuff in Bed II, Olduvai. The conclusion is inescapable that Olduwan culture and Villafranchian fauna are synchronous in time and that both are approximately 1.75 million years old.

References

1. Leakey, L. S. B., *Olduvai Gorge* (Camb. Univ. Press, 1951).
2. Leakey, L. S. B., *Stone Age Races of Kenya* (Oxf. Univ. Press, 1935).
3. Leakey, L. S. B., *Nature*, 184, 491 (1959).
4. Leakey, L. S. B., *Nature*, 189, 649 (1961).
5. Evernden, J. F., and Curtis, G. H., *Proc. INQUA Cong., Warsaw* (1961).

New Finds at Olduvai Gorge

L. S. B. Leakey*

In *Nature* of December 17, 1960, p. 1050, I reported the discovery of the bones of a hominid foot as well as some other specimens, in deposits of Bed I at Olduvai, but in a geological stratum lower than that which yielded the skull of *Zinjanthropus* in 1959.

The deposit at site *F.L.K.N.N.* I, which yielded the foot bones, the few hand bones, some tiny skull fragments, the two clavicles and the 'lissoir', has since then yielded the greater part of a hominid mandible (see Fig. 1) (found by my son, Jonathan Leakey, on November 2), as well as parts of two hominid parietals (see Fig. 2).

From the mandible, it is possible to estimate that the age of death of this individual was about twelve years. This is on the basis of present-day tooth eruption, since the second molars are in occlusal position but little worn, while there is no sign whatsoever of the eruption of the third molars. It is realized, of course, that in Lower Pleistocene times growth may have been more rapid, and that this jaw may perhaps represent an individual of less than twelve years.

The new mandible can be regarded, almost certainly, as belonging with the two parietals, the foot bones, some of the hand bones, and one of the clavicles. Since these remains represent a hominid which is stratigraphically earlier than *Zinjanthropus*, they are of considerable scientific interest.

Although detailed study has not yet been undertaken, the following facts may be placed on record:

(*a*) The overall dental pattern does not appear to be compatible with the type seen in *Zinjanthropus* or any other Australopithecine, and it seems possible that we are dealing with a quite distinct type of early hominid.

Nature February 1961.

(*b*) The lower canines, while relatively large, are wholly hominid in type and morphologically quite unlike the canines of pongids, but recall *Australopithecus*.

(*c*) The lower incisors are also hominid in their general morphology although they do, to some extent, recall the lower incisors of *Proconsul*.

(*d*) The premolars are remarkable and are unlike what is normally to be seen in the Australopithecinae. The anterior-posterior length in both the third and fourth premolars is greater than the bucco-lingual width, while the fourth premolar has very well-marked cuspules bordering the edge of a large posterior fovea.

(*e*) The first molar is well worn and has a general cusp pattern reminiscent of what can be seen in some recent Australian Aborigines, but it is of course larger.

(*f*) The second molar is much longer than the first and is remarkably elongate.

The mandible was unfortunately broken prior to fossilization, and part of the right ramus has been distorted and made to appear much nearer to the

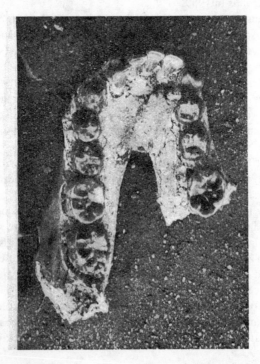

Fig. 1. The new jaw from site *F.L.K.N.N.* I Olduvai.

left half than is really the case. The *corpus mandibulare* is very massive indeed. Unfortunately, the lower margin of the mandible is missing, so that it is not possible to say anything about the lower rim of the mandible or of the symphyseal region.

The two parietals are especially remarkable because, although they apparently belong to a young individual only twelve years old (or less), they are larger than those of *Zinjanthropus*. They are remarkably thin, and exhibit no sign of a sagittal crest or of any marked temporal line. The lack of both these may, perhaps, be due in part to the youthful age. Nevertheless, these parietals suggest that we are dealing with a hominid with a larger brain capacity, as well as somewhat less specialized, than *Zinjanthropus*.

At the time of writing the communication published in *Nature* of December 17, very few stone tools had been found in this lower level; since then, more have been found.

Another discovery of outstanding interest was made on December 2. This consists of the brain case (see Figs. 3 and 4) of a hominid from Bed II at Olduvai, at Site *L.L.K.* This skull was found at a stratigraphic horizon which yields quantities of stone tools of stage 3 of the Chellean culture. It may reasonably be assumed that we have, at last, found a skull representing the makers of the Chellean culture.

The Chellean culture was the first recognized stone-age culture ever to be officially accepted by science more than a century ago, but in all the years

Fig. 2. Two frontals of a juvenile. They are a little larger than those of *Zinjanthropus*, and probably belong with the mandible.

that have followed, no authentic find representing 'Chellean man' has been made other than two teeth found at Olduvai in 1954, and reported in *Nature* in 1958. In this connexion it must be noted here that *Atlanthropus*, found by Prof. Arambourg in North Africa, was in the first instance, placed on record as being associated with Chellean tools; but this has since proved to be incorrect, since the cultural material found with them is quite clearly of Acheulean type.

This new skull from Olduvai, which comes from the well-established Chellean horizon in the gorge, is remarkable in a number of respects. It has a number of resemblances (although some of them are only superficial) to the Pithecanthropines. In other characters, however, the new skull shows considerable resemblances to the Steinheim skull from Germany, a specimen which is usually regarded as contemporary with the early phases of the Acheulean hand-axe culture and assigned to the genus *Homo*. The new skull also shows certain resemblances to two well-known African fossil skulls, those from Broken Hill and Saldhana, respectively. It is very large—209 mm. long and 150 mm. wide—and while the vault of the skull is low compared with the present-day man, it is high compared with fossil skulls from Java and Pekin. No discussion of points of detail will be attempted at present.

The third discovery made in recent months is that of an exceptionally rich living floor of a late stage of the Oldowan culture, some 20 ft. higher in Bed I

Fig. 3. Profile view of the skull of a man from Bed II Olduvai (*L.L.K.* II) found at a level which yielded abundant stone tools of Stage 3 of a Chellean culture. The skull is 209 mm. long.

than the *Zinjanthropus*-level and immediately underlying the 'marker bed' at the top of Bed I. The cultural material in this new floor is associated with a very rich fauna and is of special interest because it provides an intermediate stage between the ordinary Oldowan and stage 1 of the Chellean, as found at sites such as *B.K.* II. Moreover, the study of the fauna found here indicates that, at this level, man had more skill in hunting the large adult animals living at that time than is shown at the *Zinjanthropus*-level.

I wish to thank the National Geographic Society, which has enabled us to work in the field continuously since February 1960, with a large party. I also owe special thanks to my wife and to my son Jonathan, and to my senior assistant, Heselon, on whom the bulk of the work in this very long season has fallen. I am grateful to the Geological Survey of Tanganyika for making available the services of Dr. Pickering to carry out geological mapping on the sites, and on the Gorge as a whole. I also thank the many individuals, too numerous to name, as well as the Wenner Gren Foundation and the Wilkie Foundation, who have helped in a variety of ways to make this further season possible.

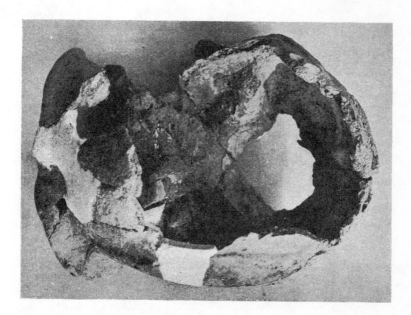

Fig. 4. View of the skull of Fig. 2 from above, to show the brow ridge area and other characters.

The Phyletic Position
of *Ramapithecus*

Elwyn L. Simons*

Recent discoveries of early Pleistocene hominids at Olduvai gorge, Tanganyika, by expeditions under the direction of Dr. L. S. B. Leakey have pushed back certain knowledge of fossil man almost to the beginning of this epoch. To the extent that the K-A date suggested for these early men, 1.75 million years, (Leakey et al. 1961) is accurate, the beginning of the "Villafranchian" provincial age, and thus of the Pleistocene itself, is shown to be considerably earlier than most previous estimates. It therefore seems appropriate that renewed attention be drawn to the only Pliocene fossil primate specimen known to this writer, which can be defended as being within, or near, the population ancestral to Pleistocene and subsequent hominids, the type maxilla of *Ramapithecus brevirostris* at Yale Peabody Museum.

This maxilla, Peabody Museum No. 13799, was collected August 9, 1932 by the Yale North India Paleontological Expedition under Dr. G. E. Lewis (Fig. 1). The geologic occurrence of *R. brevirostris* was first given by Lewis (1934) as "Either latest Middle Siwalik [Dhok Pathan Zone] or basal upper Siwalik [Tatrot Zone]." However, Lewis (1937) later determined the horizon of Y.P.M. 13799 as being within the Nagri zone, which is of Pliocene early Middle Siwalik age. Gregory et al. (1937) also indicate the level of this specimen as Nagri.

Consequently, Hooijer and Colbert (1951) seem to have erred in listing *Ramapithecus* as occurring only in the Tatrot zone fauna which they suggest as being very close to the Plio-Pleistocene boundary. Regardless of these published differences in age determination the provenance of the specimen is known, so that, at least potentially, its temporal position can be verified.

*1961 (*Postilla*, Yale Peabody Museum, November).

Faunal correlations indicate that, even in the unlikely event that *Rama-pithecus* occurs as late as the Tatrot horizon, this primate is distinctly older than the "Villafranchian" hominids of Olduvai gorge.

In spite of the significance of Y.P.M. 13799, as being possibly the earliest known hominid, it has been largely overlooked, or briefly dealt with in the more recent summaries of hominid evolution, a common conclusion being that the type is too fragmentary to permit taxonomic assignment. Actually, such a conclusion is incorrect and misleading. This right maxilla provides at least some information as to shape, size or positioning of the entire upper

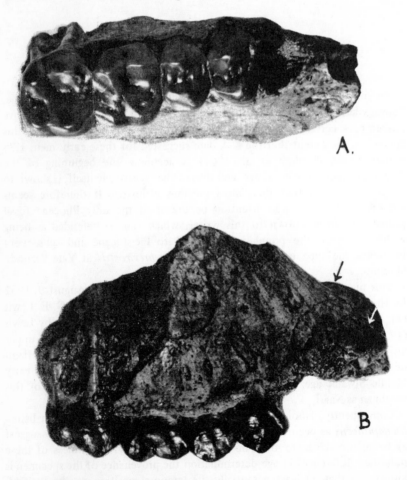

Fig. 1. Occlusal view (A) and lateral view (B) of right maxilla of type of *Ramapithecus brevirostric*, Y.P.M. 13799.

dentition except for M^3, in that alveolae of I^{1-2}, C are preserved as well as the series P^3 through M^2. Moreover the base of the nasal aperture can be seen above the incisors, and, contra Hrdlička (1935), the dental arcade can be determined as parabolic and not U-shaped, as was correctly stated by Lewis (1934) in the original description of this form (see Fig. 2). Some may think (as Hrdlička did) that extrapolating from the right maxilla alone, in order to determine that the disposition of the upper cheek teeth is in an arcuate line, instead of being arranged in the parallel series seen in all pongids, is a rather uncertain procedure. However, at one point (see arrow 1, figure 2) the maxilla reaches nearly, if not entirely to the point of the palatal intermaxil-

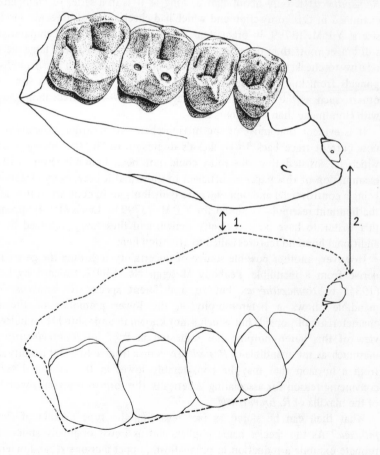

Fig. 2. *Ramapithecus brevirostris*, right maxilla, Y.P.M. 13799, and reverse of same, showing arcuate arrangement of teeth.

lary suture. Since we may safely assume that *Ramapithecus*, like other vertebrates, was bilaterally symmetrical, if the right maxilla and its mirror-image are pivoted around this point the amount of posterior divergence of the cheek tooth rows cannot be further decreased beyond the arrangement shown in figure 2 without assuming an impossibly long basal diameter for the central incisor pair (figure 2, arrow 2). In fact, the space allowed for these teeth in figure 2 (in order to be on the safe side) is intentionally made greater than it is likely to have been. Preservation of the entire length of the alveolar cavity of the right central incisor allows for comparative measurements as to its size. The central incisor root of *Ramapithecus* is only about half as long as it is in a series of chimpanzees examined in this connection and which had cheek teeth of the same absolute size as Y.P.M. 13799. In orangutans the central incisors have, comparatively, still longer roots than does *Pan*. As is well known, possession of large incisors relative to cheek teeth is a general feature distinguishing both fossil and living pongids from known hominids. In this feature of central incisor size, as in others, such as the highly arched palate, *Ramapithecus* agrees more closely with Hominidae than with Pongidae.

It is evident that most of the misapprehensions regarding *Ramapithecus* now current trace back to Hrdlička's discussion of the specimen (1935) in which he insisted that the form could not be a hominid. Even a casual examination of this paper is sufficient to show that it bears every evidence of being a controversial and non-objective contribution. In contrast to this, all of the hominid resemblances cited for Y.P.M. 13799 by Lewis (1934) appear to this writer to have been correctly drawn, and these are reinforced by the additional hominid features called to attention here.

However, another possible source of uncertainty regarding the genus may derive from a mandible, Peabody Museum No. 13807, assigned by Lewis (1934) to *Ramapithecus*, but to a different species *R. hariensis*. This mandible shows a heteromorphy in the lower premolars of the sort characteristic of pongids but which is not known in undoubted Hominidae. In view of this heteromorphy, not indicated in P^{3-4} of *R. brevirostris* and inasmuch as the mandible of *R. hariensis* comes from a different locality, and from a horizon that may be considerably lower in the section, I see no convincing reason for associating generically the form it represents with that of the maxilla of *R. brevirostris*.

What then can be stated as fact regarding the type maxilla of *Ramapithecus*? As the species name implies, and as Lewis originally stated, this primate exhibits a reduction in prognathism, upper incisor size, and in length from the alveolar border above the incisors to the base of the nasal opening, when compared to pongids of its general size, whether living or fossil. This length from nasal aperture to I^2 in *Ramapithecus* is approximately 44 per cent of the length of $P^3 - M^2$ (see arrows, figure 1) while corresponding percentages in a series of specimens of *Pan* range from 70 to 98. Specimens of *Pongo* and *Gorilla* examined fall within the range of *Pan*, in this proportion.

In addition to the foregoing differences, the upper incisors and canine, judging from their alveolae, cannot have been as large as they typically are in even the smallest Great Apes, a fact also pointed out by Lewis (1934), who remarked: "The face is very slightly prognathous, as contrasted with recent Simiidae. There are no diastemata in the dental series. The canine is small, not an antero-posteriorly elongated trenchant tusk but a hominid type with a transverse dimension exceeding the antero-posterior dimension." Lewis (1934: 163-166) fully discussed the dental characters of Y.P.M. 13799, consequently it is unnecessary to repeat this description here. In general, crown patterns resemble both *Dryopithecus* and *Australopithecus* about equally.

Without further extending the polemical atmosphere surrounding this specimen, so unfortunately initiated by Hrdlička, this writer will simply call attention to his final statement regarding *Ramapithecus*, since he appears to be the only person to have studied the actual specimen who has published doubts as to its hominid status. The significance of this remark, in the light of modern understanding of the australopithicines as hominids, seems to have been overlooked. Hrdlička (1935: 36) observed:

"The genus[*Ramapithecus*], although in the upper denture, in general, nearer to man than are any of the Dryopitheci or the *Australopithecus* cannot ... be legitimately established as a hominid, that is a form within the direct human ancestry."

This curious statement indicates that Hrdlička would now have to place the genus in the Hominidae since he regarded it as more man-like than *Australopithecus*, a genus universally accepted today by competent students as belonging to this family. Evidently if there are convincing reasons why *Ramapithecus brevirostris* should not be regarded as representing the earliest known hominid they have not been demonstrated to date.

To contend that the specimen is too inadequate for definite taxonomic assignment implies that pongids and hominids cannot be distinguished, even when reasonable information is available regarding the size, emplacement, structure and arrangement (whether arcuate or parabolic) of nearly all of the upper dentition, together with several characters of palate and face as well. Postcranial remains, if found, might make it easier to assign this primate taxonomically, but the six or seven distinct approximations to hominid morphology discussed here for Y.P.M. 13799 provide an adequate basis for associating it with the latter family. It seems illogical to choose the alternative of regarding this form as belonging to an otherwise unknown group of apes, parallelistic toward hominids but not closely related to them, when it occurs in the proper time and place to represent a forerunner of Pleistocene Hominidae.

References

Gregory, W. K., M. Hellman and G. E. Lewis, 1937. Fossil anthropoids of the Yale-Cambridge India Expedition of 1935. Carnegie Inst. Wash. Publ. No. 495, pp. 1-27, 8 pl.

Hooijer, D. A. and E. H. Colbert, 1951. A note on the Plio-Pleistocene boundary in the Siwalik Series of India and in Java. Amer. Journ. Sci., v. 249, pp. 533-538.

Hrdlicka, A., 1935. The Yale fossils of anthropoid apes. Amer. Journ. Sci., v. 229, pp. 34-40.

Leakey, L. S. B., J. F. Evenden and G. H. Curtis, 1961. Age of Bed I, Olduvai gorge, Tanganyika. Nature, v. 191, pp. 478-479.

Lewis, G. E., 1934. Preliminary notice of new man-like apes from India. Amer. Journ. Sci., v. 227, pp. 161-179, 2 pls.

Lewis, 18,G. E., 1937. Taxonomic syllabus of Siwalik fossil anthropoids. Amer. Journ. Sci., v. 234, pp. 139-147.

A New Lower Pliocene Fossil Primate
from Kenya

L. S. B. Leakey*

The object of this note is to place on record the discovery of a new fossil higher primate during excavations at a believed Lower Pliocene site in Kenya. It is just possible that the age may be uppermost Miocene. The find is of the greatest interest since it helps to bridge the gap between the numerous Lower Miocene higher primates of East Africa and the early Pleistocene Hominidae.

Lower Pliocene fossil beds with mammalian fauna are very rare in Africa and the new site at Fort Ternan, some forty miles east of Kisumu, Kenya, is believed to be the first such site to be excavated in the whole of the continent, south of the Sahara. A few North African Pliocene sites are on record.

The site was discovered by Mr. Fred Wicker, a local farmer, in an area where I have suspected the presence of Pliocene deposits ever since 1932.

Fort Ternan is only a few miles east of Koru, the Lower Miocene site where the first specimen of *Proconsul africanus* and *Limnopithecus legetet* were discovered.

I first located potential fossil-bearing strata in this region in 1932. There were beds which clearly overlay the Lower Miocene series of the Koru region, but since the whole area is one of very high rainfall, with consequent dense vegetational cover, there are few natural exposures of the rock. Prospecting for fossil beds is, in consequence, very difficult.

Mr. Fred Wicker found the first fragmentary fossils on his farm a number of years ago, but it was not until two years ago that he picked up some large limb bones, almost as large as those of Hippopotamus, which seemed to him sufficiently unusual to send down to me at Nairobi. Mrs Leakey and I went up to Fort Ternan as soon as possible, thereafter, and were shown the hill

*The Annals & Magazine of Natural History, November, 1961.

377

slope where the fossils had been picked up. Almost at once a number of other surface specimens were found by Mr. Wicker, Mr. Firth, (a neighbouring farmer who had joined us) and by ourselves. These surface finds strongly suggested that the site would repay scientific excavation but it was not until April, 1961, that sufficient funds were available, as well as the necessary trained personnel, for this work to be put in hand.

As a result of a short season's work in 1961, in charge of my senior African Field Assistant, Mr. Mukiri, more than 1,200 fossils have been found *in situ*, in a preliminary excavation at this site.

Examination of these fossils tends to confirm the idea that the deposits are of Lower Pliocene age, but final appraisal of the date must await fuller identification of the fossils. Meanwhile, the possibility of a slightly older date cannot be ruled out, since three tests by the potassium argon technique have all yielded dates of circa fourteen million years.

The fauna so far found includes mastodont material which clearly represents a species more evolved than the Trilophodonts of our Lower Miocene deposits, but which is not so advanced as *Anancus* in the Lower Pleistocene beds of Kanam West.

There is a small giraffid which seems to be ancestral to the modern genus *Giraffa* and, as such, is of very great interest.

Other artiodactyl material is common, including many antelopes represented by horn cores, mandibles, maxillae and some limb bones; there are also pig remains. A most interesting find consists of some parts of an animal which seems to stand somewhere between the Anthracotheres and the Hippopotami, with cheek teeth approaching those of the latter but an anterior dentition more of Anthracothere type. There are also a few fossils representing Carnivora and Rodentia.

It was most encouraging to find in such an assemblage that the order Primates was also represented. There are a few teeth of some kind of monkey,—as yet unstudied; a very large upper canine, scarcely distinguishable from those of *Proconsul nyanzae* of the Lower Miocene, and the important new fossil primate, which is described below.

The following is a diagnosis and preliminary description of this new Kenya Lower Pliocene primate.

Super-Family   HOMINOIDEA.
Family   Incertae sedis.
Genus   *Kenyapithecus* gen. nov.

Diagnosis.—A genus within the super-family Hominoidea, with low crowned molars and pre-molars; the upper canines are small and set vertically in their sockets. There is a well defined canine fossa, and the root of the malar element of the malar-maxillary process is set just above the first molar.

Genotype.—The type of the genus is the new species *Kenyapithecus wickeri* described below.

Species *Kenyapithecus wickeri* sp. nov.

Diagnosis.—A species of *Kenyapithecus* with the following as diagnostic characters.

The upper canines of the presumed female are small, both absolutely, as well as relative to the size of the molars and pre-molars, in comparison with the position to be seen in Pongidae and Proconsulidae.

The upper canine tooth has a small root which is set nearly vertically in the maxilla. It is compressed bucco-lingually and somewhat elongate anterior-posteriorly, so that the tooth is flattened in cross section rather than conical or pyramidal. Both upper pre-molars are three rooted and the fourth upper pre-molar is almost the same with bucco-lingually as the first molar. The crown of the fourth upper pre-molar is more complex than is usual in Pongidae and Proconsulidae, and it carries no trace of a cingulum. Anterior, mesial and posterior fovea are present on the fourth pre-molar.

The first upper molar is large relative to the size of the canines and pre-molars, but smaller than the second molar. It is low crowned, with smooth enamel and no cingulum. The second upper molar is a little larger than the first. In both the molars the bucco-lingual width and the anterior-posterior length are approximately equal.

The species has strongly developed canine fossae and the root of the malar maxillary process is vertically above the posterior half of the upper molar.

Holotype.—Two maxilla fragments and a lower molar of the same individual.

Horizon.—At present the indications given by the associated fauna and by the geology suggest a lower Pliocene, or possibly uppermost Miocene, date.

Note on the names.—The generic name is after Kenya Colony and the specific name in honour of Mr. Fred Wicker, who discovered the site where subsequent excavations revealed this interesting fossil.

Description of Type.—The left maxilla fragment is the more complete of the two, carrying the upper canine, the roots of the third upper pre-molar and the whole fourth upper pre-molar, together with the first and second upper molars—all in excellent preservation.

The crown of the third upper pre-molar is broken off at the alveolar margin and this enables it to be seen that the tooth was three rooted.

The right maxilla fragment has only the upper first and second molars present but the root of the third molar is present, the crown having been broken off at the alveolar margin. The impression of the posterior root of the fourth upper pre-molar is also preserved.

The lower molar consists of a crown only and it exhibits contact facets anteriorly and posteriorly. It occludes very well with the upper right second molar and is assumed to be the second right lower molar of the same individual as the maxillae.

Both the maxilla fragments show the well defined canine fossa, which is characteristic of the genus, and is of hominid type. The fossa is better preserved on the left side than on the right side. Both specimens show the root of the malar maxillary process as being set over the posterior half of the first molar, and both retain fragments of the palatal area, and show that it was very shallow.

The bony wall of the maxilla on the facial aspect is very thin indeed and is only preserved because the maxillary sinuses are full of a hard stony matrix. Both specimens had been broken before being embedded in the deposit in which they were found.

Since the left maxilla is the better preserved, it will be used as the basis of the description of the dentition, supplemented, where necessary, by information from the right side.

The left upper canine has the tip of the root missing and the extreme tip of the crown, (about 1 mm.) is also broken away; otherwise it is beautifully preserved.

It differs morphologically, very markedly indeed, from the so-called "small" *Sivapithecus* canine in the *Sivapithecus sivalensis* specimen which was described by Gregory, Helman and Lewis, in 1937/38 and it is also considerably smaller. It also differs both in size and morphology from any other published *Sivapithecus* upper canines of any species of which I have a record.

It is a relatively compressed canine, bucco-lingually, and has a consequent slightly exaggerated anterior-posterior length, which is further stressed by a swelling on the lower anterior margin at the point where the internal cingulum ends. There is a shallow groove on the anterior face running from this swelling to the tip, much as may be seen in upper canines of the Proconsulidae and in some upper canines of the Asiatic *Sivapithecus*, but it is much less strongly developed. The lingual face of the canine is slightly convex but lacks the strong medium ridge seen in the upper canines of the genus *Sivapithecus*, even in small females. On the posterior face there is a narrow area of wear extending longitudinally from the tip to a point just above where the cingulum ends posteriorly. This wear facet seems to postulate a lower third pre-molar of semi-sectorial type. The inner face of the crown of the canine is marked by a cingulum. The measurements of this upper canine are:—

Anterior-posterior length at the base .... 9.25 mm.

Maximum bucco-lingual width 8   mm.

Height (to which may be added about 1 mm.

for the missing tip) .... 11.25 mm.

The index $\frac{100 \text{ B}}{\text{L}}$ is 86.4

As stated earlier, the crown of the third upper pre-molar is broken off at the alveolar margin and reveals the presence of three distinct roots. The posterior buccal root was small compared with the other two.

The fourth upper pre-molar is present and in perfect condition except for a small fragment of enamel which is broken away at the anterior buccal corner. It is clear from examination of the alveolar margin, that this tooth is also three rooted.

This fourth upper pre-molar is specially interesting for a number of reasons: it differs markedly in its morphology from the corresponding tooth in *Sivapithecus africanus* described by Le Gros Clark & Leakey, and it is clearly of a different species. In the present specimen there is no cingulum at all, whereas in *Sivapithecus africanus* there is an anterior and a posterior cingulum with the latter extending to the lingual face.

The crown of this fourth upper pre-molar of *Kenyapithecus wickeri* is very wide bucco-lingually, having almost the same diameter as the first upper molar; the surface of the crown is much more complex than in *Sivapithecus africanus*.

In addition to the well defined anterior and posterior fovea, there is a mesial fovea formed as follows: a ridge runs from the tip of the lingual cusp towards the centre of the tooth and then divides into two parts which enclose the mesial fovea. This is a structure which I have not seen in any *Proconsul* or in any of the Asiatic *Sivapithecus, Ramapithecus*, or other Siwalik primates.

A slightly similar structure is to be seen in some of the less worn fourth upper pre-molars of Australopithecines.

This fourth upper pre-molar is also very much lower crowned than in the Asiatic genus *Sivapithecus*, and is comparable, in this respect, to *Ramapithecus*. It is distinctly lower crowned than the corresponding tooth in *Sivapithecus africanus*.

The contact facet between the fourth upper pre-molar and the third upper pre-molar is long, even though a part of it is missing on the chip at the external corner. This facet must have been at least 5 mm. long when intact, a feature in which it resembles *Ramapithecus brevirostris*, and a character which is certainly connected with a shortening of the face and of the molar pre-molar series becoming compressed from end to end. This type of compression is not seen in *Sivapithecus africanus*, nor in any of the Indian

species of *Sivapithecus* about which I can find record.* The measurements of
the upper fourth pre-molar are:—

Anterior-posterior length 6   mm.
Bucco-lingual diameter .... 10.25 mm.
The index $\dfrac{100\,B}{L}$ is 170.8

    The first upper molar is a large tooth relative to the size of the pre-molars
and canines, although, as stated, the bucco-lingual width of the fourth
pre-molar is almost the same as the first molar. For example, in both male
and female of *Proconsul africanus*, the canines are larger than in *Kenyapithecus wickeri*, and yet the first molar of the latter is much larger than the
first molar of either the male or female of the former. It is also relatively
larger when compared with the canines and the corresponding molars in the
Asiatic *Sivapithecus* group.

    The first upper molar has no cingulum, it is low crowned, with smooth
enamel on the three nearly equal sized cusps of the trigone and over the rest
of the crown. Prior to wear there was probably a small anterior fovea but this
anterior face has been worn by contact with the first lower molar. A small
posterior fovea can still be traced. On the lingual face, anteriorly, there is a
very tiny ledge of enamel which may, perhaps, be regarded as the last relic of
a disappearing internal cingulum. The measurements of this first upper molar
are:—

Anterior-posterior length .... 10.5 mm.
Bucco-lingual width .... 10.5 mm.
Index 100

    The second upper molar is a slightly larger tooth but it hardly differs
morphologically from the first upper molar but is a little less worn. Its
measurements are:—

Anterior-posterior length .... 12.5 mm.
Bucco-lingual width .... 12.25 mm.
Index 100

    While we do not possess a third upper molar, the roots of this tooth are
preserved on the right side, and to judge by these roots, it is almost certain

*It is not at all clear, as Professor Gaylord Simpson has pointed out to me, just what the
genus *"Sivapithecus"* of Asia really is. It seems that the species *"Sivapithecus"*
sivalensis was definitely excluded from the genus and that the genotype is *Sivapithecus
indicus.* This is another strong reason for giving the Fort Ternan material new generic
rank, for it differs from *indicus* even more than from *sivalensis.*

that the third upper molar was smaller than the second, at least, in its anterior-posterior dimension.

Combining the evidence of the two maxilla fragments, one containing P. 3 to M. 2 and the other M. 1 to the roots of M. 3, we can obtain an approximate measurement of the length of the whole molar pre-molar series. This is 41 mm., of which some 23 mm. lies behind the root of the malar element of the malar maxillary process. This is a relationship which is closely paralleled in a great many Hominidae and quite unlike the Pongidae.

The second lower molar is represented by a crown which occludes perfectly with the right second upper molar, and it is therefore presumed to be the right lower second molar of the same individual. It has a very simple crown pattern and is low crowned with smooth enamel over the cusps and no cingulum.

A most interesting feature is the position of the fifth cusp, which is set much more in the midline than is usually seen in Pongidae and Proconsulidae and is another character in the direction of the Hominidae. The measurements are:—

Anterior-posterior length . . . . 11. mm.
Bucco-lingual width . . . . 9. mm.
Index 81.8

Discussion.—In view of the likelihood that further material representing this most interesting new Lower Pliocene fossil hominoid will be found during the next season's work at Fort Ternan, the significance of this find will not be discussed in any detail here.

It must suffice to point out that, while it clearly represents a creature related, to some extent, to the lower Miocene species, which Leakey and Le Gros Clark called *Sivapithecus africanus*, it is equally clearly not a true *Sivapithecus*, as may be seen by the morphology of the upper canine and fourth upper pre-molar, and also by the presence of the canine fossa and the position of the root of the malar element of the malar maxillary process.

In all of these characters it shows a greater or lesser approach towards the structures we associate with the Hominidae. For this reason, I have purposely refrained from suggesting any family into which this new species should be placed. I am satisfied that it is not a member of the Pongidae in the sense in which I have elsewhere defined that family, but I am not sure whether it should be placed in the Proconsulidae (which I distinguish from the Pongidae) or whether it may not perhaps represent an early member of the Hominidae.

Only the discovery of further material of this species will clarify this point. For the moment we must rest content with having knowledge that the Lower Pliocene of Kenya is going to help us fill the gap in our knowledge of Hominoidea evolution.

When I started writing this note, I intended to refer these Fort Ternan specimens to the genus *Sivapithecus*, giving them only a new specific name. As my study proceeded, however, I found myself forced to abandon the generic name of *Sivapithecus* since the specimens differed in too many characters from all the described Asiatic species of *Sivapithecus*. On the other hand, the Fort Ternan specimens do show certain clear affinities with the Lower Miocene specimens which Le Gros Clark and I called *Sivapithecus africanus* in 1951. Moreover, in a number of characters the Fort Ternan material exhibits a marked tendency in the direction of the Hominidae and is certainly more hominid than *Oreopithecus*.

There is every hope of further material being obtained from Fort Ternan which will give us the answer and I have, therefore, refrained from placing *Kenyapithecus wickeri* into any family at present. On the other hand, I strongly suggest that when the new genus is allocated to a family, *Sivapithecus africanus* will have to join it there and be removed from the Pongidae.

References

Clark, W. W. Le Gros & Leakey, L. S. B. 1951. "The Miocene Hominoidea of East Africa," F.M.A. 1. *British Museum of Natural History, London*.
Gregory, W. K. 1916. "Evolution of the Primates."
———, Hellman, M. & Lewis, G. E. 1938. "Fossil Anthropoida of the Yale-Cambridge India Expedition of 1935."
Hopwood, A. T. 1933. "Miocene Primates from Kenya." *J. Linn. Soc. (Zool.) London*, 1938.
Hurzeler, J. 1958. "Oreopithecus bambolli."
Lewis, G. E. 1934. "Preliminary Notice of New Man-like Apes from India."
Robinson, J. T. 1959. "The Dentition of the Australopithecinae."

On the Mandible of *Ramapithecus*

Elwyn L. Simons*

During the past three years a number of findings have enlarged scientific understanding of the initial differentiation of hominids from pongids. These advances are the outgrowth of significant developments in the study of man-like hominoids of Miocene and Pliocene age, recovered from deposits in Africa and Eurasia. In order of their occurrence these additions to knowledge are as follows: (1) The discovery and description by Dr. L. S. B. Leakey of an African member of *Ramapithecus* [=*Kenyapithecus*] at Fort Ternan, Kenya, in deposits which have been dated by the *K/A* method as about 14 million years old. (2) The assignment to *Ramapithecus* by Simons[1] of a second maxilla (a referred specimen of *Dryopithecus punjabicus* originally figured by Pilgrim,[2] from Haritalyangar in the Nagri zone, Siwalik Hills, North India). (3) The recent determination at Yale that several known mandibles from the latest Miocene and/or early Pliocene of the Siwaliks can plausibly be referred to *Ramapithecus*. This contribution is an attempt to relate the first two of these discoveries to previously published discussions of *Ramapithecus* (Leakey,[3] Simons[1,4]) and to present new evidence showing that mandibles of the earliest hominid, *Ramapithecus*, are known from the latest Miocene and/or Pliocene of the Siwalik Hills, India.

It seems advisable initially to point out that a revision of dryopithecine taxonomy will soon be forthcoming (Simons and Pilbeam,[5] in press). Background and conclusions on dryopithecine taxonomy are presented in fuller detail in that study.

Abbreviations.—A.M.N.H., American Museum of Natural History, New York; B.M.N.H., British Museum (Natural History); C.M.N., Coryndon Museum of Natural History, Nairobi; G.S.I., Geological Survey of India, Calcutta; M.C.Z., Museum of Comparative Zoology, Harvard; N.M.N.H.P.,

*1964 (*Anthropology*, Vol. 54)

National Museum of Natural History, Paris; and Y.P.M., Yale Peabody Museum, New Haven.

Material.—The type species of the genus *Ramapithecus, R. brevirostris*, is founded upon a right maxilla (Y.P.M. 13799) from the Siwalik Hills of North India containing the root of I^2, alveolus of I^1, canine alveolus, and P^3–M^2. G. E. Lewis (written communication, 1964) states that it is probable that the specimen is not from the Tatrot as was originally indicated, but from the cuesta scarp at Haritalyangar [Nagri (?), Simons 1961: 1; Lewis 1937: 142]. Recent intensive collecting in the Tatrot (?) north of Haritalyangar by K. N. Prasad (personal communication) failed to produce any fossil Primates, although he recovered without difficulty a series of Primates at the cuesta scarp. Consequently, the occurrence of Primates in the Tatrot of the Siwaliks has not been proved. G. E. Lewis has kindly supplied the following statement regarding the collection of Y.P.M. 13799:

> Number 13799 was brought to me by a native, who took me to a spot some distance northward from Haritalyangar and insisted he found it there. To be sure it may have occurred there, but I eventually decided that he wanted to hide its true locality. After my 1937 publication, and after Krynine[6] had had such good success in petrographic studies of large rock samples from many Siwalik localities, we examined the matrix on Y.P.M. 13799 and found it to be identical with that on the collections from Haritalyangar cuesta scarp—which as Pilgrim says[2] "represents a decidedly older type than that of Dhok Pathan." I had originally intended to publish my later views, but other matters and the war intervened.

Recently Simons referred a second right maxilla definitely from Haritalyangar (G.S.I. D-185) to *Ramapithecus*.[1] This identification demonstrates the occurrence of this primate at Haritalyangar and reinforces the later view of Lewis that this site could be that of the type. An isolated upper third molar also from this site, recently recovered in India, is now under study by K. N. Prasad. It is of the proper, small size to belong to this same species. Thus, upper dental remains of three individuals have been recovered to date in India, all apparently from the Nagri zone cuesta at Haritalyangar. A fourth portion of an upper dentition representing this species is that of *Ramapithecus* [=*Kenyapithecus*] from Fort Ternan, Kenya.

Since lower jaws with dentitions are quite commonly recovered in much greater numbers than are maxillae and upper teeth in dissociated fossil concentrations of continental deposition, there is a very high probability that if as many as four separate parts of upper dentitions of this taxon have been found, mandibular materials of this species exist unrecognized among known dryopithecine specimens. Approximately four dozen binomials have been coined to date for fossils which may represent members of the Dryopithecinae. Not one of the types of any of these species include *definitely* associated upper and lower dental materials. This suggests that some of the upper and lower dentitions from these deposits with different species names may represent the same species.

The tentatively referred mandible of *Ramapithecus* cf. *R. brevirostris* (Gregory, Hellman, and Lewis[8]) represented by a cast Y.P.M. 13870,[7] does not, in my opinion,[4] belong to the genus *Ramapithecus*, a conclusion which Lewis now believes to be justified, inasmuch as the mandible was referred (in Gregory, Hellman and Lewis, 1938: 21) to *Ramapithecus brevirostris* only because of possible occlusal relationships with the holotype maxilla, whereas it was recognized that "the teeth are somewhat too narrow and the P_3 has its long axis too anteroposteriorly oriented to fulfill completely the requirements of a lower dentition of the genotype." Other reasons for doubting this reference are: (1) The specimen (G.S.I. D-618) is from a different horizon (Chinji) and locality (Salt Range) than are the maxillary materials of *Ramapithecus*. (2) Unlike most dryopithecines, this specimen has a distinct simian shelf. (3) It shows marked lower premolar heteromorphy which is not known to date in undoubted Hominidae. Should *Ramapithecus* have possessed a sectorial P_3, like that seen in G.S.I. D-618, such a lower tooth would have produced a deep wear facet on the anterior face of P_3 in Y.P.M. 13799, but no such facet exists in this specimen. In addition, the small upper canine of *Ramapithecus* figured by Leakey (not separated from P_3 by a diastema in any of the three maxillae) will not allow for functional occlusion of a sectorial P_3 such as that of G.S.I. D-618 (Y.P.M. 13870, cast). G.S.I. D-618 together with a second lower jaw (left side with damaged $P_4 - M_3$) from the upper Chinji zone near Domeli, India (B.M.N.H. M-15243) both show small size and mandibular gracility differing from all other Siwalik hominoid mandibles. In these two mandibles there is fairly marked development of the simian shelf—otherwise both fall within the metric and morphologic range of variability of *Proconsul africanus*. When B.M.N.H. M-15243 and G.S.I. D-618, both of which have been separated in the mid-line of the symphysis, are set together along this line, they show a typical pongid U-shaped dental arcade, which could not occlude with that inferred for the *Ramapithecus* palate by Simons.[4] These two specimens appear to represent in decreasing order of probability, (*a*) a new species, (*b*) a pigmy race of one of the described Eurasian pongids, or (*c*) an Indian variety of *Proconsul africanus*.

Pilgrim's discussion[2] of *Dryopithecus punjabicus* suggests a method of determining maxillary and mandibular associations in *Ramapithecus*. The material he assigned to his new species *D. punjabicus* included the type, consisting of portions of the right and left horizontal rami of the same mandible (G.S.I. D-118, and D-119), the right containing M_3 and the left M_2, and a referred maxilla (G.S.I. D-185). The subsequent taxonomic allocation of these two finds is interesting. Lewis[9] assigned the mandibular fragments to the genus *Bramapithecus*, while (as is stated above) Simons[1] referred the maxilla to *Ramapithecus*. If one, however, accepts Pilgrim's reason for placing these upper and lower dental materials in the same species, a view which I will attempt to confirm below, then the obvious implication of taxonomic work to date is that *Bramapithecus* mandibles are the lower jaws of *Ramapithecus*. Unless species distinctions can be supported, the prior binomial for this earliest known hominid must be *Ramapithecus punjabicus* (Pilgrim) 1910 and the following "species" become junior synonyms of this taxon: *Ramapithecus brevirostris, Bramapithecus thorpei, Bramapithecus* (?) *sivalensis,* and *Kenyapithecus wickeri.*

Pilgrim's Contribution.—The type mandibular fragments of *Ramapithecus punjabicus* (Pilgrim) came from a high horizon in the Chinji Zone near the village of Chinji—the referred right maxilla, G.S.I. D-185, from the Harital-yangar cuesta scarp in the Nagri zone (Pilgrim, 1915: 9, 16). In 1915 Pilgrim[2] dealt with the question of whether the two specimens could have been sufficiently separated temporally to lessen the probability of their belonging to the same species. He concluded that this was not the case. Problems regarding the rate of sedimentation, stratigraphic disconformities, and lithology in the Siwaliks are extensively discussed by Colbert.[10] From this discussion, and others, it seems clear that the rate of sedimentation while the Upper Chinji-Nagri Zones were accumulating was rapid and that there are no abrupt faunal or lithologic changes between these two zones. There is some reason to think that typical *Hipparion* may not occur in the Chinji Zone, as was reported by some earlier workers, while other authors, such as Borisiak,[11] present evidence that the Chinji has the oldest *Hipparion* fauna in Asia. These data would seem to favor a pre-Pliocene age for the Chinji. The primate materials here referred to *Ramapithecus punjabicus* come from both the Upper Chinji and the Nagri, and I would agree with Pilgrim that but one species, *R. punjabicus*, occurs in the two zones. Associated faunas of both Indian and African specimens suggest that known *Ramapithecus* lived at about the time of the Miocene-Pliocene temporal boundary. In the absence of a series of geochemically dated faunas or detailed studies of faunal correlation between mammals of the Fort Ternan and Siwalik localities, no more precise determination of the temporal position of *Ramapithecus* is possible at this time. It seems unlikely, however, that the temporal range of materials here referred to *Ramapithecus punjabicus* will ever prove to be sufficiently great to justify two or more time-successive species populations. At least I am not aware of any scientific evidence, now available, which would warrant such a conclusion.

It is well known that the reference of unassociated upper and lower dentitions to the same species has its weaknesses. However, I believe that Pilgrim's decision to do so in this case can be justified on morphological grounds. Pilgrim[2] summarized his conclusions on this point as follows:

> The dimensions of these teeth, the moderately low cusps, the complexity of the folding of the enamel, and, above all, the peculiar serrated outer edge of the molars incline one so strongly to the opinion that we have before us a maxilla and mandible which belong to the same species, that, unless fairly conclusive evidence were forthcoming of a close affinity to another genus, or of the existence of features in the maxilla, which told against an affinity with *Dryopithecus* [now, in this case, *Ramapithecus*] , I should feel fairly certain that the similarity mentioned between the mandible and the maxilla indicated specific identity.

The Yale Mandibles.—Three specimens referable to *Bramapithecus* are in the Yale collections—all are mandibular fragments with molars present (Y.P.M. Nos. 13806, 13814, and 13833). They are closely comparable to the type of *Ramapithecus punjabicus* (G.S.I. D-118-119) although, as in all other hominoids, there is some variation in the crown pattern of the molars. The four specimens have in common a thick, robust mandible in the M_{2-3} region which, however, is quite shallow vertically. In this feature they differ significantly from Eurasian and African dryopithecines, in which the mandible under M_3 is considerably deeper relative to its thickness (Fig. 1). The molars tend to be quadrate and crowded rather than anteroposteriorly elongate and spaced out as in *Dryopithecus* and *Proconsul*. The one lower molar from Fort Ternan, figured by Leakey,[3] and which he regards as belonging to the same individual as his East African *Ramapithecus* maxillae also has this shape. In Y.P.M. 13806 and 13814, M_2 and M_3 are essentially the same length. In the *Dryopithecus* group M_3 is typically longer than M_2. As in *Ramapithecus* upper molars, the individual cusps do not stand out in relief as in African and Indian pongids. Distinct, large, wear facets are present on the anterior and posterior faces of M_2 in G.S.I. D-118, Y.P.M. 13806 and 13814, and on the anterior face of M_3 in G.S.I. D-119 and Y.P.M. 13806, 13814, and 13833. Particularly in Y.P.M. 13814, the type of *"Bramapithecus thorpei,"* wear against adjacent teeth has cut deep, arcuate "contact facets" into the anterior margins of M_2 and M_3. This, together with the quadrate form of the teeth, strongly suggests that the animal must have had a short face, and a crowded tooth row which lacked diastemata. Mr. D. R. Pilbeam has recently pointed out to me that the horizontal ramus begins to turn toward the symphysis at the level of M_1 while in dryopithecines, such as *Sugrivapithecus*, the inward curvature toward the symphysis commonly does not begin until about the level of P_3 (Fig. 2). This distinction is a direct reflection of the differences between tooth arrangement in a short-faced form and that seen in long-snouted hominoids. It is interesting to note that these same features, deep anterior contact facets, subequal size of quadrate M_2 and M_3, shallow but robust mandible and lingual curvature toward the symphysis at the level of M_1, are present in the type of *"Telanthropus capensis"* and are about equally developed in several of Dart's Makapan mandibles of *Australopithecus*. Perhaps even more significant is the presence of these same features, together with other similarities, in the Lantien jaw discovered on

ELWYN L. SIMONS

GENERA AND SUBGENERA

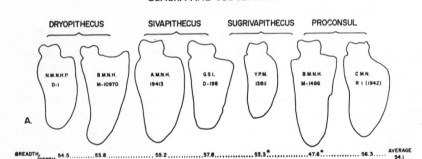

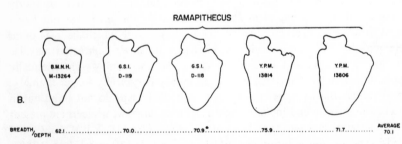

Fig. 1. Diagrammatic vertical sections of hominoid mandibles across mid-line of M_3 showing distinctly lower breadth-depth ratios in the *Dryopithecus* group (*A*) than in *Ramapithecus* (*B*). Diagrams are anterior views of left rami and reversed views of right rami.

*Depth estimated either by adding height of M^2, when M^3 missing, or by projecting the lower outline of mandible.

July 19, 1963 in Northwest China.[12] This mandible may be *Australopithecus* (s.l.), or even a member of much more recent *Homo*; whichever it is, resemblances between *"Bramapithecus"* and such hominid jaws are striking. These strong similarities reinforce the probability that *"Bramapithecus"* mandibles belong to a taxon on or near the main line of human descent. This conclusion can be reached independently without reference of these mandibles to the same species as the previously discussed maxillae of *Ramapithecus*. Nevertheless, the two sets of data are interrelated and reinforce the association of upper and lower jaws. It seems most unlikely that hominid mandibles differentiated in one species while hominid maxillae first reached the hominid grade in a different taxon. Lewis clearly recognized the hominid ties of *"Bramapithecus"* discussed above, but until more became known about *Ramapithecus* maxillae, the phyletic and taxonomic implication of structure in *"Bramapithecus"* remained uncertain. Lewis[13] commented

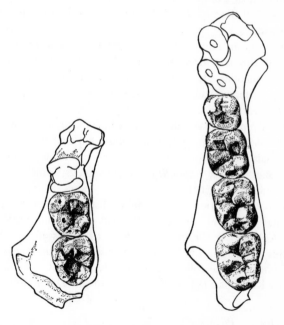

Fig. 2. Comparison of Mio-Pliocene hominid mandible (*A*) *Ramapithecus*, Y.P.M. 13814, with contemporary dryopithecine (*B*) *Sugrivapithecus*, Y.P.M. 13811. Unlike living or fossil apes, in the hominid the mandible begins to turn inward toward the symphysis at the level of M_1 and the molars are rounded with low relief. In the *Sugrivapithecus* mandible, M_3 is restored from those of other dryopithecines. Scale ×1.

perceptively in his initial discussion of *"Bramapithecus:"* ". . . the sculpture of the crowns is highly suggestive of many human molars. The deep folds, persistent in spite of severe wear, are notable features. The author . . . believes that the genus has affinities with *Dryopithecus* and was probably derived from a common stock. It may very well lie near to the stem which led to the Hominidae proper."

In his revision of 1937, Lewis[9] placed the four partial lower dentitions, discussed above, in the genus *"Bramapithecus"* but retained three different species, *"B. thorpei," "B." punjabicus* and *"(?) B. sivalensis."* Lewis' recognition of the taxonomic affinity of these materials was another important step but, in view of known variability in living Hominoidea, these materials need not indicate more than one species. For this species *"B." punjabicus* (Pilgrim) 1910 has priority. An additional specimen (here assigned to this species), B.M.N.H. M-13264, from the Attock district, Punjab is either from the uppermost Chinji or from the Nagri. Three of the finds, Y.P.M. 13833, 13834, and the type G.S.I. D-118-119, come from the Upper Chinji and one of them, *"(?) B." sivalensis,* Y.P.M. 13806, from the Nagri age cuesta scarp at Haritalyangar. Thus, at Haritalyangar as well as at Ft. Ternan, Kenya, lower teeth of this sort have been found at a locality which has yielded *Ramapithecus* maxillae. It seems most unlikely that two species were independently differentiating toward Hominidae at this time (end of the Miocene and/or early Pliocene), one of which is known only from mandibles, the other only from maxillae, but both of which occur at the same sites. I can find no morphological, temporal, or distributional evidence for thinking that all the materials belonging to the "species" listed below should not be referred to one species, *Ramapithecus punjabicus,* which was originally diagnosed by Pilgrim[14] in 1910.

In regard to the question of geographic distribution of this species, it is interesting that a right M^2 from the Pontian of Melchingen, Württemberg, assigned by Koken[15] to *Dryopithecus suevicus* shows all the characteristic molar features outlined in the diagnosis below for *Ramapithecus punjabicus.* A left M^2 from the same collection, markedly different, but also included in *D. suevicus* by Koken is a *Dryopithecus*—presumably *D. fontain.*

Systematics

Order   *PRIMATES*
Suborder Anthropoidea
Superfamily Hominoidea
Family   HOMINIDAE
Genus   **Ramapithecus**   Lewis, 1934
            Dryopithecus   Lartet, Pilgrim *(partim)* 1915:16

Bramapithecus   Lewis 1934:173
Dryopithecus   Lartet, Lewis (*partim*) 1934:171
Kenyapithecus   Leakey, 1962:690

Type Species.—Ramapithecus brevirostris   Lewis 1934[13] (considered here to be a subjective synonym of *Dryopithecus punjabicus* Pilgrim, 1910).[14]

*Generic Diagnosis.—*Differs from *Australopithecus* and members of the *Dryopithecus* group in the following general features: slightly smaller over-all size (except for *Proconsul africanus*), shallower mandible, less complex patterns of tooth crenulation, shorter face, little or no evidence of cingular or Carabelli's cusps. Incisors and canines reduced, in relation to cheek-tooth size when compared to *Dryopithecus*, but not as markedly as in *Australopithecus*; incisor procumbency intermediate.

Differs from *Dryopithecus* and other apes in showing more widely spaced and much lower crowned molar cusps, so that central or occlusal fovea of molars covers more of the crown surface of the tooth, and the sides of the upper molars (particularly) are more vertical. Also differs from *Dryopithecus* in showing a larger and lower canine fossa, an arched palate, arcuate tooth row, and much shorter rostrum.

*Specific Diagnosis.—*Same as for the genus, which is monotypic.

Referred Species.—Ramapithecus brevirostris   Lewis (1934:162), *Bramapithecus thorpei*   Lewis (1934:173), *Bramapithecus*(?) *sivalensis*   Lewis (1934:171), *Kenyapithecus wickeri*   Leakey (1962:690).

*Summary.—*Earlier discussions of the mandible of *Ramapithecus*, the oldest probable forerunner of man, have been based on a jaw which actually belongs to a species of *Dryopithecus*. Materials previously assigned to species of the genus *"Bramapithecus"* are here referred to the genus and species *Ramapithecus punjabicus*. This species probably occurred widely throughout Eurasia and Africa about 14 or 15 million years ago. Considered together, known material of *R. punjabicus* indicates a *Pan*-sized primate with short face, arcuate palate, and an *Australopithecus*-like mandible (Fig. 3). Dental and facial characters are so close to *Australopithecus africanus* as to make difficult the drawing of generic distinctions between the two species on the basis of present material. Provisionally the two genera, *Ramapithecus* and *Australopithecus*, are retained as distinct because of their considerable time separation. *Ramapithecus punjabicus* is almost certainly man's forerunner of 15 million years ago. This determination increases tenfold the approximate time period during which human origins can now be traced with some confidence.

The author wishes to acknowledge valuable discussions of the subject with W. E. LeGros Clark and D. R. Pilbeam. Figures were prepared at Yale by Miss Polly Porter and Miss Anna Held.

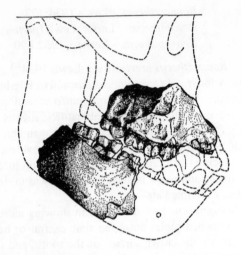

Fig. 3. Hypothetical appearance of the face of *Ramapithecus*. Maxilla
Y.P.M. 13799; mandible, Y.P.M. 13814 (reversed). Dotted outline of canine
from type of *"Kenyapithecus wickeri."* Dashed lines conjectural. Scale
X0.72.

The research reported here was supported in part by a grant in geology
from the National Science Foundation, No. GP-433, and by grants from the
Wenner-Gren Foundation of New York.

References

1. Simons, E. L. *Science,* **141**, 879 (1963).
2. Pilgrim, G. E., *Records Geol. Surv. Ind.,* **45**, 1 (1915).
3. Leakey, L. S. B., *Ann. and Mag. Nat. Hist.,* **13**, 689 (1962).
4. Simons, E. L., *Postilla,* **57**, 1 (1961).
5. Simons, E. L., and D. R. Pilbeam, *Folia Primatologica* in press.
6. Krynine, P. D., *Amer. J. Sci.,* **34**, 422 (1937).
7. The original of this mandible G.S.I. D-618 cannot now be located in the collections
   at Calcutta, therefore further comment as to the taxon which it represents will have
   to be based on Y.P.M. 13870 (cast). Simons[4] inadvertently referred to this specimen
   as Y.P.M. 13807, now M.C.Z. 8386, the type of *Ramapithecus hariensis* Lewis
   (1934), which was ultimately assigned to *Sivapithecus sivalensis* Lewis[8] and which is
   not a *Ramapithecus*.
8. Gregory, W. K., M. Hellman, and G. E. Lewis, *Carnegie Inst. Wash. Publ.* No. 495, 1
   (1938).

9. Lewis, G. E., *Amer. J. Sci.*, **34**, 139 (1937).
10. Colbert, E. H., *Trans. Amer. Philos. Soc.*, **26**, 1 (1935).
11. Borisiak, A. A., (translation) *Internat. Geol. Rev.*, **4**, 845 (1962).
12. Anon., *Illust. Lond. News*, **243** (6483), 742 (1963).
13. Lewis, G. E., *Amer. J. Sci.*, **27**, 161 (1934).
14. Pilgrim, G. E., *Records Geol. Surv. Ind.*, **40**, 63 (1910).
15. Koken, E., *Fürher durch die samlungen* (Tübingen, Stuttgart: Geol.-Min. Inst., 1905), p. 1.

Prehistory in Shanidar Valley, Northern Iraq

Ralph S. Solecki*

The archeological investigations of two sites in Shanidar Valley, northern Iraq (Figs. 1 and 2), have been made more significant through the use of interdisciplinary studies. The combined information provides concrete data regarding man and his environment in this region from the Middle Paleolithic age (perhaps 100,000 years ago) to the present.

The significance of the Shanidar Valley investigations is that here, in this one locality, there is an almost continuous sequence of human history dating from the time of the Neanderthals. The information derived from these investigations contributes to biological, paleontological, climatological, and geological studies, as well as archeological and anthropological ones—the major concerns of the project. The Shanidar data do much to elucidate man's history in a most interesting period of his existence—the time of the Neanderthals and the replacement of this long-dominant people by *Homo sapiens*.

The project is of further special interest because Shanidar lies within the area where domesticated plants and animals—the basis for the great Neolithic economic, social, and cultural revolution—appear to have been first developed. The Shanidar excavations provide data reflecting the effect on the people in this remote valley of the introduction of the new mode of living, which was dependent on the products of the fields and on tamed animals rather than exclusively on the hunt. The great alternations of climate and temperature which mark the Pleistocene, a recent geological period of the ice ages dating back more than a million years, are reflected in the cultural history.

*Science, 1963

397

The sites, Shanidar cave and the nearby village site of Zawi Chemi
Shanidar, have given us a long preface to Mesopotamian history. Thus far, the
cultural sequence for Shanidar Valley is outlined on a relatively firm basis by
carbon-14 dates from about 50,000 years ago, and by "guess dates" for
periods before that. Paleoclimatological inferences have been made on the
basis of pollen remains and of trace elements in soil studies. Osteological

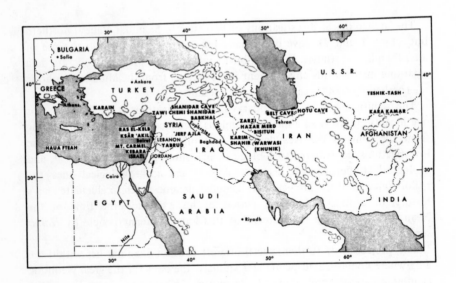

Fig. 1. Selected archeological sites in northern Africa, the Near East,
and the Middle East: Haua Fteah (Libya); Mount Carmel and Kebara
(Israel), Ksâr 'Akil and Ras el-Kelb (Lebanon); Yabrud and Jerf Ajla
(Syria); Shanidar Cave, Zawi Chemi Shanidar, Babkhal, Zarzi, Hazar
Merd, and Karim Shahir (Iraq); Belt Cave, Hotu Cave, Bisitun, and
Warwasi (Iran); Kara Kamar (Afghanistan); and Teshik-Tash (Uzbekis-
tan).

materials from seven Neanderthals and 28 representatives of post-Pleistocene *Homo sapiens* have been found. There is also a wealth of faunal data. The presence of domesticated animals in Shanidar Valley at the relatively early date of 8900 B.C. seems likely.[1]

The Sites

Shanidar cave (Fig. 3) is situated at longitude 44°13'E, latitude 36°50'N, about 400 kilometers due north of Baghdad, within the outer folds of the Zagros Mountains. The cave, of limestone-solution origin, is about 2.5 kilometers from the Greater Zab River, a major tributary of the Tigris River. The precipitous mountains there reach an elevation greater than 1900 meters. The region is relatively well wooded. There is still some wild game to be seen in the area.

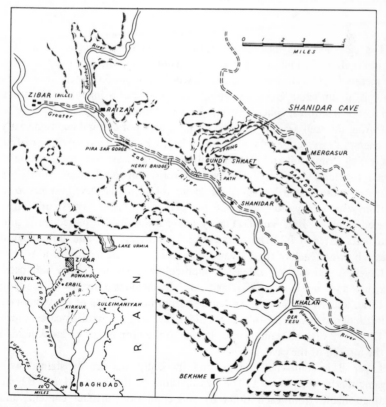

Fig. 2. Map showing the location of Shanidar Valley in northern Iraq.

Fig. 3. The limestone cave of Shanidar, seen from the south. The swallow holes at the right enter into the cave. The long grass slope in front receives nourishment from the spilled human occupational debris.

The cave lies at a measured elevation of 765 meters, facing south. The mouth is about 25 meters wide and 8 meters high, and the cave extends about 40 meters to the rear, with a maximum width of about 53 meters. Its earthen floor is about 1200 square meters in area. The cave is inhabited by several families of Kurdish shepherds during the winter months.

During the four seasons of excavation,[2] a series of cultural deposits nearly 14 meters deep were explored down to bedrock. The deposits consist of an easily dug loamy soil and material indicative of at least five major rockfalls. These rockfalls were very effective man-traps—apparently they caused the death of most of the Neanderthals so far found in the cave. From top to bottom the occupation sequence includes four major layers, arbitrarily labeled layers A, B, C, and D (Fig. 4). Layer B was divided subsequently into two parts, B1 and B2. There are cultural, stratigraphical, and chronological breaks between each of these layers, so far as can now be determined.

Layer A consists of extensive, multicolored, dry and dusty ash beds, hearths, and black organic-stained soil. It includes remains of modern, historic, and Neolithic age. As deduced from observations of contemporary Kurdish-herdsmen occupation at Shanidar cave and neighboring caves, much of the heavy organic staining must be due to the dropings of livestock herded in the interior of the cave.

Layer B is somewhat thinner and markedly less heavily stained with organic matter than layer A. The two divisions of this layer, B1 and B2, are distinguishable from each other by soil coloration, artifact content, and carbon-14 dates. The upper part, B1, is Proto-Neolithic[3] and is dated at about

8650 B.C.[4] The lower part, B2, is Mesolithic (or very late Upper Paleolithic) and is dated at about 10,000 B.C.[5]

Shanidar B1 is contemporary with the basal layer of the Zawi Chemi Shanidar village site, which has a carbon-14 date of about 8900 B.C.[6] The artifact contents of cave and village layers are quite similar. In addition to bone artifacts and chipped stone implements, larger tools of ground stone, such as querns, mortars, and hand rubbers, were found. These indicate that some sort of vegetal foods, possibly acorns or even cereal grains, were prepared as part of the diet. The find, in the cave, of fragments of matting or basketry, the oldest yet known, suggests that collecting baskets may have been used. Twenty-eight skeletons were associated with the B1 layer in Shanidar cave; of these, 26 were found in a cemetery group. Associated with the cemetery were platforms of stones[7] and an arc-like alignment of flat stones (Fig. 5).

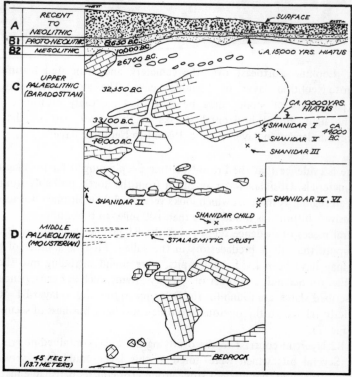

Fig. 4. Schematic cross section of the Shanidar cave excavation, showing the major cultural layers, the pertinent radiocarbon dates, and the relative positions of the Shanidar Neanderthals.

Fig. 5. Looking northeast over the cemetery and associated features in the Proto-Neolithic layer of Shanidar cave. The stone wall and the rough pavements of stones may be part of a mortuary custom of this age. The light, broad horizontal streaks in the upper part of the section are ash lenses in layer A, the Recent-to-Neolithic layer.

There is evidence that the Proto-Neolithic people ranged far for manufacturing materials. Obsidian was brought in from the north, probably from the Lake Van region. A material which looks very much like bitumen was used as an adhesive;[8] bitumen is found more than 100 miles to the south.

Several pieces of evidence suggest that the B1 peoples had a more assured food supply than their predecessors in the valley. First, a number of pits, which may have been food storage pits, were found intruding into the B2 layer (Fig. 6). Second, a number of "luxury" items, such as beads, pendants, and inscribed slates, are found for the first time in the cave in layer B1—items not strictly related to the onerous and time-consuming business of securing a living (Fig. 7).

The B2 layer, in contrast to the overlying B1 layer, contained no grinding stones. Several pits which were noted in this layer could have served as storage pits for food that was not stone-ground (of course, perishable material such as wood could have been used for preparing food). The artifact assemblage is different from that found in layer B1. It includes a large number of microliths of the "geometric" type, carefully made and reflecting

Fig. 6. A stone-filled pit with four associated boulder querns and quern fragments in the Proto-Neolithic layer of Shanidar cave. These indicate food grinding and probably food storage.

an expert and sophisticated flint-chipping industry (Fig. 8). It is inferred from the technological and cultural level of these people that they were more oriented to the hunt than their followers a thousand years later. We may also assume that they had a more complex technology and economy than their predecessors at Shanidar.

Layer C is easily distinguishable from layer B on the basis of stratigraphy and artifact remains (Fig. 9). The top part of this layer has been dated by the radiocarbon method at about 26,700 B.C.;[9] the bottom part, at about 33,100 B.C.[10] Thus far in the excavations we have been unable to find remains linking layers B and C. There is an abrupt change of industries, from a blade-tool type reminiscent of the Upper Paleolithic "Aurignacian" (here called "Baradostian")[11] in layer C to the more highly evolved microlithic industry of basal layer B. The stone equipment of layer C indicates a high degree of skill in the woodworking crafts (only a few worked bones were found). Expecially numerous are the burins, which are characterized by several types of working-bits. No human skeletal remains have been found in this layer, but it is assumed that these people were a variety of ture *Homo sapiens*.

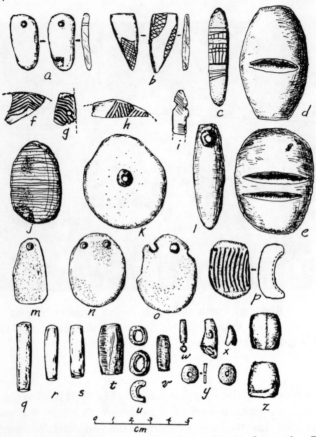

Fig. 7. Pendants, beads, and other objects from the Proto-Neolithic layer at Shanidar cave (*a–d*) and Zawi Chemi Shanidar village (*e–z*). *a*, Shell pendant; *b*, incised slate tablet; *c*, incised slate pebble; *d*, single-grooved plano-convex steatite stone object; *e*, double-grooved steatite stone object; *f–h*, incised fragments of bone tools; *i*, carved fragment of bone tool; *j*, flat pebble bearing parallel incised scratches; *k*, flat single perforated pebble pendant; *l*, elongate single perforated pebble pendant; *m*, flat single perforated green stone pendant; *n*, *o*, double perforated limestone (marble?) pendants; *p*, small steatite object with single U-shaped groove in which there are nine deeply incised cuts; *q–s*, cut tubular bone beads; *t*, barrel-shaped steatite stone bead; *u*, three squat steatite stone beads; *v*, tubular limestone (marble?) bead; *w*, small tubular cut bone bead; *x*, perforated animal teeth (probably *Cervus elaphus*); *y*, two flat disk beads of indeterminate material; *z*, two broad bone beads.

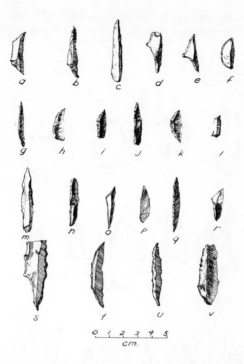

Fig. 8. Various forms of finely executed points and side blades of flint from the upper and lower subdivisions of Layer B (Proto-Neolithic and Mesolithic horizons) at Shanidar cave. They are pressure retouched. With the exception of *m*, a "Gravettian" type point, and *s*, a single-shoulder based point, all the specimens shown are blunted-back retouched on one side. Some of them were probably side blades for composite implements. From the points, at least, it is inferred that the bow and arrow were known—a great technological advance.

Layer D (Fig. 10) is the thickest layer in the cave (about 8.5 m). There is evidence of heavy occupational concentration toward the middle of the layer. The Mousterian artifacts include rather typical points, scrapers, and knives made on unifacial flakes (Fig. 11). Seven Neanderthal skeletons [six adults (numbered from I to VI) and one child (unnumbered)] were found in the upper third of the layer.[12] Since only about one-tenth of the cave has been excavated thus far, more human remains are likely to be found in future seasons. Shanidar Neanderthals I and V were found near the top of layer D, in the level dated approximately 44,000 B.C.[13] T. Dale Stewart, of the U.S.

National Museum, is studying the adult skeletons.[14][15] The late Muzaffer
Senyürek, of the University of Ankara, studied the skeleton of the Shanidar
child.[16]

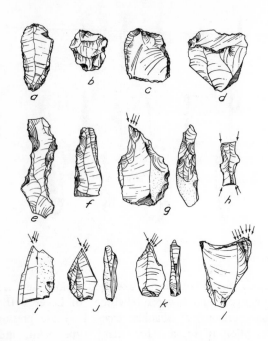

Fig. 9. Flint artifacts from layer C (Upper Paleolithic, Baradostian
horizon) at Shanidar cave. They were made by percussion striking and
pressure retouching, principally on blades. These artifacts indicate a
heavy preoccupation with wood-working (very few bone implements
were found). A fireside activity requiring special talents is clearly
shown by the diversification of the tool kit, indicating gouging, incis-
ing, cutting, shaving, and scraping arts, specialized forms being found within
each group. a, End scraper; b, "Circular" scraper; c, side and end scraper
combination; d, "nosed" steep scraper on a blade core; e, notched or
"strangled" blade; f, chisel-ended implement; g, combination nosed burin (or
graver) and end scraper; h, multiple-ended burin; i, angle-struck burin; j,
stepped-bit "bec de flute" type burin; k, nosed-bit "bec de flute" type burin;
l, heavy bitted burin with polyhedric facets.

Fig. 10. The Shanidar cave excavation, looking west toward the "find" spot of Shanidar II in the keyway pit. The deepest part of the excavation is at right.

Investigation

Several approaches are currently being studied for investigating the Shanidar materials, and each of these opens new phases of research. Three broad avenues of investigation are discussed here. The first is the establishment of a chronological framework to serve as support for the study (Fig. 12). Comparative studies of the Shanidar sites and of other sites of the same age in the same broad geographical zone also are made. The second approach is the study of populations that lived in the Valley, from perhaps 100,000 years ago, to find what can be learned of them and their movements from their ancient leavings. The third is investigation to find where the Shanidar Valley fits in the great food-production revolution that supposedly took place in southwestern Asia.

Chronological Framework

Archeology without the backdrop of a time scale has little meaning. The cultural-temporal positioning of the occupations on the basis of the artifact typology was accomplished first. The chronology was fixed by 16 carbon-14 dates from all four layers at Shanidar cave and by one from Zawi Chemi Shanidar. The samples were dated by four different laboratories in studies of which several were duplicate checks.[17] The dates range from about A.D. 1750 for layer A to about 48,000 B.C. for layer D. Several obsidian samples from layers B and C were also dated.[18]

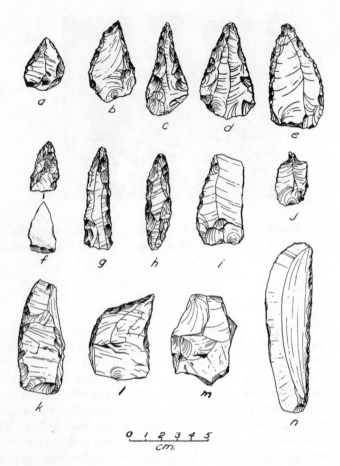

Fig. 11. Examples of artifacts from layer D (Middle Paleolithic Mousterian horizon) at Shanidar cave. They are percussion struck, and made on unifacial flakes of flint. These represent the simplest implements at Shanidar cave, presumably used for tipping spears, as skinning knives, and as simple wood-working tools. No Levallois prepared cores were found, although many of the artifacts exhibit "facetted butt" preparation on their basal ends. *a–e*, Typical Mousterian points; *f*, "Emireh"-type point with basal inverse retouch; *g*, elongated Mousterian point; *h*, double-ended point; *i*, convex-edged sidescraper; *j*, borer; *k*, convex-edged sidescraper on a thick flake; *l*, assymetrically shaped point or *"déjeté"* type sidescraper; *m*, flake core; *n*, unusually long sidescraper and knife combination.

On the framework of this chronological scale, the climatological data obtained from studies of noncultural materials in the deposits were arranged. We enlisted the aid of a palynologist, Arlette Leroi-Gourhan of Paris, whose findings (nine samples) were independently corroborated, with one exception, by trace-element analyses of the soils (five samples), made by Bruno E. Sabels of the University of Nevada.[19] These analyses indicated marked fluctuations of climate in the late Pleistocene (Fig. 13), bearing out the geological observations made elsewhere in Kurdistan by Herbert E. Wright, Jr., of the University of Minnesota.[20][21]

Data for the 8.6-meter level (the lowest for which there is information), well into the Mousterian layer, indicate a climate much warmer than that in the area today and growth of the date palms (*Phoenix dactylifera*) not far away.[22] Data for the 7.5-meter level show a reversal to an exceedingly cool climate and growth of fir trees (*Abies*) in the area. Pollens near the top of layer D, at depths of 4.25 and 4.35 meters, suggest a return to warm climate about 44,000 B.C. Findings for layer C suggest a change from a dry, steppe environment near the start of the Upper Paleolithic Baradostian occupation, at about 34,000 B.C., to a wet and cold climate near its end, at about 25,000 B.C. Data are lacking for the next 15,000 years, to the base of layer B. However, findings for the two parts (B1, B2) of layer B indicate a relatively cool climate changing to a warmer one similar to the present climate. A culture horizon comparable to B1 at Zawi Chemi Shanidar was also evidence of warmer conditions.

We are painfully aware that the minimum four conditions postulated by Edward S. Deevey, Jr.,[23] as requisite for the application of pollen analysis to the problems of prehistory are only half satisfied at Shanidar. Lacking are a "standard pollen sequence" and a "knowledge of the regional plant ecology." But a start has been made toward a climatological sequence for Shanidar Valley.

The question at this point in the studies is this: If the suggestions of climate changes are correct, where do the alternations at Shanidar fit into the Pleistocene climate sequence? The dated part of the cave chronology, to about 48,000 B.C., can be checked against generalized curves. Beyond that, there is some doubt. An attempt to date the Shanidar cave deposits below the oldest carbon-14 determinations can be made by rough extrapolation on the basis of guessing the rate of accumulation of cultural deposit in feet per 1000 years.[24-27] Assuming a constant rate of cultural deposition of about 1.25 feet per 1000 years, we guess that the Shanidar cave deposits began accumulating close to 100,000 years ago. The chronological fit of the projected curve with Flint and Brandtner's interpretations of climate change since the Last Interglacial[28] is better than the fit with Zeuner's or Emiliani's

A TENTATIVE CHRONOLOGICAL CORRELATION OF SELECTED SITES IN THE NEAR AND MIDDLE EAST AND NORTH AFRICA*

TIME SCALE B.P.	LIBYA — HAUA FTEAH	PALESTINE — MOUNT CARMEL AND KEBARA	LEBANON — KSÂR 'AKIL AND RAS EL-KELB	SYRIA — YABRUD AND JERF AJLA	IRAQ — SHANIDAR CAVE, ZAWI CHEMI SHANIDAR, AND OTHER SITES IN NORTHERN IRAQ	IRAN — CASPIAN CAVES, WARWASI AND BISITUN	AFGHAN — KARA KAMAR	GENERAL LEVEL OF CULTURE
10,000	LAYER XIII (10,600 B.P.)[1]	KEBARA LAYER B; EL-WAD LAYER B		YABRUD AND JERF AJLA	CAVE SHANIDAR: LAYER B-1 (10,600 B.P.)[6], LAYER B (12,000 B.P.)[6], LAYER B-2 — ZAWI CHEMI (10,800 B.P.)[6]. Open Sites: KARIM SHAHIR, M'LEFAAT, GIRD CHAI. Cave Sites: ZARZI, HAZAR MERD B, BABKHAL (U), PALEGAWRA	HOTU AND BELT (11,500 B.P.)[7]; WARWASI	TRENCH-A LEVEL 4 (10,580 B.P.)[7]	PROTO-NEOLITHIC (Simple food production, "luxury items" equipment, and microliths)
15,000	LAYER XVII (18,400 B.P.)[1]	KEBARA LAYER C	KSÂR 'AKIL COMPLEX 1	YABRUD SHELTER III				MESOLITHIC (Microlith and backed-blade industries)
20,000		EL-WAD LAYER C			Hiatus			
25,000		EL-WAD LAYER D	KSÂR 'AKIL (28,500 B.P.)[3] (6.50-7.00m)		TOP LAYER C (28,000 B.P.)[6]			UPPER PALAEOLITHIC (Blade, burin, and end-scraper industries)
30,000		KEBARA LAYER D; EL-WAD LAYER F		YABRUD SHELTER II LAYERS 2-5		WARWASI		
35,000	LAYER XXV (34,000 B.P.)[1]	KEBARA LAYER F (34,700 B.P.)[2]	KSÂR 'AKIL COMPLEX 2	YABRUD SHELTER II LAYER 6	BOTTOM LAYER C (35,000 B.P.)[6]		LOWER LOESS (>34,000 B.P.)[7]	
40,000		ET-TABÛN LAYER B (39,500 B.P.)[2]	KSÂR 'AKIL COMPLEX 3 (44,000 B.P.)[4] (16m)	JERF AJLA TRENCH A (43,000 B.P.)[7]	Hiatus			
45,000	LAYER XXXII (46,000 B.P.)[1]	ET-TABÛN COMPLEX 3 (44,000 B.P.)[2]; ET-TABÛN LAYER C			TOP LAYER D (46,000 B.P.)[6]. Cave Sites: SPILIK, HAZAR MERD C, BABKHAL (L)	WARWASI		MIDDLE PALAEOLITHIC (Flake, point, and side-scraper industries)
50,000			RAS EL-KELB BASAL LAYER (>52,000 B.P.)[5]	YABRUD SHELTER I	UPPER LAYER D (50,000 B.P.)[6]. Open Sites: TARJIL, SERANDUR, TELEGRAPH POLE 26/22	BISITUN BASAL LAYER		
55,000								
60,000					(Base of Shanidar Cave estimated 100,000 B.P.)			

interpretations[29] (Fig. 13). The deepest pollen sample (8.6 m) and the corresponding trace-element sample (8.3 m) which reflect a very warm climate could correspond with Flint and Brandtner's "Eem," or Last Interglacial. The next Shanidar curve position could be interpreted as corresponding with their Early Würm stadial. The much disputed Göttweig Interstadial[29] in their analysis corresponds with the climatological evidence from the lower part of layer C and the upper part of layer D: a colder climate about 20,000 years ago is indicated at Shanidar. The gap between layers B and C falls in what is called the Würm Maximum (etc.), in the European Alpine sequence. The Zagros Mountain glaciers advanced down the slopes during this interval, causing in all probability a lowering of temperatures and a retreat of the flora and fauna.[21] Man could not tolerate such an icebox very long (the glaciers came down to elevations of about 1500 m), and he sensibly left for the Florida of his time. According to the inferred Shanidar climatological data, the climate had improved greatly (from man's stand-point) by 10,000 B.C., and by about 8000 B.C. had changed to a warmer, postglacial climate very much like that of today.[21][30]

Unfortunately, no other pollen or trace-element climatological studies have been made for this range of prehistorical time in the Near East, and thus there are no data with which the Shanidar data can be compared.[31] Changes in climate have been established on faunal evidence; such evidence, however, even in natural (noncultural) contexts is recognized as being of secondary reliability.[29]

One of the best-known examples of climate sequence based on faunal evidence from a Near Eastern archeological site is at Mt. Carmel.[32] Primarily involved are two fauna, a cool-wet-loving deer and a warm-dry-loving gazelle. Zeuner[33] adapted the Mt. Carmel faunal-frequency chart in his correlation with the European late Pleistocene sequence. This touched off a debate which is still alive as fresh data are gathered.[20][34-36] Especially illuminating are

◄——————

Fig. 12. A tentative chronological correlation. The dates given for the various sites are round numbers based on carbon-14 determinations reported as follows: 1) C. B. M. McBurney, *Advan. Sci.* 18, 496 (1962); 2) K. P. Oakley, *ibid.* 18, 415 (1962); 3) J. Perrot, in R. J. Braidwood and G. R. Willey, "Courses Toward Urban Life," *Viking Fund Publ. No. 32* (962), p. 150; 4) J. Franklin and S. J. Ewing, personal communication (Sept. 1962); 5) D. A. E. Garrod and G. Henri-Martin, *Bull. Musée de Beyrouth* 16, 4 (1961); 6) R. S. Solecki (see text); 7) C. S. Coon, *The Seven Caves* (Knopf, New York, 1957), pp. 210, 252, 253, 315. Layers without carbon-14 dates are given relative positions in their respective sequences.

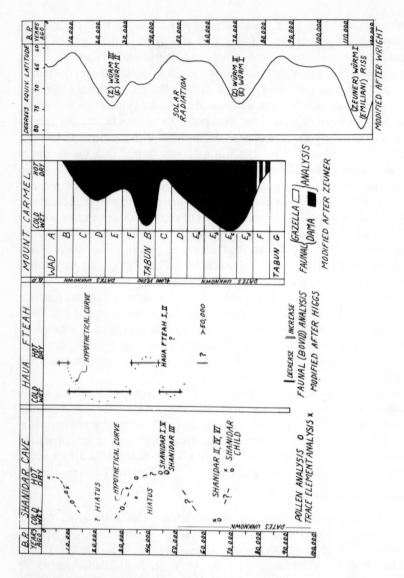

Fig. 13. Inferred climatic changes in the Near East, proposed on the basis of indicators from three paleolithic sites, in north Africa, the Levant, and the Zagros Mountains, compared with the solar radiation curve for the upper Pleistocene.

Hooijer's[37] investigations of the deer and gazelle frequencies from Ksâr 'Akil, in the Lebanon. These throw some doubt on the climate interpretations from the Mt. Carmel sequence.

Another late Pleistocene climate sequence, based on faunal evidence, primarily the large bovines, has been offered for the North African and Mediterranean area.[38] [39]

Concerning faunal curves, Hooijer's admonition[34] is pertinent: "What the vertebrate palaeontologist does rather more than anything else when studying the 'fauna' of an occupation site is sampling the history of the menu of the local population of prehistoric man." Today, you cannot find a Kurd at Shanidar who will eat snails or the flesh of boars, even though both abound. These are restatements of the observation that the fauna of an area, as identified in archeological contexts, is passed through the filter of human occupation. Cultural selection of fauna in a particular region, however, is obviously dependent upon the existing faunal inventory, which must have first passed through the screen of natural environment.

Of import to the Shanidar study is a comment by Charles A. Reed of Yale University, who has studied Shanidar faunal data from three excavation seasons. He says that the remarkable thing about the fauna of Shanidar cave is that outwardly all of the bones look to be of the same age and of recent data, having the appearance of a "single-age, post-Pleistocene fauna".[40] The bones or faunal evidence, therefore, suggest that the climate at Shanidar did not change a great deal from Middle Paleolithic times on. Yet the primary climatological data, the available pollens, show otherwise. At present there is no ready explanation of this contradiction. Broadly speaking, animals are less sensitive to climate change than plants. Furthermore, some animals, such as sheep, are less sensitive to change than others.[39] [41] Could this be the root of the problem at Shanidar? Or is it that here, as in the Mediterranean area,[34] [37] the hunters had access to a large region with a very wide range of environmental conditions from which to draw their game animals?

We must wait until a regional sequence of pollen data has been obtained from the Shanidar area before we can say that the climate-change yardstick can be applied in the Near East with precision. Nevertheless, in the two faunal curves and the admittedly incomplete pollen curve of Shanidar (Fig. 13), some broad correspondence can be seen, with one notable exception. The plot for Tabūn B in the Mt. Carmel diagram, indicating a wet and cold climate, is not in accord with the other curves. It occurs at about the time the Mousterian cultures in this part of the Near East were dwindling.

Human Populations of Shanidar Valley

Study of human populations of the Shanidar Valley is a complex process, its complexity compounded by incompleteness of the Shanidar, or related investigations and by a lack of data. However, some general observations can be made on the basis of the available Shanidar data.

The Mousterian layer seems to have been built up by a series of Neanderthals who were relatively stagnant culturally; there were 2000 generations of them in the perhaps 60,000 years of its accumulation. Preliminary analysis of the tool types, from bottom to top, indicates that, except for the brief vogue of what looks like the "Emiran" type point,[42] there were no changes in the deposit. These basally inverse retouched points were found in the middle of a heavy occupational zone at a depth of about 8.5 meters—a zone which, as noted earlier, is probably evidence of a climate warmer than that of today. Neither fauna nor culture seem to have been much affected by the change to a very cool climate that is indicated by remains at a depth of about 7.5 meters. About this time (about 60,000 years ago), three of the six adult Neanderthals (Nos. II, IV, and VI) whose skeletons have been recovered were killed, all crushed by rocks (Fig. 14). Shanidar III, found at a depth of 5.4 meters, lived in a warmer climate perhaps 50,000 years ago. Shanidar I (Figs. 15 and 16) and Shanidar V were found at a depth of about 4.3 meters in a horizon dated about 44,000 B.C., also in a warm environment. Physical violence, compassion for the living,[43] and a certain regard for the dead are reflected in the skeletal finds. Stewart[14][44] has shown that the Shanidar Neanderthals have morphological features similar to the Tabūn skeletons of Mt. Carmel, which postdate the Shanidar Neanderthals by at least 5000 years. Stewart has also shown, on the basis of his studies of the skulls of Shanidar I and II, that an almost classic Neanderthal skull form was retained over a period of at least 15,000 years. The form was seemingly unaffected by the climatic changes inferred here. The carbon-14 dates recently obtained for Tabūn B (about 39,500 years ago) and Tabūn C (about 41,000 years ago)[45][46] suggest that the Mt. Carmel sequence falls almost entirely within the Last Glaciation (Würm in the Alpine sequence).

There are certain differences in tool types between the Mousterian cultures of Mt. Carmel and Shanidar—for example, the absence of the Levallois core technique at Shanidar[47] and evidence of the technique at Mt. Carmel. This undoubtedly must have some basis in the difference in environment. The recently obtained dates for Mt. Carmel point up the difficulties in making cultural correlations on the basis of industry typologies[48] and negate my conclusions from typological comparison of the Mt. Carmel and the Shanidar

Fig. 14. The skull of Shanidar II, as it appeared when discovered, crushed under a rockfall. The skull is lying on its right side, face to the front. The stone to the left was found directly over the left temple. This individual lived in a cool climate.

Fig. 15. The skull of Shanidar I, dated about 44,000 B.C., as it looked in the Shanidar laboratory after removal from the cave. The vertebrae are in place. This individual lived in a warm climate.

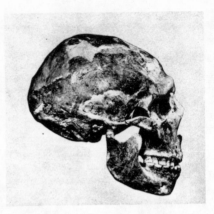

Fig. 16. The skull, restored, of Shanidar I. [Smithsonian Institution]

Mousterian.[47] If the Mt. Carmel dates were some 6000 years older, they would make the cultural sequences, at least, match better with those of other sites in the Near East.

Viewed broadly, the Shanidar Mousterian is a reasonably good example of the Mousterian culture horizon which ranged from Western Europe and North Africa to Uzbekistan[49][50] and Central Asia[51] in a rough ellipse around the Mediterranean, Black, Caspian, and Aral seas.[52] An interesting parallel can be drawn between the Shanidar and the Teshik-Tash Mousterian,[49][50] where, in similar mountainous environments, the principal animals hunted were goats. In the Iraq-Iran area, an occupation closely related to the Shanidar Mousterian occurred at the shelter-cave sites of Hazar Merd, Babkhal, Spilik, Bisitun, and Warwasi, and occupations less closely connected, at the open sites of Tarjil, Serandur, and Telegraph Pole 26/22.[53][54] Hazar Merd and Bisitun, at least, appear to be statistically related to Shanidar.[55]

The Mousterian lingered on longer at Mt. Carmel than it did in the Zagros Mountains, a finding that upset former chronological estimates for Mt. Carmel.[56] The terminal date for the Mousterian has been set at about 35,000 to 40,000 years ago in the Levant;[45] this is about the same as the date established for the beginning of the Upper Paleolithic III Baradostian of Shanidar. The date for the end of the Mousterian in Libya has been set at about 35,000 to 40,000 B.C.[57] The Mousterian came to Haua Fteah and to Shanidar at about the same time, but for some reason it seems to have been late in appearing at Ksâr 'Akil and Mt. Carmel. One must conclude that the Acheulian industries lingered on until quite late at Mt. Carmel, if the inferred chronology is true (Fig. 13). The Mousterian was part of an abrupt introduction, possibly stemming from Africa.[58] But neither the spread nor the final extinction of this culture was uniformly smooth. The carbon-14 dates hint that the final Mousterian cultures occurred at the same time as initial Upper Paleolithic occupations in the Near East.

What happened eventually to the last Shanidar Neanderthals is not known. It is hardly likely that unfavorable climate was a contributing cause of their departure. The possibility that they were eliminated by a prehistoric catastrophe cannot be ruled out. There is no evidence, but perhaps the Upper Paleolithic true *Homo sapiens* contributed to this extinction at Shanidar. However, if the Neanderthals had been bested in combat (and this surely would have been an unequal fight), it might be expected that the newcomers would have taken over their homes.[59] There seems to be evidence of cultural intermixture of the Upper Paleolithic and the Mousterian Middle Paleolithic in a transitional industry (the Emiran) in the Levant,[60] and similarly, passage of the Mousterian culture into the Upper Paleolithic Perigordian I in France.[61] But such was not the case at Shanidar. After, at most, a lapse of 10,000 years, the new occupants of Shanidar cave, the Baradostian people, took over a wilderness restocked with game, with no one to dispute their hunting territory claims.

On the basis of their tool inventory, it appears that these Upper Paleolithic peoples were most closely related to the Southwest Asian and European blade- and burin-using populations.[11 62 63] The Baradostian industry is unique in Iraq, although it has been reported from Warwasi cave in western Iran.[64] Nothing is known of cave or "home" art. It looks as though the Baradostian people had adapted their hunting methods to local conditions and pursued the same game animals (mainly goats) as their Neanderthal predecessors in Shanidar Valley. Probably they drove these gregarious herbivores over cliffs or trapped them in blind canyons nearby.

In the four known caves in the Zagros area which contain a Mousterian occupation overlaid by a Mesolithic one, only Shanidar and Warwasi caves have an intervening Upper Paleolithic occupation. There are more numerous, related occupations to the west in the Levant. There the closest Parallels to the Baradostian are at Yabrud (shelter II, layers 4 and 5) in Syria, at Abu Halka (layer IVc) in Lebanon, and at Mt. Carmel Wad E in Palestine—or what R. Neuville[65] calls Upper Palaeolithic III.[11] The Upper Paleolithic had a longer and more complete cultural history in the Levant than in the mountain hinterland of the Zagros area. While it is evident that the Baradostian did not have the time spread of the Mousterian, a more likely explanation of the sparseness of distribution for the Zagros area is a lack of population. It is possible that this interior mountain environment necessitated a special economic adjustment.

About 26,000 B.C., it is surmised, the climate became too cold for man at Shanidar and he left. The next occupation was not until about 15,000 years later. No barren soil layer was noted between layers B and C with which this hiatus can be correlated. This apparent desertion of Shanidar in the later Upper Paleolithic is paralleled at other dated and undated sites in the Near East, from Kara Kamar[66] in Afghanistan to southern Turkey.[67] There may well have been a low population density during the peak of the Last Glaciation, between about 13,000 and 23,000 years ago.[68] This is borne out by the dwindling number of sites even in the historically rich area of the Levant, where the Upper Palaeolithic stage V of Neuville[35 65] is clearly defined in only two sites, both in Palestine (Mt. Carmel Wad C "Atlitian," and el Khiam E). The hiatuses occur between the period of blade and burin industries of the Upper Paleolithic and the Mesolithic of the very late Pleistocene. In neighboring Soviet Asia we find a similar situation, with even longer hiatuses between the Mousterian and the Mesolithic.[50 69] After the close of the Last Glaciation, about 9000 to 10,000 B.C., there was a rash of Mesolithic settlements. As in the Near East, they blossomed over what is now Soviet Asia like desert flowers after a rain, taking advantage of an apparent cultural vacuum, meeting with little or no resistance. Surely something new must have been added to the economy, or new techniques and innovations must have broadened the economic base, contributing to this evident population spurt.[70]

The date of this movement, at least in this part of the Near East, was about 10,000 B.C., and the movement probably lasted not more than one and a half millennia. There are ten known sites of this relatively brief culture horizon (generally belonging to the "Zarzian"[71]) in the Iraq-Iran Zagros Mountain area in contrast to the lone pair of known Baradostian sites, spanning a period about five times as long. The Mesolithic layer B2 of Shanidar cave is one of these culturally related "Zarzian" sites; the others are components in the cave sites of Zarzi, Hazar Merd, Babkhal, Palegawra, Hajiyah, Barak, and Warwasi and in the open sites of Turkaka and Kowrikhan.[53 54 64 72] Outside the Zagros Mountain area, on the Caspian Sea in Iran, are the Belt and Hotu caves,[35 42 73] which have occupations of comparable date and culture.

The origins of this Mesolithic culture are not definitely known. Certainly it did not stem from the Baradostian at Shanidar. It could have come from the Levant, but related cultures to the north beyond the Caucasus area may have been just as compelling.[62] This people marked the end of the true hunters and gatherers, analogous to the Azilians and Tardenoisians in Europe prior to the Neolithic cultures. The sudden abundance of snail shells, the marked discoloration of the soil (from vegetal stuffs?), and the suggested presence of pits and basins in the Mesolithic layer of Shanidar cave suggest that these people were successfully launched on the road of experimentation with nontraditional food.

The cultural analog to the qualified "Zarzian" horizon in the Levant is the "Kebaran" of the Upper Paleolithic VI stage.[62][63] In North Africa, the analog to this culture horizon is the Oranian, which appears to date from later than 15,000 to 12,000 B.C. in the Maghreb.[27][36] It is possible that Oranian-related cultures swung eastward along the Mediterranean and inland through the Zagros arc and on eastward? It is too soon to say, but we are on the threshold of knowing. If this were true, then the movement of the later Proto-Neolithic horizon would be an interesting phenomenon to trace. The matter of the relationship of "Zarzian" to the open-air sites of the Ukraine, a thousand miles away, is still not clear.[62]

The next culture horizon in Shanidar Valley is known from the Proto-Neolithic occupation at the cave (layer B1) and at the open site of Zawi Chemi Shanidar.[74] These sites were probably seasonally occupied. Related components are found at such sites as Karim Shahir, M'lefaat, and possibly Asiab.[53][54][64][72][75] The evidence from Zawi Chemi Shanidar shows that this culture, especially, was well on its way toward full food production; the domesticated sheep was already known—an innovation probably brought in from some other area.[1] In the Levant the analogous Proto-Neolithic culture seems to have been the Natufian of Palestine.[76] A more distant analog is the Capsian culture in North Africa (Maghreb), emergent there sometime after 9000 B.C.[36] The interrelationships among these widely dispersed cultures, like those for the previous Mesolithic horizon, are not yet positively shown, but the thread of cultural similarities cannot be dismissed.[77]

The contrast between the Mesolithic and the Proto-Neolithic cultures at Shanidar is very marked. The compelling problem is that of determining the origin of the Shanidar B1-Zawi Chemi Shanidar culture horizon (Proto-Neolithic), with its focus on economic change. It may be that the preceding Shanidar B2 type culture and its Mesolithic equivalents elsewhere were for some reason, possibly ecological, already heavily predisposed toward experimental food collection and preparation of such edibles as acorns, nuts, and wild grass seeds. Social changes must have accompanied the new mode of life, but inferences about this are somewhat more difficult to make. At any rate, it is an inescapable fact that a food-production revolution of a sort is evidenced at Shanidar cave layer B1 and at Zawi Chemi Shanidar. It did not evolve directly out of Shanidar B2, but the change probably took place not very far away.

This great revolution seems to have occurred at just about the time of an abrupt world-wide rise in temperature.[78] Undoubtedly the same sort of climatic change had occurred before in man's history, but without a similar aftermath, so far as we know. Presumably, man did not have the right combination of mental, technological, and social attributes earlier in his development to search out and utilize radically new ways of getting a living, or else he was not in an area where the proper combination of ecological factors obtained. But given these, a kind of trigger was needed to make him depart from being a perpetual "lotus-eater," forever dependent upon hunting and gathering for his existence. In the area under discussion, the rise in temperature could have served as just such an indirect stimulus. The same sort of shock stimulus and subsequent concatenation of events was felt in the American Southwest at about the same time (about 8000 B.C.),[79] [80] where, paralleling developments in the Near East, there were shifts to an economic base more dependent upon food gathering, especially the gathering of vegetal foods, than on hunting. The hallmark of the so-called American Desert Culture was the flat milling stone, or quern, and the gathering basket.[80] At Shanidar and related sites we find evidence of the introduction of querns and hand milling stones [also, at Shanidar cave, baskets (?), and at Zawi Chemi Shanidar, possibly some kind of reaper (Fig. 17)[8]], indicating vegetal foods. The wild goat, known since the first occupation at Shanidar cave, was now of minor importance as compared to the sheep, which was found domesticated in Shanidar Valley. The stange was set for a "mixed-farming" economy.

Fig. 17. (Left) A knife, 20.9 centimeters long, made of a flint blade held with a tarry substance in a bone handle, found in the Proto-Neolithic cemetery at Shanidar cave. (Right) A laterally grooved bone handle, 21.7 centimeters long, which presumably held flint blades, from the Proto-Neolithic layer at the Zawi Chemi Shanidar village site. This was probably a sickle for cutting grasses.

As for the Desert Culture of the American Southwest, it seems that food production did not take hold there as it did in the Near East. Lacking was the combination of potentially domesticable animals and wild cereal prototypes, which in the Near East were the touchstone to civilization.[81]

References and Notes

1. C. A. Reed, *Z. Tierzüchtung Züchtungbiol.* **76**, 1 (1961), pp.31–38.
2. For the 1951 season see R. S. Solecki, *Sumer* **8**, 127 (1952); ——, *ibid.* **9**, 60 (1953). For 1953, see R. S. Solecki, *Smithsonian Inst. Ann. Rept.* **1954**, 389 (1955) [reprinted in *Sumer* **11**, 14 (1955)]; ——, *Sumer* **9**, 229 (1953). For 1956–57 see R. S. Solecki, *Smithsonian Inst. Ann. Rept.* **1959**, 603 (1960); ——, *Sumer* **13**, 165 (1957); ——, *ibid.* **14** 104 (1958). For 1960 see R. S. Solecki, *Trans. N.Y. Acad. Sci.* **23**, 690 (1961).
3. The terms *Paleolithic, Mesolithic,* and *Neolithic* are not precisely defined but serve as a useful nomenclature for establishing broad cultural perspectives in prehistory.
4. Sample W-667 is dated 10,600 ± 300 years ago [R. S. Solecki and M. Rubin, *Science* **127**, 1446 (1958); M. Rubin and C. Alexander, *Am. J. Sci. Radiocarbon Suppl.* **2**, 183 (1960)].
5. Sample W-179 is dated 12,000 ± 400 years ago [M. Rubin and H. E. Suess, *Science* **121**, 481 (1955)].
6. Sample W-681 is dated 10,870 ± 300 years ago [R. S. Solecki and M. Rubin, *Science* **127**, 1446 (1958); M. Rubin and C. Alexander, *Am. J. Sci. Radiocarbon Suppl.* **2**, 184 (1960), date the same sample (W-681) 10,800 ± 300 years ago].
7. The platforms, associated with evidence of fire, were probably of ceremonial origin.
8. R. S. Solecki and R. L. Solecki, "Two bone hafts from the Proto-Neolithic horizon at Shanidar, Northern Iraq," in preparation.
9. Sample W-654 is dated 28,700 ± 700 years ago [M. Rubin and C. Alexander, *Am. J. Sci. Radiocarbon Suppl.* **2**, 184 (1960)].
10. Sample GRO-259 is dated 35,080 ± 500 years ago [letter from H. DeVries (1 Aug. 1959)].
11. R. S. Solecki, thesis, Columbia University (1958).
12. ——, *Trans. N.Y. Acad. Sci.* **23**, 690 (1961).
13. Sample GRO-2527 is dated 46,000 ± 1500 years ago [R. S. Solecki, *Smithsonian Inst. Ann. Rept.* **1959**, 629 (1960); letter from H. DeVries (1 Aug. 1959)].
14. T. D. Stewart, *Sumer* **14**, 90 (1958) [reprinted in *Smithsonian Inst. Ann. Rept.* **1958**, 473 (1959)]; *Yearbook Am. Phil. Soc.* 1958), pp. 274–278.
15. *Bibliog. Primatol.* **1**, 130 (1962) (Adolph H. Schulz anniversary volume); *Sumer* **14**, 104 (1958); *ibid.*, in press.
16. M. Senyürek, *Anatolia* **2**, 49 (1957); *ibid.* **2**, 111 (1957); "A Study of the Deciduous Teeth of the Fossil Shanidar Infant," *Publ. Univ. Ankara, No. 128* (1959).
17. The samples were dated at the Laboratory of Physics, University of Groningen, Groningen, Netherlands; the Lamont Geological Observatory, Palisades, New York; the U.S. Geological Survey, Radiocarbon Laboratory, Washington, D.C.; and the Geochronological Laboratory, London Institute of Archaeology, London University, London, England.
18. I. Friedman, R. L. Smith, C. Evans, B. J. Meggers, *Am. Antiquity* **25**, 476 (1960). I believe, on the basis of the evidence, that obsidian dates older than those of layer B are not reliable.
19. R. S. Solecki and A. Leroi-Gourhan, *Ann. N.Y. Acad. Sci.* **95**, 729 (1961).

422   The Fossil Record

20. H. E. Wright, Jr., in *Prehistoric Investigations in Iraqi Kurdistan,* R. J. Braidwood and B. Howe, Eds. (Univ. of Chicago Press, Chicago, 1960), pp. 1–184.
21. ——, *Eiszeitalter Gegenwart* 12, 131 (1961);*Ann. N.Y. Acad. Sci.* 95, 718 (1961).
22. Previously, date palms had not been found, in an archeological context, in Mesopotamia before Sumerian times.
23. E. S. Deevey, Jr., *Am. Antiquity* 10, 135 (1944).
24. R. S. Solecki, unpublished manuscript.
25. C. B. M. McBurney has hit upon the same generalization from carbon-14 dates, using a more involved method.[26] [27]
26. C. B. M. McBurney, *Advan. Sci.* 18, 494 (1962).
27. ——, *Nature* 192, 685 (1961).
28. R. F. Flint and F. Brandtner, *Am. J. Sci.* 259, 321 (1961).
29. H. E. Wright, Jr., *Bull. Geol. Soc. Am.* 72, 933 (1961).
30. This would substantiate Dr. Wright's observation for climate change in Kurdistan.
31. Willem Van Zeist's "Preliminary palynological study of sediments from Lake Merivan, S. W. Iran" (unpublished manuscript, 1961) is not applicable here.
32. D. A. E. Garrod and D. M. A. Bate, *The Stone Age of Mount Carmel* (Oxford Univ. Press, Oxford, 1937), pp. 1–240.
33. F. E. Zeuner, *Dating the Past* (Methuen, London, 1958), pp. 1–516.
34. D. A. Hooijer, *Advan. Sci.* 18, 485 (1962).
35. F. Clark Howell, *Proc. Am. Phil. Soc.* 103, 1 (1959).
36. C. B. M. McBurney, *The Stone Age of Northern Africa* (Penguin, London, 1960), pp. 1–288.
37. D. A. Hooijer, *Zool. Verhandel.* 49, 1 (1961).
38. E. S. Higgs, *Advan. Sci.* 18, 490 (1962); —— and D. R. Brothwell, *Man* 41, 138 (1961).
39. E. S. Higgs, *Proc. Prehist. Soc.* 27, 144 (1961).
40. C. A. Reed and R. J. Braidwood, in *Prehistoric Investigations in Iraqi Kurdistan,* R. J. Braidwood and B. Howe, Eds. (Univ. of Chicago Press, Chicago, 1960), p. 165.
41. K. Kowalski [*Folia Quarternaria* 8, 1 (1962)] finds that small rodents are very useful indicators of climate in cave sections. No such study has been made as yet at Shanidar Cave.
42. R. S. Solecki, *Smithsonian Inst. Ann. Rept.* 1954, 389 (1955).
43. Compassion for the living is indicated by evidence of care of the infirm and wounded (one individual, at death, was recovering from a stab wound in the rib) and by evidence of surgery (an arm, useless since birth, had been cut off above the elbow).
44. T. D. Stewart, *Science* 131, 1437 (1960); paper delivered at American Association of Physical Anthropologists meeting; *Smithsonian Inst. Ann. Rept.* 1961, 521 (1962).
45. K. P. Oakley, *Advan. Sci.* 18, 415 (1962).
46. I believe that the "guess date" of "as early as 37,000 B.C." [D. R. Brothwell, *Proc. Prehist. Soc.* 27, 155 (1961)] for the Skhul finds of Mt. Carmel is within the limits of credibility.
47. R. S. Solecki, *Smithsonian Inst. Ann. Rept.* 1959, 603 (1960).
48. F. Bordes, *Science* 134, 803 (1961); ——, in *Evolution of Man,* S. Tax, Ed. (Univ. of Chicago Press, Chicago, 1960), vol. 2, pp. 99–110.
49. H. L. Movius, Jr., *Bull. Am. School Prehist. Res. No. 17* (1953), pp. 11–71.
50. ——, *Proc. Am. Phil. Soc.* 97, 383 (1953).
51. V. A. O. Ranov, *Akad. Nauk Tadjikstan SSR Stalinabad* 1, 89 (1961); ——, in *Noveishei etat geologicheskogo razvitiia territorii Tadzhikistana* Dushanbe, U.S.S.R., (1962), pp; 35–65.
52. F. E. Zeuner, in *A History of Technology,* C. Singer, E. J. Holmyard, A. R. Hall, Eds. (Oxford Univ. Press, Oxford, 1954), vol. 1, pp. xlviii–lvix. The distribution can be extended around the Caspian Sea and eastward.

53. R. J. Braidwood and B. Howe, in *Prehistoric Investigations in Iraqi Kurdistan*, R. J. Braidwood and B. Howe, Eds. (Univ. of Chicago Press, Chicago, 1960).
54. R. J. Braidwood, *Advan. Sci.* 16, 214 (1960).
55. This conclusion is based on a rough statistical estimate for Shanidar Mousterian. It looks like a "typical" Mousterian.
56. R. S. Solecki, *Trans. N.Y. Acad. Sci.* 24, 712 (1959).
57. C. B. M. McBurney, *Advan. Sci.* 18, 494 (1962).
58. ——, in *Neanderthal Centenary*, G. H. R. von Koenigswald, Ed. (Drukkerij, Utrecht, Netherlands, 1958), pp. 1–325.
59. In the Levant area the Upper Paleolithic had evolved through two stages (U.P. I, U.P. II) before the Baradostian appeared in the Zagros.
60. D. A. E. Garrod, *J. Roy. Anthropol. Inst.* 81, 121 (1951).
61. F. Bordes, in *Neanderthal Centenary*, G. H. R. von Koenigswald, Ed. (Drukkerij, Utrecht, Netherlands), pp. 1–325.
62. D. A. E. Garrod, *J. World Hist.* 1, 13 (1953).
63. ——, *Bull. Soc. Prehist. Fran.* 54, 439 (1957).
64. R. J. Braidwood, *Iranica Antiqua* 1, 2 (1961).
65. R. Neuville, *Arch. Inst. Paleontol. Humaine* 24, 1 (1951).
66. C. S. Coon and E. K. Ralph, *Science* 122, 921 (1955); C. S. Coon, *The Seven Caves* (Knopf, New York, 1957), pp. 1–338.
67. I. K. Kökten, *Belleten* 19, 271 (1955); M. Senyürek and E. Bostanci, *ibid.* 22, 171 (1958); E. Bostanci, *Anotolia* 4, 129 (1959); ——, *Belleten* 26, 233 (1962).
68. M. Rubin and H. E. Suess, *Science* 123, 442 (1955). Haua Fteah was evidently occupied during the height of the Last Glaciation (see [26]).
69. H. L. Movius, Jr., *Actes Congr. Intern. Quaternaire*, 4[c] (1953), pp. 3–20.
70. P. N. Tretiakov and A. L. Mongait, *Contrib. Ancient Hist. U.S.S.R.* (Russian Translation Series of the Peabody Museum of Archaeology and Ethnology, Harvard Univ.) 1, 1 (1961); A. Mongait, *Archaeology in the U.S.S.R.* (D. Skvirsky, trans.) (Foreign Language Publishing House, Moscow, 1959), pp. 1–429.
71. The name "Zarzian" was given these sites by R. J. Braidwood and B. Howe [*Prehistoric Investigations in Iraqi Kurdistan*, R. J. Braidwood and B. Howe, Eds. (Univ. of Chicago Press, Chicago, 1960), pp. 155, 180; *Science* 127, 1419 (1958)] after D. A. E. Garrod's site in Iraq [*Bull. Am. Prehist. Res.* 6, 13 (1930)].
72. R. J. Braidwood and B. Howe in "Courses Toward Urban Life," *Viking Fund Publ. in Anthropol. No. 32* (1962), pp. 132–146.
73. C. S. Coon, *Cave Explorations in Iran in 1949* (University Museum, Philadelphia, 1951), pp. 1–124; *Proc. Am. Phil. Soc.* 96, 231 (1952).
74. R. L. Solecki, "Zawi Chemi Shanidar, a Post-Pleistocene Village in Northern Iraq," in preparation.
75. The distinctiveness of Shanidar Cave layer B1 should correct the impression that, after the "Zarzian," caves were not inhabited by the Zawi Chemi Shanidar peoples [see [53], and R. J. Braidwood, *Science* 127, 1419 (1958)].
76. D. A. E. Garrod, *Proc. Brit. Acad.* 43, 211 (1957); Garrod calls Natufian a "Mesolithic Culture." J. Perrot, in "Courses Toward Urban Life," *Viking Fund Publ. in Anthropol. No. 32* (1962), pp. 147–164.
77. There are rough correspondences in the timing, the basic tool kit, luxury goods, and certain economic traits which hint at a kind of unity, as yet undefined, and a widespread culture horizon in the African Mediterranean area and Near East.
78. W. S. Broeker, M. Ewing, B. C. Heezen, *Am. J. Sci.* 258, 429 (1960).
79. R. S. Solecki, "Clues to the Emergence of Food Production in the Near East," in preparation.
80. J. Jennings, "Danger Cave," *Soc. Am. Archaeol. Mem. No. 14* (1957).

81. The fieldwork discussed in this article was made possible by grants from the American Philosophical Society, Columbia University, the National Science Foundation, the Smithsonian Institution, and the Wenner-Gren Foundation and by the generous cooperation of the Government of Iraq and the Iraq Petroleum Company. I thank Rose L. Solecki and James H. Skinner for critical reading of the manuscript and Alan Mann for help in its preparation.

Recent Discoveries of Fossil Hominids in Tanganyika:
At Olduvai and Near Lake Natron

L. S. B. Leakey and M. D. Leakey*

Excavations were continued at Olduvai Gorge throughout 1963 with funds generously provided by the Research Committee of the National Geographic Society, Washington, D.C. Some work was also undertaken at a new site on the western side of Lake Natron. The main work at Olduvai was concerned with the cultural sequence and stratigraphy of Bed II, Olduvai, but a little work was carried out in Bed I and also in Bed IV. We thank the U.S. National Geographic Society for financial support.

During the period under review a number of hominid remains have been found, some of which are of outstanding importance.

(A) In the early part of the year, work was continued at site V.E.K. IV where fragments of a thick hominid skull were found by Miss M. Cropper in 1962. A number of additional fragments of this skull, including a damaged palate, were recovered. This specimen has not yet been examined. Its possible relationship to the fossil human remains found at Kanjera in 1931–32 is likely to be of interest. This specimen is catalogued as Olduvai, Hominid No. 12.

(B) In October 1963, part of the vault of a small skull associated with the greater part of a mandible and parts of both maxillae, was found at site M.N.K. II. The lower third molars are fully erupted but as yet unworn, the upper third molars are just emerging from the alveoli. A late adolescent age is therefore indicated. The parts of the skull preserved include most of the occipital bone, which articulates very nicely with the two parietals, of which the right is the more complete; there are also a part of the frontal and parts of both temporals (Figs. 1 and 2). The mandible contains all the cheek teeth and

*Nature, April 1969.

Fig. 1.   The new hominid skull from site *M.N.K.* II Olduvai. Profile view.

Fig. 2.   The new skull. Occipital view.

both the canines in good condition, and all four incisors are present but the crowns are somewhat damaged (Fig. 3).

This specimen exhibits all the special morphological characters which could be seen in the juvenile mandible from Olduvai from *F.L.K.N.N.* I and the associated parietals, which were briefly described in *Nature* (189, 649; 1961, and 191, 417; 1961). The new specimen is recorded as Olduvai Hominid No. 13.

(*C*) A few fragments of a cranial vault of similar form to (*A*) here, but probably a younger individual also from site *M.N.K.* II. This specimen is listed as Olduvai Hominid No. 14.

(*D*) Three teeth of an adult—probably a male—were also found at site *M.N.K.* II, but in a deposit stratigraphically overlying that which yielded (*B*) and (*C*) here.

All these three specimens come from deposits which are approximately midway in Bed II but which appear to antedate the appearance of hand axes.

Fig. 3. The mandible associated with the skull from *M.N.K.* II Olduvai (left) next to the juvenile mandible found in 1960 from *F.L.K.N.* I.

(*E*) Considerable parts of the cranial vault, as well as most of the teeth of a young adult, in which the third upper and lower molars are just coming into occlusion. This specimen had been washed out by heavy rainfall at site *F.L.K.* II, Maiko Gully; it had, moreover, been afterwards trampled on and very badly broken up by herds of Masai cattle before it was discovered by one of our senior African staff. It is derived from deposits 3—4 ft. above the marker bed at the top of Bed I.

Parts of this specimen had been washed a long way from the original site and others had been carried away attached by mud and clay to the feet of cattle. The work of recovery and piecing together the hundreds of fragments will continue for some considerable time. The maxillary teeth of the right side, some of the mandibular teeth and parts of the frontal of this specimen are seen in Figs. 4 and 5.

The importance of this particular find is that it provides the greater part of the frontal bone, with the supra-orbital region, of an individual in which the teeth clearly show that it belongs to the same morphological group as the *F.L.K.N.N.* I juvenile of 1960 and the specimens listed here, rather than to the Australopithecine sub-family as represented by *Zinjanthropus*, or the South African representatives.

In addition to the five individuals represented in the material listed here, a sixth important discovery was made in January 1964, in deposits with a fauna of Middle Pleistocene age lying on the west side of Lake Natron some fifty miles north-east of Olduvai Gorge. Initial exploration of this area was carried out under the leadership of my son, Richard Leakey, who was later joined by Mr. Glynn Isaac, who took charge of the scientific side of the work. Mrs. Isaac, Mr. Richard Rowe and Philip Leakey also took part, as well as a number of our African staff.

On January 11 one of our African staff, Mr. Kamoya Kimeu, located a magnificent fossil hominid jaw *in situ* (see Figs. 6 and 7). This jaw, unlike specimens (*A*), (*B*), (*C*) and (*D*) here, represents an unmistakable australo-pithecine and provides, for the first time, a mandible representing this sub-family from East Africa.

It will be recalled that in earlier notes in *Nature* and elsewhere, we have stressed the fact that the juvenile and the other fossil remains from site *F.L.K.N.N.* I, found in 1960, did not represent an australopithecine such as *Australopithecus (Zinjanthropus) boisei*, but were wholly distinct and different. It was stated that these must be thought of as representing a contemporary and primitive hominine branch of the Hominidae.

We refrained from giving a scientific name to the material from site *F.L.K.N.N.* I—the juvenile and the female—together with other specimens representing the same type (the molar tooth from site *M.K.* I) until there were better data on which to decide just where to place this type of hominid

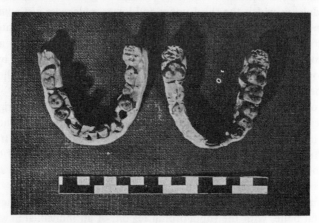

Fig. 4. The maxillary teeth (right) and mandibular teeth (left) of the broken skull from site *F.L.K.* II, Maiko Gully.

Fig. 5. Part of the frontal of the broken-up skull from *F.L.K.* II, Maiko Gully.

in the taxonomic sequence. The new material found in 1963 makes it possible to draw conclusions and to give a diagnosis for a new species of the genus *Homo*. This diagnosis and a preliminary description by Leakey, Tobias and Napier follow this article.

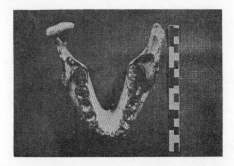

Fig. 6. A new mandible of *Australopithecus (Zinjanthropus)* type from the new site west of Lake Natron, north-east of Olduvai.

Fig. 7. Side view of the mandible of *Australopithecus (Zinjanthropus)* type from west of Lake Natron.

A New Species
of the Genus *Homo*
from Olduvai Gorge

L. S. B. Leakey
P. V. Tobias
and
J. R. Napier*

The recent discoveries of fossil hominid remains at Olduvai Gorge have strengthened the conclusions—which each of us had reached independently through our respective investigations—that the fossil hominid remains found in 1960 at site *F.L.K.N.N.* I, Olduvai, did not represent a creature belonging to the sub-family Australopithecinae.†

We were preparing to publish the evidence for this conclusion and to give a scientific name to this new species of the genus *Homo*, when the new discoveries, which are described by L. S. B. and M. D. Leakey in the preceding article, were made.

An examination of these finds has enabled us to broaden the basis of our diagnosis of the proposed new species and has fully confirmed the presence of the genus *Homo* in the lower part of the Olduvai geological sequence, earlier than, contemporary with, as well as later than, the *Zinjanthropus* skull, which is certainly an australopithecine.

For the purpose of our description here, we have accepted the diagnosis of the family Hominidae, as it was proposed by Sir Wilfred Le Gros Clark in his book *The Fossil Evidence for Human Evolution* (110; 1955). Within this family we accept the genus *Australopithecus* with, for the moment, three sub-genera (*Australopithecus, Paranthropus* and *Zinjanthropus*) and the genus

Nature, April 1964.
†See also *Nature* of March 7, pp. 967, 969, and preceding articles in this issue.

Homo. We regard *Pithecanthropus* and possibly also *Atlanthropus* (if it is indeed distinct) as species of the genus *Homo*, although one of us (L. S. B. L.) would be prepared to accept sub-generic rank.

It has long been recognized that as more and more discoveries were made, it would become necessary to revise the diagnosis of the genus *Homo*. In particular, it has become clear that it is impossible to rely on only one or two characters, such as the cranial capacity or an erect posture, as the necessary criteria for membership of the genus. Instead, the total picture presented by the material available for investigation must be taken into account.

We have come to the conclusion that, apart from *Australopithecus (Zinjanthropus)*, the specimens we are dealing with from Bed I and the lower part of Bed II at Olduvai represent a single species of the genus *Homo* and not an australopithecine. The species is, moreover, clearly distinct from the previously recognized species of the genus. But if we are to include the new material in the genus *Homo* (rather than set up a distinct genus for it, which we believe to be unwise), it becomes necessary to revise the diagnosis of this genus. Until now, the definition of *Homo* has usually centred about a 'cerebral Rubicon' variably set at 700 c.c. (Weidenreich), 750 c.c. (Keith) and 800 c.c. (Vallois). The proposed new definition follows:

Family   HOMINIDAE (as defined by Le Gros Clark, 1955)

Genus   *Homo*   Linnaeus.

Revised diagnosis of the genus Homo. A genus of the Hominidae with the following characters: the structure of the pelvic girdle and of the hind-limb skeleton is adapted to habitual erect posture and bipedal gait; the fore-limb is shorter than the hind-limb; the pollex is well developed and fully opposable and the hand is capable not only of a power grip but of, at the least, a simple and usually well developed precision grip;* the cranial capacity is very variable but is, on the average, larger than the range of capacities of members of the genus *Australopithecus*, although the lower part of the range of capacities in the genus *Homo* overlaps with the upper part of the range in *Australopithecus*; the capacity is (on the average) large relative to body-size and ranges from about 600 c.c. in earlier forms to more than 1,600 c.c.; the muscular ridges on the cranium range from very strongly marked to virtually imperceptible, but the temporal crests or lines never reach the midline; the frontal region of the cranium is without undue post-orbital constriction (such as is common in members of the genus *Australopithecus*); the supra-orbital region of the frontal bone is very variable, ranging from a massive and very

---

*For the definition of 'power grip' and 'precision grip', see Napier, J. R., *J. Bone and Joint Surg.*, 38, B, 902 (1956).

salient supra-orbital torus to a complete lack of any supra-orbital projection and a smooth brow region; the facial skeleton varies from moderately prognathous to orthognathous, but it is not concave (or dished) as is common in members of the Australopithecinae; the anterior symphyseal contour varies from a marked retreat to a forward slope, while the bony chin may be entirely lacking, or may vary from a slight to a very strongly developed mental trigone; the dental arcade is evenly rounded with no diastema in most members of the genus; the first lower premolar is clearly bicuspid with a variably developed lingual cusp; the molar teeth are variable in size, but in general are small relative to the size of these teeth in the genus *Australopithecus*; the size of the last upper molar is highly variable, but it is generally smaller than the second upper molar and commonly also smaller than the first upper molar; the lower third molar is sometimes appreciably larger than the second; in relation to the position seen in the Hominoidea as a whole, the canines are small, with little or no overlapping after the initial stages of wear, but when compared with those of members of the genus *Australopithecus*, the incisors and canines are not very small relative to the molars and premolars; the teeth in general, and particularly the molars and premolars, are not enlarged bucco-lingually as they are in the genus *Australopithecus*; the first deciduous lower molar shows a variable degree of molarization.

Genus   *Homo*   Linnaeus
Species   *habilis*   sp. nov.

(*Note:* The specific name is taken from the Latin, meaning 'able, handy, mentally skilful, vigorous'. We are indebted to Prof. Raymond Dart for the suggestion that *habilis* would be a suitable name for the new species.)

A species of the genus *Homo* characterized by the following features:

A mean cranial capacity greater than that of members of the genus *Australopithecus*, but smaller than that of *Homo erectus*; muscular ridges on the cranium ranging from slight to strongly marked; chin region retreating, with slight or no development of the mental trigone; maxillae and mandibles smaller than those of *Australopithecus* and within the range for *Homo erectus* and *Homo sapiens*; dentition characterized by incisors which are relatively large in comparison with those of both *Australopithecus* and *Homo erectus*; canines which are proportionately large relative to the premolars; premolars which are narrower (in bucco-lingual breadth) than those of *Australopithecus*, but which fall within the range for *Homo erectus*; molars in which the absolute dimensions range between the lower part of the range in *Australopithecus* and the upper part of the range in *Homo erectus*; a marked tendency towards bucco-lingual narrowing and mesiodistal elongation of all the teeth, which is especially evident in the lower premolars (where it expresses itself as a marked elongation of the talonid) and in the lower molars (where it is accompanied by a rearrangement of the distal cusps); the sagittal curvature of the parietal bone varies from slight (within the hominine range) to moderate (within the australopithecine range); the external sagittal curvature of the occipital bone is slighter than in *Australopithecus* or in *Homo erectus*, and lies within the range of *Homo sapiens*; in curvature as well as in some other morphological traits, the clavicle resembles, but is not identical to, that of *Homo sapiens sapiens*; the hand bones differ from those of *Homo sapiens sapiens* in robustness, in the dorsal curvature of the shafts of the phalanges, in the distal attachment of *flexor digitorum superficialis*, in the strength of fibro-tendinous markings, in the orientation of trapezium in the carpus, in the form of the scaphoid and in the marked depth of the carpal tunnel; however, the hand bones resemble those of *Homo sapiens sapiens* in the presence of broad, stout, terminal phalanges on fingers and thumb, in the form of the distal articular surface of the capitate and the ellipsoidal form of the metacarpo-phalangeal joint surfaces; in many of their characters the foot bones lie within the range of variation of *Homo sapiens sapiens*; the hallux is stout, adducted and plantigrade; there are well-marked longitudinal and transverse arches; on the other hand, the 3rd metatarsal is relatively more robust than it is in modern man, and there is no marked difference in the radii of curvature of the medial and lateral profiles of the trochlea of the talus.

Geological horizon. Upper Villafranchian and Lower Middle Pleistocene.

Type. The mandible with dentition and the associated upper molar, parietals and hand bones, of a single juvenile individual from site *F.L.K.N.N.* I, Olduvai, Bed I.

This is catalogued as Olduvai Hominid 7.

Paratypes. (*a*) An incomplete cranium, comprising fragments of the frontal, parts of both parietals, the greater part of the occipital, and parts of both temporals, together with an associated mandible with canines, premolars and molars complete on either side but with the crowns of the incisors damaged, parts of both maxillae having all the cheek teeth except the upper left fourth premolar. The condition of the teeth suggests an adolescent. This specimen, from site *M.N.K.* II, Olduvai, Bed II, is catalogued as Olduvai Hominid 13.

(*b*) The associated hand bones, foot bones and probably the clavicle, of an adult individual from site *F.L.K.N.N.* I, Olduvai, Bed I. This is catalogued as Olduvai Hominid 8.

(*c*) A lower premolar, an upper molar and cranial fragments from site *F.L.K.* I, Olduvai, Bed I (the site that yielded also the *Australopithecus* (*Zinjanthropus*) skull. This is catalogued as Olduvai Hominid 6. (It is possible that the tibia and fibula found at this site belong with *Homo habilis* rather than with *Australopithecus* (*Zinjanthropus*). These limb bones have been reported on by Dr. P. R. Davis (*Nature*, March 7, 1964, p. 967).

(*d*) A mandibular fragment with a molar in position and associated with a few fragments of other teeth from site *M.K.* I, Olduvai, Bed I. This specimen is catalogued as Olduvai Hominid 4.

Description of the type. Preliminary descriptions of the specimens which have now been designated the type of *Homo habilis*, for example, the parts of the juvenile found at site *F.L.K.N.N.* I in 1960, have already been published in *Nature* by one of us (**189**, 649; **191**, 417; 1961). A further detailed description and report on the parietals, the mandible and the teeth are in active preparation by one of us (P. V. T.), while his report on the cranial capacity (preceding article) as well as a preliminary note on the hand by another of us (*Nature*, **196**, 409; 1962) have been published. We do not propose, therefore, to give a more detailed description of the type here.

Description of the paratypes. A preliminary note on the clavicle and on the foot of the adult, which represent the paratype (*b*), was published in *Nature* (**188**, 1050; 1961) and a further report on the foot by Dr. M. H. Day and Dr. J. R. Napier was published in *Nature* of March 7, 1964, p. 969.

The following additional preliminary notes on the other paratypes have been prepared by one of us (P. V. T.).

Description of Paratypes

(*a*) *Olduvai Hominid* 13 *from* M.N.K. *II*. An adolescent represented by a nearly complete mandible with complete fully-erupted lower dentition, a right maxillary fragment including palate and all teeth from P^3 to M^3, the latter in the process of erupting; the corresponding left maxillary fragment with M^1 to M^3, the latter likewise erupting; the isolated left P^3; parts of the vault of a small, adult cranium, comprising much of the occipital, including part of the posterior margin of *foramen magnum*, parts of both parietals, right and left temporosphenoid fragments, each including the mandibular fossa and foramen ovale. The distal half of a humeral shaft (excluding the distal extremity) may also belong to Olduvai Hominid 13. The *corpus mandibulae* is very small, both the height and thickness at M^1 falling below the australopithecine range and within the hominine range. All the teeth are small compared with those of Australopithecinae, most of the dimensions falling at or below the lower extreme of the australopithecine ranges. On the other hand, practically all the dental dimensions can be accommodated within the range of fossil Homininae. The Olduvai Hominid 13 teeth show the characteristic mesiodistal elongation and labiolingual narrowing, in some teeth the L/B index exceeding even those of the type Olduvai Hominid 7, and paratype Olduvai Hominid 6. The occipital bone has a relatively slight sagittal

curvature, the Occipital Sagittal Index being outside the range for australopithecines and for *Homo erectus pekinensis* and within the range for *Homo
sapiens*. On the other hand, the parietal sagittal curvature is more marked
than in all but one australopithecine and in all the Pekin fossils, the index
falling at the top of the range of population means for modern man. Both
parietal and occipital bones are very small in size, being exceeded in some
dimensions by one or two australopithecine crania and falling short in all
dimensions of the range for *Homo erectus pekinensis*. The form of the
parietal—antero-posteriorly elongated and bilaterally narrow, with a fairly
abrupt lateral descent in the plane of the parietal boss—reproduces closely
these features in the somewhat larger parietal of the type specimen (Olduvai
Hominid 7 from *F.L.K.N.N.* I).

(*b*) *Olduvai Hominid 6 from* F.L.K. *I*. An unworn lower left premolar,
identified as P_3, an unworn, practically complete crown and partly developed
roots of an upper molar, either M^1 or M^2, as well as a number of fragments of
cranial vault. These remains were found at the *Zinjanthropus* site and level,
some *in situ* and some on the surface. Both teeth are small for an
australopithecine, expecially in buccolingual breadth, but large for *Homo
erectus*. The marked tendency to elongation and narrowing imparts to both
teeth an *L/B* index outside the range for all known australopithecine
homologues and even beyond the range for *Homo erectus pekinensis*. The
elongating-narrowing tendency is more marked in this molar than in the
upper molar belonging to the type specimen (Olduvai Hominid 7) from
F.L.K.N.N. I.

(*c*) *Olduvai Hominid 8 from* F.L.K.N.N. *I*. Remains of an adult individual
found on the same horizon as the type specimen, and represented by two
complete proximal phalanges, a fragment of a rather heavily worn tooth
(premolar or molar), and a set of foot-bones possessing most of the
specializations associated with the plantigrade propulsive feet of modern man.
Probably the clavicle found at this site belongs to this adult rather than to the
juvenile type-specimen; it is characterized by clear overall similarities to the
clavicle of *Homo sapiens sapiens*.

(*d*) *Olduvai Hominid 4 from* M.K. *I*. A fragment of the posterior part of
the left *corpus mandibulae*, containing a well-preserved, fully erupted molar,
either M_2 or M_3. The width of the mandible is 19.2 m level with the mesial
half of the molar, but the maximum width must have been somewhat greater.
The molar is 15.1 mm in mesiodistal length and 13.0 mm in buccolingual
breadth; it is thus a small and narrow tooth by australopithecine standards,
but large in comparison with *Homo erectus* molars. There are several other
isolated dental fragments, including a moderately worn molar fragment.
These are stratigraphically the oldest hominid remains yet discovered at
Olduvai.

Referred Material

Olduvai Hominid 14 *from* M.W.K. *II*. (1) A juvenile represented by a fragment of the right parietal with clear, unfused sutural margins; two smaller vault fragments with sutural margins; a left and a right temporal fragment, each including the mandibular fossa.

(2) A fragmentary skull with parts of the upper and lower dentition of a young adult from site *F.L.K.* II, Maiko Gully, Olduvai, Bed II, is also provisionally referred to *Homo habilis*. This specimen is catalogued as Olduvai Hominid 16. It is represented by the complete upper right dentition, as well as some of the left maxillary teeth, together with some of the mandibular teeth. The skull fragments include parts of the frontal, with both the external orbital angles preserved, as well as the supraorbital region, except for the glabella; parts of both parietals and the occipital are also represented.

Implications for Hominid Phylogeny

In preparing our diagnosis of *Homo habilis*, we have not overlooked the fact that there are several other African (and perhaps Asian) fossil hominids whose status may now require re-examination in the light of the new discoveries and of the setting up of this new species. The specimens originally described by Broom and Robinson as *Telanthropus capensis* and which were later transferred by Robinson to *Homo erectus* may well prove, on closer comparative investigation, to belong to *Homo habilis*. The Kanam mandibular fragment, discovered by the expedition in 1932 by one of us (L. S. B. L.), and which has been shown to possess archaic features (Tobias, *Nature*, 185, 946; 1960), may well justify further investigation along these lines. The Lake Chad craniofacial fragment, provisionally described by M. Yves Coppens in 1962, as an australopithecine, is not, we are convinced, a member of this sub-family. We understand that the discoverer himself, following his investigation of the australopithecine originals from South Africa and Tanganyika, now shares our view in this respect. We believe that it is very probably a northern representative of *Homo habilis*.

Outside Africa, the possibility will have to be considered that the teeth and cranial fragments found at Ubeidiyah on the Jordan River in Israel may also belong to *Homo habilis* rather than to *Australopithecus*.

Cultural Association

When the skull of *Australopithecus* (*Zinjanthropus*) *boisei* was found on a living floor at *F.L.K.* I, no remains of any other type of hominid were known from the early part of the Olduvai sequence. It seemed reasonable, therefore, to assume that this skull represented the makers of the Oldowan culture. The subsequent discovery of remains of *Homo habilis* in association with the Oldowan culture at three other sites has considerably altered the position. While it is possible that *Zinjanthropus* and *Homo habilis* both made stone tools, it is probable that the latter was the more advanced tool maker and that the *Zinjanthropus* skull represents an intruder (or a victim) on a *Homo habilis* living site.

The recent discovery of a rough circle of loosely piled stones on the living floor at site *D.K.* I, in the lower part of Bed I, is noteworthy. This site is geologically contemporary with *M.K.* I, less than one mile distant, where remains of *Homo habilis* have been found. It seems that the early hominids of this period were capable of making rough shelters or windbreaks and it is likely that *Homo habilis* may have been responsible.

Relationship to *Australopithecus (Zinjanthropus)*

The fossil human remains representing the new species *Homo habilis* have been found in Bed I and in the lower and middle part of Bed II. Two of the sites, *M.K.* I and *F.L.K.N.N.* I, are geologically older than that which yielded the skull of the australopithecine *Zinjanthropus*. One site, *F.L.K.* I, has yielded both *Australopithecus (Zinjanthropus)* and remains of *Homo habilis*, while two sites are later, namely *M.N.K.* II and *F.L.K.* II Maiko gully. The new mandible of *Australopithecus (Zinjanthropus)* type from Lake Natron, reported in the preceding article by Dr. and Mrs. Leakey, was associated with a fauna of Bed II affinities.

It thus seems clear that two different branches of the Hominidae were evolving side by side in the Olduvai region during the Upper Villafranchian and the lower part of the Middle Pleistocene.

The Olduvai Bed I Hominine
With Special Reference to
its Cranial Capacity

P. V. Tobias*

On February 25, 1961, Dr. L. S. B. Leakey announced the discovery of the greater part of a juvenile hominid mandible, as well as parts of two parietals, at the site *F.L.K.N.N.* I in Bed I at Olduvai Gorge, Tanganyika.[1] Pending further examination and the recovery of more bones of this hominid, these remains have hitherto been referred to as pre-*Zinjanthropus*, since the horizon from which they were recovered is a little lower than the *Zinjanthropus* horizon. Leakey pointed out that the remains were larger than those of *Zinjanthropus* and claimed that they represented a hominid with a larger cranial capacity. Later, he went further and attributed the juvenile remains, not to an australopithecine, but to "a very remote and truly primitive ancestor of *Homo*".[2]

Most definitions of man (hominine or 'euhominid') have hinged about a critical 'cerebral Rubicon', set variously at 700 c.c. (Weidenreich), 750 c.c. (Keith, Robinson) or 800 c.c. (Vallois). However, it seems likely that ranges of cranial capacity overlap within the Hominidae and that no clear-cut dividing line exists. Even between the pongids and hominines, there is almost an overlap, since one large male gorilla has a capacity of 752 c.c. (Schultz 1962), while the smallest hominine capacity hitherto reported in an apparently normal member of *Homo erectus (Pithecanthropus)* is 775 c.c. It was therefore of interest to estimate the probable cranial capacity of the juvenile cranium of pre-*Zinjanthropus* from *F.L.K.N.N.* I.

Although the two parietals are incomplete, reconstruction of the missing parts was easy, because the entire coronal and temporal borders are present

*1964 (*Nature*, April)

on the left bone and the entire lambdoid (or occipital) border on the right. In addition, the anterior part of the sagittal border is present on the left parietal and the posterior part of this border on the right. The first reconstruction of the biparietal part of the calvaria was made by Dr. Leakey and myself; later a second reconstruction was made by Mr. A. R. Hughes and myself (Fig. 1).

Using the biparietal vaults thus reconstructed, Mr. Hughes and I made two partial endocranial casts, each representing that part of the cranial cavity enclosed above and at the sides by the parietal bones (Fig. 2). The front, back and sides of the endocast were set by the borders of the articulated, reconstructed parietal bones. The basal aspect of the endocast was made to follow the concavo-convex contour of the temporal margins of the parietals.

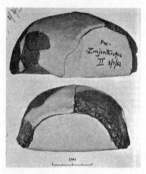

Fig. 1. **Recons**tructed biparietal arch of the Olduvai hominine from F.L.K.N.N. I, seen from above.

Fig. 2. Partial endocranial cast within the biparietal arch of the Olduvai hominine from *F.L.K.N.N.* I. Above, anterolateral view (as seen from in front and to the right); below, view from behind. (In the upper photograph, a dotted line has been added to demarcate the endocast more clearly from the edge of the plaster-reconstructed portion of the right parietal bone.)

Each of the two finished products was accepted as representing the volume of the tunnel-shaped space enclosed by the parietals. The volume of each of the two partial endocasts was determined five times by water displacement: the endocast based on the first biparietal reconstruction yielded five values ranging from 362 to 364 c.c. with a mean of 363.6; the endocast based on the second yielded five values ranging from 362 to 365 c.c. with a mean of 363.4.

The problem now was to estimate what proportion of the total endocranial volume might be constituted by the biparietal endocranial volume. In order to provide a basis for making this estimate, four endocranial casts of fossil hominids were selected, in which the total volume had been reliably determined and on which the outline of the parietal bones was unmistakably detectable. Two were endocasts of australopithecines (the Taung specimen and *Zinjanthropus*) and two of *Homo erectus* (one each from Java and Pekin). From each of these four endocasts, biparietal partial endocasts were made and the volumes determined by water displacement five times each. For each cast, the mean values thus obtained were then expressed as a percentage of the known total volume (Table 1).

TABLE 1. PROPORTION OF ENDOCRANIAL VOLUME
ENCLOSED BY PARIETALS

Specimen	Total endocast volume (A)	Partial endocast mean volume (B)	B/A (per cent)
Australopithecus africanus (Taung)	520	294	56.54
Zinjanthropus boisei (Olduvai)	530	288.6	54.45
H. erectus erectus ('*Pithecanthropus* I'—Java)	935	469.6	50.22
H. erectus pekinensis ('*Sinanthropus L* III' —Pekin)	1,030	562.8	54.64

The values for the ratio B/A per cent range from 50.22 to 56.54, a remarkably small range when one considers the known variability of the parietal bone in modern man and the varying size of the four endocasts selected.

These percentages have been used to estimate a range of possible values for the total capacity of the Olduvai juvenile from *F.L.K.N.N.* I. From a mean value for the partial endocast of 363.4 c.c., the following total capacities have been computed:

If B/A = 50.22, total capacity = 723.6; if B/A = 56.54, total capacity = 642.7; if B/A = 53.96, total capacity = 673.5 (mean of the four percentages in Table 1).
If B/A = 53.38, total capacity = 680.8 (mid-value between 50.22 and 56.54).

The estimates range from 642.7 to 723.6 c.c., with central values of 673.5 and 680.8. All these values lie in the area between the largest known australopithecine (530 c.c.—or 600 c.c. as the estimate for an adult corresponding to the Taung child, Tobias[3]) and the smallest known *Homo erectus* capacity (775 c.c.).

Whichever of the estimated values one accepts confirms what Leakey had claimed and what the measurements on the parietal bones had indicated, namely, that the *F.L.K.N.N.* I juvenile had a more capacious cranial vault than any australopithecine. This capacity, coupled with the non-australopithecine curvature of the parietal, and the many non-australopithecine features of the teeth and mandible, as well as the characters observed by Napier[4] and Day and Napier[5] in the post-cranial bones, all point to a total morphological pattern which is outside the range for the Australopithecinae and close to, if not within, the range for the Homininae. If the capacity of 675–680 c.c. were accepted as compatible with hominine status, the juvenile individual from *F.L.K.N.N.* I must be accepted as representing a hominine, intermediate in morphology between members of the genus *Australopithecus* and those of *Homo erectus*. The full evidence on which this conclusion is based will be presented elsewhere, as well as a definition of the taxonomic status of the Bed I juvenile believed to belong within the Homininae. Meanwhile, it may be stated that the non-australopithecine, hominine features which characterize the juvenile are apparent as well in the mandibular fragment and molar tooth from *MK* I, near the base of Bed I; in the remains of a second individual, fully adult, from the site *F.L.K.N.N.* I in Bed I; in several teeth and other remains found on the *Zinjanthropus* horizon at *F.L.K.* I in Bed I and clearly not belonging to *Zinjanthropus*; as well as in remains from Bed II to be described elsewhere.

I thank Dr. L. S. B. Leakey for placing the Olduvai hominid fossils at my disposal for examination. I also thank Mr. Alun R. Hughes, of the Department of Anatomy, for his assistance. This work was supported by the Wenner-Gren Foundation for Anthropological Research and the South African Council for Scientific and Industrial Research.

References

1. *Nature,* 189, 649 (1961).   4. *Nature,* 196, 409 (1962).
2. *Nature,* 191, 417 (1961).   5. *Nature,* 201, 969 (1964).
3. *Nature,* 197, 743 (1963).

Bone Smashing by
Late Miocene Hominidae

L. S. B. Leakey*

The Upper Miocene fossil beds of Fort Ternan have yielded many hundreds of fossil bones of an extensive extinct mammalian fauna.[1] Most of these bones are not badly broken up and frequently bones are uncovered during excavation lying in natural articulation (Fig. 1). In this photograph can be seen (*a*) a complete skull of a hornless bovid with the mandible articulated on the extreme right; (*b*) a large femur and tibia in articulation, bottom right; (*c*) the bones of the hind leg of an antelope comprising femur, tibia, astragalus and calcaneum, in articulation; (*d*) part of an articulated vertebral column. There are also a variety of bovid mandibles which have come apart at the symphysis and other unbroken bones.

In striking contrast to this situation, there are in the same deposit, and at the same level, small areas of fossils where the bones have been broken up, and where the damage includes excellent examples of depressed fractures of the types usually associated with "a blunt instrument" (Fig. 2). In this photograph can be seen: (1) a tibia broken across the shaft and with a depressed fracture at the proximal end (Fig. 3); (2) part of a bovid skull with the maxillae intact, but the premaxillae and also the brain case have been broken away; (3) an "antler" of a deer-like creature attached to a fragment of brain case, but the rest of the skull is missing; and (4) a large broken tibia.

Before the 1967 season, I had begun to suspect that these areas of broken-up bones had some special significance in relation to the known presence, at the Fort Ternan site, of the Upper Miocene hominid *Kenyapithecus wickeri*. During the 1967 season, additional finds included a small broken bovid skull with a beautiful example of a depressed fracture (Fig. 4)

Nature, May 1968

Fig. 1. Part of the excavation showing skull and mandible of a bovid, on the right; large femur and tibia in articulation, bottom right; the bones of a leg of an antelope in articulation, centre; and part of an articulated vertebral column, left.

Fig. 2. View of another part of excavation where all the bones are broken. On the left, a tibia broken across the shaft with a depressed fracture; beneath it a bovid skull with the back of skull and premaxillae broken away; bottom right, part of large broken tibia; above right, "antlers" of deer-like creature with part of skull.

Fig. 3.   Details of the broken tibia with depressed fracture from Fig. 2.

which resulted in the removal of the occipital region of the brain case and exposed the brain cavity. We also recovered a peculiar lump of lava exhibiting several battered edges, and with every appearance of having been used to smash bones (Fig. 5).

The available evidence presented here therefore strongly suggests that the Upper Miocene hominid *Kenyapithecus wickeri*[2] was already making use of stones to break open animal skulls in order to get at the brain and bones to get at the marrow. The new finds (which will be dealt with in detail in a fuller report), when taken in conjunction with the fact that at the base of bed I at Olduvai *Homo habilis* already had an extensive kit of different types of stone tools,[3] most strongly suggest that we can expect to find evidence of the making of stone tools during the Pliocene.

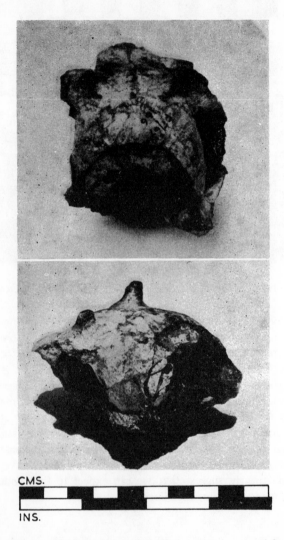

CMS.

INS.

Fig. 4. Two views of the small bovid skull showing depressed fracture with a
semicircular outline that has removed back of skull.

The work at Fort Ternan has been carried out with the aid of grants from the Research and Exploration Committee of the National Geographic Society, Washington.

References

1. Leakey, L. S. B., *Ann. Mag. Nat. Hist.*, Series 13, 4 (1961).
2. Leakey, L. S. B., *Nature*, 213, 155 (1967).
3. Leakey, M. D., in *Background to Evolution in Africa* (edit. by Bishop, W. W., and Clarke, J. D.) (University of Chicago Press, 1967).

Fig. 5. A view of one angular edge of lava lump with extensive damage as a result of battering.

Epilogue

L. S. B. Leakey

Discoveries in the field of anthropology have been taking place faster and faster as the years have gone by, and we might almost describe the speed with which this has happened as an inverse geometric progression. The finds made in the last ten years exceed those of the previous 100 and, quite possibly, those of the next one year may exceed those of the past ten. This is due to two things. One is the fact that there are many more trained workers in the field, and the second, that modern technical developments make sites which were previously difficult to reach, accessible, and discoveries at those sites more probable.

Each new discovery, which is due to scientific investigation, rather than to chance finding in the course of commercial undertakings, represents, or should represent, a new basic fact, and the basic fact of a discovery is not something which alters as time goes on and more discoveries are made. On the other hand, when a new discovery is made, it leads inevitablv and, moreover, justifiably to new interpretations. These interpretations should never be confused with the facts. They inevitably must change as more fundamental information on the same overall problem becomes available.

Let me give two examples of what I mean by this. In 1959 my wife, Mary Leakey, discovered fragments of teeth sticking out of the cliff face at Bed I of Olduvai. This led, first, to the uncovering of the greater part of a complete skull, *Zinjanthropus*, and thereafter to the exposure at the level from which the skull was taken, of an extensive stone age living floor of the Oldowan culture. This was littered with stone tools, as well as with broken-up animal bones and teeth. The facts of this discovery were clear. Here was a skull whose structure and dental morphology proclaimed it to be an Australopithecine. This Australopithecine had been found in direct association with the living floor, and the culture on the living floor was the primitive Oldowan.

449

At that time, moreover, no other type of hominid had been found in Bed I, Olduvai. All of these things were facts. From these facts it seemed to be reasonable to conclude as an interpretation that *Zinjanthropus* represented one of the hominids who had been the makers of the Oldowan culture. Since at that time the accepted definition of man was "a primate that makes tools to a set and regular pattern," it was a reasonable further interpretation to consider that *Zinjanthropus*, although morphologically an Australopithecine, must be ranked by definition as a man. As he seemed to be a tool-making man there was a distinct likelihood that he represented an ancestor of man today. The facts set out earlier have not changed, but within a few months of the discovery of *Zinjanthropus* the whole of our interpretation had to be changed. The reason for this change lay in the discovery of further facts; namely, that in the same geological horizon in Bed I, and even at the actual site where the *Zinjanthropus* skull was found, there was clear evidence of the co-existence of another hominid which was much more like man of today in his overall morphological picture. These new facts necessitated saying, immediately, that it was no longer certain that *Zinjanthropus* represented the makers of Oldowan culture. It was now possible either that the original interpretation was correct, or that the new hominid represented the maker and *Zinjanthropus* did not, or even, thirdly, that they both represented makers of this primitive culture. The same discovery, since it presented us with a much more manlike creature than *Zinjanthropus* living at the same point in time, wholly removed the likelihood that *Zinjanthropus* could any longer be regarded as an ancestor of *Homo sapiens*.

To give another example of the essential difference between facts and interpretations, we may cite the discovery of an occipital bone with a primitive paleolithic culture and certain amount of fauna at Verteztoles in Hungary. The facts were clear. A large and massive hominid occipital had been found associated with artifacts and with fossil fauna. Initial theories based on these facts suggested that the human bone represented *Homo erectus*; that the culture was akin to the Oldowan, and that the fauna was indicative of a Lower Pleistocene age. More detailed study of the material later showed that none of these three interpretations was really valid; but the facts upon which the interpretations were based have not altered.

In recent years, whenever a new discovery of importance has been made, it has become accepted practice to make a preliminary announcement in the scientific press. Inevitably, such a preliminary announcement cannot give the total facts upon which the conclusions are drawn, because it appears in a scientific journal such as *Nature* or *Science* the editors of which have to restrict the amount of space given to any communication, in any given issue.

The object of a preliminary report of this kind is to make available some general information, as soon as possible, to fellow workers so that they can, if they wish, either write for more information or come to view the specimen themselves. An unfortunate tendency has developed of late, for anthropologists who are mainly engaged in University teaching, rather than in actual field studies, to start lengthy discussion and criticism on the basis of these preliminary reports, often without even viewing the original specimens, or casts thereof. This sort of controversy, often accompanied by dogmatic pronouncements, must be deplored. What we need, and need badly, is more and more good field work, and less dispute about discoveries until the detailed reports about them are made available. When the detailed reports appear discussion and dispute about the information is justified.

Inevitably, a certain amount of general speculation must take place at each and every stage of our knowledge of early man, simply because without it we cannot formulate textbooks for students or deliver meaningful lectures which will stimulate interest. For example, now that we know that at the end of the Miocene and the beginning of the Pliocene there existed a hominid who was not yet a man, but nevertheless leading to man, both in East Africa and in India, we can and indeed should, speculate as to the possible relationship of this stock to the various hominids which we know were in existence at the beginning of the Pleistocene. The Kenya representative of this Miocene hominid is *Kenyapithecus wickeri.* We know that he had small canine teeth, an arched dental arcade, a short face, a canine fossa, and remarkably manlike central incisors. All of these characters are rather more suggestive of ancestry for *Homo habilis* than for the Australopithecines; some of the latter are characterized by a lack of canine fossa and by very reduced canines and incisors.

In view of the fact that *Kenyapithecus wickeri* has been shown to have been using lumps of stone to batter open bones and skulls of contemporary animals, it is distinctly probable that he developed more and more along the carnivorous diet behavior patterns which later characterized *Homo habilis*, but which is not true of the Australopithecines.

The fact that Asia has a Mio-Pliocene primitive hominid, *Ramapithecus*, certainly opens the possibility that this stock may have given rise to some more evolved hominids in Asia. We must therefore expect some interesting finds in Asia in the next few years.

In this book we have deliberately omitted reference to a number of finds which stood somewhat by themselves like the Heidelberg mandible, the finds at Fontechevade, Solo, Combe Capelle, Mapa, and Ternifine, etc. This omission does not mean that these finds are not of very considerable importance, but rather that a great deal more work is essential before we can set them properly into the framework of the jigsaw puzzle. For example, there are many anthropologists, today, who treat the Heidelberg jaw as representing an European *Pithecanthropus* although such an interpretation does not really seem to fit its morphological characteristics. Similarly, while some people, including the writer, regard the Swanscombe fragments as proto-*Homo sapiens*, others like Arambourg, regard it as another *Pithecanthropus*. The Solo skulls are regarded, by some, as a final derivative of the Java and Peking man complex, but others see in Solo man no more than an aberrant and over-specialized local variant of *Homo sapiens*. Still others see in this group of skulls the possibility of a cross between *Homo sapiens* and the Pithecanthropines.

All of the above examples show that a vast amount of work is waiting to be done. It must be hoped that many who read this volume will be willing to dedicate themselves to this detective work with enthusiasm. Only about one millionth of the surface of Africa has as yet been explored from the anthropologist's point of view. Even less is known about Asia, while for those who want to concentrate on the later fields of evolution there is the American field where man must have lived for about 100,000 years and yet we only know about him during the last 10,000 to 15,000 years!

Finally, let me say to those who contemplate joining the ranks of scientists searching for early man, "don't expect an easy life; don't expect quick results; don't expect rapid recognition; and certainly don't expect ever to be wealthy. The work is exciting. There is always a new discovery awaiting you just around the corner. So go to it and take part."